As I Please

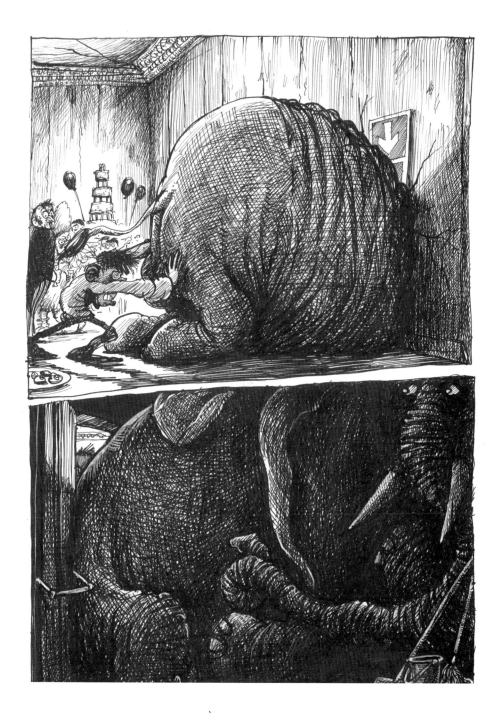

MARTIN ROWSON

As I Please

and Other Writings
1986–2024

With a Foreword by Kevin Maguire
and an Afterword by Chris McLaughlin

LONDON NEW YORK CALCUTTA

Seagull Books, 2024

Unless otherwise stated, all illustrations in this volume are by Martin Rowson
The illustrations in the frontmatter belong to the series *The Elephant in the Room*

Foreword © Kevin Maguire
Afterword © Chris McLaughlin
Remaining texts and illustrations © Martin Rowson
This compilation © Seagull Books

ISBN 978 1 80309 450 2

British Library Cataloguing-in-Publication Data
A catalogue record for this book is available from the British Library

Typeset and designed by Diven Nagpal, Seagull Books, Calcutta, India
Printed and bound in India by Hyam Enterprises, Calcutta, India

For Patricia, in gratitude for her clear eye and continued factotum services.

In memory of Michael Foot, friend, inspiration, fellow multitasker, who spread himself to the condition of the sublime.

And, as ever and with all my love, for Anna, Fred and Rose.

CONTENTS

Foreword by Kevin Maguire   *xxv*

As I Please . . .

Dr Faustus . . . **3**   World Cup . . . **4**   Pinochet . . . **7**

Tribune's 60th Birthday Party and Gordon Brown . . . **10**

Millennium . . . **13**   Jill Craigie . . . **16**

Countryside . . . **18**   What If . . . **21**

Twin Towers . . . **24**

Faith Schools . . . **28**

Queen Mother's Death . . . **30**

May Day . . . **33**   Jubilee . . . **36**

Berlin . . . **38**   USA . . . **42**   Bali . . . **44**

Saatchi . . . **47**   Orwell . . . **50**   Campbell Gag . . . **52**

Tory Sacrifice . . . **55**   Xmas . . . **58**

Chechen . . . **60**

US Elections / Fallujah . . . **63**

Twenty-Four-Hour Drinking . . . **66**

Iraq Hegemony . . . **69**   The Thing . . . **71**

Lefties . . . **74**   Blair Embarrassment . . . **77**

Syd Barrett . . . **81**   Speculation . . . **84**   Class War . . . **87**

Olympics . . . **90**   NI Hope . . . **93**   Offence . . . **95**

50th Birthday / Stop the War . . . **98**   Anarchism . . . **101**

Viruses . . . **104**   Militarism . . . **107**

Zoo . . . **110**   Murdoch . . . **112**

Climate Change . . . **115**

Pope . . . **118**

Michael Foot . . . **121**

Omens . . . **124**   Osborne . . . **127**

Rioting . . . **130**   Disraeli . . . **133**   Greece . . . **136**

Banality of Evil . . . **139**   Theft . . . **142**   Goderich . . . **145**

Media Lens . . . **147**   Zombies . . . **150**

Doctor Who . . . **153**

Scottish Referendum . . . **155**

Christian Country . . . **158**   BBC . . . **161**

Scottish Vote . . . **163**   Hobbyism . . . **166**   Potemkin . . . **169**

Hebdo . . . **171**   Buildings . . . **174**   Corbynmania . . . **177**

Cavell / Tory Patriotism . . . **180**   Bowie . . . **182**

Jeremy Corbyn's New Year Message, Modestly Re-imagined . . . **185**

Philosophy . . . **188**   Moscow . . . **191**

Cult . . . **194**

Labour Rancour . . . **197**

Brexit . . . **200**   Political Idiocy . . . **203**

Fascism . . . **206**   Life . . . **209**

Weaponizing Embarrassment . . . **211**   Johnson . . . **214**

Sexual Harassment . . . **217**

Other Writings

The Paragon of Animals, Lower than Vermin   **223**

Is Judge Dredd a Fascist?   **225**

The Album   **228**

Afterword to *The Waste Land*   **232**

We Are the True Outsiders of Journalism   **236**

Adoption   **242**

Drawing Some Difficult Conclusions   **248**

High Importance of Being Low   **250**

Waitemata   **256**

Is God a Hedgehog?   **261**

Selections from *Mugshots*   **264**

Mission Impossible: *Tristram Shandy*   **275**

The Towers of Babel   **281**

Syd Barrett, the Death of England and the End of Time: 10 May 2007   **287**

My Three Mothers   **295**

The Dog Allusion: An Excerpt   **301**

The Cartoonist's Secret Code   **304**

Giving Offence: An Excerpt   **307**

Rude Awakening   **323**

Luck of the Draw   **330**

Let's Kill Uncle   **336**

Drawing Out the Dark Side   **340**

William Hogarth   **350**

Otto Dix: *Der Krieg*   **362**

Charlie Hebdo   **372**

James Gillray   **380**

Massacres in Paris   **391**

Art Is a Serious Business   **396**

The Communist Manifesto as a Graphic Novel   **401**

The Ground-breaking Squiggles of Saul Steinberg   **405**

The *New York Times* Cartoon Ban   **409**

As If . . .   **412**

Foreword to Roland Elliott Brown's *Godless Utopia*   **416**

Covid Days: *Plague Songs*   **420**

The Dolorous Countenance of Angela Merkel   **431**

Johnson on the Way Back?   **434**

The Love Songs of Late Capitalism: An Excerpt   **439**

The Prejudices That Haunt Us   **448**

Communards   **452**

Cartooning the Tory Years   **455**

Afterword by Chris McLaughlin   **467**

Acknowledgements   **469**

Foreword
Kevin Maguire

If the pen truly was mightier than the sword, then so too would be a cartoonist's pencils and brushes.

Martin Rowson wields both masterfully as a highly skilled literary and graphic chronicler of our condition, the acclaimed cartoonist consistently producing prose considerably more readable than many a lionized writer and the successful author regularly creating glorious images that few scribblers could even dream of matching.

The book in your hands is an engaging and compelling collection of Rowson's monthly columns in the left-wing *Tribune* journal—where, for 20 years, he filled the coveted 'As I Please . . . ' slot occupied by the great political writer George Orwell over two spells between 1943 and 1947—as well as work for a string of other publications—some of them mainstream, such as the *Guardian* and the *Independent*, while a number are from obscure American underground magazines you may struggle to name, never mind find. Those pieces are none the worse for appearing in rags with microscopic circulations. What they all share is Rowson's caustically acerbic confrontation with the wrongs of the world.

His is the broadest range of subjects, from high politics to low morals; ideological fights to petty squabbles; Britain's divisive class system to the mass assassination of *Charlie Hebdo* secularists; London Zoo to even *Doctor Who*, the enduring BBC travels of a regenerating time lord yet to return in a police box TARDIS spacecraft to encounter Orwell himself.

Forever punching up, not down, Rowson's targets are those who exercise power over the powerless. He's rooted on the democratic left, an internationalist but definitely no party propagandist; the likes of Labour prime minister Tony Blair, the invader of Iraq, shown no mercy and given as deserved a kicking as any Conservative Party leader or reactionary on the right of the spectrum.

The elan of Rowson's vivid writing is a glorious pleasure, as satisfying as his brilliant cartoons are to savour, whether reading these bite-sized columns or sitting down for the full meal of a book or novel he's authored.

Whether intended or not, he encourages us to think for ourselves. His arguments challenge us; at the same time, they make us laugh and get angry and usually leave us wanting more. To float like a butterfly and sting like a bee page after page, if I may borrow and adapt a rather famous description, encourages a reader to return again and again.

One of the most enjoyable aspects of reading a provocative column he's written is to start without quite knowing where Rowson will go, let alone finish. Perhaps the columnist himself occasionally doesn't know the final destination when opening the laptop lid to deliver a stipulated world length and hit the deadline. Predictability is the enemy of creativity. Hostile political opponents level a number of charges at Rowson. Boring will never, ever feature among them. Some think he could start and win an argument in an empty room. He probably has.

I witnessed Rowson charming a curious, somewhat sceptical audience in a deindustrialized Tyneside town in England's kept-behind North. He won them over with wit, intellect and forthrightness, seasoned with a little humility and admission of fallibility. The mainly working-class people of South Shields who departed their homes on a chilly Thursday evening, forsaking the *One Show* and *Emmerdale*, were typical of the very folk who Rowson believes deserve to be treated with greater fairness, decency and respect by those who misrule over them. They loved him, eyes opened wide by the unexpected champion from London.

Back in the day, Rowson sketched the great and the not so good frequenting the Gay Hussar restaurant in London's Soho, a renowned haunt of lefties. The young Michael Foot at a corner table heard from the Soviet ambassador that Hitler would invade his country. Tom Driberg propositioned Mick Jagger. It was that type of restaurant. The rich collection of drawings is now under the protection of the National Portrait Gallery after a protracted wrestling match with unloving owners who shut the place but wanted to retain arguably the most valuable fixtures and fittings from its history.

I recall that one of Rowson's subjects, perhaps it would be accurate in this instance to label the political bruiser a victim, asked why he was presented unsympathetically. The aggressive fixer was on pretty reasonable eating, drinking and chatting terms with Rowson, I might add. 'Because,' replied the author of this collection, 'I draw as I see and find.' And writes too, ferociously, honestly, without fear or favour. The keyboard the pen gave way to would be as inadequate as the pencils and brushes in an actual sword fight, but they remain formidable weapons in the battle for hearts and minds. Enjoy.

Kevin Maguire is a Daily Mirror *associate editor and* New Statesman *columnist.*

As I Please . . .

Columns Written for *Tribune*
1998–2017

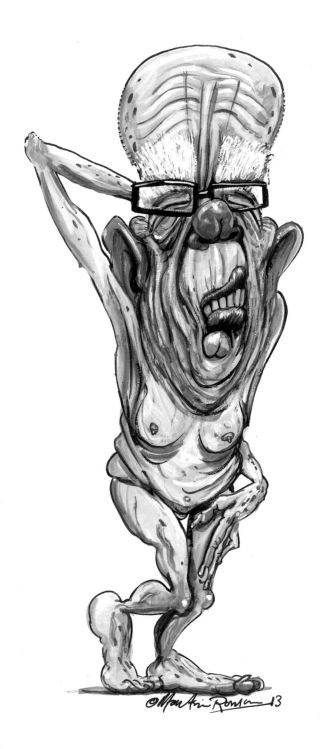

2013

Dr Faustus . . .

April 1998

It always pains me to have to point out when this government gets something horribly and hopelessly wrong, but that, after all, is what friends are for. Moreover, when I see life seeking to imitate art, I cannot remain silent when it is obvious that someone should really have made the effort to have read the source material more carefully, if only to spare the prime minister further embarrassment.

As it is, New Labour's current re-enactment of *Dr Faustus* is way 'off-message'. In Christopher Marlowe's original, the necromancing doctor makes his pact with the devil according to a strict contract meticulously observed by both parties. For 24 years Faustus is attended and served by Mephistopheles who grants Faustus all he demands, including, memorably, Helen of Troy. In return, at the end of the 24 years (Act 5 Scene 5) Mephistopheles comes to claim Faustus' soul at the stroke of midnight, and off they go to Hell together.

In the cool new New Labour version, however, diabolical liberties have been taken with the original. Faustus (a boyishly winsome Leonardo DiCaprio–style performance from Tony Blair) and his sidekick Wagner (portrayed with muscular bravado by method-school stand-by Alastair Campbell) can hardly pass a day enjoying supreme power over the temporal world without Mephistopheles (Rupert Murdoch—rather typecast) turning up demanding another hunk of his supplicant's soul. However, even with a typical, if cavalier, disregard for the integrity of the classics, decency alone should demand that Mephistopheles hold off until, say, halfway through Act 3.

Even more worrying for purists is New Labour's reinterpretation of the Faustian pact, which is the central and defining dramatic device of the tragedy. In the original, Mephistopheles, although he is the Prince of Lies, is true to his word and faithfully serves Faustus, delivering him whatever he wants for the stipulated 24-year-long pact. But what precisely has Murdoch delivered? The modern Prince of Lies is not stupid, whatever else he may be, and even he must have known that it would have been ridiculous for the *Sun* to have backed John Major in the last election, having spent the previous four years destabilizing him. This is quite apart from the fact that most *Sun* readers were probably going to vote Labour anyway, whatever the paper's conclave of serious-minded and incorruptible leader-writers may have enjoined them otherwise to do.

In fact, the *Sun*'s support for New Labour is an entirely unquantifiable thing, as ethereal as the demonic ectoplasm invoked during the dark rites of black masses. To look, for a moment, into another pit of hell, it has been widely reported that on election night, *Daily Mail* editor Paul Dacre, watching vast swathes of Middle England fall to New Labour, cried out (with the cry of an anguished soul being dragged by succubi down a hell-hole): 'Fuck! These people are all *Daily Mail* readers!' All of which begs the question: 'How many seats did the *Sun* win for Blair? One? Ten? Fifty? The electoral arithmetic after 1 May last year make these figures look like small change. Add to this Murdoch's long tradition of backing winners and dumping losers, and his side of the bargain begins to look increasingly tawdry. Moreover, for those *Sun* readers who like to reflect on such things, the apparent (or, if you prefer, obvious) cynicism of Murdoch's rating might indeed prove to invalidate any future political advice the Digger's fallen angels offer their readers.

Last year, the Labour campaign exhorted the electorate to vote for change. I wonder whether voters imagined the only change on offer was a change of logo and personnel among those given leave by British capitalism to mind the shop and, in effect, meant business as usual for the biggest bogeyman in global capitalism. If anything, Murdoch's demonic countenance is rendered more, not less, infernal by the utter banality of his product. But rather than the prime minister mortgaging his soul in order to help Mephistopheles win another zillion TV stations and another squillion newspapers to churn out simultaneously poisonous and anodyne cack, what would it cost Blair to tell Murdoch to sod off? Murdoch has succeeded in demonizing himself so completely I wonder if anyone reads his newspapers any more without silently dismissing everything in them as merely another commercial gambit by the Boss. Then again, at five-to-midnight, as Mephistopheles manifested himself with a whiff of sulphur in his study, Faustus cursed the Devil and recanted and went to Hell anyway.

World Cup . . .

July 1998

Being a totally unreconstructed hangover from the gender-politics-obsessed early 80s, I have always strenuously maintained that football is merely the stinking smegma beneath the shrivelled foreskin of the withered phallus of the patriarchy, and, as a consequence, the World Cup has left me cold. Honestly, I couldn't give a toss about England or Scotland's hopes in France, even less so about the wearisome parade of key matches between Chad and the Faroe Islands that have been disrupting television schedules for what now seems like months. I don't even get particularly worked up about the predictable outbreaks of hooliganism (and the equally predictable bleatings of disapproval from our political masters) apart from a vague regret that the fascist Right continues its political hegemony over the hooligan element among football fans, when a bit of crafty agitprop might have these pissed-up working-class warriors diverting their crapulous rage into building barricades and tearing down the Temple of Capitalism. Some hope.

Part of the problem with such a deranged analysis is that a lot of the hooligans arrested after the Marseille riot turned out not to be 'working class' (in the old, workerist vanguard definition) at all, with many of them holding down 'respectable' and highly paid jobs (until the prime minister gets them sacked, that is), without a trace of social deprivation to justify their yahoo antics. This puzzled some liberal commentators who have clearly never considered how vile a cocktail is produced when you mix alcohol, testosterone and male bonding among young men retarded in late adolescence. What is puzzling is the apparent acceptability if you remove the alcohol.

It has long been recognized in certain circles that the middle-class WASP male is one of the most rapacious creatures to have stalked the planet since the late Cretaceous period. Just look at the history of imperialism and all the little imperialisms that have followed in its wake. It often seems that everything the White middle-class male looks at he must then claim as his own. Take rock 'n' roll, expropriated from its African American creators, then expropriated again from its mainly working practitioners by big business. Or consider the revolting final consequences of the radical liberation movements of the 60s. What was the response of White middle-class men to feminism? To insist, by the early 80s, that men, too, were victims; moreover, by agitating for equal treatment. Hence, a whole generation of weedy dickheads loping off to the woods to beat drums and 'bond'. Germaine Greer even suggested recently in an *Observer* article that transgenderism was just another aspect of the male imperial imperative. Her compelling argument can be summed up neatly as, 'I mean, why should bloody women be the only ones allowed to have women's bodies, we're gonna have those too.'

Football is the latest trophy of working-class culture to be expropriated by a middle class who have nothing much except money and so buy up and corrupt everything they behold. Thus, Nick Hornby's *Fever Pitch* (1992), which has burdened a rather daft game of two halves with so much psycho-babbling bullshit, its main purpose now seems to be as a therapeutic tool to help confused middle-class boys come to terms with their inner feelings. Thus (and this is the other side of the same coin) the thraldom of Premier League football to the interests of big business which flogs overpriced merchandise and overpriced seats to the fans, hardly believing their luck that so many suckers could have been born at the same minute. Thus, inevitably, Rupert Murdoch's Sky TV. A couple of years ago, Sky ran a particularly cynical poster campaign at the announcement of the new football season, with the tagline 'Football is your religion: We understand, it's ours too.' I don't quite understand how that got past the Advertising Standards Authority, when it is obvious to everyone that money

The Guardian, June 1998

is Sky's religion and football merely another means for Rupe to extend his monopolistic hold over the British people and increase his profits.

Anyhow, does any of this sound at all familiar? A group of culturally alienated middle-class White boys observing a cohesive bastion of working-class culture, taking possession of it and then changing it out of all recognition to the point where its working-class creators are no longer welcome to join in? Interestingly enough, New Labour repeatedly trumpets its ordinary, blokeish credentials by citing the enthusiasm of its wonks for football, whether its Tony doing 40 consecutive headers with Kevin Keegan or Ed Balls sneaking away from his computer models of endogenous growth theory to watch the footie with the lads, or Gordon bunking off from the economy sliding into recession to watch Scotland play in France. Which presumably means we are meant to admire testosterone and male bonding as the guiding forces of the New Labour project. Personally, I am still waiting for them all to get pissed.

Pinochet . . .

October 1998

General Pinochet, mouldering in the London Clinic, seems to have had the peculiar effect of a particularly efficacious emetic on the finest minds in the establishment, forcing them to spew all manner of extraordinary poisons over the rest of us in a revolting maelstrom of sanctimoniousness and long-digested prejudice. That serial moralizers should be the most voluminous vomiters should surprise no one.

The archbishop of Canterbury, being Primate, is a prime example. (When I say he is a primate, I obviously have no intention of libelling blameless orangutans and gorillas, harming no one as they roll about in their own filth.) George Carey is clearly a very silly man heading a rather silly church, but even he surpassed himself in calling for 'compassion' in dealing with Pinochet. I suppose in that great melon head of his, Carey imagined he was being too true to the tenets of his faith which call for forgiveness and compassion in dealing with one's enemies. However, unless I am hideously in error (and burn me, George, if this is so), there is not more joy in heaven over sinners, who, far from repenting, impose a deal on their victims that allows them to sin, then get away with it, and, rather than showing any hint of repentance or remorse, buy their ties at Burberry's, receive an annual Christmas hamper from the Adam Smith Institute and take tea and rock cakes with Margaret Thatcher.

Which brings us to Thatcher's own pool of puke. I find myself at a total loss to understand the workings of Lady Thatcher's mind. One minute she is calling for fallen women to take the veil and be immured in convents, which is entirely consistent with a Christian morality that has always been hard on fornication and, in particular, women as the tools of Satan than on anything else. But the next minute, she is off with whatever pass for fairies in the lecture halls of the military–industrial complex. Surely, even she can see the glaring obscenity of as good as saying that the life of one member of the Special Air Service (SAS) is worth the lives of roughly sixty Chilean victims of Pinochet's terror, especially when the whole point of Pinochet for his British and American groupies was that he got rid of inflation. Even the Tories are now embarrassed by Thatcher, except for those sad little chaps who take beans on toast in The Presence and suffer from whatever variant on the Oedipus complex makes you sublimate your urge to have sex with your grandmother. But the Tories are only embarrassed because Thatcher says what they all think but dare not say out loud. Instead, in the last week, we have had an ever-flowing torrent of noxious verbiage issuing from commentators in the *Times*, the *Telegraph* and the *Daily Mail*, from former Tory ministers, even from the new touchy-feely Blairite Express.

The line is roughly this. The man is a monster but he did wonders with the economy (on the basis that one per cent off the rate of inflation roughly equals 1,237 Chilean victims of Pinochet's terror). He stood down from power of his own free will and made way for democracy (on the basis that one moment of despotic realization of the inevitable roughly equals 893 Chilean victims of Pinochet's terror). They argue that bringing Pinochet to book will endanger trade with Chile, and, therefore, endanger British jobs (one ground-to-air missile roughly equals 68 Chilean victims of Pinochet's terror), and that, in any case, all this happened years ago and the present government is just re-enacting the childish student enthusiasms of its members' youth. One call to grow up and live in the real world equals . . . well there is probably not time enough to count the victims of that particular poisonous homily.

While we might reflect once more on how wonderful it is that Tories only ever express concern about a threat to British jobs when somebody tries to stop them selling the machinery of death to their foreign fascist friends, we should not forget that what the Labour government has done is genuinely brave. Not just in as much as it is exactly the opposite of what I expected it to do, nor that, for once, the government has chosen not to be cravenly supine at the feet of establishment opinion. What the government has done is strong on morality and low on rhetoric. Albeit dressed in legal camouflage, the arrest of Pinochet is a magnificent statement of the sanctity of human rights, and, moreover, the legal arguments now being argued over the extradition suggest they may be setting a precedent braver than they can imagine. Pinochet's lawyers argued, on the first day of the hearing, that if Pinochet were answerable for his crimes in a different jurisdiction, then—heaven help us all—no statesman or political leader would be safe anywhere in the world. Doesn't that prospect bring a warm glow to your heart?

The Guardian, October 1998

Tribune's *60th Birthday Party and Gordon Brown . . .*

March 1999

One of the less obvious pleasures of working for *Tribune* is that you occasionally get invited to parties where, if you're lucky, you get a chance to speak to some of the paper's more celebrated and glamorous supporters. It was thus shortly before last May's election, at *Tribune's* 60th birthday party, that I was telling Gordon Brown to forget all the complicated economic models Ed Balls had been explaining to him so conscientiously and to understand instead that economics was an art, not a science. He shouldn't, therefore, worry about all that frightening cack the shamans and mountebanks in the policy units told him, but instead sublimate all economic theory to his political objectives and ameliorate the condition of the poor as his first priority. He smiled winningly the smile you smile at jabbering drunks at parties and replied 'Why do you always draw me so fat?'

While Gordon may not be so fat any more, the trouble now is that, soon, most of the rest of us won't be either. But rather than dwell on the countless millions of personal tragedies that the coming depression will bring as trade contracts, jobs vanish and banks collapse, perhaps, instead, we should revisit a local political tragedy with as strong a whiff of Aeschylus to it as of economic meltdown.

When Tony Blair tells us, both blithely and blindly, that There Is No Alternative to the Labour Government's Economic Policy, we must assume he does this because he and Gordon Brown genuinely believe that the neoliberal new world order is more than just another subjective analysis of how to order things for the best. Instead, startled and mesmerized in the white-hot glare of an empirically based scientific truth, the government has, literally, no alternative than to go along with it. It's just a shame, then, that the whole edifice should be collapsing just as we're enjoined to worship at its altars of rubble and spite.

It's even more of a shame that a whole political class, even one as craven and opportunistic as New Labour, should have failed to understand that economic theory has always been the junior partner to political will. It just so happens that, since the Enlightenment, one of the slicker political tricks has been to pretend that the economic aspects of a political agenda are enshrined in empirical scientific truth and are therefore unanswerable because they are *objectively true*. Marx did this brilliantly with the invention of dialectical materialism and was honoured in the Soviet Union (along with Stalin, for a while) as the 'Greatest Scientist in History'. The neoliberals did it brilliantly as well. However, the downside is when people actually believe you. Then, like New Labour, all you can do is stand Marx on his head, whisper 'All philosophers hitherto have sought to change the world; the point, however, is to explain it,' and, with your

Tribune, 1997

economics neutered, fumble along as best you can when you realize you've castrated your politics as well.

Before we take one final look at the neoliberal, monetarist agenda before it crumbles away to nothing, allow me a brief digression about another *Tribune* party. It was three Christmases ago, and Will Hutton was wondering what to write in his *Guardian* column in the dead week between Christmas and New Year. I suggested, for a laugh, that he propose a new school of left-wing monetarism, strong on controlling the money supply, but just as strong on defending the welfare state, so instead you control public spending by slashing Trident, the monarchy, tax breaks for the rich and so on. He, too, smiled that smile you smile at jabbering drunks, but I think I was making a valid point. Because what defines late-twentieth-century economic liberalism is that it will only fit in with a right-wing political agenda, because it is merely a 'scientific' tool of that agenda. However many desiccated calculating machines argue over statistics, it cannot be gainsaid that monetarism, neoliberalism and that frayed paper tiger globalization are not 'challenges to be met' but just another way (and I can say this in *Tribune* with impunity) for the Boss class to stomp on the people. When Brown and Blair signed up to the New Orthodoxy, they had, despite crossing their fingers and whistling like hell, bought in to the whole of the rest of the agenda, to rigorous control of public expenditure by targeting welfare and the poorest sections of society, to denigration of the state and the public sector, to denigration of trades unions and the apotheosis of managementism, to downsizing, to job insecurity, to ever-widening pay differentials and inequalities in wealth, to short-termism, to scorched-earth speculation, to greed. And however much they may try to regulate and control it, New Labour will learn, if they haven't already, that there is no such thing as Capitalism with a Human Face.

As I write this, Gordon Brown is hawking his newly rediscovered conscience about the central banks and economic forums of Europe, trying to persuade anyone who'll listen that now is the time to cut interest rates to avoid the coming recession. At the beginning of the last recession, Sir Edward Heath referred to Nigel Lawson as his 'favourite one-club golfer', meaning that, hitched up to neoliberalism, the only economic tool the chancellor had was interest rates. Gordon Brown must be the first golfer in history to want to carry on playing after he's thrown away his only club. And in the middle of the Great Depression, in his inauguration address, President Roosevelt, forced through necessity to abandon the economic strategies New Labour have so recently embraced and instead embrace a strategy and ideology New Labour abandoned for short-term electoral gain, said, 'We have nothing to fear except fear itself.' Unless Brown and Blair stop being consumed by fear of the discredited champions and practitioners of a collapsing right-wing project, we should all be very, very frightened indeed.

Millennium . . .

November 1999

Frankly, I'm amazed. I never thought we'd see power shared and devolved in the Six Counties of the North of Ireland, not because the divide between the two 'traditions' was too wide and deep to be bridgeable, but because it seemed increasingly obvious that all the politicians involved found it more interesting, self-fulfilling and, to be honest, easier just to leave things as they were. In a way, you can't blame them. Now that normal politics have finally arrived in this sectarian statelet founded on the principle of Carson's gang refusing to give up their weapons, politicians who previously strutted on a world stage, shook hands with American presidents, partook of Evian and brioche at 10 Downing Street, won Nobel prizes and rode high on the hog on *Newsnight*, will now find themselves little better than parish councillors, finding ways to fix broken paving stones and deliver meals-on-wheels in a chilly backwater on the outer edge of Europe.

No wonder, then, that for 30 years they preferred to let the Brits get on and do the boring stuff while they carried on striking their murderous poses for as long as possible on The Brink. The originating struggles of the Civil Rights Movement long ago disappeared beneath republicans scooping out Catholic informers' eyeballs with teaspoons, loyalists burning babies in their cots so they could wave bunting and strut through a housing estate, unionists refusing to compromise for a second from their principled position of oppressive hegemony over their Catholic neighbours and British governments pretending they weren't seeking a negotiated settlement and sending out death squads. Well, having achieved neither the United Irish dream of 1798 and 1916, nor Carson's 1921 nightmare of a perpetually Protestant Ulster, I hope they're all very pleased with themselves. Mobile Library Service Resumed. Not (Too) Many Dead.

Forgive me my rather acid tone. It seems only appropriate at the burnt-out end of probably the vilest century in human history that, in my last column of the millennium, I should come on a tad unforgiving. And yet, and yet . . .

While quantitatively we're about to depart a century of unparalleled savagery and carnage, qualitatively it could be argued that, in the West at least, we have never, ever had it so good. Indeed, looking forward from the middle of the nineteenth century, a socialist time traveller might easily believe that, by the end of the twentieth century we had attained the New Jerusalem, or at least the outer suburbs. Think about it for a moment. Within the lifetime of many *Tribune* readers, the quality of life in this country has changed out of all recognition, and for the better. For most of the nineteenth century, the progressive political agenda was defined by a struggle for the

extension of the franchise and for democracy, which was finally ineradicably won with the 1948 Representation of the People Act. Harnessed to that political struggle were the social campaigns of the great Victorian and Edwardian socialists for improved health care, housing and education, along with the creation of a welfare state to protect the weakest in society. To a very large extent, these battles have also been won.

Advances in medicine alone mean that life today is, simply, safer than it was a hundred years ago. When my stepmother started working as a trainee nurse in 1941, her first job was boiling bloodstained handkerchiefs in a vast cauldron in a TB isolation hospital. Now TB, along with diphtheria, polio, smallpox and most other infectious diseases have either been eradicated or rendered manageable. Likewise, advances in simple domestic technologies have liberated millions of people and not simply the 'housewife' of advertising folklore. When *Tribune* was founded, as many as a third of the workforce were employed in domestic service, condemned to a life of servile drudgery. That world has gone completely and is as incomprehensible to us today as every man on the street wearing a hat, kneejerk deference for our 'betters' or thousands of people a year choking to death in London's smog.

In short, we have been emancipated from the harsher brutalities of life, to such an extent that we hardly even notice how unimaginably comfortable and privileged we are. Instead, we keep up a steady level of complaint about the minutiae of levels of healthcare, education and social provision our grandparents could only dream of or fight for. It's significant, moreover, that the foundations for this great emancipation were all laid down by Beveridge, Butler's 1944 Education Act and Bevan's creation of the National Health Service before the century was even half over.

So, what have we done since? For 50 years, politicians, unable to conceive of anything better, have kicked the NHS, education and the welfare state around as so many political footballs. In the same way, the politicians of Northern Ireland, realizing early on that the unyielding republican and unionist war aims were unattainable, struck poses for decades because they could think of nothing better to do. In the meantime, we've created a consumer society which, while immensely comfortable, is also shallow, soulless and unsustainable. Our mid-Victorian time traveller would recognize, as we should, that the war will remain only half-won while power and wealth remain in the hands of a few, profit-driven despoilers of society, culture and our natural world. This century's seen us freed from the tyrannies of brute existence. Next century, let's finally start redistributing the wealth and the power. Happy New Year.

Jill Craigie . . .

December 1999

I'm writing this at the end of the week when Jill Craigie died. I got to know Jill in recent years when she and Michael Foot would attend *Tribune*'s regular beanos in the excellent Gay Hussar restaurant in Soho. The last time we met, early last summer before she became ill, she was telling me how much she yearned for a fully reformed second chamber of Parliament, so Michael could, with honour intact, become a member and she could, also with honour, get him out of the house and no longer have to prepare him three cooked meals a day. More seriously, she also outlined her development as a socialist. With typical passion and incisiveness, Jill described herself as belonging to a strand of the socialist movement now almost completely occluded, but nonetheless potent and attractive for all the slow attrition of expediency over principle and, indeed, hope which has given us New Labour. When she said she was a William Morris socialist, I knew exactly what she meant.

In these fallen times, William Morris tends to mean wallpaper and gift tags in the Victoria and Albert Museum shop, but his legacy is far, far more important than that, and we forget it at our peril. It's not just about upholding the principle of useful labour as opposed to useless toil (a precept, incidentally, originally from John Ruskin, whose book *Unto This Last* was held by most of Attlee's cabinet to be the greatest influence on their personal political development); nor was it simply about the morally uplifting qualities of art made available to everyone, irrespective of class or perceived ability. Morris not only said, rather wonderfully, 'If a chap can't compose an epic poem while he's weaving a tapestry, he had better shut up, he'll never do any good at all,' but also, after reading *Das Kapital*, that 'this is awfully easy stuff.'

In short, Morris was fun, he thought everyone else should have fun, and recognized that industrial capitalism is no fun at all. That's why he constantly alluded back to the pre-industrial never Neverland of the Middle Ages.

As I've already said, this strand of the Labour movement has been almost completely obscured as New Labour has willingly surrendered to the apparent final triumph of global capitalism. In this new millennium, there will be the temptation, to which many smart dunderheads will fall, to see global capitalism as the summit of economic, political, cultural and human endeavour. Many, I'm sure, will herald the latest stage of history as (yawn) the End of History, as we enter on a thousand years of rule by money to match the thousand years of Christ's rule on earth prophesied in the Book of Revelation. The unread dicta of whoever the latest smooth and bespectacled guru is to grace the prime minister's bedside table may be less lurid than the apocalyptic ravings of Saint John the Divine on Patmos, but they're probably about as accurate in terms of analysis and conjecture.

WILLIAM MORRIS ABSENT-MINDEDLY WALLPAPERS OVER GEORGE BERNARD SHAW IN THE PARLOUR AT KELMSCOTT MANOR.

Scenes from the Lives of the Great Socialists (London: Grapheme, 1983)

The truth is that global capitalism is wheeling us all in an admittedly rather stylish handcart straight to hell. The short-termism and rapacity of the profit motive and the timidity of our elected leaders in even addressing the consequences of unrestrained capitalism mean that we are now heading for an environmental Armageddon entirely of our own making and that, as a species, we've probably got another 50 years before we've made the planet intolerable for anything approaching the comfortable but wasteful, unequal, unjust and unsustainable model the West has presented to the rest of the world as the paradigm for human existence. Globalization, in short, in inseparable from global warming.

Of course, however enticing Morris' vision of a medieval, socialist future might be, it's not likely to happen. What we have left, however, is the ability to recognize that things needn't—moreover, shouldn't—be as they are, and the best way of focusing that recognition is to get back to Morris and ask the simple but devastating question: 'Just how much *fun* is all this?' If we want our children and grandchildren and their descendants to have even the opportunity of having fun, we need to change entirely the way we order human affairs.

It goes without saying that almost all politicians evince adolescent levels of seriousness and pomposity in going about their business, so it's clearly up to the rest of us, when we've stopped laughing at them, to point out how little fun there is in predicating economics on the ludicrous idea of constant growth, of measuring that growth by car production, of reducing the value of everything to the level of a share price, of sublimating all activity to the accumulation of more money.

And if we must protest in order to survive, let's make sure we have some fun at the same time. In order to reclaim the planet, you can't do much worse than to start by reclaiming the streets. Then, of course, we can set about reclaiming the Labour Party.

Countryside . . .

February 2001

Among my many shortcomings, I recognize that perhaps my worst is my indestructible metropolitan snobbery. Born, bred and living in London, I've always been suspicious of the English countryside. I also recognize that this prejudice marks me apart from many of my fellow citizens who continue to maintain a sentimental nostalgia for somewhere the vast majority of them abandoned generations ago. That migration is probably the source of our collective yearnings for rural idylls: a mass desire to return to the land from which our ancestors were, usually forcibly, torn by a complicated series of economic and social factors, leaving us dreaming of readmittance to a simpler, earthier Eden.

Of course, the Tory Party and its paramilitary wings the *Daily Mail* and the Countryside Alliance have long made it their business to assume that the soul of England—or, more precisely, Middle England—resides outside where nearly all the English—and particularly, and significantly, the Black, Brown and Yellow English— live. But in this Arcadian fantasy of corn dollies and cricket on the village green, several things get forgotten. For instance, if it's a return to nature you're after, in almost all of England you're on a hiding to nothing. The English countryside is probably the least natural on earth. By felling the forests, our neolithic ancestors started the process which has continued unabated ever since. From feudalism through the enclosures to agribusiness bulldozing hedgerows and amalgamating fields into windblown prairies, nature has been subjugated to the needs of humankind and, more to the point, money. So where there appears to be nature, in a Capability Brown country park, it's ersatz, and where there is nature, it's exploited to destruction. It's becoming increasingly clear, for instance, that last autumn's floods were more the result of current farming methods than of the increasing vicissitudes of global warming: the move to the cultivation of winter wheat means that, with the advent of the (hardly unexpected) autumn rains, fields that would previously have been covered with ploughed-in stubble which would, to an extent, have soaked up the water, are now bare and vast patches of naked soil, thousands of tons of which get washed away into rivers and their flood plains, now covered in all that ticky-tacky housing sprawl. Meanwhile, that same winter wheat cultivation means that the habitat in which ground-nesting songbirds previously thrived is, quite simply, no longer there: the stubble and furrows which protected them from predation have become bare, open killing fields. When Vaughan Williams sentimentalized the timeless allure of the English countryside a hundred years ago with *The Lark Ascending*, it's unlikely that he foresaw that the way of life of the sturdy yeomen he was memorializing would one day be responsible for driving skylarks to the brink of extinction.

Of course, it's horribly unfair for any town dweller like me to blame the besieged 'folk' who actually live in the countryside for any responsibility for their own predica-ment. Isn't it? According to the Countryside Alliance and any number of Tory spokes-men, the vast majority of us simply fail to understand what living in the country is like, and so are complicit in destroying this 'way of life' by, among other things, imposing an intolerable burden of bureaucracy and red tape on simple rustic efforts to feed us ungrateful townies. That said, it's always rather reassuring to know that the food we eat isn't poisonous, and no amount of red tape seems to have hindered a couple of Eddie Grundies in Northumberland from illegally importing meat which they then illegally fed (after failing to prepare according to the legal guidelines) to their pigs, which they then illegally exported.

Daily Mirror, September 2002

Interestingly enough, when the current foot-and-mouth outbreak was raised on *Any Questions* last weekend, Billy Bragg observed, quite reasonably, that the vast urban majority might be more sympathetic towards the plight of the countryside and its inhabitants if they did the same in response and made at least some attempt to understand why most English people thought that hunting foxes with dogs was barbaric and should be banned. He was met by his rural audience with unanimous hostility, which rather proves the point. After hundreds of years of exploiting and despoiling the land and creatures they loudly claim stewardship over, it's hard to feel too sorry for a group of people who insist that a minority hobby almost all of their fellow citizens consider abhorrent is more important than everything else, and that all their other problems are everyone else's fault and part of a deliberate campaign of cultural extermination. Especially when the alleged aggressors, if they think of their self-proclaimed victims at all, tend to think of stately homes, country cottages and clotted cream.

Well, that's Middle England for you, whatever that mythical place may be. The next time you hear the *Daily Mail* or William Hague evoke this never Neverland when shouting a loud hurrah for fuel protestors or peasant farmers or masters of foxhounds, think instead of J. R. R. Tolkien's Middle-earth, an unreal world of goblins and trolls, with a history, culture and language entirely made up by its author.

What If . . .

May 2001

As the Oklahoma bomber Timothy McVeigh sits in his federal penitentiary awaiting the consummation of his almost sacramental auto-sacrifice at the shrine of the US military–industrial complex, time, I think, for a little game of 'what might have been'.

Think back to the late 80s. In the Soviet Union, Gorbachev is continuing with his policies of dismantling both the old Stalinist empire in Eastern Europe and the terror apparatus of the state. Meanwhile, Reagan's re-armament programme has plunged the federal government deep into deficit. But let's now tweak history a tad to see what happens when the emerging neoliberal new world order gets its first shock with the stock-market crash of October 1987. Just pretend that the panic is greater than it was, worst of all in the banks, who, fearing a general banking collapse, call in the US government's debts. The federal government naturally defaults and is bankrupted. At this point, in California, the new technology companies—many with Japanese backing and a Pacific rather than Atlanticist Cold War frame of reference—start thinking politically as well as merely commercially as all those Pentagon contracts disappear because the federal government has no money to pay for them. With a massive hike in federal taxes, more and more Americans join the growing tax strike, as history has taught them is the founding American way. More to the point, the Californians, seeing a brighter future on the other side of the Pacific, secede from the Union, and, in one of those mysterious, unfathomable but defining moments in history, the United States rapidly collapses, with each state seceding in turn, and with absolutely no public support for an already discredited federal government using armed force to halt the disintegration. Reagan thus becomes the last president of the United States and sinks into senile obscurity. And Washington DC fulfils the manifest destiny foretold by Gore Vidal's grandfather, Senator Gore of Oklahoma, who said of the federal capital's new buildings, 'they'll make wonderful ruins'.

So what then? The rich, money-making parts of the former United States (as we now learn to call it) rapidly regroup, with California and New York State being the leading partners in the new Western Confederacy and Eastern Confederacy of Independent States. Texas tries to go it alone and is reannexed by Mexico, while the remaining 40 or so states break down into lawlessness and almost permanent minor border warfare. The 10-foot-high fence stretching the length of the new Mexican border succeeds pretty well in repelling economic migrants from the north, although an occasional former professor of economics from Chicago slips through to scrape a barely living wage as a domestic houseboy in Acapulco. The Branch Davidians prosper in Waco because no one cares, and anyway they're indiscernible from all the other tin-pot micro-governments made up of former militiamen and gangsters oscillating between fanaticism and corruption that pepper what was once called Middle America. Washington State votes, in Proposition 591, to become part of Canada, meaning that Bill Gates and Microsoft come under the suzerainty of the Queen and the Commonwealth. The missiles meanwhile rust in their silos in Utah, heavily guarded by troops of the United Nations (which has decamped to Moscow).

That move is necessitated by the obvious fact that the Soviet Union is now the 'sole remaining superpower', to repeat an annoying phrase much beloved of the media. And yet the removal of the greatest threat to world peace has had an effect on the Soviet government few of the more hawkish members of the now defunct US administration might have anticipated. The group of young reformers surrounding Gorbachev seize the opportunity to slash military spending, reinvest in and fundamentally reform the Soviet economy. The gamble works, and the first free elections in the Soviet Union see Gorbachev returned at the head of a hugely popular reformed Communist Party government promising domestic prosperity, a free press and a Truth and Reconciliation Commission to investigate the former crimes of the state, while the former head of the KGB languishes in prison awaiting trial. In rapid succession the Soviet Union and

the newly independent states of Eastern Europe join the EU while their neighbours in the West, with the addition of Canada, Mexico and the Eastern Confederacy join the reformed Warsaw Pact. Somewhere an idiot writes about the End of History. A series of unforeseen historical accidents lead to a growing belief that state socialism, albeit now with a more human face, has triumphed over free-market capitalism because it is intrinsically morally better. Sleek, smooth young men from Gosplan start journeying to the former USA to give advice to the emerging nations of the Midwest on planned-economy reforms. The new state-socialism world order rigorously regulates the multi-nationals until many voluntarily liquidate themselves (in an unfortunate turn of phrase) and become state-owned enterprises, committed to public ownership and common benefit instead of private greed . . .

And there the dream fades, and we return to reality, to George W. Bush, to rapacious global capitalism, to disintegrating public services, to Greed as our terrible, all-consuming God . . . If only, if only . . .

Twin Towers . . .

October 2001

Last week, along with my friends and colleagues Steve Bell and Dave Brown, I was inducted into a very distinct kind of journalistic hall of fame when we all made it to the *Daily Telegraph*'s 'Useful Idiots' column, for apparently bringing comfort to 'the enemy'.

Still, at least they succeeded in totally misrepresenting the *Guardian* cartoon which earned me my exalted place in the pantheon of appeasers, defeatists and fellow travellers of terrorism. I won the accolade for suggesting a moral equivalence between Bush and bin Laden, by depicting them as boxers about to start a bout under the tutelage of the Grim Reaper himself. What they didn't bother mentioning was that Old Death himself was urging them to beat up the patsy, an already bowed and bloodied figure representing the world. So far, I would have thought, so even-handedly liberal.

To be honest, I'm getting sick (to death, I might say, but more on that in a minute) of the babel of conflicting opinion that's billowed up over the Earth since the appalling atrocities of 9/11. I no longer want to hear about moral superiority, moral equivalence, historical ironies or how, as quite a few of my natural political allies have said, the Yanks had it coming.

The dust that settled over Lower Manhattan after the immolation and collapse of the World Trade Center towers contained, never forget, all that was left of thousands of human beings: an aerosol of vaporized people that has its exact parallel in the murder and subsequent desecration of the bodies of millions of Jews whose physical

The Guardian, September 2001

remains ended up, as the end product of the Nazis' production line of death, as ash flushed into the shallow ponds of Auschwitz. To say that the bond dealers, tourists, secretaries, janitors, firefighters and all the rest who perished in the twin towers of the World Trade Center 'had it coming to them' as patsies—as 'legitimate targets'—for the real and alleged crimes of their government is exactly the same as the millennia of scapegoating Jews which culminated in the systematic, production-line extermination of European Jewry. It simply won't do as any kind of decent, human response, ever.

That's not to say everyone should shut up, but that the instigating horror, like all the previous horrors our frequently vile species commits against itself, almost needs to be taken out of context and witnessed in silence. The consequences of the tragedy, however, should enjoy no such immunity, and thus my brief turn in the *Telegraph*.

In answer to their charge that I was implying moral equivalence between Bush and bin Laden, I reluctantly put my hands up. Moreover, my true feelings would probably get me into even deeper waters with the churchy fogeys of Canary Wharf. Because Bush and Blair *are* like bin Laden, not just in their repeated willingness to slaughter innocent bystanders in order to prove a blunt political point to those bystanders' political leaders. They also, through their avowed adherence to a monotheistic, absolutist belief system based in the denizens of Bronze Age Judea trying to make sense of life and death, believe not only in life after death, but that that pig in a poke will somehow be better than this Vale of Tears we all inhabit. It may make life more comforting, but it also, obviously, makes life cheap. I, on the other hand, tend to the opinion that, it being the only thing we have, human life is a currency which should never be devalued, least of all by callous fucks who place ideas, beliefs, opinions or principles above the humanity which, in our kilogram of over-evolved brain, has, ironically, formulated that murderous melange of mostly superfluous opinion in order to fill the empty days of our lives.

Jonathan Swift, as so often, had it right in the 'Digression on Madness' in *A Tale of a Tub* (1704). All the philosophers, he argued, separated from their followers, would be good for nowhere except Bedlam. 'For what man in the natural state or course of thinking, did ever conceive it in his power to reduce the notions of all mankind exactly to the same length, and breadth, and height of his own?' And that madness goes across the board, be it bin Laden, or Milošević, or Bush, or Hitler, or Stalin, or Pol Pot, or McDonald's and the Coca Cola Company. In short, the only way for the mass of humanity to survive in relative harmony is to tolerate other people's opinions.

Am I then advocating quiescence in the face of madness? Far from it. Although this may serve to undermine all I've written above, my favourite passage from Voltaire is the seldom-quoted story of the Emperor of China who, about to order the crucifixion of a group of Jesuits, says, he's doing this not because he is intolerant, but because they are.

The Guardian, September 2001

Faith Schools . . .

November 2001

Like the prime minister, last week I travelled down the Road to Damascus, and, unlike him but as is only correct on such a thoroughfare, the scales were lifted from mine eyes and I have undergone a complete conversion from opinions previously voiced in this column. For yea, I am now an ardent enthusiast for this government's programme of increasing the number of faith schools in our community. This may strike my regular readers, regularly nauseated by my vehement atheism, as the worst kind of apostasy, but the example of two recently established faith schools in our borough has forced me to change my mind. The thing is, they really are centres of excellence where the children lucky enough to be selected—sorry, to be offered a place—receive an education which, instilled with core spiritual values, is literally working wonders.

It's true that I wasn't previously aware of a large Aztec community in our borough, but I'm delighted to say that Quetzalcoatl High is going to change all that. Unfortunately, we were too slow off the mark to get a letter signed by three Aztec priests confirming that we regularly participated in Aztec devotions and thus guarantee our daughter a place at the school (which is obviously massively over-subscribed), but our cannier friends tell us amazing things about the school. Its success can be put down almost entirely to the central role given to Aztec spirituality in the curriculum, from the compulsory services held each day at sunrise to the previously unexplored areas of butchery and weaving hummingbird feathers as essential components in the personal development of each student's social and communitarian skills. In short, what the teacher-priests at Quetzalcoatl are instilling in their pupils is the idea of discipline and individual sacrifice for the good of the community as a whole, to levels previously unimaginable in secondary education in this country.

Although our daughter has missed out on an Aztec education (though it must be said that she's on the waiting list for transfer, and they do have a surprisingly high turnover of pupils), we did manage to get her a place at the other excellent local faith school, which I believe is the first exclusively druid school to have received public funding in Britain for several millennia. Earth Goddess (Primitive Wiccan) Community College is as enthusiastic as Quetzalcoatl in making spiritual values central to the children's education, and in similar ways. Nothing can show this better than last week's Halloween PTA event, held to celebrate the Celtic New Year. Mere words can hardly describe the magnificent sense of togetherness displayed on the faces of teachers, children and parents as we danced and ululated, our chants harmonizing with the screams of the teachers, children and parents from other local faith schools as they were burnt alive in the blazing 60-foot-high wicker man erected in the school playground.

The Happiness Manifesto (Toronto: Black Eye Books, 2002)

Now you may think that human sacrifice has no part to play in our children's education. I must disagree. What, after all, could be nobler than the idea of little children, many of them as young as 11, being slaughtered as an act of devotion to the common good? As the god-priest-headteacher at Quetzalcoatl puts it in the school's prospectus, the core values of respect and duty can find no better means of expression than individual pupils having their still-beating hearts carved out of their chests, whether voluntarily or as an alternative to detention, particularly as it is a central tenet of the Aztec faith that, without this sacrifice, the sun will fail to rise each morning. Moreover, the introduction of hallucinogenic paste as the only thing available in the school tuck shop means that, above all, the pupils are *happy* for the entire duration of their inevitably short school careers. Likewise, at Earth Goddess, the whole school, and the wider school family, were actively involved in the fundraising drive—selling mistletoe and crudely carved plasticine phalluses—to build the new Stone Circle Killing Ground, and the altar stone itself was, to everyone's delight, inaugurated by the deputy head herself being sacrificed beneath the Head of Physical Education's flint knife.

All this can only be healthy. It teaches, as I've said, the ideas of duty and sacrifice, and helps us understand the world and its diverse peoples better than we might previously have done. And, of course, it chimes with the zeitgeist. To coin a phrase, Death is the new Life. Whether it's commodity brokers, janitors and firefighters in New York or babies in Afghanistan, the sooner we appreciate that they are merely sacrifices to a higher order of things we can never begin to comprehend, the happier a place the world will be.

Queen Mother's Death . . .

April 2002

On Easter Sunday, just hours after the Queen Mother's death, I was in Stratford-upon-Avon, birthplace of our national poet and, for many, spiritual as well as geographical centre of England. A rather tatty yellow RSC flag hung limply, at half mast, from the flagpole on top of the Shakespeare Memorial Theatre, a building judged by many to be totally inadequate for the purposes of modern theatre (not least because of the lousy view you get of the stage from the cheap seats) and fit only for demolition. Others, many of them knights of the realm, are horrified by these plans for demolition and rebuilding and blacken the names of their opponents in the more popular press. You can take that as any kind of metaphor you choose, but let's move on. Outside, in the thin drizzle, the subjects of this ancient land were reacting to the Queen Mother's death as you'd expect. They were buying ice cream or antiquarian books from the book 'fayre' in the condemned theatre, watching buskers on unicycles juggling scythes, making balloon animals and parading (as they do every Sunday, to the dismay of many of Stratford's population) their roaring, great big motorbikes by the score. Moving among them, I failed to register any collective feeling of grief or mourning or even a vague, sniffy sadness of the kind you could cut with a knife after the death of the Queen Mum's errant former granddaughter-in-law.

Which is odd, as the denizens of Stratford that day—knee-jerk Tories and foreign tourists in pretty equal measure—are, presumably, the constituency for whom this national period of mourning has been arranged. It's certainly not intended for sneering cynics like me, which is perhaps why the only palpable emotion I'm aware of is a desperate falseness of tone.

Any death is tragic to a lesser or greater degree, and that of someone aged 101, peacefully, in their sleep, is probably the least tragic you can hope for, and being the least poignant is least likely to provoke an outpouring of sympathetic grief or pity in anyone outside the deceased's immediate family. That's one reason why the national outpouring of media emotionalism strikes such a false note. Another reason is that the Queen Mother's death is being used—has been planned to be used for decades—as a transparently cynical operation by the British establishment to keep us bought in to the increasingly shabby myth of monarchy and, consequently, in our place. What's odd is that it isn't really working.

Certainly, every newspaper, with a very few exceptions, has bombarded us with endless eulogies, presenting the Queen Mother as some mystical amalgam, in her wit and 'common touch', of Dorothy Parker and La Pasionaria. Much has been made of how she stayed in London during the Blitz and got bombed by her husband's compatriots and her brother-in-law's potential sponsor. This, it is generally accepted, was good for morale. (Likewise, Stalin stayed in Moscow during the war, but, alas, didn't live to see over 3000 of his grief-stricken people crushed to death in a stampede at his funeral.) And? What else? Considerable flutters on the gee-gees, opening shopping centres, being the presiding matriarch of the most dysfunctional non-fictional family of the twentieth century, the fact that she wasn't the thin fascist witch who propelled her husband to the throne and (I'm reliably told) fuelling herself, like her younger daughter, with gin to ameliorate the daily bloody awfulness of being 'royal' seem, ultimately, to be this old lady's only claims to our affection.

And yet, even as I write this, the *Daily Mail* and its fellow establishment patsies are rounding on the pinkoes in the BBC (if only, if only) for failing to be sufficiently deferential, sorry, respectful during their coverage last Saturday because Peter Sissons was wearing the wrong kind of tie and, presumably, failed to pull his own head off in a very public display of grief. Meanwhile, Prince Charles—now free of grandmotherly

Red Pepper, April 2011

disapproval to marry his mistress—opines about his 'magical' grandmother and her 'bond' with the people of this 'ancient land'. This is the kind of quasi-mystical and mawkish 'blood and soil' stuff one more usually associates with Charles' Nazi-leaning uncle David. And this was suitably matched by Monday night's 'news' that gamekeepers from the royal estates were mounting an all-night vigil around the Queen Mother's coffin in Windsor, in a fairy-tale conflation of *Babes in the Woods* and *Snow White and the Seven Dwarfs*, but like the fairy-tale story of the House of Windsor, tinged with the deeply sinister cadences of the Brothers Grimm.

Sticking with fairy tales that go wrong, Diana was another stubborn aristocratic gel with too much time on her hands who could pull the same trick of making her less fortunate fellow citizens feel she was just like them, thus ensuring that they would keep her and themselves firmly in their very different places. It was her unexpected death, and the spontaneous response from the people (and the general sense of embarrassment once we'd got over it), which has rendered the Queen Mother's long-expected death and the establishment's meticulously planned and carefully choreographed funereal rites now seem so utterly bogus and irrelevant. I think, finally, we may have outgrown fairy tales. A nation yawns and, to echo Bagehot's hideously overused phrase (funeral next Tuesday), daylight rushes in and shows an empty room, motes of dust settling on a scuffed and slightly stained parquet floor.

May Day . . .

May 2002

How did you spend May Day? I know it's a couple of weeks ago now, but I enjoyed myself so much that I'm going to tell you how I spent mine. I was working, but being a cartoonist, I was also having fun, and my work that morning was to find some rioting anarchists and draw them. I didn't have much luck at first, although I did enjoy helping to stop the traffic in Park Lane along with some cyclists, people dressed up as Esso tigers and lots of jolly, laughing policemen, who eventually and good naturedly 'moved us on'. Then I watched some crusties in cardboard top hats try to trespass in Grosvenor Square. As they only numbered seven young people and a dog, their mass political action didn't quite come off, but you have to admire them for trying. Then it was off to that old Tribunite haunt, the Gay Hussar in Soho.

There I drew those two great stalwarts of the Labour movement, Rodney Bickerstaffe and Jack Jones, who were, for the record, drinking absinthe and champagne. And a few hours thereafter I finally wandered down to Trafalgar Square to sketch the May Day rally. By the time I got to Nelson's Column, most people had gone home, but you can't keep a good hack down, so, in the interests of serious journalism, I paddled to the middle of one of the fountains and clambered up on top to interview some young people squatting there. They consisted of three young hippy women, a resting actor and a truanting schoolboy called Shaun who lives in a care home and had bunked off to join the fun for the third year running. The actor, incidentally, was stark-bollock naked, as he insisted was his right as a citizen. He's also, he told me, lived completely without money for the last four months, bartering and pilfering the food supermarkets throw away each night to make ends meet. This lifestyle and his nakedness, were, he insisted, political acts, and I couldn't disagree.

It was delightful, sitting up there in the warm spring drizzle, serenaded by the gentle thrumming of the police helicopters overhead and sharing a joint with my new friends. After a while, the actor and the schoolboy both started complaining of having overfull bladders, and demurred when I suggested that, obviously, they should just piss over the parapet into the fountain below. I then bet young Shaun 20 quid that he didn't have the bottle. I'm pleased to report that he won the bet, to the loud applause of the dwindling crowd of protestors and tourists. As the actor eschews money, he relieved himself anyway, making a small human contribution to the ocean of pigeon waste that traditionally bedecks the heart of the capital.

It must be said that their political agenda, beyond nudity, no money and pissing in public, was hardly sophisticated. Basically, they want to be left alone by the global capitalists in order to do what they want to do, which essentially means having fun according to their own lights. But its naivety doesn't invalidate their programme, if you can call it that. The point is that they want everyone else to be left alone so they can have fun too, and were prepared to make a very public stand (and get extremely cold) in order to say so.

After a while I bade my pals adieu and toddled off to my final political encounter of the day, which was far less uplifting, not that Mo Mowlam doesn't know how to have fun. And at the launch of her book *Momentum* (boomboom!) was cuddling those political giants Mick Hucknall and Graham Norton just to prove the point. That was about the level of political discourse that night, apart from the electrifying collective knowledge that Mo hates Peter, Gordon and Tony's guts.

Well, so what? How does any of this add to the political debate? In Mo's case, not at all, as typically of a (former) denizen of the heart of New Labour that debate has long since descended to the level of backbiting gossip. My cycling, truanting and naked comrades, however, are the ones running with the true agenda, and making deadly serious political points crucially by having fun. With the conventional politics of the political elite, old or new, as dull and out of touch as a Sunday afternoon in the suburbs, no wonder that next day the citizens of Hartlepool elected a monkey as mayor.

The Guardian, May 2001

Jubilee . . .

May 2002

Twenty-five years ago, a neighbour came round to my parents' house and asked my father if he's supporting the moves to have a street party to celebrate Her Majesty's Silver Jubilee. 'On the contrary,' my father replied, 'I will do everything in my power to prevent it from happening. Moreover,' he yelled at the neighbour's fleeing back, 'I'll hang up banners saying "Death to the German Usurpress!" ' Now this I could relate to: my dear old anarchistically-minded dad was linking arms across generations and class divides with Johnny Rotten to say Stuff It. Lots of us did. And the common legacy the Silver Jubilee gave my generation is the memory of how blissful it was that week to be alive, to see the Sex Pistols' 'God Save the Queen' reach number one, and how equally blissful it was that 'the establishment' were so frightened as to be foolish enough to fiddle the figures to deny the Pistols their prize. The point was that that jubilee, and the system of monarchy it sought to celebrate, was still worth rebelling against, still had the potency to make our gloriously inarticulate punk catcalls worth the candle. This time round I'm not quite so sure.

The problem is that the monarchy is now such a ragged paper tiger that efforts to remove it come a very long way down my agenda of things that are worth bothering to get out of bed to do. Like reforming the House of Lords or banning foxhunting, the softness of the quarry spoils the sport, and the only significant thing about any of them is that failure to get on and do something about them shows just how frightened and feeble 'New' Labour really is. So should we really care that Tony Blair's tongue rolls out like a red carpet each time he sees the queen coming? I think, on balance, we probably should.

Another thing my father told me was that we had to get rid of the monarchy because it was the cock crowing on top of the dung heap, and that no radical change would be possible in this country while the whole ludicrous edifice remained. And of course he was and is right. Since the last jubilee we've learned to laugh more heartily at our Royal Family than at any time since the Regency, at the adulterous princes, the burning palaces and the pissed-up or pissed-off princesses. And if we don't laugh, we smile indulgently at the funny old things, or enjoy the delicious campness of a good parade, or queue up to look at a lying-in-state from the same motives that make us queue up to get a fast thrill at Alton Towers. None of us, I suspect, 'loves' the queen in any way more meaningful than we 'love' the gift shop at the Tower of London. Although no more do most of us hate her.

What's wrong with the jubilee it that it's intended to remind us that we're actually meant to *adore* this short German woman. She is, after all, the personification of the

The Guardian, June 2002

nation. But it won't wash because, if we bother to think about it, most us know that really she's the personification of the creaking, ossified but still immensely powerful establishment that would have sold us out to Hitler and has shown itself again and again since the war to be both cowardly and useless in serving the interests of the majority of Her Majesty's subjects. That's why Tony's fawning, dull street parties in the drizzle and the buffed-up brocade on a Lord Lieutenant's epaulettes all add up to a self-consciously amnesiac celebration, not of the nation, not of England, its history or its people, but of a senile feudalism designed to keep us asleep. Once upon a time it brought a happy slumber in which we'd smile in our sleep at dreams of glory. Now I suspect it has more in common with a coma brought on by boredom. But the point is that when you're asleep, *nothing happens.*

Significantly, my republican father is my adoptive father, and although I've inherited his republicanism, it's because of argument rather than the genetics that is the mainstay of the monarchy. I'm fleeing the country to avoid this jubilee, rather than stick a safety pin through my nose and yowl like I did 25 years ago. Maybe that's because I've grown up a bit. I won't be around to see how much England has as well.

Berlin . . .

June 2002

Last week I was in Berlin—which groans under an almost unendurable weight of history—in order to avoid the jubilee, which bore the burden of history like dandruff on a soufflé. When I was last in Berlin in 1987, the city was fossilized in a standoff which had started in 1945 and showed no signs of ever ending. Walking in the Tiergarten, we watched as a jeep drove past, containing an American, British, French and Russian serviceman, just like something out of *The Third Man*, made 40 years before. I remember observing to my wife that although this was ludicrous, its absurdity was on the cusp of turning from a burden of history into 'heritage', where the horrors of the past are sanitized in order to be made palatable to schoolchildren or repackaged as tea towels on sale in the giftshop. Fifty or a hundred years hence (and we had no reason at that point to assume that anything was going to change, short of apocalypse or, as things turned out, Gorbachev) that jeep, with its occupants in their antique uniforms, would be as poignant and chilling as the Changing of the Guard at Buckingham Palace. Half a mile away the Reichstag was still a blackened hulk, and beyond it, in the no man's land between the Wall and East Berlin, rabbits hopped and would doubtless continue to hop around the top of Hitler's bunker, dodging the landmines and the barbed wire.

Now, of course, all that has changed. Standing next to the Reichstag last Monday, I tried to explain to my 13-year-old son that, in his life time, the bus we saw coming westwards down Dorotheenstrasse would have been stopped by gun emplacements, tripwire and a concrete wall. He found the idea incomprehensible and, from his point of view, it is. Not just the absurd obscenity of the whole thing but also because the hardwired Manicheanism of the Cold War is now as dead and meaningless for him and his generation as a suit of armour in the Tower of London is for me.

But Berlin still wears its history like a scab. The Nazi heritage, the Stalinist heritage, the Cold War heritage, all contribute to make Claud Cockburn's judgement on Berlin still valid: that a single pine tree in Berlin at midday is far more terrifying than an entire French forest at midnight. But with that legacy of horror comes its interest. Our host, who fled, aged four, to West Berlin with her family two months before the Wall went up, said she still missed the edge, and the edginess, Berlin had before 1989: being a Berliner scored you an immense number of cool points, because it was interesting. Now, she said, Berlin is getting more and more like Dortmund. Which points to an unsettling yet enduring human trait, simultaneously disastrous and yet compelling. Our lives are mostly dull and boring, and so we can't stop ourselves constantly yearning for what looks like glory, the torchlit parades or barricades, the marching armies or the struggle for freedom. That's what informed most of European history for most of the last century.

Meanwhile in London, in my absence, a million people turned out to celebrate the jubilee and watch pomp rock and marching bands, while the grumbles of republicans (like me) failed to generate much interest. In neither case do I detect the prospect of either a White Monarchical Terror or Red Revolution. The fact is the British monarchy ceased to have a historical role 300 years ago, was instantly transformed into heritage and so stopped being interesting. The monarchy exists, after all, on sufferance: we chopped off Charles I's head, and dethroned his son James II, and the inherent legacy of the Whig Revolution is that we could always do the same if they ever dared to get interesting again. In Europe, however, the traumas of history are far more recent and still itch, as all those dull European Social Democrats are finding out to their— and probably our—cost. Despite the attempt to heritage up Berlin's past so that you can now buy Red Army caps and badges next to Checkpoint Charlie, presumably manufactured in sweatshops by Kurds and Romanians, according to our host, those same 'guest workers' are regularly hunted through the Stalinist blockhouses of East German towns by gangs of bored young men. What Brecht called 'the old bitch' of Nazism is, I fear, still sufficiently interesting to far too many Europeans still so maddened by their history to have forgotten everything about it. Suddenly Brian May on top of Buckingham Palace looks a lot less nauseating.

USA . . .

September 2002

My son Fred's innate anti-Americanism is coming along nicely, despite his love for all things American. He's aware of the irony involved here, but that doesn't stop him from asking 'Why does George Bush think he's emperor of the world?'

The short answer is that he is, which explains why everyone else on the planet sits somewhere on a sliding scale of feelings about the Yanks from mild resentment at their brashness to murderous hatred, with Tony Blair off the scale accusing everyone who doesn't evince blind subservience to the will of the American Imperium of knee-jerk anti-Americanism. To a very small degree he's right. Given a choice between American democracy, leavened with huge, indigestible lumps of McDonald's culture and Enron-style capitalism, and the bleak, death-worshipping theocracy of America's latest most high profile and, in the short term at least, successful opponents, there is no choice.

And yet, and yet . . . Let's ignore for the moment those large swathes of the world that were actually attacked last century by the United States or its stooges—Iraq, Iran, Vietnam, Cambodia, Korea, Japan, Sudan, Somalia, Lebanon, the nascent Soviet Union, most of mainland Europe, China, a lot of Latin America—and instead look at one of the few countries that wasn't: ourselves. And yet, as some smart arse observed last week when the 'Star-Spangled Banner' was sung in St Paul's Cathedral, that anthem was written during the War of 1812, when we bombarded Washington and burnt down the White House. In this era of strained ironies, that's a nice one to start off with. But considering the 'Special Relationship', and the anti-American resentment that either undermines or underpins it, you don't really need irony to help you focus on the realities.

Which are these: In the twentieth century, Britain bankrupted itself fighting two European wars, one futile, the other essential to the survival of humanity. The Americans bailed us out, and we're still, literally, paying them back. The 'Special Relationship', then, is that of resentful debtor and contemptuous creditor. Except that stating it so baldly is rather vulgar, and so, instead, the British establishment dressed the relationship up as something almost spiritual, or at least tribal. The Americans, in short, are us. Or at the very least our wayward and bumptious kin, transferred to the New World to have a second chance at perfecting the manifest destiny of the English. Indeed, there's a lot to be said for the idea that the American Revolution was merely the successful continuation of our failed Puritan, republican revolution. And then reflect that America, as a concept, is the exact opposite of the tribal, blood and soil, Heimat concept of nationhood that has pertained so bloodily in the irredeemable Old World, precisely

The Guardian, September 2002

because it isn't another renewable England, but a babel of renewable Germanies, Hungaries, Italies, Russias, Lithuanias, Jamaicas, Mexicos, Japans, Chinas, Koreas, Jewish Pales, Scotlands, Irelands and so on, and on. That's why (in spite of all those pained British reminders about the ironies inherent in the 'War on Terror') significant numbers of Americans supported Irish republicanism, but also why, at the same time, the bankrollers chose not to move to the Falls Road and indulge completely in the old, gory European nationalist fantasy of blood, soil and homeland.

If this is sounding horribly like a love letter to America, in part it is, however mawkish we might find current displays of American patriotism. But remember that there's nothing wrong with the right kind of patriotism. Here, that's a love of the England of Wat Tyler, the Levellers, Milton, Blake, William Morris, the Tolpuddle Martyrs, the International Brigades and (widening the field) Bevan and Keir Hardie, not forgetting Tom Paine. He stands in the American pantheon too, along with Thomas Jefferson, Abraham Lincoln, Joe Hill, Paul Robeson, Martin Luther King, Jerry Rubin and many, many others. And if I'm being absurdly romantic as the latest deformed, greed-driven mutation of the American Dream threatens to incinerate more babies in less fortunate, faraway countries, just consider this, written about Richard Nixon by Hunter S. Thompson: 'This country is probably the highest compliment ever paid to the human race, but just how low do you have to sink to become president of the United States of America?'

Bali . . .

October 2002

Last Saturday's mass murder in Bali is yet another instance of our species' unending war against itself. We must assume that the people who blasted 200 or more other people into bloody bits did so because they believe that slaughtering strangers will make the world a better place. It is always thus, for while I don't for a moment under-estimate humankind's capacity for inhumanity for its own sake, when you clear away the blood and bones you'll usually find, in the wreckage, a manifesto laying out a pro-gramme for transcending our current condition. Politically motivated murder is not, despite what we might think, either cynical or psychotic, but the exact opposite: it's the very best sentiments of humanity—our dreams, our hopes, our inextinguishable belief that, through our own actions, we can change and improve the course of our destiny and that of all our fellow human beings—that inexorably leads to people doing the worst thing they can do to other people, which is kill them.

Before they were driven out by American bombs and their own people, the Taliban government in Afghanistan certainly thought their bleak and bloody theocracy offered a programme for those people which was blissfully good, because it had been provided by God Himself, and you can't get much better than that. And if some people fail to see the obvious goodness of whatever programme it is you're peddling, what option do you seriously have, when a better life for everyone is clearly in jeopardy, than to get the wreckers out of way, in the obvious way? This kind of casuistry is disgusting but universally and eternally seductive, and you can see it applied by Hitler, or Pol Pot, or Osama bin Laden, or Joseph Stalin, or Henry Kissinger. The list is endless.

Admittedly, baser, more selfish motives operate as well, but I think the number of murderous despots who slaughter people purely in order to ensure their own survival is few. Saddam Hussein is probably one, although it's not hard to imagine that he thinks that his necrocratic government is just as good for the terrorized people of Iraq as it is for him. George Bush is more difficult, although it's not impossible to believe that he thinks bombing babies and desecrating the grief of the relatives of the victims of 9/11 by using it as an excuse to pursue a dynastic grudge war against Iraq is as good for the people of America, who nearly voted him into office, as it is for his family's Omertà and the bank balances of his rich friends in the oil business.

Tony Blair certainly seems to believe that he is a force for moral good in this world, and it probably never even occurs to him that he's been responsible for the deaths of more people he's never met than any British prime minister since Churchill. Even if he ever did think such thoughts, it wouldn't be hard for him to say that the end justifies the means which, in truth, it often does. However much we deplore the collateral damage (a popular euphemism for blasting babies into a bloody goulash), only the most callous kind of moral mountebank would argue that in all cases we should stand aside and just weep. And that applies as much in the case of interventionist wars dedicated to regime change as it does to any other instance of taking action against human evil. No one, I think, now questions the actions of the Soviet Union, Britain and the US which forced regime change on Nazi Germany, or Tanzania forcing regime change on Amin's Uganda, or Vietnam forcing regime change on Pol Pot's Kampuchea.

Nonetheless, you have to carry a very precise moral depth gauge once you elect to start wading through a swamp of other people's blood and guts. At the Tribune Rally in Blackpool earlier this month, Christopher Hitchens made a compelling and powerful argument for military action against Saddam Hussein, because to stand aside and continue merely to watch and weep over the continuing suffering of the Iraqi people was morally indefensible. Listening to him, I found it hard to disagree, but as I said to him afterwards, although his plan to use the American Imperium as a patsy to impose

Tribune, October 2002

international socialism around the world was a novel idea, it had a flaw. Climb to your moral high ground, certainly, but be very careful when it's obvious to everyone that your enforcer is still digging ever deeper to find his. Hitchens was about to explain things more precisely when Chris Mullin intervened and suggested they nip out for a drink, and Hitch duly scarpered. He did, however, take his leave of me with a high five and the heartening valediction, 'Stay cool!' As things stand at the moment, I'm finding that rather hard to do.

Saatchi . . .

Just before the turn of the millennium I was asked by a national newspaper which cultural artefact of the last thousand years I'd destroy if I had the opportunity. My choice was the Saatchi collection. This was partly because I can't stand the output of all those Kaspar Hausers who stumbled, blinking, out of Goldsmiths' College in the late 80s imagining that Marcel Duchamp, the Dadaists, the surrealists and the rest of that noble crew had never happened; moreover, if the typical shallow, vain, faux-shocking stuff we see is the best they can conceive of, then roll on postconceptualism, with empty galleries full of nothing at all as the artist (in Rotterdam) hasn't thought it up yet.

Even then, of course, Saatchi would buy the empty space for half a million quid, which was the main reason I wanted to bomb his fabled collection into atoms (and just think: all that formaldehyde would go up like buggery!). The Saatchi collection has practically nothing to do with art, and everything to do with the power of patronage, whereby one man's taste defines a market, and where that man's aesthetic judgement was honed in the white heat of advertising, the Industry of Lies, which also helped give us 18 years of Tory rule. Ironically, despite the Tories' abiding addiction to the pornography of the free market, the art market post-Saatchi is almost pre-capitalist, aspiring towards the condition of a Medici-style monopoly, rather than a Murdoch one.

I'm sure it's just an oversight that Saatchi's own contributions towards art and design—the magnificently mendacious 'Labour Isn't Working' poster and, eighteen years later, Tony Blair's hauntingly prescient 'Demon Eyes'—aren't nestling in his collection alongside Tracey Emin's unmade bed and Damien Hirst's sawn-up livestock. (To digress for a moment, absolutely the worst thing about giggling chancers like Hirst is that they don't do their own butchering.) Nonetheless, in its new home in County Hall, Saatchi's acquired crap has reached new levels of repulsiveness.

Independent Magazine, 1993

It's not the art itself—the rotting cow's head getting stinkier by the minute in a large tank of live bluebottles, or Myra Hindley's portrait made from children's hand prints, or the aforementioned enfant pathétique Tracey Emin's suggestive deployment of vegetables—that offends. Mostly, now, it's just dull. It's the location. In panelled halls and chambers where mostly good and mostly underpaid (by Saatchi and the Britart brats' standards) public servants spent 60 years improving the quality of the lives of Londoners, we now have a private monument to one rich man's vanity. Rather than County Hall housing, educating, transporting and serving the people, the people (maybe that should read 'the consumers' or 'the clients') are now expected to pay an £8.50 entry fee as a tribute to bolster Saatchi's estimate of his own impeccable good taste.

If I were you, I wouldn't bother. I got in free last week when I went to cover some media knees-up on a journalistic assignment, and I'm still feeling depressed by the experience. Although I should imagine Saatchi put as much thought into his choice of location as Hirst applied to placing a pickled shark in a tank (that is, not much), in practice it's his greatest act of iconoclasm, a final smirking symbol of the destruction Saatchi and his smarter clients sought to wreak on the public sector in favour of private greed, elevating individual desire above the needs of the community. And, of course, the Saatchi collection's new home on the South Bank is, more consciously, a direct attack on Tate Modern, which, whatever else you may think about it, is a publicly owned, free gallery.

That, however, begs another question. Is Saatchi's loot a gallery at all? Some people have commented that the Britart sensation is now terribly hackneyed and old hat, and Saatchi's collection is less a gallery than a museum, chronicling trends in art of a decade or more ago. I'd go further than that and say that it's neither a gallery nor a museum, but a mausoleum. Centuries from now grave robbers will push their way through the rubble and the webs of giant spiders, dodge past the eternally burning tanks of formaldehyde to enter the holy of holies, wherein will lie the preserved remains of this latter-day Tutankhamun (in a tank), clutching bags of money and one of Nigella's cook books, and surrounded by his grave goods.

And the robbers will see that there is absolutely nothing of any value there (apart from some rather nice veneer on the walls), and nip over the river to pillage the abandoned Museum of Parliamentary Democracy in Westminster.

Orwell . . .

June 2003

Anniversaries make for easy journalism. Confronted with those acres of empty space, and with unforgiving deadlines making it imperative to fill them, nothing is easier than finding out that it's 50 years since the queen got crowned, or Tony Blair got born, or, as we've seen recently, 100 years since the birth of George Orwell. Squatting as I am on what was originally his column, it would be ungracious of me to complain too much about this summer's Orwell Fest, and *Tribune* had a better claim than most to make whoopee and celebrate its most illustrious former contributor. Nonetheless, I have a gut feeling that Orwell would have been slightly uncomfortable about the mild stench of personality cult that's been in the air in recent weeks, with TV programmes, radio broadcasts, new biographies and, in the papers, acres of newsprint now crammed full of words.

Still, we've all had a bit of a laugh at the latest revelations about Orwell's nark list of suspected fellow travellers which he provided to the spooks. The list itself, as is usually the case, exposed Orwell not to charges of hypocrisy or McCarthyite cravenness, but as being all too human. I was especially delighted to see *New Statesman* editor Kingsley Martin and *New Statesman* Grand Old Man J. B. Priestley there, showing it for what it really was: a dying man's way, by whatever means necessary, of getting even with the people he hated. Disgraceful and unforgivable, perhaps, but also entirely understandable. Journalism, along with politics and life itself, is a rough old trade, and, in any case, I'm not aware of either Martin or Priestley suffering unduly as a consequence.

Someone who would have acted in exactly the same way was Evelyn Waugh, the centenary of whose birth falls this October, so brace yourself for even more acres of print about him. Apart from being almost exact contemporaries, Orwell and Waugh make an unlikely couple, although in fact they held each other in high regard as writers and were among the best satirists the twentieth century produced. More than that, their satires were counter-intuitive, if you limit yourself exclusively to an examination of the satirist. Orwell, hard man of the left, fatally skewered Stalin's Soviet Union, the left's chief false god; Waugh, the blustering Catholic Tory reactionary, not only chronicled the excesses and absurdities of his class (or the one he aspired to) in his early novels, but also, in his *Sword of Honour* trilogy, wrote one of the darkest ever exposes of the stupidities of British-imperialist vanity, along with pointing up the ludicrous futility of the Catholic casuistry of his hero Guy Crouchback (for whom read Waugh himself) and, for good measure, chucked in a nice satire on his own mawkishly nostalgic novel, *Brideshead Revisited*.

Scenes from the Lives of the Great Socialists (London: Grapheme, 1983)

No one, however, has ever claimed that Waugh was a prophet of anything (his face was firmly set looking backwards). Orwell has been less lucky, both in the powers of foresight attributed to him by future generations and in the bloody awful TV programmes to which, if nothing else, he bequeathed a catchy title. But Orwell was a satirist, not a prophet, and I'm reminded of the eighteenth-century bishop who said, after reading *Gulliver's Travels*, that he didn't believe a word of it. The enduring power of Orwell's satire demonstrates that nothing much changes, that human politics has always been debauched by power and that humankind has an infinite capacity for inhumanity. 1984, after all, was not actually like *1984*, except that it continued to be like 1948. Unfortunately for Orwell, his act of deliberate, satirical dyslexia has condemned him to a glib role, imposed on him by lazy journalists.

Nonetheless, if you're still on the lookout for a British author (also born in 1903) to provide paradigms applicable to our modern world, I'd advise you to reread John Wyndham. Perhaps because he was writing science fiction, I suspect that Wyndham won't get the anniversary jubilee he deserves; he was too popular, his chosen genre not quite decent, but he's hardly dated at all. *The Day of the Triffids*, after all, is about a world where nearly everyone has been blinded by a weapon of mass destruction, and then terrorized by intelligent, carnivorous genetically modified crops. And in *The Kraken Wakes*, invading aliens inhabiting the ocean floor melt the polar icecaps, resulting in a fifty-foot rise in sea levels. Filling the papers with speculations about the lives of dead authors is all very well, but don't forget that it stops us being told about the forthcoming, inevitable and still largely ignored bigger story of global warming.

Campbell Gag . . .

September 2003

Earlier this summer, two days before David Kelly allegedly committed suicide, I was standing in London's fashionable Soho when I was verbally assailed by the prime minister's former director of communications. I'd just presented Michael Foot with a large cartoon to celebrate the 'Gay Hussar' leg of the great man's 90th Birthday Footathon, and back out on the pavement a photographer approached me asking if I had a business card as he wanted to contact me later. Personally, I eschew such vanities, so I told the snapper I could write my details down in the small sketchbook I carry most places, and was doing so when Alastair Campbell walked out of the Gay Hussar and bellowed at me.

'Isn't that fucking typical? Martin fucking Rowson signing fucking autographs! What a tosser!'

I insisted that I was doing nothing of the kind, but he wouldn't let it lie. ''Course you are, you wanker! You fucking love it, don't you?' he opined, continuing in this vein for some time until something else caught his attention.

Now many of you, having read the newspapers and formed a firm view of Campbell's sinister and shadowy role in the dark triumph of New Labour, will think that this was typical; just the kind of foul-mouthed bullying this demi-devil had turned into his trademark, striking terror into the faint, fragile hearts of all those delicate and sensitive souls who spend their empty days writing haikus for what used to be called the Tory Press. As ever, things are slightly more complicated, and not as they seem.

The point, I suddenly realized in Greek Street, is that Campbell was *trying to be funny*. True, as a comic schtick it's more *Derek and Clive* than Dorothy Parker, but we play with what we're dealt, and just because his sense of humour is rather primitive doesn't mean that Campbell, like everyone else, can't use humour as a social tool to make people like and trust him. The problem is, his rough, joshing kind of jokes tend to do exactly the opposite. Combine this with his almost insane levels of loyalty to those, like the late Bob Maxwell, who deserve it least, and you have the man in a nut-shell.

Not that I'm offering another apologia for Campbell. In my slight acquaintance with him, he's lied directly (and pointlessly) to me twice, though one of those lies may have been a joke, when (after I encountered a terrible triumvirate of Campbell, Rod Liddle and Boris Johnson at some knees-up or other) he said, jerking his thumb at Johnson, 'How dare you say I swear! I never swear, not even to Tory cunts like him!' That said, his reputation as the Prince of Darkness, like Mandelson's before him, is as undeserved as they wished it was true.

Put simply, he was an over-loyal bag carrier whose flair for brutal badinage made him a handy stooge for the media to hate, leaving his master to grin boyishly and melt hardnosed editors' hearts. As John Biffen said of Bernard Ingham, 'the sewer, not the sewage'.

Before Bush and Blair launched their illegal attack on Iraq, I asked an unnameable Numer 10 source (hooray!) why Blair was being so reckless in pursuit of such a potentially dangerous policy. My source, who is very close to Campbell and the Blairs, said, with some desperation in their voice, 'Tony thinks he's right.'* Which made me guess

---

* For the record, all these years later I think I can safely reveal that my source was Fiona Millar, Alastair Campbell's partner.

Alastair Campbell drawn from the life at
THE GAY HUSSAR
21st May 2002

with Fraser Kemp in ¼ profile.

Martin Rowson '02

Mugshots (London: Methuen, 2005)

that a lot of people around Blair were convinced he was wrong, but got on with their jobs of selling the policy, of being the sewer.

Is that why Campbell finally bridled when Gilligan tried to stitch him up, yet again, as Blair's stooge? For the record, my hunch is that the two people who will come out worst from Hutton will not be Blair and Campbell but Andrew Gilligan and, ironically enough, Dr Kelly himself. Although no one who sees Hutton as a useful stick to beat the government wants to hear this, Kelly repeatedly broke the terms of his contract in saying whatever he felt like to anyone who'd listen, and then went 'ballistic' when the Ministry of Defence 'betrayed' him for exposing his betrayal. And it seems to me that was something he couldn't live with. At least he had a choice, unlike thousands of Iraqis and growing numbers of British and American soldiers, into whose deaths we are not, it seems, to have any kind of inquiry, maybe because we already know why they died and are dying: because Britain is a vassal state of the USA and does what it's told, especially when our prime minister is reduced to a delusional monomania born of a heightened sense of his own self-righteousness. Which may indeed be the reason why, as he might put it himself, Campbell's finally fucked off.

Tory Sacrifice . . .

October 2003

By the end of the week I'm writing this, Iain Duncan Smith may have been cemented into his doomed leadership of the Conservative Party, or may be a rapidly fading memory in a footnote in the whimpering end of the story of the most successful political party in history. It doesn't really matter either way, as the Tories are now looking suspiciously like some strange Melanesian cult of serial godslayers. Without getting too anthropological about it, there are exact parallels between the Conservative Party and those ancient vegetation myths that have informed and fuelled most religions, including Christianity, since time immemorial. Having emerged from the wreckage of the English Civil War as the party advocating the divine right of kings, they've believed for centuries in the importance—indeed, the divinity—of leadership, bolstered by an unquestioning loyalty to the leader. At the end of the day (which is where we are now), that boils down to faith, pure and simple. Thus, Duncan Smith's pathetic last-ditch defence of his pathetic leadership, where he demands loyalty not because he's any good or has any hope of ever being any good, but solely because he is 'the leader', and loyalty, along, I suppose, with worship, is what leaders get because they're leaders.

The Guardian, April 2013

However (and the ironies here are lost on no one), when he calls for loyalty to himself, everyone knows that Duncan Smith was previously serially disloyal to John Major, thus contributing to the Tories' bloody defeat in 1997 and Major's own destruction as leader.

In fact, if you can bear to look at the history of the Conservative Party for even a minute, it soon appears less like a political party and more and more like the blood-spattered clearing round a gnarled old fetish tree deep in the jungle, with successive godkings' heads arranged on poles, their entrails draped over the arcane accoutrements and vestments of Tory religious observation. Chamberlain, Eden, Douglas-Hume, Heath, Thatcher, Major and Hague have all been sacrificed by their followers, those who once worshipped them, in order to propitiate the terrible natural forces of electoral misfortune and maybe make the sun shine tomorrow.

As I said, this is pretty straightforward vegetation-myth stuff. The problem now is, first, that the redemptive, fertilizing blood of the slain godkings has soaked the ground in the sacramental killing fields so deep it's now a gory swamp incapable of sustaining any kind of life, and second that, as the juju doesn't appear to be working any more, there's a dwindling number of potential and willing sacrificial victims. And who, honestly, can blame them?

There's something else, though. The Tories are debauched not just by their dogged and dogmatic adherence to the Führerprinzip, but also, like the rest of us, because of the legacy of their former she- Führer.

Margaret Thatcher destroyed the Tory Party far more effectively than she's ruined the Labour Party. True, Blair is a Thatcherite in all regards, from his economics to his faith in his own unswerving rectitude, but the Labour Party he was elected to lead bridles against his leadership for good, honest ideological reasons. The Tories sacrificed Thatcher because she was mad and they were frightened she'd lose them the next election. And power—on her terms—was all they had left. In slashing and burning British manufacturing (to destroy the working-class basis of Labour support), she almost accidentally let the flames consume everything else as well. But that wasn't only the Old Labour shibboleths of the welfare state and the public sector. She destroyed Old Tory England too. You might say not a moment too soon, but just look what she gave us instead of spinsters, pissed on warm beer, cycling unsteadily to evensong: a million Mondeos crawling into the IKEA carpark on a Sunday morning. In short, Thatcher bought our complicity in her laissez-faire counter-revolution with rampant consumerism, the promise (if you're lucky, you work hard and keep quiet) that you can have whatever you want whenever you want it. And that's how you'll be happy.

In theory, it sounds perfect. In reality, it's cursed us as a nation to suffer from an insatiable craving for perfection, whether it's perfect miracles on the NHS, perfect schools, perfect TV, perfect sex partners, perfect coffee, perfect cars, perfect and electable leaders of the Conservative Party or, in the end, perfect happiness. With the result that all of us, across the board, will never be content and never, ever be happy again. Least of all the Tories.

Xmas . . .

December 2003

Last weekend I went with the family to see the latest James Bond movie, *Die Another Day*. Ignoring for a moment the film's interesting if almost imperceptible anti-American, post-9/11 subplot, just as it started my 12-year-old daughter held up a nugget of popcorn and pointed out its startling resemblance to Tony Blair. Although I doubt that this discovery will lead to the same kind of pilgrimages you get when someone spots a simulacrum of the Virgin Mary in a tortilla in Yucatan, it has potential. Who knows, but in centuries to come the Filmworks Greenwich may have evolved into a popular shrine to Our Tony of the Popcorn with (given the nature of the fare available in most multiplexes) a miraculous spring of Diet Pepsi bubbling up between the rows of seats, with the power to cure the poorly yet credulous of all known ailments, while the lump of popcorn itself will be set in a reliquary of solid gold and depleted uranium. And every 15 December (the feast day of Saint Rose of Lewisham) the holy snack will start to glow with an eerie puce light, and the people will behold it in wonder.

Or maybe not, depending on whether you consider the Age of Miracles to be past. A lot of people in high places clearly think that it hasn't, as recent insights into the spiritual life of the prime minister's wife have shown us. If Cherie Blair has faith in the efficacy of caking yourself in mud in order to be 'reborn' in a shack in Mexico, then why not a miraculous piece of popcorn? It's no more ludicrous, and no less likely to be 'true', than the dicta of the Catholic Church, to which she is a keen adherent. Which begs another question we should ask, as we all carefully arrange our Christmas cards according to the strict rules of feng shui: Do the Blair children, or indeed the Blair adults, still believe in Father Christmas?

This is a tricky one, I know, and S. Claus is a slippery customer. The original Nicholas may or may not have been a bishop in Asia Minor during the fourth century (Common Era, thank you very much), who may or may not have brought back to life three murdered children in a tub of brine, or alternatively may or may not have thrown three children's heads (or bags of gold) through the windows of three girls he was seeking to save from a life of prostitution. What we do know is that his emblem is three balls.

Tribune, December 2002

The image of Father Christmas as a jolly, white-bearded fat man was actually the invention of Thomas Nast, a nineteenth-century American cartoonist, who also gave us the Republican elephant and the Democrat donkey. However, his Santa borrowed heavily from longstanding images of Father Christmas, dressed in green and red, wearing a crown of holly and mistletoe and, when thinner and much more sinister (and with form as long as your arm for scoffing kids in the bleak midwinter), clearly meant to be a Siberian shaman. His current dress code of red and white is either an ancient race-memory of the pigmentation of hallucinogenic mushrooms used in shamanistic rituals or, far more likely, the corporate colours of the Coca-Cola Company, imposed on him in an early-twentieth-century advertising campaign. If that thought leaves (like the product) a nasty commercial taste in your mouth, remember that the main ingredient of coke in its early days was cocaine, and we're nearly back into the realm of drug-induced transcendence and very, very primitive shamanism. The reindeer are part of that as well, in case you were wondering.

So, just as the Virgin Mary and most of the saints are Christianized versions of pre-existing goddesses or local gods, the fat fool in his grotto in the shopping centre is merely the latest incarnation of a very ancient and very pagan seasonal demon. Which is fine by me, and should be fine with the Blairs, considering all the other bullshit, spiritual and otherwise, they seem to believe in.

I don't even have any problem with the 'commercialization' of Christmas: stripped to its essentials, it's a universal midwinter pagan potlatch festival when, if we can, we all engage in an excess of eating, drinking and spending to make us feel better when it's cold and dark and rather frightening outside. So forget all that Christian rubbish, and enjoy! Oh, and if you feel compelled to contemplate the tearless baby in his manger among the ox shit, without wishing to ruin it for you I should just point out that he dies at the end. Happy Christmas.

Chechen . . .

September 2004

What do you think is the best justification for killing children? Revenge? Revenge for the actions of their parents? Revenge for the actions of a government you decide they and their parents topsy-turvily represent? As deliberate targets in a wider struggle to achieve what you perceive to be freedom and justice? As deliberate targets in pursuance of more abstract political or theological opinions? Because, regretfully, they happen to be in the way of the aforementioned pursuit of freedom, justice, your politics or your theology? Because they happen to be in the way of your speeding car? Because they happen to be in the way of your geopolitical objectives which you seek to achieve through a (deeply regrettably) imprecise military strategy we might, for the hell of it, term 'shock and awe'? Because they happen to be in the way of your unending Global War on Terrorism?

Or maybe you think the best justification for killing children is (again and obviously regrettably) because they or their parents obstinately refuse to cohere to the dictates demanded by a strict adherence to the principles of your economic theory. Or because they're less important than strictly adhering to the principles of your economic theory. Or because they're less important than the realization of your political objectives (see above). Or because they, and indeed everyone, is secondary to the purity of your abstract political theories. Or because everyone, obviously, is less important than God. Or because (tricky, this one) they are individually less important than the ultimately happy lives that will be led one day by other children once you have achieved your political, theological or economic goals which (regrettably, as it happens) you can only achieve through killing children.

Although, of course, you may think that killing children is best justified because they can sometimes be naughty. Or because they cry. Or whinge. Or make too many demands. Or are inconvenient. Or are too expensive. Or you can't get a babysitter. Or you're hungry. Or you need their bedrooms to take in lodgers. Or lovers. Or to house you collection of religious texts. Or political texts. Or nationalist texts. Or skulls. Or bombs. Or because you want to turn it into a gym, so you can work out and tone up your bod the better to be able to contribute fully to the struggle to achieve your political, theological or economic goals through killing children.

Then again, you might best justify killing children because they're short. Or perhaps, despite their shortness, because they prove exasperatingly difficult to stack when you confine a large number of them into a relatively small space. Or maybe their shortness serves as an unspeakable provocation, once more reminding you of the primacy over God's universal design of Newtonian physics, with its vile secularist pseudo-theories about gravity and so on, which also conspires to make your bombs, strung up like lethal fairy light between basketball hoops, fall to the ground with fatal results for both you and the children you're trying to stack, thus effectively disrupting your attempts to achieve your political or theological goals.

Or it could just be that the best justification for killing children is that they make unacceptable claims on your limited and diminishing supplies of water (and mark my words, we'll hear this one with increasing frequency in the years to come). Or because the brand of trainers you manufacture has gone out of fashion and the children whose little fingers sew them together have no further economic function, and while not

The Guardian, September 2004

really actually killing them, you are now, understandably, quite indifferent to their fate. In fact, that's probably the best justification for killing children: you, yourself, would never dream of killing children in a million years, but you're so distracted by other more pressing matters, like cabinet reshuffles or the inadequacy of proper structures within your social services department, that you're effectively prevented from stopping other people doing it.

Although, honestly, the best justification for killing children must be that, otherwise, one day, they might grow up, with the genuine risk that they themselves will then start killing children. Isn't it? Moreover, as they're going to die eventually anyway, and as you've already established that your own life is of little importance when set against your political, theological or economic theories, particularly if one or any of those already guarantees that when you're dead you're not really dead at all, surely the most sensible thing to do is to cut out the middle man by relieving the children of all those empty years to come, of pain, strife, boredom, disappointment, anger, frustration and everything else which proves beyond question that this earthly life isn't worth a scrap of the tattered, blood-spattered paper your chosen manifesto is written on. Isn't it? No, I don't buy it either.

US Elections / Fallujah . . .

November 2004

In the assault on Fallujah, which is in full spate as I write this, two interesting symmetries are in play. The first one is obvious, although underplayed in all the coverage: that part of this Final Battle, this neo-con Armageddon, is a civil war, Iraqi against Iraqi. And it goes deeper than that. Many of the commanders as well as the foot soldiers on both sides are former comrades under Saddam, who now either still wear their Ba'athism on their sleeves or have long since hidden their party cards at the back of a drawer. Which side is Vichy, which the Maquis, which side the putative liberators, depends, I suppose, on your point of view.

The other symmetry is more obvious. We know all about the 'foreign fighters' and the jihadists fighting their own final battle against the infidel in the defence of Fallujah and, they imagine, the true faith. On the other side, before the assault we had a lot of reports of the prayers of GIs and their stated commitment to fight 'evil' by journalists 'embedded' with the American forces. (A brief digression here. Did you know that, factoring in its duration, more journalists have been killed in the Iraq adventure than in any comparable war? In the new American Imperium, it seems that journos have only two choices: between being 'embedded' and being embedded in the ground.)

From an individual point of view, it's understandable that poor young men who volunteered for action might seek the protection of a higher power at the prospect of possible death. But of course, following President Bush's 're'-election, it goes deeper than that.

Much has been made of Karl Rove's brilliant electoral strategy in getting out the religious vote, and the rest of the world has gazed in wonder at so many people voting against the evidence of their own eyes and, very often, against their own economic self-interest. America, we're told, is now irreconcilably divided. To put it simply, the two Americas can be defined as the constitutionalists on one side, offering the eighteenth-century Enlightenment, Philadelphia vision of the American dream, and the Christians, referring further back to the seventeenth-century Pilgrim Fathers, Salem model. And I can offer my own evidence for this.

You may remember that in my last column for *Tribune* I jovially prophesied that, immediately following the Presidential election, a new American Civil War would break out between those Christians and constitutionalists. This struck me as such a good joke that I repeated it in a cartoon published in the *Guardian* the day before America went to the polls. Here I should point out that my cartoons are also published on the *Guardian*'s excellent website, which gets about two million hits a week in America, and that they also helpfully insist that my email address appear beneath each published cartoon. Anyway, the consequence was that I received a deluge of hate email from very, very angry Republican voters, most of it foul-mouthed, abusive and, mostly, deeply ignorant. Many of my unbidden correspondents seemed to think that Neville Chamberlain was some kind of pinko Euro-weeny (these were the ones accusing me of appeasing the towelheads, whose authors seemed unaware of the fact that the Republicans were opposed to the American entry into the Second World War or that Dubya's granddaddy Prescott Bush happily did good business with the Nazis). Others asserted that if America hadn't saved my sorry ass back then I'd now be speaking German, although in fact I'd probably be speaking Russian. But what struck me about them all was the purity of their *rage*.

I have no way of knowing the denominational bent of my critics, but their vehement support for Bush and his programme of fear, despair, incompetence and lies suggests they were at least willing to go along with the Salemists and all their baggage of unquestioning obedience and unforgiving, unloving intolerance. But why are they so angry? They've run the world for the last four years and will again for the next four. And then I recognized the symmetry. These were the voices of the dispossessed and hopeless. Just like their Muslim opposite numbers, these people have been consistently underserved and betrayed by their leaders. The Middle East is strewn with the wreckage of the failure of Ottomanism, pan-Arab nationalism, smaller nationalism, Ba'athism,

The Guardian, December 2004

dictatorship and, where it's happened, fierce Islamism. America, on the other hand, has been debauched by corporatism, capitalism, greed and the deadening, literally sickening pale redemption offered by raw consumerism. Huddling amidst the ruins, many people's only hope seems to be to paint themselves into a transcendental corner, where the only way out is up to heaven. Except, on the evidence, heaven isn't there, and it becomes growingly obvious what the *con* in 'Neo-con' is actually short for.

Twenty-Four-Hour Drinking . . .

January 2005

I'm writing this a year to the day since my father died, which provides me with an excuse to pass on an anecdote he told me many years ago. When he was a medical student at Barts Hospital in the late 40s, he took part in one of those weird student rites of passage popular then as much as now, which entailed the initiate buying an alcoholic drink over the bar of different licenced premises for every hour out of the 24 hours of a single day. He told me that this was comparatively easy from about 5 a.m. onwards, with plenty of pubs around the various London markets serving their purpose until lunchtime, and from 3 until 5 in the afternoon he and his tottering companions filled the breach by blagging their way into a couple of low Soho drinking dens. 5 p.m. till 11 was a doddle, and some more blagging in other West End clubs and hotels took them up to about 2 in the morning. After 2, however, things became tricky, and, according to my father, they ended up driving to Maidenhead in the middle of the night in order to complete the task before adjourning back to Smithfield in triumph.

I share this with you because it shows that 24-hour drinking is nothing new, and, for that matter, never has been. Just to widen our historical perspective, there's a delightfully disgusting passage in William Langland's fourteenth-century allegory about the Peasants' Revolt, *Piers Plowman*, where the figure of Gluttony vomits forth a pool of puke so foul and malodorous that not even a 'Hertfordshire dog' would eat it. I've no idea what the twenty-first-century curs of Nottingham and Manchester make of half-digested Bacardi Breezers and premier export-strength lagers, but it's salutary to reflect for a moment on the furore that's suddenly (and rather late in the day) erupted around what is, basically, a rather minor devolutionary reform.

Unsurprisingly, this has largely been orchestrated by the *Daily Mail* and primarily, I suspect, to continue its marketing strategy of selling papers by terrifying its readership with an apocalyptic vision of armies of drink-maddened teenage chavs bringing England to its knees. But it also demonstrates once more a wonderful kind of typically English, and specifically reactionary, hypocrisy.

The person I blame, you'll be glad to hear, is Margaret Thatcher. Her foul legacy still poisons almost every aspect of British life, up to and including 'New' Labour's continuing misplaced infatuation with a market-based political strategy the electorate whole-heartedly rejected almost eight years ago. Thus, the absurd Alan Milburn graces us with the spectacle of a kind of Thatcherite pissing contest as he attempts to make our flesh creep with promises of how irredeemably wedded to the market the next 'New' Labour government will be.

But Thatcherism destroyed more than just the Labour and Conservative parties. In pursuit of her narrow class interest, and in revenge for the post-war welfarist settlement, she systematically destroyed the manufacturing industry, the unions it sired and its communities of workers along, most importantly, with their sense of dignity. Simultaneously, she and her governments deliberately underfunded the public sector and denigrated those who worked there. Remember the kulturkampf against teachers, nurses, ambulance drivers, social workers and all the rest of the people who helped cement society (which she said didn't exist) into place, what might usefully be termed the non-commissioned-officer class of foremen and ward sisters and shop stewards who actually ran things. But that wasn't perhaps her greatest crime; that lay in what she offered in compensation, which was the democratization of greed.

What had previously been the preserve of rich young idiots in Nazi regalia was now on offer to everyone who was willing or compelled to abandon their dignity for a tawdry, empty dream of rampant consumerism, production predicated on nonsense management theory and the triumph of a deranged creed that you can have whatever you want, whenever you want it. History became heritage (with a gift shop); factories and pits were replaced by call centres; passengers and patients became customers; state provision was subsumed into 'internal markets' and life, in short, became Shopping.

It's no wonder that, dignified only by designer labels and new generation mobile phones, the children of the electorate Thatcher debauched should elect to get pissed out of their heads at every available opportunity. What's odd is that her loudest cheerleaders, who thought they had most to gain from her scorched-earth policy of vengeance and spite and did so much to help her implement it, still haven't worked out that the England she destroyed was their England too, and can't quite understand why they keep gagging as they watch hundreds of TV channels offering equal measures of cheap tat and humiliation cynically dressed up as entertainment, and all of it for sale. And the only comforting thought is that at least her millionaire son is now a convicted criminal. I think I need a drink . . .

Iraq Hegemony . . .

February 2005

Three hundred years ago, the English were a byword throughout Europe for cruelty to animals. Hidalgos in Castile and peasants in the Kingdom of the Two Sicilies would blanche when they heard of the depths of barbarity the English would sink to in tormenting their fellow creatures for fun. In addition to cock-fighting, dog-fighting, burning cats in baskets, bear- and bull-baiting and hunting anything with four legs or wings that moved was the exquisite refinement whereby gentlemen of the nascent Enlightenment would, after dinner and when the ladies had withdrawn, stroll out onto the terraces of their newly built Palladian mansions and, with the Capability Brown landscape stretching out into the gloaming before them, toss live chickens into a pond full of ravenous pike built specially for the purpose.

Of course, over the years society's attitudes change. The paradigm shift away from a full and fulfilling enjoyment of cruelty to animals can be seen as part of a more general shift in social and political hegemony away from the countryside to the town. Bentham and Mill stated, in their different ways, that the moral health of any society can be judged by its attitude to animals, but they did so because they were, to a large extent, cheerleaders for that hegemonic shift. A huge majority of the English now deplore the blood-thirsty appetites of rural communities who they'd recognize—if they thought about it at all—as a class left behind by history. And throughout history, of course, power has constantly been moving from one group to another, whether as a result of industrialization, commerce, urbanization, depopulation, climate change, disease, war or revolution.

However, before we get too Marxist about the whole thing, there are occasions when a desired (as opposed to unsought) hegemonic shift can be accelerated, when power or ownership of whichever means of production you choose can be transferred as a result of the intervention of outside factors; when, if you like, a *catalyst* is brought into play.

We have recently had the opportunity to observe a textbook example of this in the shift in hegemony from a previously dominant group to its formerly dominated counterpart in Iraq. The majority Shias would probably have had to wait forever to wrest power from the minority Sunnis if they hadn't struck on the bright idea of using a catalyst, in this case the full military might of the American Imperium. Luckily for the cunning Shia, they found an American administration made up in equal parts of naive wide-eyed Christian idealists, old-fashioned Yankee imperialists and ever older-fashioned capitalist looters, each sufficiently gullible to lap up the Shias' schtick about weapons of mass destruction and the rest of it to the point where they'd do the dirty work and be, in short, the catalyst for a historic shift in power.

Given the momentous nature of this hegemonic shift, 100,000 or so civilian casualties is probably a small price to pay, and certainly a lower price than would have been paid in any internal attempt at seizing power from the Sunnis. As for them, if I were a Sunni, I'm not sure I wouldn't be fighting by any means necessary—including deploying religious crazies to chop contractors' heads off on webcams—in a last-ditch effort to hold on to my hegemony.

There is, however, a fly in the ointment, which arises from the volatility of the chosen catalyst. The defining dumbness of the Bush administration, already manifested in Rumsfeld's novel strategies of victory through under-manning and under-planning, threatens to screw up the whole enterprise because that hotchpotch of naive idealists, imperialists and looters seem to think that they have an intrinsic worth, rather than just being useful patsies for anyone cleverer than them. The last thing the new Shia power elite in Iraq needs is for the patsies to start alienating the 100 million Shia to the east, particularly when, as seems very likely, they'll be essential allies in the forthcoming struggle with the corrupt Sunni despotisms to the west as the Islamic world sinks into its very own Thirty Years' War.

Talking of which, a sideshow to Europe's Thirty Years' War, when Protestants and Catholics slaughtered each other with unprecedented savagery, were the English Civil Wars which culminated in us chopping off our king's head. That regicide, as well as defining another historic hegemonic shift, was another reason why Spanish grandees and Sicilian serfs viewed the English as barbarians. The evolving irrelevance of the restored monarchy has marked the continuing power shift, to the point where the only point of the royal family is to make us get sniffy and go 'aaaaah'. But now, with the forthcoming marriage of the Prince of Wales and his mistress, most people who care seem to be going 'uuuuurgh!' instead, suggesting that that particular long historical process might finally be coming to its end. On the whole, I think it's wiser not to ask the Americans along to accelerate it.

The Thing . . .

May 2005

The nineteenth-century radical William Cobbett called it 'The Thing', a nicely vague and slightly sinister term for what we now call 'The Establishment' or 'The Elite', that critical mass of kings, nobles, prelates or politicians and their courtiers or sycophants who, thanks to some turn in history countless millennia ago, control our destinies. Of course, The Thing takes many forms. The Versailles model under the absolutism of Louis XIV is one manifestation; Tony Blair's touchy-feely faux-populism, praised without question by portly post-Stalinists like David Aaronovitch, is another. A bureau-cratic European super-state, doodled with an almost anal intensity into being by patri-cian old buffers like Valéry Giscard d'Estaing is a third.

But the most interesting thing about The Thing is not its apparently infinite capacity to adopt a thousand different faces or masks, but its rigidity and inability to adapt. This is odd, considering that The Thing is, however inhumanly it behaves, a human construct, and humans are an extraordinarily adaptable species. Or maybe I'm wrong. Maybe The Thing is, after all, there by divine right or else sanctified by the holy mysteries of history. Whichever way, what The Thing signally fails to do is shift in parallel with the changing moods of the human beings it finds itself, for those foggy historical reasons, in charge of.

Actually, that's not quite right. What The Thing can't do is evolve smoothly. At any particular time The Thing's current form is never quite fully adapted to its political environment, but it invariably fails to evolve to suit that environment until it's almost too late and it's staring complete non-viability and therefore imminent extinction in the face. It's only then that it makes a sudden, startling evolutionary shift, more Lamarckian than Darwinian, and somehow or other manages to survive, albeit in an apparently different form. That's what happened in this country in the 90s. Everyone knew that the Conservative Party, for centuries the outward political form of The Thing, had become entirely vestigial and therefore useless (it still is, but has yet to work this out). Thus, in a sudden shift, the appearance of The Thing changed, as the various component creatures contributing to its symbiotic makeup withered away and dropped off to be replaced by seemingly new ones. So while The Thing used to consist of masters of foxhounds, hereditary peers and Richard Littlejohn, it's now made up of media luvvies, life peers and David Aaronovitch. But even so, The Thing still never quite manages to catch up, so in its current, post-election morphology once more it is inevitably out of step with its political environment. That said, there's no real point in trying to blame The Thing: Tony Blair is no more capable of adapting away from being irredeemably New Labour (or was it irrepressibly? iridescently? irri-tatingly? who cares?) than a dodo could suddenly adapt wings to fly away from the Portuguese fishermen bashing its tiny brains out.

The forces that fuel the engine of evolution are many and varied. Round these parts they tend to take the form of voting, even though The Thing itself is far from happy about this. You'll remember how lengthily the various parasites living in The Thing commented on the ineffectiveness of the inexorable mechanics after last month's election, even though the result was a beautifully articulate expression of the collective will (Labour—yes; Blair—no). Likewise, after last Sunday's French referendum, many more of those slimy creatures clinging to the stringy warts on The Thing's back have

The Guardian, May 2005

complained that the French people who voted 'no' voted the wrong way for the wrong reason (and I won't bother quoting Brecht again quite yet). But actually the French 'nonards' were quite right. If they were voting against anything, they were voting against The Thing which, in France as in Europe more generally, is once more reaching that stage of senescent non-viability. Whether you choose to see The Thing in the form of Chirac, a president most people voted for because they didn't want him less than they didn't want the fascist Le Pen, or as a European Constitution redrafted by an elite of bureaucratic committeemen into a lengthy behemoth of unreadable, incomprehensible irrelevance, it amounts to the same thing, or 'Thing'.

Despite the fact that I can't quite think at the moment of any sustainable territorial political construct that's been created by anything apart from war, conquest, dynastic marriage, insurrection or revolution, the European 'project' should be able to do better than this. Its abiding problem, however, had always been that the debate about it, on both sides, has consisted exclusively of beefy rumblings between different groups of worm-like creatures in The Thing's distended lower gut, a debate from which most decent people have rightly recoiled in disgust. What the European Constitution should say, succinctly, is 'Neither Washington nor Beijing, but a Peaceful and Prosperous Europe'. Unfortunately, at this stage of its evolution, the thing is that The Thing is too stupid to realize it.

Lefties . . .

June 2005

Now here's a salutary story I first heard some years ago from, I think, our very own Ian Aitken. Two old lefties are sitting in a pub in Hampstead, probably The Flask, sometime in the late 50s. The first old lefty slams his pint down on the table and shouts at his erstwhile comrade 'I can't see how you could possibly have stayed in the Party after Hungary!', when a third old lefty on his way to the gents says 'And I can't see how either of you could have stayed in the Party after the Molotov–Ribbentrop Pact!' At which point the barman leans over the bar and bellows 'Well I can't see how any of you wankers could've stayed in the Party after Kronstadt!'

Although Kronstadt probably doesn't mean much any more to most people, Trotsky's suppression of the rebellion by the sailors at the Kronstadt naval base in Petrograd is just another of those perennial fault lines on the left that split comrade from comrade. As the Kronstadt rebels had previously provided the vanguard for the Bolshevik Revolution in October 1917, their liquidation by Trotsky's Red Army in 1921 is chillingly emblematic of the endless cavalcade of purity, betrayal and expedience masquerading as principle and the ceaseless compromises which in turn divide lefty from lefty.

I mention all this because I'm currently concerned about the soul of my old friend and former *Tribune* colleague Nick Cohen. Actually, Nick's fine. I saw him last week at an unimpeachably liberal-lefty book launch and, despite being slightly tubbier than the last time we met, he was blooming. Nonetheless, Cohen is apparently now lost to us on the left, at least according to Peter Wilby, former editor of the *New Statesman*. To be honest, I find it rather hard to accept Wilby as the sole arbiter of pure leftyism—after all, he edited the Staggers under Geoffrey Robinson's ownership, which began with a purge which included the aforementioned Ian Aitken as well as *Tribune's* resident whipping boy Paul Anderson, and having Christine Odone as your deputy hardly strikes me as being the defining stamp of pure lefty thought. But of course, we all know that the real reason for Cohen's departure into outer darkness is his stance on Iraq.

Of all the possible points of no return for lefties—and you can take your pick from a vast smorgasbord of points of principle, from Kronstadt via Clause IV to Kosovo and beyond—Iraq is probably the trickiest, and points up some of the complexities in being a lefty in the first place.

To simplify things with a couple of gross simplifications, please allow me to qualify Marx by saying, first, that all history hitherto is the history of struggle for hegemony, and likewise to paraphrase Lord Acton by observing that all power aspires towards the condition of despotism. The role of leftyism throughout history has been to stand in honourable opposition to these two inexorable trends, to oppose those who seek or exercise power to exploit and control those in their power, and once in a position of political power itself to rein in the abiding tendency towards despotism. Struggles for equality, justice and the rest are parts of the process, and not the purpose of the process itself.

Which points out the singular problems thrown up by Iraq. Cohen and others have repeatedly attacked sections of the left for appearing, in their opposition to the Iraq War, to support a murderous fascist thug in the form of Saddam Hussein, and thereafter in appearing to side with the Islamo-fascists now fighting the US-led occupation of Iraq, in Iraq and, as we've seen to our cost, elsewhere. And he's quite right. But, confusingly, so are his opponents who say that, in opposing one form of hegemony, he's sided (like Christopher Hitchens and David Aaronovitch) with the US brand of hegemony which, fatally, combines aggression, simple-mindedness and, as a lot of poor Black citizens of New Orleans have discovered (somewhat later than their equally powerless counterparts in Iraq), almost breath-taking levels of blasé incompetence.

You should never underestimate the stupidity of human beings, particularly the ones who think they're being clever when they come up with a pat definition and

Illustration from Mark Seddon, *Standing for Something* (Hull: Biteback, 2011)

explanation for everything and then elevate this as a principle high above the messy realities on the ground. Which is another way of saying that lefties should be smart enough to be able to believe five contradictory things before breakfast: that you can support Muslim communities suffering prejudice and oppression (in Burnley or Kosovo) while abominating their co-religionists in power, or struggling for hegemony, in Afghanistan or Iraq, while simultaneously abominating ill-conceived and poorly planned military actions to overthrow that hegemony, while still supporting the immediate victims of that hegemony in their own struggle to free themselves from it, frequently by whatever means necessary, which include using someone else's hegemonic power to do the job. But, at the end of day, you can do no worse than follow the money (and the power), and then bitterly oppose the bastards who are hoarding it.

And if all that leaves you feeling rather confused, it probably should. As Trotsky himself wrote, 'History has different yardsticks for the cruelty of the Northerners and the cruelty of the Southerners in the [American] Civil War [. . .] let not the contemptible eunuchs tell us that they are equals before a court of morality!' Which, obviously, he wrote to justify his suppression of the Kronstadt rebellion.

Blair Embarrassment . . .

January 2007

It is reported that, in November 1990, as Margaret Thatcher's cabinet waited to file into her office to tell her the game was up, Kenneth Clarke said: 'I hope this doesn't last for too long; I have a very low embarrassment threshold.' It doesn't really matter whether he actually said it or not (and his central role in John Major's government suggests that the threshold wasn't actually that low). We all get the point. And one can only wish that Gordon Brown had stolen this quality of Clarke's, along with all his economic policies, back in 1997. If he had, we wouldn't be in the mess we are now.

I've said it before, and might as well say it again for all the attention anyone pays it, but Tony Blair has resigned, in disgrace, because of the abject failure of his Iraq adventure. He's just taking a very long time to do it: so long, in fact, that no one has noticed.

That, I imagine, is the point. If he stretches it out long enough, by the time he finally goes he's probably hoping that something else will come along to guarantee that when he dies, he won't have the word *Iraq* carved on his o'er brimming, if dodgy, heart. It may yet work, although I doubt it, and in the meantime, adhering as ever to the template of Greek tragedy, the instigating error works its way through to final catharsis in the worst possible way for the tragic hero.

The Guardian, July 2003

It's the bestselling flaw of Blair's personality that he wants, above all, to be loved by those whose opinion he values. That list includes George Bush (or any American president), Rupert Murdoch, global capitalism and history. It doesn't include the Labour Party or, apparently, the people of this country. And yet the inexorable workings of the grinding engine of tragedy mean that catharsis will only come once he reaches a point of self-awareness as a direct result of the horrible things that befall him. Earlier variants on this have included the death of loved ones, being harried by the Furies and so on.

In Blair's case it has been for him to become ridiculous, and, therefore, embarrassing.

His silence over Lebanon, his Quixotic obsession with frantic 'reform' (with high-blown rhetoric, as ever, an easy alternative to action), his prolonged silence over the circumstances of the quasi-judicial murder of Saddam Hussein: all these were, and are, both ridiculous and embarrassing.

But it gets worse, because that's all it can do, as it duly did with his speech on board a battleship last week, talking up the efficacy of his continued policy of liberal interventionist armed response (I'll let you work out the acronym for yourselves.) Of course, Blair isn't alone among civilian democratic politicians in being seduced by the cheap allure of militarism. So far, he hasn't fallen quite as low as Thatcher, who evinced an unsuspected fondness for driving tanks, or the ridiculous oaf Michael Heseltine, whose fondness for uniforms almost equalled Mussolini and Idi Amin's, or the even more ridiculous Michael Portillo, whose notorious Special Air Service speech was both utterly fatuous and border-line fascistic.

Nonetheless, having run out of options like Thatcher before him (in 1982, at least, when, pre-Falklands, she was the most unpopular prime minister since records began), Blair has khakied himself up to sing a battle hymn to military options.

In part, I agree with him: there's a little Palmerston in many leftist hearts. But that's another part of his tragedy. Iraq was probably the right war, but fought by the wrong people at the wrong time, and Blair's credulity and hopefulness suckered him, and us, and thousands and thousands of now dead Iraqis, into a war planned and executed by idiots.

Worse, while the triumph of hope over experience is often an attractive trait, in Blair's case it just comes across as delusional. Worse still, the repeated assertion that the Iraqi people (or the ones left alive) are better off now, along with the stale mantra that democracy alone blesses them with a kind of unperceived yet understood grace that more than compensates for the murder, mayhem, discomfort and fear which colour their everyday lives, sounds madder and madder with every repetition, particularly as they now have a government of incompetent sectarians who can't even organize a lynching properly.

There was always a hint of madness to Blair's militarism: remember how he sold his policy of standing 'shoulder to shoulder' with America before Iraq, by saying that we owed them for the 'blood sacrifice' of the Second World War.

There was something chillingly deranged about that phrase, even though you could dismiss it as just more meaningless bombast.

But the hotly and widely debated madness of Blair isn't now the issue. What matters now is how much longer we are prepared to let him act out his tragedy in public before it all just gets too embarrassing for Brown, the Labour party and the rest of us to stand.

Syd Barrett . . .

May 2007

On the day that Margaret Thatcher resigned in November 1990, I cracked open the champagne. However, on 10 May this year, when her political heir Tony Blair announced his forthcoming resignation, the bubbly lay unopened and I went to the Barbican for a tribute evening to Syd Barrett instead.

Barrett, for those of you who don't know, was the founding genius of Pink Floyd, who, according to myth and legend, gobbled too much acid during the Summer of Love, went irreversibly insane and, after recording with some difficulty two albums of sublime opacity, disappeared from view for the next 35 years before dying on 7 July last year. Apart from the legacy of his own musical output—the solo albums *The Madcap Laughs* and *Barrett*, almost all of Pink Floyd's first LP *The Piper at the Gates of Dawn* and the closing track 'Jugband Blues' on their second album—Barrett is probably best remembered by most people as the inspiration behind the post-Syd Pink Floyd's squillion-selling albums, *The Dark Side of the Moon* and *Wish You Were Here*.

The lyrics and much of the music were written by Roger Waters, Syd's old school friend, who replaced him as front man when the band dumped its increasingly demented founder. Under Waters, Pink Floyd were transformed from the hippy English whimsicality they exemplified when Syd was in charge, owing more to Edward Lear than to Timothy Leary, into the 'Greatest Band in the World'. Daft, childish songs about hallucinating cats or paeans of praise to bikes and pet mice were replaced by globally popular hymns of portentously gloomy, adolescently introspective misery and angst. Thanks entirely to royalties from his reissued backlist from the 60s, to many people's amazement Syd left £1.7 million in his will, published last week, although there's not really any evidence that he ever spent much of it on either himself

or his semi in Cambridge. Roger Waters, who aged 15 was the chair of Cambridge Youth CND and who in 2002 performed at a benefit concert in aid of the Countryside Alliance, now lives in the Unites States with his fourth wife and is worth somewhere in the region of £100 million.

Syd Barrett's myth has a potency that cuts in all sorts of different directions. First, in the profligacy of dead hippies at the end of the 60s—from Brian Jones, through Jimi Hendrix, to Jim Morrison—Syd is the one who was 'lost' (as almost everyone who mentions him terms it) but lived on; although the ultimate romantic kudos of actually being dead eluded him, he scored high in the romantic stakes by being mad, being variously described as a basket-case acid casualty or schizophrenic (in fact, he was probably neither). Both of these factors added to his allure; not gone, but beyond reach; not dead, but as good as, yet with the faintest tantalizing hope every-burning in his fans' hearts that, one day, he might return.

I've got a bike, you can ride it if you like... R.I.P.SYD!

Then there's the Manichean dimension. In the Syd myth, Waters is the bad guy. When Syd got weird, it was Waters, it is said, who froze him out of the group and then abandoned him (although neither of these things is necessarily true). Worse, he changed Pink Floyd's direction, from its joyous silliness under Syd to the magnificent miserabilism which led to its worldwide success and all those millions and millions of pounds.

You'll be familiar with the template. The good guy dies—or gets killed or sidelined—and all he leaves behind is a yearning, intangible, slightly sniffy feeling of what might-have-been-but-never-was, with everything rendered doubly, deliciously tragic by the certain knowledge of what we got instead. It's Danton and Robespierre, Trotsky and Stalin, Lennon and McCartney. And, each time, the fantasy—the snatched-away possibility—is always inevitably better than the hard reality. The little men—unimaginative, mediocre or murderous—always seem to triumph.

This is how myths embed themselves in our minds and, although the antitheses to Barrett wasn't the guillotine, the gulag or Mull o'Kintyre, it was, probably despite Waters' best intentions, the slow victory of the commercial, commodified society we now live in. Beyond the myth, there's a strong suggestion that, rather than being simply mad, Barrett chose to opt out of the commercial machinery of the pop industry which, like everything else, operates under the current hegemony of the accountants.

I almost included Tony Blair and Gordon Brown in that list of mythic opposites, but that doesn't quite work. Although Blair conforms exactly with what we might term 'Roger Waterism', having become an international brand trading on vacuous pomp, Brown, too, is of the accountants' party. Still, I had a good night out the day Blair said he was finally going to quit. The only low point was at the end of the first half, after we'd listened to the likes of Kevin Ayers and Captain Sensible sing songs from Syd's oeuvre, when Roger Waters came on as an unannounced guest and proceeded to play one of his own dreadful, moody dirges. Half the audience stood up to applaud wildly, but a significant part stayed stubbornly seated and, up in the balcony, there was a concerted chorus of Syd fans shouting: 'Fuck off'. 'Fuuuuck ooooooff'.

There's hope yet.

Speculation . . .

October 2007

When I was on a trip to New York a year after 9/11, a friend of mine who lives in Greenwich Village told me, in tones of disgust mingled with incomprehension, that the biggest tourist attraction in Manhattan was now Ground Zero, the scarred but otherwise now-totally-empty site of the World Trade Center. He was disgusted by the prurience of it all (as were we, so we didn't go), but also couldn't quite get his head round why tourists were going in their hundreds of thousands to see something that wasn't there.

Of course, it wasn't quite as simple as that. Metaphysics usually isn't. But as they flocked through streets still thronging with roadside stalls selling a plethora of 9/11 kitsch (including paintings on velvet of the burning twin towers—I saw several of these with my own eyes), it's obvious that these sight-seers were off to see lots of different things, some of which were there and some which weren't. They were going to see a historic site, a vast and terrible memento mori, the location of a memory, the site of a hope, a vacancy that was filled with despair or a hideously palpable ghost.

But though this pilgrimage to a void was explicable, it was also beyond question pretty weird, even if it remains typical of our times. For instance, a couple of weeks

Tribune, October 2007

ago I listened to the prime minister's monthly press conference, in which he was treated by senior and serious political journalists a bit like Lord North after he lost the American colonies. Without quite suggesting that Gordon Brown had bits of baby flesh caught between his snaggly yellow teeth, the savaging the hacks gave him was proportionate to him having committed some monstrous crime of almost unimaginable awfulness, the result of which was that he was but hours away from being hounded from office in total and eternal disgrace.

In fact, as we know, what he'd done was not do something. As with the tourists gawping at Ground Zero, the press pack was howling round a vacuity or emptiness; in other words, a void. In this case it was the non-election, an event that was now a non-event, and therefore did not exist. As it happens, I don't know anyone who wanted an election in November anyway. There is no general feeling abroad of impatience for the opportunity of change, like there was in 1997. Indeed, if there was a general feeling of anything, it was a mixture of indifference and slight irritation that quite soon we'd be expected to trudge out in the dark and damp to vote in an unnecessary and meaningless contest between the two almost identical wings of the Institutionalized and Permanent Thatcherite Revolutionary Party. The irritation arises from the fact that if we don't vote, we'll then be browbeaten by our leaders for Letting Down Democracy (This, like drinking more than a thimble full of wine once every six months, is something else which is All Our Fault and nothing whatsoever to do with our leaders.)

This obsession with the non-existent—a bizarre kind of media and political meta-physics which exists solely in the invisible realm of the yet-to-be—is present all around us. You can see it in the endless speculation that dominates both print and broadcast journalism; you can hear it first thing every morning when the top story on BBC Radio news is about a report *about* to be published, a speech to be made *later that day*, a meeting someone is *going to* have with someone else. Partly this is because of the current nature of journalism, driven mad by 24-hour news, where you can't tell if the hyperactivity is a symptom of the media's attention-deficit disorder or *vice versa*; partly it's because it's safer than actually reporting and analysing the facts, as I can obviously *speculate* that the prime minister might possibly be a werewolf with far greater legal impunity than I could report it as verifiable fact.

But mostly, of course, this frenetic and hysterical atmosphere, whipped up about things which haven't happened, is because by and large the utter blandness and apparent interchangeability of Brownism and Cameronism makes it seem as if there's nothing else happening anyway. Thus, apart from natural disasters or the beastliness of foreigners, the news agendas are dominated by the latest speculation about the future, whether it's the likelihood of universal obesity or climate change or economic meltdown or whatever.

Of course, you and I know that there is a whole raft of things that need to be reported, but which aren't. The same things need to be addressed by our politicians too, but we seem to have reached a point where the media and political elites in this country are so detached and deracinated that they live in perfect symbiosis feeding off each other while being simultaneously completely disconnected from us, their consumers and electors. How long this will go on for before our boredom and irritation gets through to them, I don't know. But meanwhile expect more and more exquisite, crass and entirely irrelevant metaphysical speculation about how many marginal constituencies or prospective Lib Dem leaders you can fit on a pinhead.

Class War . . .

March 2008

Ten years ago, we were reliably informed that the class war was over. 'New' Labour was thoroughly embourgeoized, and you may remember John Prescott announcing that we were all now middle class. So maybe it's not that surprising that the BBC should devote an entire season of programmes to the 'White Working Class', almost as if just noticing that they're still there was a major scoop.

You don't have to be an unreconstructed old Marxist to acknowledge that class has provided the defining fault line in British politics for centuries. Much of the history of the twentieth century was fuelled by class war, albeit often heavily disguised as something else, and for most of the last 100 years the working class was on the winning side, even though it seldom seemed so. But see how things have changed. The First World War saw the power of the aristocracy finally broken, after it had bungled its way to the slaughter of up to a million working class Britons on the Western Front (even though the mythology tended to concentrate on poetic middle-class subalterns); after the Second World War, Attlee's Labour government fundamentally changed the power balance of the nation in favour of the majority of its citizens, now entitled as of right to proper education and healthcare, as well as the opportunity to succeed in life in ways previously denied them.

However, class runs much deeper than mere material advantage or disadvantage. Wider university access, to take just one example, may have catapulted many working-class children into the middle classes, but the working class remained a solid cultural entity, with its own traditions and values, as well as a strong sense of identity, with much of it linked to the wider struggle for justice.

But then we got Thatcher, who, motivated by vengeance, launched a full-scale assault on the working class. Again, it's not Spartist to describe her policies as class war

Classy!

The Guardian, April 2013

in its rawest form: through the deliberate use of unemployment, trade-union law and the underfunding of the public sector, Thatcher systematically destroyed the authority of an entire stratum of the working class represented by teachers or trade union officials or district nurses or a dozen of other groups who were central to that sense of class identity and cohesion. That cohesion was further eroded by a fresh onslaught of rampant, credit-based consumerism in the late 80s, cheered on by a pliant press with a fundamentally anti-working-class agenda, typified by the *Sun* under the editorship of Kelvin McKenzie, alumnus of Alleyn's, a public school in South London.

But that wasn't all. Thatcherism successfully peddled the lie that material prosperity outweighed all other considerations, including class identity. The chance to debauch yourself shopping at IKEA at midnight gave the illusion of social mobility into the middle class, but all those millions who took the trip travelled lightly, dumping a great deal of the baggage that defined them as infinitely more than merely units of production or consumption. Worse, those left behind, deprived of the example of positive and proud working-class role models, were left to collapse into a kind of irredeemable underclass.

Worse still, battered by Thatcherism, the entirely beneficial kind of middle-class guilt exemplified by the likes of Attlee (and Michael Foot and Tony Benn) got dissipated and distracted. Part of it got channelled instead into a commendable concern for single issues, but forgot that poor ethnic minorities are just as much a part of the working class as their White neighbours. Spiralling yet further downwards, the inevitable tensions that result from deprivation and exclusion made a lot of middle-class progressives, now manifested in 'New' Labour, give up on the White working class entirely, dismissing them as an inherently racist electoral irrelevance.

Personally, I blame the media. The BBC's 'White' season may be a serious (as well as deeply patronizing) examination of the working class, but that doesn't mean they're absent from our screens. In fact, the working class are there all the time, as a freak show. The once-radical Channel 4 seems for years to have based its entire schedule on laughing at the proles, whether on *Wife Swap* or *Neighbours from Hell* or *Big Brother* or *Shameless*.

A rare Channel 4 producer who still had a sense of shame explained this to me a couple of years ago. Almost all media organizations in this country depend on the labour of extremely poorly paid young people who then tend to rise up the ranks. As my producer friend told me, these organizations would be able to meet all their inclusivity quotas on ethnicity and everything else if they simply improved the pay, so that it wasn't just the well-educated children of rich, middle-class families who could afford to work there. As it is, it seems that the class war truly is over, and what we're watching is the victors' mopping-up operations.

Olympics . . .

April 2008

A few weeks ago, I bumped into my old mate Bill Hagerty at the Sports Journalism Awards, where he greeted me with the following words. 'Bloody hell! What are you doing here? You and sport go together like a horse and shotgun!' It was an entirely reasonable question. Although I was there ostensibly to hand over this year's Sports Cartoonist award, the truth is that all sport bores me rigid. Partly this is because I'm no good at any of them, and an hour or so freezing on a touchline aged 11 is enough to define most people for a lifetime. I've also long held the opinion that all organized sport is inherently fascistic, and therefore to be treated with disdain and contempt, although that doesn't mean that thereafter I want to stop anyone else enjoying themselves in whatever way they choose.

Nor does it mean that I don't recognize that sport, as a cultural phenomenon, is very interesting indeed. Like most human activities, there's a great deal more to it than you might imagine: just on the anthropological level, organized team sports clearly encompass tribalism, ritual, repressed sexuality, displaced or rechannelled warfare, the symbolic creation and overthrow of elites and all the rest of it. And it goes a lot further than that. Just to take professional football as an example, while it takes in all of the above, it's also served in the last 25 years as a yardstick for the triumph of capitalism, with the expropriation, exploitation and corruption of yet another manifestation of working-class culture by both the middle class and wizened gangsters like Rupert Murdoch in order to make themselves even more money.

Naturally enough, both its fans and its participants like to pretend that sport enjoys a detached purity which allows it to be justified entirely and exclusively by itself. This is the aspect of sport which annoys me more than any other. But although everyone from English cricketers touring apartheid South Africa to the Chinese government protest at length that sport has nothing to do with politics, this is just another all-too-human instance of wilful self-deception. The truth is that sport *is* politics, in both its high and low sense. This includes trying to hop or skip higher or further than anyone else all the way down to shadow diplomacy and surrogate warfare, and of all the sporting events that ever have been or ever could be, the Olympics are absolutely the most political.

It was ever thus. In antiquity, the original Olympic Games were (literally) naked politics; in their modern incarnation, inspired initially by a rather sinister kind of Nietzschean, Hellenistic triumph of the physical superman, they've remained so. And although admitting as much would probably break the spell, diffuse the magic and

The Guardian, July 2008

ruin the fun, it's the Olympics' political dimension that makes them even remotely interesting. Without Jesse Owens magnificently disproving the lies of Aryan physical superiority, the 1936 Berlin Olympics would have been memorable only as a gaudy exercise in Nazi propaganda, and therefore just as nauseating yet dreary as the Spartakiads that typified Soviet totalitarianism, with all those hormonally enhanced athletes and sad, desexed little gymnasts. The 1968 Mexico City Olympics are mostly remembered because of Tommie Smith and John Carlos' Black Power salutes from the victors' podium and the further evidence they provided of the cravenness of the International Olympic Committee, who suspended Smith and Carlos from the US team and expelled them from the Olympic Village. That, of course, happened after the IOC had decided to proceed with the games despite the massacre by Mexican police of 300 protesting students 10 days before the opening ceremony.

And in a way it's the repeated assertion of the bogus division between sport and politics, particularly by the dunderheads who always seem to end up in sports administration, that gives the Olympic Games any credibility at all, because of the way it unwittingly exposes all the ironies and hypocrisies it seeks to hide. After all, Beijing only got the games because the IOC was reflecting the emerging new geopolitical realities of the twenty-first century, and dutifully kowtowing to the next superpower on the block. Beijing wanted them because it isn't quite yet in a position to ignore the rest of the world's disgust at its record on human rights and so sought the fig leaf of international respectability. But instead of providing the money-shot propaganda both parties intended, the whole thing is descending into brutal farce with a kind of horrible inevitability.

In the first few weeks of Gordon Brown's premiership, when he hesitantly started to pick at the ragged edges of Blair's legacy by dumping super casinos, my wife suggested that Brown's then popularity would go through the roof if he just had the guts to cancel the 2012 London Olympics. I agreed with her wholeheartedly, although I now think we'll profit more from all the other kinds of shame we're bound to expose ourselves to when they go ahead. Meanwhile, given his record since those illusory lotus days last summer, we can only stand back in wonder that Gordon didn't drop the Olympic torch and set fire to his feet outside Number 10 last Sunday.

NI Hope . . .

October 2008

A couple of weeks ago I spent the night in Belfast, doing a gig for the Slugger O'Toole Political Awards where I was drawing the winners as they won—and what they won was my drawing of them. This could have been a tricky—indeed, dangerous—assignment, as quite often politicians of every stripe don't particularly like the way I portray them, but as things turned out everyone seemed delighted, all the way from the delightful female DUP Councillor of the Year to the impressively dour Sinn Fein Assembly Member who won the Up and Coming Politician prize.

This universal approval of my handiwork was a first for me. The Awards themselves were another first, this time for Northern Ireland, as this is the first time in 40 years everyone across the province's abysmal political divides has felt confident enough to stand in the same room as each other, having a drink, sharing a joke and celebrating each other's achievements. It was also the first time I'd ever been to Belfast, so it was good to see first-hand the setting for all those horrendous events I and every other cartoonist have been covering for longer than most of us can remember. To enhance my enjoyment, the Awards' organizers arranged for me to go on a black-cab tour of the city. This is now an established part of the Belfast Experience, originally set up by a cabbie who's also a former member of the UDF, but is now married to a Catholic and has Irish-speaking children. My cabbie was a Catholic called Pat (though he told me in the bad old days he used to tell his Proddie fares that he was called Billy the moment he drove into a loyalist area), and we had a fine old time of it, driving through the pouring rain up the Falls Road, down the Shankill and over to Short Strand, trying to work out between us what the hell any of it had really meant.

Of course, the ultimate legatee of the Horrors of History is Heritage (usually with an illuminated capital H, thank you very much), and in these easier times, it's tempting to look at all those famous, murderous murals painted on the end walls of their slums by both communities and see them slowly, thankfully, aspiring towards the condition of gift-shop kitsch, the kind of thing you could reproduce on the packets of fudge on sale in the Troubles Visitor Centre gift shop. They're not quite there yet, as the 60-foot-high 'peace walls' still attest, but it probably won't take long: say another 30 or 40 years. That said, in the pub after the Awards dinner, I suggested to the dour young Shinner that the whole bloody mess could have been sorted in 1971 if someone had had the presence of mind to get the rival muralists together and fly over a couple of sales reps from Windsor and Newton to get them to discuss materials. In my experience among cartoonists, nothing unites as effectively as the common analism of what materials you use, and these extraordinarily gifted young artists would soon have for-

The Guardian, May 2014

gotten how much they hated each other as they compared how different paints and brushes worked on crumbling brickwork.

This appeal to the redemptive power of art was, of course, a joke, although with serious intent behind it. To his credit, my new found friend from Sinn Fein laughed, albeit rather nervously. But I also believe very strongly in the redemptive powers of laughter as well. There's also redemption to be found in hope. And the most hopeful things I saw in my drive round Belfast, though far less artistically accomplished than all those famous murals, were some slogans daubed on hoardings round an undeveloped building site on the Shankill. These weren't sectarian, but indicative of the return of proper politics to Northern Ireland: 'Homes for Ordinary People, Not for Yuppies!'

There's also hope to be found in the prospect of those Yuppy flats now never being built. And as we watch capitalism's latest final crisis unfold, not trying too hard to resist the temptation to scream 'Told you so!' as well as laugh ourselves silly, hope abounds everywhere. As the criminally mad and unjust hegemony of the last 30 years crumbles away, it's not just the long overdue humbling of our hubristical masters we should be savouring, but also the inevitable consequences of us all being obliged to produce and consume less that we don't need, stop striving ceaselessly for never-ending growth irrespective of the social or environmental cost, and basically just slow down a bit so we've got room enough for hope instead of merely expectation.

And while there's hope, I hope that this won't be my last column for the last edition of *Tribune*. Hope to see you next month.

Offence . . .

January 2009

Something strange happened to me last week. It's my job to produce hard-hitting visual satire of current events, but anything I ever say or draw about Israel—which last week's events in Gaza demanded of me—automatically brings with it a specific kind of double jeopardy. I know in my bones, before I've drawn the first line on the paper, that I'm storing up trouble ahead. This is because of the formidable fire power not just of the Israeli army, but of the Israel lobby too. In the past, even the tamest caricature of Ariel Sharon has elicited emails accusing me of producing the vilest anti-Semitic cartoon since the closure of Julius Streicher's Nazi hatesheet *Der Stürmer*, neatly if somewhat boldly asserting that any criticism of Israel equates me with one of the more prominent cheerleaders of the Holocaust.

This is a longstanding and largely effective tactic, even if the idea that the state of Israel is synonymous with worldwide Jewry is a false syllogism, as is the insistence that any and all criticism of Israel is automatically evidence of anti-Semitism. It's worse if you're actually Jewish and don't unquestioningly support everything Israel does. Then you're a 'self-hating Jew' or, according to Melanie Phillips, part of a repulsive movement she dubbed 'Jews for Genocide'. In other words, little better—and probably worse—than a Nazi.

I suspect the people who say things like this know it's not actually true, but understand how insults work. Two and a half years ago I did an admittedly savage cartoon about Israel's disastrous incursion into Lebanon. Mostly thanks to the aforementioned Melanie's website publishing my email address and fomenting her readers to give me a piece of their mind, I received a deluge of thousands of emails, most of which read, pithily enough, 'Fuck off, you anti-Semitic cunt.' Now, it must be said that I've always worked on the basis that if I can't take it, I shouldn't give it, but this onslaught rattled me. It wasn't the Tourettic tone of the emails, but the accusation that I'm an anti-Semite, which I'm not. But an insult isn't an insult if it accuses you of being something you actually are, and the point of hurling such insults is pretty obvious. It's to make people you disagree with (adopting my correspondents' shtick) to shut the fuck up and go away, either in shame, fear or embarrassment. And thus, to all intents and purposes, you win the argument.

As I said, this is an effective tactic, even if it's a dumb strategy, and it's been very popular in recent years for any group, from Zionists to Islamists to atheists, to use the excuse of being 'offended' as an offensive weapon to force their opponents to shut the fuck up by returning the offence in spades. If you think about it, Mad Mel's 'Jews for Genocide' crack is infinitely more offensive than anything any non-Zionist Jew has ever said, but the nature of the game means that it's unlikely, in all her sour self-righteousness, Mel's going to shut the fuck up any time soon. (Would that she were, along with a list of other sourly self-righteous pundits almost infinitely long, including David Cameron when he talks about the state of the economy, because everybody knows his party is directly responsible for the mess we're in, up to and including debauching the Labour Party into hurtling headlong down the same blind alley.)

Anyway, back to that strange thing that happened to me. Last Wednesday, the *Guardian* published a cartoon of mine called 'Balance Reporting' (a dig at one of the Israel lobby's most vociferous websites) showing the Grim Reaper holding a set of scales, one side laden with hundreds of Palestinian coffins and the other with about nine Israeli ones. In the cartoon the latter appears to be heavier because the Reaper's got his thumb on it. I thought it was quite a good image, but still hunkered down in expectation of another tsunami of hate emails making all the usual accusations in the usual way.

However, all I got was one email, purportedly from an Israeli army officer, which praised my work but thought that maybe I'd got hold of the wrong end of the stick. Interestingly, it was a very long email—far longer than something knocked off in a fox hole outside Gaza City—and my man had neglected to delete the job title 'Project Manager' after his name, which suggests that, apart from a personalized first paragraph, this was a form email being sent to any Western journalist the Israeli spin machine noticed.

Maybe this is the beginning of a new, gentler tactic. Maybe I'm just no longer worth the effort of being told to shut the fuck up. But either way, what I've been writing about is merely a side show, if hitherto an extremely ugly one, to the real story, which is the old story about the unrestrained flexing of power and the consequent accruing of piles of corpses. Although it must be said that my email correspondent insisted that the Israeli army went out of its way to try to avoid civilian casualties as it pursued its entirely justified and defensive action. Which, I suppose, puts an entirely different complexion on the whole thing, and the Israelis aren't the brutal, callous, hegemonic mighty military machine their actions would have led the world to believe. It's just possible, if he's right, that they're simply completely bloody useless.

50th Birthday / Stop the War . . .

February 2009

Six years ago this Sunday, on 15 February 2003, between one and a half and two million people marched—or, in most cases, ambled—through the streets of London in order to tell Tony Blair that they didn't want to be party to an American-led invasion of Iraq. As we all know, he preferred listening to voices in Washington, or possibly even in his head, to those coming from the streets. As we also know, his selective deafness had dire consequences not just for the hundreds of thousands of people who are now dead as a result, be they Iraqi civilians or British or American soldiers, but also for his premiership and his reputation.

Still, as Blair has told us repeatedly ever since, he did what he did because he thought both it and he were 'right'. That, as he's also often said, is what 'leaders' do. Which I suppose must be right too. After all, we have these people to lead us, by the nose if necessary, in whichever direction they think 'right', a decision they come to because of their greater wisdom, experience and judgement. Which (to go full circle) is why they are the leaders and we are the led.

Except, as ever, it's not quite as simple as that. You may remember that a few months ago I mentioned a book I'd just read by an American anthropologist called Christopher Boehm. In *Hierarchy in the Forest*, he argued that, unlike almost all of our primate cousins, we humans are not—or, more to the point, were not—hierarchical in the same way as chimpanzees, gorillas or baboons. By studying the ethnographic record, he realized that pre-agricultural peoples on every inhabited continent not only don't exhibit social hierarchies of the kind we now endure, but actively go out of their way to prevent the hierarchies, and the leaders at their summit, from emerging. He called this structure 'counter-hierarchical' and further argued that it was an evolved mode of behaviour which is also present in bonobos, our closest genetic relatives. But more interesting still, he triangulated from his findings and suggested that, until the advent of the settled communities that arose because of agriculture, this was how all previous humans had lived, for around 95 per cent of our time on the planet.

As is only appropriate as we celebrate Charles Darwin's 200th birthday, as well as the 150th anniversary of *On the Origin of Species*, which demonstrated how we humans are interwoven into the whole tapestry of life on Earth, it's worth repeating that this shows what kind of animals we actually are, and how we're meant to be. In the wild, so to speak, humans are strictly egalitarian. But this is merely a consequence of a deeper human motivation, which is altogether more heartening than the kind of brutal, collectivist egalitarianism you might conjure up in your mind, following nine thousand years or so of being both conditioned and coerced by the imposed hierarchies of civilization. In our natural state we successfully strove against the emergence of hierarchies in order to protect our individual personal autonomy. In other words, we acted collectively to stop ourselves being individually terrorized into submitting to the will of putative leaders.

And that, in a nutshell, is the bedrock of all human history hitherto, back to around 7000 BCE. Before then, there were no leaders. Or, as the anthropologists would have it, no alpha males.

Now, of course, with the benefit of civilization and technology, which have resulted not only in more or less permanent exploitation, inequality and warfare but also the probable rendering of the planet as uninhabitable, we have leaders to show us the way. But the question arises—sticking with an anthropological turn of phrase—of just how alpha those alpha males (and females) actually are. Because it's now obvious that our recent leaders who've droned on most about 'leadership'—that is, Thatcher, Blair and Brown—showed all the signs of behaving like cringing baboons fawning to the City of London in order to avoid a clip round the ear from the well-heeled alpha males therein.

The Guardian, February 2003

In Thatcher's case, this is understandable, though unforgivable. As the 'leader' of a party committed to the maintenance of hierarchies, she torched manufacturing in order to terrorize any challenge to the hierarchy from the unions or the working class into submission, meaning there was only the financial sector left to fuel the economy. But Blair and Brown's abject surrender to Thatcherism, and their subsequent subservience to the hierarchy their party was created to undermine, is far more unforgivable. Then again, Blair has beta male written all over him, along with a potential for lackeyism, which cost countless Iraqis far more than a banker losing his bonus.

Which brings us back to the Stop the War March. It happened to take place on my 44th birthday, and even a banker could probably do the simple maths involved to tell him that that means that this Sunday I'll be 50. Which is no big deal in itself, although it's enormously gratifying to enter my sixth decade to the clatter of the latest elite of idiots tumbling from their false hierarchy. Twitching the strands of DNA that stretch back through the millennia to our ancestors, such a response is only—and truly—human.

Anarchism . . .

April 2009

There's an old and largely forgotten anarchist slogan which goes something along the lines of 'Tear it down! It doesn't need rebuilding!' That has a pleasingly nihilistic ring to it: the old anarchist idea of destruction for its own sake which was typified by their strategy in the nineteenth century of what was called 'propaganda by the deed'. This would entail a vanguard of anarchists (in the public imagination wearing wide-brimmed fedoras and capacious cloaks, carrying a spherical black bomb with the word 'bomb' written on it) undertaking symbolic acts of terrorism in the belief that by example they would inspire the masses spontaneously to rise up and overthrow their oppressors. You know, like blowing up the Archbishop of Zaragoza or someone. Indeed, pursuing this policy, anarchists succeeded in murdering not just archbishops, but also tsars, kings, capitalists and American presidents, as well as a depressingly large number of bystanders, although at the end of the day they had little to show for it.

Nonetheless, for about a hundred years, from the failed revolutions of 1848 to the Spanish Civil War, anarchism was a potent political force, and a far more effectively terrifying spectre haunting both Europe and America than communism, which languished for the most part in sectarian bickering until Lenin's Bolsheviks seized the main chance and staged the coup d'état which history refers to as the October

Revolution. After that, the anarchists in Russia were consigned, in Trotsky's memorable phrase, to the 'scrapheap of History', although in practice, in both Russia and, later, in Spain, this meant that they were liquidated by the Bolsheviks.

History is a fickle old tart at the best of times, and these days we prefer not to remember the passionate hope millions of people placed in anarchism to liberate them from the tyranny of kings, churches and the violence inherent in the state. We forget about the thousands of anarchists who attended the Russian anarchist Prince Kropotkin's funeral in 1921, or the quarter of a million mourners for the Spanish anarchist Buenaventura Durruti in Barcelona in 1936, after he was killed by a stray bullet following his anarchist militia's relief of Madrid, which had been besieged by fascists prior to the arrival of the eponymous 'Durruti column'.

Indeed, *Tribune* readers of a certain age may only recognize 'Durutti column' as the name of a Mancunian post-punk band cobbled together by the late Tony Wilson, who called themselves—misspelling it as 'Durutti column'—not after the anarchist militia leader, but from a slogan on a 1967 poster produced by the slightly preposterous groupuscule of exhibitionists who formed the Situationist International and who spelled the name wrong in the first place.

Which in itself is highly emblematic of the fate of failed political movements: revolutions repeat themselves not, like history, as farce, but as brand names, pacified spectacle or a knee-jerk signifier of cool. Just consider how Franz Ferdinand expropriated the iconography of Soviet Futurism for the cover of their first album, or how Joe Strummer, signed up to CBS, used to ponce around in a Red Brigades tee-shirt.

And so it is with anarchism, or at least those who style themselves anarchists these days. For me, the most telling image from last week's G20 meeting was of the crusty young man smashing a window of the Royal Bank of Scotland, surrounded by probably hundreds of photographers. This was 'propaganda by the photo-opportunity', a weird kind of symbiosis between the media and people who claim to want to change the world, but seek to do so by parading themselves as a media-friendly freak show.

I suppose this tactic has certain merits, although there's always a danger that the host body will eventually be completely engulfed by its parasites and the demonstrators will all be snappers and hacks, a bit like those cells of the American Communist Party in the 50s where the cadres finally realized that every single one of them was an FBI agent provocateur. That said, it doesn't mean that we shouldn't all be actively seeking to tear it down, or that it needs rebuilding.

Remember, what the G20 achieved was merely the recharging of the batteries of the life-support machines keeping global capitalism just about alive, albeit currently in what looks like a permanent vegetative state. What none of the world's 'leaders'

Daily Mirror, October 2019

have embraced for a moment is the idea of grabbing this golden opportunity to forge something new from the self-inflicted wreckage. Something, for instance, which might halt or even reverse our suicidal addiction to carbon, institutionalized inequality or, for that matter, permanent economic growth.

Then again, the G20 was, in reality, not much more than just another spectacle, although in the long term it might prove infinitely more destructive than the capering antics of the cosy mob who think a friendly punch-up in Threadneedle Street constitutes 'tearing it down.'

Viruses . . .

May 2009

As I write, highly civilized human beings are flying overhead, brimming with highly uncivilized viruses that are trying to kill me. Those viruses, in turn, gestated thanks to the husbandry practices of other highly civilized human beings with regard to uncivilized pigs.

They—the viruses, that is—do not feel any enmity against me as an individual, nor I against them, though a third group of highly civilized human beings are currently working their socks off to devise new and cunning means of preventing the viruses from killing me, which will probably involve, in the long run, killing the viruses.

Aeroplanes as a vector of death is an old trope and covers everything from high-altitude bombing to the spread of AIDS to facilitating flying to faraway, sun-kissed resorts which require the native population to service the tourists and, therefore, find themselves in the path of tsunamis, which then kill them. The aeroplanes are, of course, the product of the ingenuity of yet another group of highly civilized human beings, but there you go.

As I write, a school about three miles from me (which is also, co-incidentally, the alma mater of Kelvin MacKenzie) has been closed because several of the pupils have been diagnosed as being infected by the viruses whose kin are undoubtedly hitching rides around the world on aeroplanes of the type which transported one of the school children halfway round the world and back in order to get a better tan, unwittingly returning home incubating some of the viruses.

As I write, thankfully none of the children are dead, although many of the viruses maybe.

Many of the pigs are certainly now dead, along with many hundreds of thousands of other pigs in countries far distant from the instigating swine, populated by highly

The Guardian, July 2009

civilized human beings whose porcine charges are thousands of miles from the particular viruses that are trying to kill me.

And, as I write, it's also 30 years and a day since Margaret Thatcher was first elected prime minister of Great Britain, which includes England, your England. And hopefully you'll have noticed my allusion to the essay of the same name written by George Orwell at the height of the Blitz. As he wrote, all around him unfolded one of the greatest cataclysms in history, killing thousands of highly civilized human beings in the vicinity closest to him and millions more the further you looked. Almost all of them were killed by other highly civilized human beings, for what that's worth.

Domestically, and as I write, the latest greatest cataclysm to befall us has killed no one. Nor did the previous greatest cataclysm to befall us, entirely the fault of highly civilized human beings, stop other highly civilized human beings from continuing to jaunt across the planet and get infected by the viruses that are trying to kill me. But then cataclysms of the kind highly civilized human beings seem constantly to yearn for, with a thrill of potential oblivion, aren't what they used to be. And neither, of course, is the England Orwell wrote about.

That, as we know, was killed stone dead by Margaret Thatcher, and her heirs in New Labour did nothing much to try and either revive the corpse or recreate something better but still recognisably in its image. Instead, she and they rebuilt England, or parts of it, as a vast Potemkin village, the artificial and unpopulated settlements erected in order to impress Catherine the Great, although in this case the hollow facades were intended to fool the inhabitants. The rest of England they left to rot.

As I write, for 30 years and a day not just England but the world has been subjugated by highly civilized human beings who, it's true, have tried to and succeeded in killing many other highly civilized human beings, but have also been culpable in buttressing systems of agriculture which often prove deadly, an economic system which, when it worked, was unbelievably callous and wasteful and an analysis of highly civilized human beings which barely acknowledges that such people exist. Instead, they gave many of us the opportunity to be desperately self-indulgent, our endless binges leavened by a neurotic obsession with every hint of cataclysm that emerged, be it global warming, swine flu, bird flu, obesity, financial meltdown, the breakdown of society, all the way up to the possibility of being offended by what someone else says. You could call this state of mind cataclysmism, and at the moment it seems to encompass Gordon Brown every time he pratfalls on a pinhead.

So, as I write, I might easily be about to be killed by the latest cataclysm, though I doubt it. And yet my optimism doesn't stop me feeling constantly queasy. But I put that down to the fact that, as I write, it seems almost inevitable that, following the next election, we'll get just another bunch of highly civilized idiots in the form of David Cameron's cataclysmists.

Militarism . . .

July 2009

George Orwell, the most celebrated former tenant of this column, got it right in 'England, Your England' about militarism and the English. We're just not very good at it. Whereas other nations—most other nations, as it happens—make a fetish of their armed forces, our emotions are mixed, mingling pride, ingratitude, sentimentality and a certain level of embarrassment. Despite our extraordinarily bellicose history, since medieval times we've only tolerated one military dictator, in the person of Oliver Cromwell, even though there have been any number of candidates for the post, all the way from Marlborough to the madmen who wanted to stage a coup against Harold Wilson's Labour government in the late 60s.

This is all rather odd, given our status as all-time top warmongers. Over many centuries we fought each other (at the Battle of Towton on Palm Sunday in 1461, the number of dead at the end of the day equalled roughly one per cent of the country's entire population, and the River Ouse ran red with blood through York for a month); we also fought our neighbours and eventually conquered, and then held through military subjugation, a quarter of the land surface of the Earth. And yet, apart from school children once upon a time parroting the dates of battles or the preponderance of eligible, marriageable but apparently non-combatant army officers in the novels of Jane Austen, ours is not a particularly militarized culture. In England, you'd never witness the kinds of scenes I saw, aged 16, in Toledo the year Franco died, of jackbooted cadets from the Guardia Civil's staff college outside town pushing respectable citizens from their tables in cafes in the main square. In fact, the closest you get to anything like that is round midnight in garrison towns on Saturday nights, before the Military Police turn up with the billy clubs and marshal the drunks back to barracks.

Of course, there's a healthy dose of English hypocrisy in all of this. Rudyard Kipling, too often dismissed as merely the jingoistic laureate of empire, caught it perfectly with the lines:

For it's Tommy this, an' Tommy that, an' 'Chuck him out, the brute!'
But it's 'Saviour of 'is country' when the guns begin to shoot.

Nor should we forget the last verse of 'The Young British Soldier':

When you're wounded and left on Afghanistan's plains,
And the women come out to cut up what remains,
Jest roll to your rifle and blow out your brains
An' go to your Gawd like a soldier.

The Guardian, July 2009

Which might lead you to conclude that nothing much changes, whether it's the perpetual lot of the poor bloody infantry, the harsh but enduring realities of geopolitics or the eternal capacity of civilian politicians to get young and, if non-commissioned, usually poor men to do their fighting and dying for them. But you also might choose to reflect on the timelessness of the poignancy and the pathos; that our failure to embrace militarism as much as we might—and as much as a powerful cabal of generals and journalists might want us to—arises, albeit inconsistently and with typical muddle-headedness, from our grief and our sense of shame trumping all those baser emotions triggered by a good parade.

The grief we feel at the death of the scantily equipped teenagers recently killed in Afghanistan is different from that we might have felt on hearing of the death last weekend of Harry Patch, over six times their age and the last surviving serving soldier from the Great War. But it's also, in many ways, identical. Patch, merely through his longevity, came to embody all the ordinary soldiers of that war, particularly the million who, unlike him, were dead by the time he was 18. True, these days the shame and the grief kick in quicker, and just dozens of dead over a week can now fuel thoughts about the futility of the whole enterprise. In Harry Patch's war, the generals and the journalists could easily accommodate 66,000 casualties on the first day of the Battle of the Somme without complaining about the equipment or thinking that maybe, just maybe, they should call it a day.

And maybe it was that degree of steady callousness—though it's always a mystery whether our ruling elite are motivated by malice or idiocy, or both—which inspired Prince Charles to describe Harry Patch, a conscript who railed in great age about the pointlessness of the whole war, as the last representative of 'our noblest generation'. How nobility manifests itself in industrial carnage is anyone's guess, though I imagine Prince Charles, happily embedded in the gilded heart of the military–monarchical complex, thinks he means vague and vaguely uplifting things like sacrifice, honour and patriotism, those words which, along with human corpses, compost militarism at its most mawkish.

Although I can't stop myself from thinking there's a higher nobility, whether 90 years ago or last week, in following George Bernard Shaw's notorious advice written in 1914: that the troops should probably shoot their officers and go home.

Zoo . . .

October 2009

I don't know if I've ever told you this, but I'm very fond of London Zoo. So fond of it, in fact, that I've spent nearly two decades actively involved in its governance and administration, ever since, as part of a group of rebellious members of the Zoological Society of London, I played a part in an insurrection against the decision, in the early 90s, to close the place. Well, we won that one. Not only didn't London Zoo close, but we also succeeded in shifting its whole ethos away from being merely another 'visitor attraction' to being a global centre for the conservation of wildlife and the natural world.

So, if any of you persist in believing that London Zoo is still an Auschwitz for animals, there solely to provide cheap and cruel thrills for gawping humans, I'd respond by insisting that, on the contrary, it's more like the apotheosis of welfarism, about protection rather than exploitation.

Of course, none of this is necessarily truly 'natural'. But again, I'd counter arguments against the existence of zoos, and in the following ways. Once more it's about protection. Any free-market bunny hugger out there (and there are quite a lot of them, believe me) who thinks the animals of London Zoo would be better off liberated from their enclosures should then take a minute or two to count the subsequent roadkill on Baker Street. Because the reason these animals need protection, as well as conservation, is that there's hardly any 'natural' left, entirely thanks to us. Which points to another reason why we both have and need zoos. It's because of how unnatural we, as a species, have become: we're sanitized, deracinated and denatured; urban humans, enclosed behind the bars of an infinite number of real and metaphorical concentric cages, yearn for the company of animals. This is partly, I suspect, so that we can make a stab at reconnecting with what we've lost.

Anyway, last week I went to a talk at the Zoo about conservation in the year 2050. And it's not looking good. Most of the world's fisheries will have been trawled to extinction, and what seafood there is will mostly consist of squid and algaeic slime. The world's human population will have increased 50 per cent from its current level to 9 billion, which will require a consequent doubling in land used for agriculture. That land is currently occupied by virgin rainforest which contains most of the planet's terrestrial animal and plant species, so they too will become extinct, massively reducing Earth's biodiversity. A majority of all those new people will live in cities, and the demand for fresh water for both them and all the new agriculture will lead, with a horrible inevitability, to massive water shortages and, consequently, water wars. Jordan already has no surface water left. The Himalayan glaciers have already nearly gone, so we won't just have water wars, but a water *nuclear* war between India and Pakistan. And all that happens without even beginning to factor in climate change.

Lower than Vermin: An Anatomy of Thatcher's Britain (London: Arrow Books, 1986)

It gets worse. Although nearly all those extra three billion people will be poor and non-White (adding to the one billion of our fellow human beings already living below starvation levels), their suffering will be our fault. That's because the world remains enthralled to a Western, Anglo-Saxon economic system, itself the narrowest possible model of all possible modes of human and non-human interaction, which is predicated solely on the shortest of short-termism, combining a lust for personal consumption and personal greed. This is reflected in our politics, which is constrained into a tiny arc of a much wider spectrum, where most of our politicians are institutionally blinkered from seeing the bigger picture.

One of the speakers last week was a United Nations economist who showed us a bar chart of global expenditure this year. The US stimulation package was the biggest, and about a third bigger than the global arms trade, but that was only about a fifth larger than bankers' bonuses on Wall Street *alone*. But the bill for bankers' bonuses was still 25 per cent bigger than *the whole of aid to the non-Western world*. So once more, the most destructive type of short-term greed is literally more valuable than collective human action to help billions of people help themselves out of the kind of poverty that compels them into reproductive cycles which compound their immiseration.

Is there any hope? Not at the moment there isn't, although I modestly proposed to several other members of the audience afterwards that if we were serious about wildlife conservation, we should kill all the doctors and then all the farmers, and after a couple of admittedly turbulent generations the few remaining bands of hunter-gatherers would live in perfect ecological harmony with the natural world. I was, of course, being satirical. My real fear, however, is that in 40 years' time, and with a straight face, they'll be calling that kind of thing 'modernization' and 'restructuring' . . .

Murdoch . . .

November 2009

When I first started working in newspapers in the mid-80s, whenever I met other journalists for a drink, sooner or later the conversation would turn to the hottest topic of the time, more important even than our perfidious editors or, indeed, ourselves. Instead, we'd earnestly debate the motion, Who is Madder, Maxwell or Murdoch?

Initially, to be sure, most contributing hacks would plumb for Maxwell, while conceding that both of them were clearly mad in a general megalomaniac-stroking-a-white-cat-in-a-secret-underwater-base kind of way. However, although Maxwell was a bully and (it transpired to no one's surprise) a crook, with an obvious eating disorder and likely alcoholism to boot, I always dissented at this point. On the contrary, I'd say, Murdoch is much more truly, deeply mad than Maxwell could ever be, and my evidence went like this.

You first had to understand that Murdoch's real first name is Keith, named after his father Sir Keith Murdoch, a regional newspaper magnate in the very small media pond of Australia between the wars. However, instead of bearing a manly, no-nonsense, rugged name like Keith in the unforgivingly machismo Australia of the 30s, little Murdoch was known by his second given name, the infinitely less rugged Rupert, with all that a wussy moniker like that implies. Thus, I'd continue, you should see Rupert's entire life as a titanic psychological battle to reclaim his denied Keithness. After his father's death (and after Rupert's time at Oxford when he kept a bust of Lenin on his mantlepiece in a text-book piece of youthful rebellion) the yearning for Keithness grew exponentially: it turned, eventually, into a global struggle to win his dead father's approval by not only asserting his fundamental Keithness, but also to out-Keith the original Keith through massive overcompensation. Thus, whereas Keith Sr only owned the *Melbourne Age*, KeithRupert was compelled, rather pathetically, to own every other newspaper on the planet. Then, finally, dead Keith could acknowledge that his son was worthy to be a Keith too, and the terrible inner screaming might stop at last.

So far, so much psychobabble. But don't forget that Rupert is also incredibly grand by Australian standards. While craving his dead father's approval, he also had to kill him all over again by denying this at every turn: thus the son of Sir Keith became, he avowed, a committed republican; he sought further to reject his father by abandoning his nationality; the little boy who was sent to Australia's best schools before going to Oxford deliberately besmirched his parents' world of sherry with the high commissioner and charity tea parties by dragging his father's profession as deep into the gutter as it could go. Indeed, the print unions' strike newspaper the *Wapping Times* got hold of an eminent psychologist to analyse Rupert, and he concluded that Murdoch's propensity for surrounding himself with fawning lowlifes like Kelvin MacKenzie, David Montgomery, Andrew Neil or, latterly, Piers Morgan and Rebekah Brookes, was a classic act of transference by which he symbolically sought out shits in order to defy Dame Elisabeth Murdoch's attempts to potty train him.

(This faecal dysfunction goes further. I was working on *Today* when Murdoch bought the paper from Lonrho, and as we were waiting for the new editor David Montgomery the deputy editor George Darby gave me a crash course in how the Murdoch empire functioned. It was a standard hierarchical pyramid, George explained, with Rupert at the top, supported by his regional Gauleiters, whom he'd treat like shit; they, in their turn, would treat the editors beneath them like shit, who'd do the

The Morning Star, September 2009

same to the journos, in spades, and the journos would then serve up shit to the readers. In short, it was a vast fountain of shit, all emanating from little Rupe, torn between the need to do his whoopsie in the correct receptacle to earn his parents' love and the overwhelming urge to smear it all over himself and everything in sight. Then Monty walked into the room—although I initially mistook him for the postboy— and George was unceremoniously sacked within half an hour.)

It gets worse. Publicizing his recent, rather disappointing biography of Murdoch, the *Vanity Fair* journalist Michael Wolff told a BBC Arts programme that interviewing Rupert was very difficult, because when he raised issues that others might think defined the man and his works—like the dishonesty of the journalism, the craven surrender to anyone who'd offer him any kind of commercial advantage, the disproportionate political influence he exerted—Rupert would stare at him in blank incomprehension. Wolff implied that Murdoch was quite simply incapable of understanding why the consequences of his actions should be a problem. This defining insensitivity to others—whether it be a failure of empathy or self-interest masking a pathological degree of selfishness—suggests that, on top of everything else, Murdoch is clinically as well as morally autistic. And that helps explain a lot else. Three marriages in, this 78-year-old toddler (whose mother, significantly, is still alive) can only relate to other people in a specific, highly controlled and ritualized way. All the latent pratfalls of human interaction have been magicked away through the simple expedient of reducing the basis all relationships to fear and worship. Moreover . . .

Sorry. Please excuse me. Ignore all of the above. I've absent-mindedly been attacking someone for their personal disabilities, and that would never do, would it now?

Climate Change . . .

December 2009

Whichever way you look at it, Christmas is a wonderfully delusional time of the year. Whether it's believing in Father Christmas, or in the dubious obstetrics in Bethlehem two and bit thousand years ago, or deluding yourself that rampant commercialism mostly fuelled by personal debt will bring you happiness, none of it really stands up to close scrutiny. Even a tipsy feeling of general bonhomie towards your workmates (if you're lucky enough to be in work) is, at heart, a delusion which dissipates with the next morning's hangover, when you're likely to recognize the true nature of things with a hideous clarity.

Still, many people have observed that humankind cannot bear too much reality, so none of this is really that harmful. Indeed, regular readers of this column may be surprised, given how often I've advertised my fierce atheism, to hear that I really like Christmas. We need a good, albeit delusional, midwinter festival to cheer us all up, whatever delusion we ultimately pretend justifies it. But beyond the gluttony, the drunkenness, the turkey and the tat, there remain other delusions which can't be dismissed so lightly.

As I write this, the Copenhagen Climate Change Conference is about to enter its second, final week. Whether or not this particular bleak midwinter is warmer than usual, and irrespective of how large its carbon footprint ends up being, this international jamboree has been either hyped up as the most important conclave in the history of humanity, or dismissed as a monumental waste of time trumped up by a sinister conclave of deliberately delusional megalomaniacs. On the one side stands science, pure and simple. Except that science, even if you're not a climate-change denier, is neither pure nor simple, and we should be as wary of worshipping science as we would be of kowtowing to any of the other hegemonies we have imposed upon us. It was science, remember, that previously gave us phlogiston theory, eugenics, the atom bomb and Zyklon B, and its dumb cousin technology that's got us into the mess we're in now. Or so they say.

But the point, of course, is that in the end science is merely a consensus of observation. Despite the shortcomings it shares with all the other gods human beings have elevated onto the altars of their own opinions, just contrast it with its detractors. Because on the other side, despite their laudable objections to being bamboozled by yet another elite, the average climate-change denier is standing shoulder to shoulder with Nick Griffin, Melanie Phillips, Saudi despots, multinational oil companies, Russian oligarchs, Third World kleptocrats, conspiracy theorists and the kind of smirking right-wing contrarian who writes for the *Spectator* these days. However furiously they blog or hurl abuse at the columnists (or the cartoonists, thank you very much) on the *Guardian* website's Comment Is Free talk boards, what the deniers fail to ask themselves is the question we should all be asking ourselves all the time: cui bono? Who, in other words, benefits from either side of the argument? Is the melting of the icecaps a lie invented purely to guarantee the rather paltry state funding received by hairy young men in pokey labs in the University of East Anglia? Or is it really happening because of the avarice and lust for ever greater power of an already enormously rich and powerful elite?

Which brings us to the hub of the matter. Science is a tool, but the point is the politics. Just as people like Richard Dawkins have wasted years trying to disprove god through science, so in the bogus debate surrounding climate change the science can

be bandied about forever. But as with religion, it all boils down to opinion (dressed up, in the case of religion, as 'faith'). And opinions are the province of politics. It may be no comfort that your ideals are ultimately 'unprovable'; but that doesn't invalidate them. So we should view climate-change science as merely the portal to a deeper and, in a way, 'truer' politics, at the heart of which lies the kernel of all politics, which is the struggle between power and freedom.

At the end of the day—which may be sooner than you think—the deniers are handing a further carte blanche to rapacious exploitation and despoilation of the natural world as well as its human inhabitants, to increasing wealth for a tiny elite, to increasing inequality and ever increasing immiseration of the majority of humankind. Which leads us to another area of science, dealt with in Richard Wilkinson and Kate Pickett's *The Spirit Level* and Oliver James' *Affluenza* among many others, and which proves that unequal societies are bad for everyone: they madden us, sicken us, drive us into addiction, desperation and crime.

So, delude yourself on any number of fronts if you like: delude yourself that our current economic model is the right one, that never-ending growth is an unarguable good, that massive overpopulation and eternal exploitation of the planet is sustainable or that industrialization—invented to accelerate the transfer of wealth from the many to the few—hasn't caused climate change. But if you do, it won't make you happier. So on the whole give me the delusions of Santa in his sleigh, the little baby Jesus and goodwill to all men, even if only for a week or so, and as happy a Christmas as possible to you all.

Pope . . .

February 2010

His Holiness the Pope smiled his slightly lop-sided and foxy smile and waved from the window of the Popemobile as it made its stately way up Whitehall, delighted but still rather amazed at the size of the jubilant, cheering multitude. When he had first announced his state visit to Great Britain, just seven short months ago in February 2010, such a reception had seemed more than just unlikely: not only did he expect to be confronted by the kind of indifference common to those unhappy lands where soulless secularism appeared to have triumphed, but the hostility of the zealots of equality legislation had promised much worse. That, now, had all changed, and as he continued to smile and wave, he thought back to the extraordinary events that had presaged Britain's reconversion to Rome and re-entry into the communion of the Universal Church.

Of course, the comforts of orthodoxy and discipline always thrive in troubled times, although the domino-like collapse of the economies of Greece, Spain, Portugal, Ireland, Italy, Croatia, France and Austria—all predominantly Catholic countries— could, in other circumstances, have resulted in different outcomes had anyone had the time to make a connection between faith and fiscal laxity. Likewise, the City Riots at Easter could, maybe, have led to a collapse in the faith in all kinds of authority. As it was, when most of the mightiest banks announced bonuses for their staff in excess of all the money in existence, the fury at the rest of the population was as much at this further proof of the bankers' innumeracy as it was in response to their avarice, even though the subsequent razing to the ground of the Square Mile of the City of London— for the historically minded its still smoking embers remained a potent evocation of the Great Fire of 1666, those last three digits also containing an ominous hint at apocalypse—had resulted almost immediately in the total collapse of the British economy as well.

But His Holiness knew that these circumstances alone would not have led to the miracle he now witnessed. For that, he could thank the actions of just one man.

It had been shortly after giving evidence to the Chilcot Inquiry into the Iraq War that a familiar figure had furtively entered a suburban Catholic Church by a side door, interrupted the local priest conducting a coffee morning for young mothers and begged on his knees that the priest immediately hear his confession. The priest had smiled apologetically at the mothers, promised not to be too long and led the figure away to a confessional box further down the nave. It was what happened next that spilt into the realm of the miraculous.

Twenty-nine hours later, the priest finally ran screaming from the confessional, and with a valedictory cry of 'Jesus Christ! He hasn't even got to the 1997 election yet!', fell dead to the floor. (The priest in question was now undergoing beatification as a prelude to canonization, while the spring of sparkling water that erupted where he'd fallen was now proven to be a most efficacious cure for acne.) The needs of the supplicant were paramount, however, and soon relays of hundreds of priests were hearing his ongoing confession round the clock. Moreover, it was rapidly calculated that, in order to achieve absolution, the supplicant would require an almost infinite supply of rosary beads on which to say the Hail Marys, and thus it was that the Church's wealth was diverted into kickstarting the moribund British economy with a massive programme of investment in the manufacture of religious artefacts.

Furthermore, given His Holiness' own dogmatic reaffirmation of the role of purgatory in personal salvation, the unprecedented step was taken to allow chantries to be established to pray for the soul of the supplicant prior to his death, so monumental was the challenge. These were endowed not just by the church, but also by the

The Guardian, September 2010

supplicant himself, whose various highly remunerative jobs thankfully required no actual input from him, even being the new goodwill ambassador for Ambre Solaire and the latest incarnation of Ronald McDonald.

Soon, the half of the working population which weren't busy stringing beads were now monks and nuns, praying nonstop to intercede on behalf of the supplicant's soul. Before leaving Rome, His Holiness had learned that seven months of ceaseless work and prayer was, according to the wisest theologians, beginning to pay off, and they had calculated that so far all this spiritual labour had remitted his sins sufficiently to knock as much as 37 seconds off his time in purgatory.

Given its new economic dependency on the Holy Mother Church, it was only a matter of time before Britain admitted its 600 years of error, and so it was that His Holiness was now on his way to the ceremonial burning of the Act of Supremacy in Parliament Square. The rain continued to fall in torrents, although since the anathematization of climate science, none knew why. Through the murk, His Holiness could just make out the figures of Rowan Williams, Harriet Harman and Richard Dawkins tied to stakes for the auto-da-fé, although he also noted with growing dismay the difficulty Ann Widdecombe and others appeared to be having with the soggy matches . . .

Michael Foot . . .

March 2010

At *Tribune*'s 60th birthday party in 1997 I asked Michael Foot and Jill Craigie if they agreed with me that, when the Thatcher Memorial pit came to be dug, it should be supported on either side by symbolic representations of David Owen and Tony Benn. Jill instantly endorsed my fantasy, although Michael was more circumspect: 'I couldn't possibly comment, but you may have a point . . .'

Imagine my surprise, then, when last Wednesday, about half an hour after Michael's death had been announced, on *The World at One*, the two people the BBC deemed most appropriate to give an immediate comment were . . . David Owen and Tony Benn. Admittedly, their contributions weren't as nauseating as David Cameron's later that day, but only marginally less so. For anyone who knew Michael—which I had the immense privilege of doing for the last 18 years or so of his life—choosing the two men who'd effectively destroyed his leadership of the Labour Party to sing his encomia might appear to be the final revenge of the establishment he despised, but I suspect it was simply down to sloppy journalism (which he also abominated). Anyway, both

Benn and Owen (who Michael really, truly loathed) came up trumps and stuck to the approved script, confirming that with his death we had lost the greatest orator of a now bygone lost political age. They also agreed (again, sticking to the official line) that he was a fundamentally decent man, perhaps too decent to be an effective leader. Of course, we know how both of them repaid his decency, but nonetheless neither was wrong, although at the same time neither of them was entirely right either.

Because merely garlanding him as a great orator doesn't do Michael justice. Certainly, he was great speaker—the noise of his voice alone, quite apart from what it said, was capable of being both inspiring and deeply comforting—but then again Hitler, to give him his due, was a pretty effective orator too, as have been countless demagogues throughout history. But Michael was, to my ears and eyes at least, the very opposite of a demagogue, just as he was the antithesis of the kind of neurotically sanitized and manicured politics embodied by New Labour or David Cameron. And that's because he was on our side.

By that I don't mean that he was narrowly on the side of a small arc of the left, or of the Labour Party more generally (although I sometimes despaired at his loyalty—manifested through muteness—towards Labour's latest mutation, just as his older friends despaired at his loyalty to avatars of Lucifer like Lord Beaverbrook or Enoch Powell). He was on the side of humanity. Infinitely lovable himself, he recognized that, in general, people as a whole are lovable too and deserve much better than they usually get. As I say, he was our side.

So, it came as no surprise when he once told me that he considered his greatest achievement in the politics of government to have been the setting up of the Health and Safety Executive. Like his friend and fellow Welsh MP Leo Abse, who added to the real, quantifiable sum of human happiness by masterminding legislation on divorce, adoption and homosexual law reform, he'd achieved something which genuinely improved people's lives, far more than any amount of great oratory.

But, for my money, his greatest political achievement lay in the rest of his long political life, the years as a serial rebel, because there too he was on our side. And that's because the best part of politics is and always has been not in seeking to usurp power, but in trying to thwart it, by harrying it, obstructing it and, most of all, mocking it. Because Michael was always on the side of the satirists as well, be it his beloved Dean Swift and William Hazlitt, or his erstwhile colleague George Orwell, or his great friend the cartoonist Vicky. Or, for that matter, cartoonists in general, whom he appreciated, admired and supported more completely than any other politician I can think of. As he once said to me, with a mischievous cackle, the thing the Labour leadership hated most about *Tribune* was the cartoons.

Michael Foot's 90th Birthday — Martin Rowson '03

And that mischievousness—his sense of fun—is something else which placed him firmly on our side, and which also imbued him, even in great age, with a defining youthfulness. Indeed, he was the youngest old man I've ever known, and displayed it over and over again, whether through the twinkle in his one good eye, his barking laugh or his standard form of greeting, which remained that weird clenched fisted, arm-wrestling Commie handshake.

The last time I saw Jill, a few months before her death in 1999, she told me that, at heart, she and Michael were William Morris socialists. In short, they believed in fun for all. So it's worth repeating Walter Pater's line about Morris: 'To burn always with this hard, gem-like flame, to maintain this ecstasy, is success in life.' Which will do very nicely. Because, whatever glib and amnesiac political commentators might say, Michael's life, in and out of politics, was a triumphant success. And although, like me, he had no time for extra-dimensional ideas of life after death, the affection he inspired, for all the reasons I've given above, means his life, in our hearts and minds, still has a long way to run. It was a joy to know, not just the politician, but the man too.

Omens . . .

May 2010

Walking the dog in our local park in recent weeks, I've noticed something I haven't seen for years. It's long been part of the shtick of cheaper stand-up comedians to riff on about the inherent hilarity of things from their childhoods: old kids' TV programmes, sweets that no longer exist, like Olde English Spangles, or—and this is a particular favourite—white dogshit. Naturally, for comedy to work it needs to contain a grain of truth, and sure enough, I have vivid memories of seeing white dogshit everywhere in the 60s and 70s. Then the white shit disappeared. But now it's back, left to bleach and petrify by irresponsible dog owners right in the middle of my neighbourhood.

There's probably an obvious reason for the return of the white dogshit. In these straitened economic times, the people who don't scoop their pooch's poop have reverted to buying the cheapest available dogfood, the kind that contains the chemicals that whiten their shit.

However, after an election campaign in which all the parties stubbornly refused to engage with reality, I see no reason whatsoever to buck this anti-empirical trend and much prefer the following fantasy analysis.

Britain just got brokener...

The Guardian, May 2010

The white dogshit was nothing less than an omen from the gods, warning of the return of the Tories.

Well, who knows? What I do know is that an election fought by fantasists continuing to peddle the dicta of a failed as well as foul economic system inside a disgraced and disgusting political establishment calls for a whole lot more than simple straightforward reporting. What it needs, in fact, is equal if not greater levels of fantasy. So with my eyes tight shut and whistling like hell, here is what the election result should have been, as opposed to what it appears to be. Given our weird times, what follows will probably end up as real anyway.

But first we need to establish the defining principle of the entire campaign, which is that everyone deserved to lose, like in a libel action between Mohamed Al-Fayed and the Hamiltons, or a debate between Christopher and Peter Hitchens.

That said, the fantasist and satirist in me demands more. So while Labour deserved to lose, they should have done so for entirely different reasons. Rather than seeing a bunch of disconnected, washed-up, backbiting Blairite bastards, we should instead view the whole pathetic, lacklustre campaign as the Labour Party at its compassionate best. Having finally recognized that Gordon is far too honourable a man to ever abandon the high office he felt it his duty to fill, despite clearly hating every second of it, the rest of the party (with Mrs Duffy's help) finally engineered a scenario in which Gordon could honourably step down as leader. So here we get the fantasy result: Labour loses just enough so Gordon can go off to be a junior lecturer somewhere and live happily ever after.

But if Labour deserved to lose, the Tories deserved to lose more. On the evidence of weeks of his studied yet unconvincing matey gaucheness, Cameron must have been the worst PR man in history. True, he no longer blushes when telling complete lies, but I suspect that this is because, as the heir to Blair, he actually believes all that bullshit about Big Societies and the CEO of Carpet Warehouse being a greater economist than Keynes. But otherwise, his face has two settings: 'charming "guy" convincing home-counties mother that he's good son-in-law material' or 'French aristocrat in a tumbril trying to comprehend the incomprehensible' (The latter setting was much in evidence in the second TV debate, after Clegg had fouled up the planned coronation). Anyway, in this case the fantasy result is: Tories win 80 per cent of the popular vote but only 12 Commons seats, and continue to oppose electoral reform.

But the best fantasy result is the one I hoped had a chance of actually happening: a Parliament so balanced and hung that forming a government proves completely impossible. Nonetheless, enough consensus is reached to pass two pieces of pressing legislation, the Great Reform Act of 2010, and a supply bill. In the latter case, after frantic horse-trading support is found from across the party spectrum for savage cuts in public expenditure, but without equivalent increases in corporation tax, income tax, exchange controls or anything else that might squeeze the rich as well as just soaking the poor. Then, with the fingerprints of almost all of them over a document that finally proves in whose interests they really govern, the MPs suddenly remember that they've changed the electoral system . . .

I've always rather liked that line of Marx's about history repeating itself, first as tragedy, then as farce. It recognizes the central role that laughter and ridicule plays in politics, and hollow, mocking laughter might prove the best option right now. What's less clear is which slice of history will end up repeating itself: 1974, 1931, 1922 or 1832. Or, for that matter, 1641. Just for the moment I've still got my eyes shut and I'm still whistling, like everyone else. Wake me up when the shooting starts or the IMF turn up. Or, on second thoughts, don't . . .

Osborne . . .

October 2010

Here's a story about George Osborne you might find instructive. About five years ago I was emailed by a minion at Bell Pottinger, a PR racket named after and run by Tim Bell, Margaret Thatcher's favourite ad man. They were proposing to organize an exhibition of my work at the Westminster Bookshop, similar to one that Denis MacShane got together in 1998 and which was opened by Peter Mandelson. Better yet, they even had someone lined up grandly to open this one, in the form of George Osborne, MP!

I replied to the email in the following terms. First, I wasn't quite sure who George Osborne was, apart from being a character in Thackeray's *Vanity Fair*, and second, I wasn't in the business of providing the fig leaf of having a sense of humour to ambitious young Tory politicians. That said, however, I would go along with their little plan so long as I could sell my work, invite my mates and make a speech.

They instantly agreed to all my conditions and so, about a month later, the big night arrived. My work was propped up on shelves around the bookshop, my mates duly arrived and commenced on the serious exercise of hoovering up as much of Lord Bell's free booze as possible, and then George arrived, trailing behind Tim Bell. They both had a little look round, then George and I mounted the steps up to the mezzanine level and George made a speech. Cartoons, he said, were absolutely splendid things, and these were all jolly good, and though he didn't see any of himself round the walls, doubtless I would draw him in time. He concluded with some bland pronouncement I no longer remember, and it was now my turn to speak.

The Guardian, October 2010

I started off by saying that the reason I hadn't done any cartoons of him was that, until this evening, I had no idea what he looked like, and until a few weeks previously I'd never heard of him. This, I continued, was because of the abject hopelessness of the Conservative opposition, who through arrogance and self-indulgence had left the real job of opposition to the cartoonists like myself and Steve Bell, who was also enjoying his ennobled namesake's largesse. However, I went on, should the dark day ever arrive when he, George, managed to climb to the top of the greasy poll (he gave an enthusiastic bark at this point), then it was only fair to warn him that every day of his life my colleagues and I would be emphasizing his weak chin, that weird cleft in his nose, his bad skin and everything else about his appearance, while also depicting him eating babies while wading thigh-high through a vast lake of human blood and shit. And I finished off by telling him that if he didn't fancy a future of crying himself to sleep every night, he still had time to retire from public life and get into interior decoration or run a pet shop or something.

It was at this point, with his lower lip trembling slightly, that the future chancellor of the Exchequer suddenly burst out: 'I wasn't expecting this kind of thing!'

In truth, I now felt slightly sorry for him. I'd been ungracious and mean, and my mates were still hoovering up Lord Bell's booze, so as he was leaving, I expressed my thanks and apologized for being a bit hard on Osborne. However, Bell just snarled, 'Needs a bit of toughening up . . .' and swept out.

I've told you all this because we need to understand various things about George Osborne, this government's economic Vandal-in-Chief. First, he's almost a victim of his own ambition, one of those Tory boys like Cameron or Portillo before them who was specifically groomed by the Tory Establishment—in his case in the form of Tim Bell—for greater things, in ways as toe-curlingly sinister as anything that happens in cyberspace. Second, he's actually a bit of a wimp, and with an unfortunately unlikable face. Which is why, as a politician, he's chosen the gambit of his old sparring partner and sailing companion Peter Mandelson, which is to disguise all your other shortcomings behind the mask of a pantomime villain, realizing that you'll never get anywhere by using charm. (Cameron is the exact opposite, though his public persona is as false as Osborne's.)

If you combine these two aspects of his character, Osborne suddenly becomes both more and less terrifying. He's less terrifying because it's just an act, the calculated malevolence purely there to cow the rest of us into compliance with his programme of Thatcherite orthodoxy. However, where he becomes more terrifying is when you realize that, essentially, when you factor in the unswerving and—more dangerously—unquestioning devotion to a failed and discredited doctrine, he really and truly doesn't know what he's doing.

I keep thinking the same two thoughts about this government. The first is that they haven't really thought any of it through, despite the coalition's constituent parties having had 13 and 80 years respectively to fine tune their policies. The second is a mental image, of the type cartoonists experience, and it's of an 11-year-old boy sitting in front of an Enigma machine and repeatedly hitting it with a hammer, just to see what might happen. There is, in other words, a stench of deranged naivety surrounding Osborne, Cameron and Clegg, and I fear we might be hearing the phrase 'I wasn't expecting this kind of thing' quite a lot in the next few years, as they survey the wreckage . . .

Rioting . . .

December 2010

The past, as we know, is another country, and they do things differently there. Take, for example, the Wilkesite Riots of the 1760s, when the London mob responded to an incompetent and unpopular government's hounding of the radical rake John Wilkes by smashing the windows of every fine town house that failed to display either a banner declaring 'Wilkes and Liberty' or a copy of the notorious issue 45 of Wilkes' magazine the *North Briton*, which ministers had charged with seditious libel (as well as arresting Wilkes on general, unspecified warrants and the chancellor of the Exchequer, a fellow habitué of the Hellfire Club, challenging him to a duel). Indeed, one tumultuous evening, part of the mob spotted a coach containing the Austrian ambassador, representative of one of the most reactionary and oppressive governments in Europe, dragged the unfortunate diplomat from his vehicle, upended him and wrote the number '45' on the soles of his shoes and then smashed his carriage to matchwood.

A few years later, during the Gordon Riots of 1780, the London mob stormed and destroyed Newgate Prison, an action which many who took part—including the young William Blake—subsequently considered the equivalent of the storming of the Bastille nine years later, and were left to reflect ruefully on how the crowd's revolutionary fervour dissipated once it had sacked a distillery in Fleet Street.

And 40 years after that, during the coronation of Prince Charles' great-great-great-great-grand-uncle George IV, the mob were so disgusted by the king's treatment of his ex-wife, Caroline of Brunswick, that on her behalf they tried to break down the doors of Westminster Abbey with a battering ram.

Of course, in those days rioting mobs were more or less accepted by the establishment as part of the political process. Hardly anyone had the vote, and the aristocracy ruled entirely in its own interests; it was therefore considered reasonable to allow the people to let off some steam now and again, and if a few windows got broken and it was wisest to hide in your cellar if you lived in the smart parts of town, well, that was

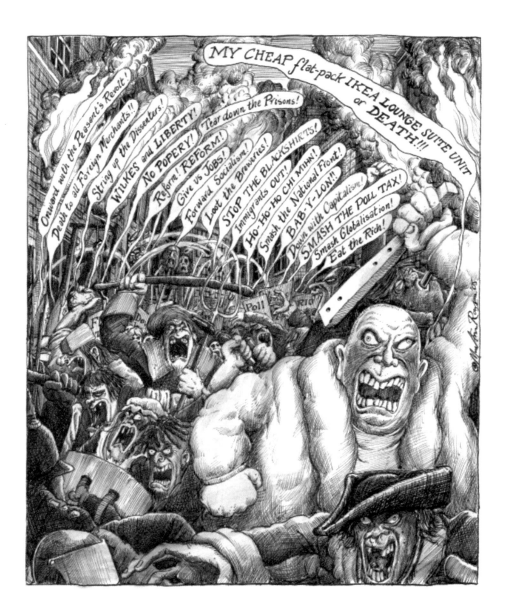

Time Out, April 2005

better than the way they did things in France, before or after the Fall of the Bastille. So what should anyone expect when, once more, you have an unmandated government, governing solely in the interests of the elite, who demonstrate the futility of voting when part of it performs a complete volte face over the policy that allowed it to win as many seats as it did? As with the poll tax, when an arrogant and complacent government blithely displays its utter contempt for us, the people, the streets are about the only place left to go.

But a decade or so of relative calm means that many people have forgotten how to do public disorder. So while many MPs are now perhaps too young to have seen *Doctor Zhivago*, they should probably reflect on the fact that pictures of children being subjected to cavalry charges usually ends up playing rather badly in the country as a whole. Nor have the police or the government yet worked out that the unled and unstewarded demonstrators *least* likely to cause trouble are the ones too naive or insufficiently nimble to escape being kettled. In other words, the young people held against their will in the freezing cold for up to 10 hours by policemen dressed as Imperial Stormtroopers from *Star Wars* are the respectable middle-class professionals of tomorrow: the doctors, teachers, lawyers, bankers and—oh yes—politicians who have now been thoroughly radicalized by Tory and Lib Dem lies and police stupidity.

Although it's always just possible that things aren't quite as they seem. It's likely, of course, that the police really are as dumb as we've always assumed, and so it was that which allowed the Tory Central Office to be stormed and occupied, thousands and thousands of middle-class children to be brutalized into radicalism and the heir to the throne's safety to be hideously compromised.

But it's also worth reflecting that the leaders of this government, despite their fine education and a gift for tactical cunning, might themselves really be much, much stupider than we ever dared fear. I know that Cameron, Osborne and Clegg are all terribly posh, but is it altogether wise, this late in the game, for the upper classes to start waging war on the bourgeoisie, particularly through their children? At a time when we're told we have to more or less discard all the worthwhile bits of the state to save future generations from the shame of sovereign debt, does it quite make sense to tell those same generations that they can now expect a lifetime of personal debt?

And, to return to the police, you would imagine that beneficiaries of the best classical education money can buy might have remembered, as they set about slashing police numbers, what every Roman emperor knew instinctively, even if it was literally the last thing that crossed their minds: the one thing you never do is piss off your own Praetorian Guard.

On which comforting note, let me wish all of *Tribune's* readers a very merry Christmas. Next year is going a lot more interesting than many people yet realize.

Disraeli . . .

March 2011

Here's an interesting passage from *Sybil* by Benjamin Disraeli, Michael Foot's favourite Tory:

> The real cause of [the Dutch] invasion [of 1688] was financial. The Prince of Orange had found that the resources of Holland were [. . .] inadequate to sustain him in his internecine rivalry with the great sovereign of France [. . .] The prince came, and used our constitution for his purpose: he introduced into England the system of Dutch finance. The principle of that system was to mortgage industry in order to protect property: abstractedly, nothing can be conceived more unjust; its practice in England has been equally injurious [. . .] [and] pursued more or less for nearly a century and a half, has ended in the degradation of a fettered and burthened multitude. Nor have the demoralizing consequences of the funding system on the more favoured classes been less decided. It has made debt a national habit; it has made credit the ruling power [. . .] it has introduced a loose, inexact, haphazard, and dishonest spirit in the conduct of both public and private life; a spirit dazzling and yet dastardly: reckless of consequences and yet shrinking from responsibility. And in the end . . . the moral condition of the people has been entirely lost sight of.

Forgive me for quoting that at such length, but over a century and a half after the founder of the modern Conservative Party wrote it, it's worth savouring. It is, after all, an indictment of banking and 'financial services' every bit as telling as Marx's more general critique of capitalism, written a decade or so later. Moreover, it's part of a specifically Tory analysis, which Disraeli himself sought to use to inform his unsuccessful attempt to forge an alliance between the landowning gentry and the workers, in order to thwart the capitalists after the repeal of the corn laws.

As such, you'd think it might appeal to Disraeli's Tory heirs, born of the class he spent a lifetime aspiring to join. Considering that David Cameron is descended in a direct line from William IV and that George Osborne will one day inherit an Irish baronetcy, both of them, along with a lot of the rest of the cabinet, and with only minor costume changes, could have walked straight out of an Anthony Trollope novel.

But to think that would be to make the same serial error as Disraeli himself. He may have led the Conservative Party, but he never quite understood it, while it never entirely trusted him. True, most Tory leaders find themselves in the same position, Cameron more than many. But Cameron nonetheless has that dominant Tory gene

Morning Star, November 2010

which defines the DNA of conservatism. Instinctively, in common with lackeys everywhere, Tony Blair and beta-level baboons, he worships power.

As I've written in this column before, the Tories originally emerged as a loose parliamentary block in support of the later Stuarts and their attenuated concept of the divine right of kings. Through the centuries, the party mutated into the party of Anglicanism, monarchy, aristocracy, landowners, capitalists, businessmen, shopkeepers, entrepreneurs, Britain and bankers, while many of these groups should, in theory, be mutually hostile. But the quality they've all had, when the Tories have claimed to represent them, is power, pure and simple, and with neither need, nor room, for ideology.

It was her commitment to ideology that made Margaret Thatcher so distinctly un-Tory, and that fuelled her equally un-Tory contempt for the kind of deference the Tory grandees expected from her. Instead, they got the sack. Cameron, however, is profoundly Tory in his freedom from ideology, whatever it may look like from outside the comfortable acres of rolling pasture and parkland in his mind. But viewed through their eyes, I suspect Cameron and Osborne are dismantling the state simply because they genuinely believe that the rich and powerful are better at running everything because . . . well, because they're rich and powerful, obviously.

So, anyone with clear vision can see that the main 'enemies of enterprise' at present aren't the civil service or regulations preventing cowboys from building schools likely to collapse on their pupils, but the banks. And yet Cameron and Osborne are unlikely to do anything to punish, stigmatize or even rein in the banks, whatever Disraeli may have said about them, because their reflex response to power is too ingrained. Nor will they do anything except go out of their way to accommodate the ever-expanding, balefully banal empire of trash of Rupert Murdoch and his family, and for the same reason.

Add to that Cameron and Osborne's breath-taking capacity for brazen lying and you have the final proof of the truth of my analysis. Words, quite simply, don't matter. The function of humans is to fawn to and flatter the rich and powerful, and everyone knows that you don't really mean what you say when you flatter someone. So the meaning of language becomes redundant, and it's reduced merely to noise.

What other possible explanation can there be for Britain's prime minister, having already declared war on his own civil service, telling his supporters in Cardiff last weekend that, in promoting the arms trade, he will unashamedly 'hustle for Britain'? Or did he truly mean that his office now amounts to little more than a rent boy turning a trick down the Dilly? But then the horrible thought suddenly occurs that maybe he did . . .

Greece . . .

June 2011

We've just got back from a week in Greece, where we stayed in the Mani, the middle of the three peninsulas that hang down from the Peloponnese, where the landscape has that strange yet comforting capacity to look like it's been mail ordered straight out of a classical catalogue, with cypresses jutting darkly upwards against a hillside of olive groves.

The most your average tourist probably knows about the place, though, is the road from the airport in Kalamata (home of the eponymous olive) to Stoupa, the area's top resort, a bay of gritty beaches, apartment blocks and tavernas.

And yet if you drive south from Stoupa, you begin to experience more than just sun, sand, sea and souvlaki. It's a barren, mountainous landscape, suiting the reputation of the inhabitants, who for 400 years prevented the Turks from ever fully conquering the peninsula.

During the Greek War of Independence, the women of Pyrgos Dirou, their men at the front fighting the Turks in the north near Kalamata, drove off an Egyptian Ottoman army trying to land from the south, armed only with stones, pitchforks and sickles, killing two-thirds of the invaders before they fled.

This fierceness also fed a rough kind of local justice, unmediated by outsiders. Grievances were settled by vendetta, which often fed revenge upon revenge between families, lasting decades and sometimes centuries.

Thus, the weird architecture typical of the Mani, of high war towers dotting the hills, some literally next door to each other, like in the village of Vatheia, where warring neighbours built their towers higher and higher to intimidate and get an advantage over the enemy.

When an English naval captain was exploring the area in the early nineteenth century, he steered well clear of Vatheia after he'd been told more than a hundred men had been killed during the latest vendetta. Not for nothing is the Mani believed to be the source of the word 'maniac'.

A 15-minute drive further south round hairpin bends brings you to a small bay, looked over by a ruined church, previously a temple to Poseidon where the pious or the credulous still leave small offerings on the stone altar, these days in the form of packets of stinky Greek cigarettes or miniature bottles of Ouzo or Metaxa brandy. And between the temple and the bay, down a rocky little path, there's a shallow, over-grown cave containing a pool of stagnant water.

This, you'll be pleased to hear, was marketed in antiquity as the entrance to Hades, though an Italian tourist in the second century CE recorded his scepticism, frankly

Seconds...

doubting whether the dead would be able to pass through the tiny hole at the back of the cave.

All of which just goes to show that Greece is no stranger to hucksterism, foreign interventions, international bullying, violence, intimidation, chaos or the promotion of ludicrous garbage as orthodox truth, and hasn't been for millennia.

Which puts the country's current predicament into some kind of historical context, even if this is little comfort to the Greeks at the moment, assailed as they are by the modern Furies of free trade and the Maenads of the market.

Last week, our hosts offered us a different explanation for the Greeks' current crisis than the orthodox neoliberal line about feckless peasants sated by the public sector lying their way into the eurozone, and then bankrupted by their own greed.

The truth of the matter, it seems, is that traditionally most Greeks were strangers to personal debt, given that interest rates had historically (and unaffordably) been around 30–40 per cent. This, we were also told, was why second-hand goods still remain comparatively expensive, because of Greek thrift.

With the prospect of eurozone membership, however, Brussels and the markets had forced Greek interest rates to plummet, with personal debt consequently exploding.

In a land where tax is often uncollectible, the subsequent deficit, exacerbated by the ratings agencies employed by the banks and bond markets to guarantee that extra pound of flesh, has now led to the imposition of VAT at a rate of 27 per cent, which will spark a further spiral of inflation, bankruptcy, unemployment and ultimate immiseration that makes the misfortunes of Oedipus or Orestes look tame in comparison.

That, though, is only a very slightly exaggerated example of what seems to be the default setting for this stage of capitalist decadence. The old, failed orthodoxies are firmly back in place, especially with nihilist zealots such as George Osborne happily surrendering the sovereignty of the state to the whirlwind of the markets, at the same time devolving the pooled strength of sovereign debt to the fragility of the kind of exploding personal debt that will inevitably follow on from his fiscal recklessness.

And there was further proof that we're now meant to be nothing more than mere playthings of the gods in red braces as we came home from Gatwick via London Bridge.

There, almost finished, stands the Shard, London's latest capitalist Tower of Babel, a gargantuan version of the war towers of the Mani and soon to be filled with bankers, dealers, traders and all sorts of other maniac devotees of their (and, tragically, our) strange cult of lies and thunder. Where, oh where are the heroic rock-throwing women of Pyrgos Dirou when you need them?

Banality of Evil . . .
July 2011

It's a brilliantly, terrifyingly precise phrase, both encapsulating and enshrining the potential within the dullest, least prepossessing people you can think of to behave with almost unimaginable inhumanity and cruelty. A less familiar phrase is the 'evil of banality', although it should fill us with just as much terror and disgust as its apparent obverse.

To understand this further, please consider for a moment three of the more prominent pantomime villains of recent years, men who have either assiduously cultivated or just don't care about their images as ruthless, conniving bastards—Rupert Murdoch, Peter Mandelson and Simon Cowell.

Murdoch, for the most part, we know about. His reach is, he'd like us to believe, universal; his ambition monopolistic and hegemonical. Governments rise and fall at his behest (we're told) and his utter, rapacious ruthlessness in achieving his aims is notorious and blithely indifferent to any consideration of either moral or legal restraint.

Similarly, Mandelson ripped through the Labour Party and the media with almost cavalier indecency in pursuit of his goals, in the process destroying much of what he touched at the same time as he sought to promote it, all against a background hum of a slavish fascination with the rich that almost equalled his estimations of his own dark powers.

Meanwhile Cowell, although perhaps ultimately a lesser demon than the other two, has nonetheless built up a media empire based on peddling people's dreams to the population as a whole, simultaneously inflaming the nation into a baying mob while also fleecing it every which way by gulling the mob into dialling premium phone lines to further enrich Simon Cowell. The dreams, meanwhile, are simply an accessory instantly disposable through the mob's or Cowell's caprice, which he camps up like the queen of the night.

In other words, these three are clearly all very bad men, and each in his own way a modern despot, a terrifying tyrant of monstrous proportions. Well yes, obviously, but there's another, possibly better way of looking at them, too. Thus, Murdoch is actually a wizened octogenarian mummy's boy having a lifelong tantrum about getting his own way, who has marshalled the world's greatest media organization to flaunt minor inconveniences like national laws in order to do . . . what, precisely? Become king of the world? Have a billion serfs build a million-mile-high gold and granite statue of himself? Not a bit of it. Instead, his hubris has hollowed out his organization

The Guardian, July 2011

in pursuit of a scoop about which D-list celebrity is being knobbed by which fading football star.

Similarly, did Mandelson leave all that damage in his wake to effect some seismic political change, thus empowering him to build a huge secret underwater headquarters to further his plans of world domination, stroking his white cat? Um . . . well, what his ultimate political achievement proved to be was to safeguard an already moribund economic system from any kind of change at all. As for Cowell, having at last created the McLuhanite monster of total media control, what manner of Orwellian nightmare does he then impose? Regimented ranks of humanity endlessly hymning the praises of Simon Cowell? The moon renamed Simon to reflect his glory? Nope. He just wants to swamp the pop charts for a week or so with some skinny adolescent of indeterminate gender crooning a hopelessly dull, mindless middle-of-the-road power-pop ballad. What these big, bad men share, in other words, is a desperate and rather pathetic poverty of ambition. Where the evil comes in the triumph of their banality is in the damage to other people they commit to achieve it and the good their actions preclude, because they've filled up all the available space in newspapers, television and politics with trash.

Because evil isn't just what happens when good men do nothing. It's also what befalls us all when dull men big up the banal and don't care about the consequences. The current and ongoing despoliation of the planet, alongside the degradation and immiseration of billions of its human inhabitants, is less about the tyranny of mighty men, and more about the primacy of the bottom line as defined by boring accountants.

In Adam Curtis' recent wonderful series on BBC 2, *All Watched Over by Machines of Loving Grace*, he concluded with the observation that the philosophy with which the elite justify their actions defines us humans as nothing more than selfish, solipsistic automata, predestined to act accordingly. In fact, as I've pointed out many times in this column, all the evidence suggests that instead we're actually cooperative, kindly, egalitarian and, on the whole, rather loveable. Not that that would suit the agenda of what I'll term, just for now, as the Banalarchs. Apart from anything else, as a vision of humanity it's far too interesting and exciting.

Theft . . .

February 2012

When the supreme governor of the Church of England says that the established church is here to help establish all faith, you know that something is getting seriously out of kilter. Given the fact that the only reason the Church of England was established in the first place was as a bulwark against Papism and as an institutionalized instrument of persecution of non-conformists, such a piece of revisionism is pretty rich even by the standards of hypocrisy and double-think hardwired into the British establishment. But when the queen, the personification of the establishment, her status the apotheosis of the burdens of history, says things out loud so cravenly at odds with what history has taught us you begin to wonder whether reality itself is starting to fray at the edges.

Still, Her Majesty's shameless dicking around with the truth last week chimes with other current monuments to self-delusion. You know, like the prime minister snuggling desperately into his PR comfort blanket in the apparently sincere belief that if you only listen to people who agree with you, then magically everyone else will agree with you. Then again, this is just part of one of New Labour's sole abiding legacies, outlined by Tony Blair in his autobiography and spat back at Ed Miliband during Prime Minister's Questions a few weeks ago: that if something is unpopular, you know it's right.

Of all the bullshit and blathering bollocks that Blair stank up the air surrounding himself with, this is perhaps the most totally fatuous and yet strangely brilliant. If you convince yourself that everyone else's opinion that your actions are abhorrent and profoundly mistaken only proves how righteous and correct they are, then you can then do absolutely anything you want. In fact, the worse it is, the better it is. In many ways, this is a piece of sublime, if foul, genius, even if it's also the mantra muttered by paedophiles and rapists through the ages. It's funny, though, how it only seems to work if your policies are abhorred by people less powerful than you are.

And there's the rub: we all remember how Blair was unbelievably courageous at beating up his own party and its supporters by doing the opposite of what they elected him to do, but can you remember him ever courting unpopularity with media moguls, financiers, American presidents or monarchs? But here's a thought, and some advice for our current prime minister. As things get worse and worse, as they will however much he keeps gurning for the cameras and browbeating the BBC, how about doing something the power elite find deeply unpopular but which is popular, perversely, with the populous in general? In which case, why not try this for size?

The three defining moments of English history which laid down the course of future centuries were all extraordinarily audacious acts of theft. The first was the

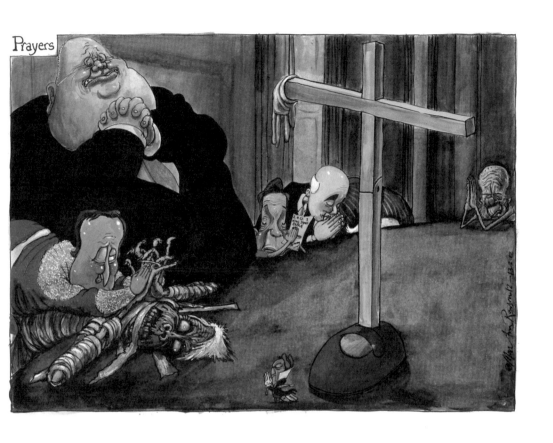

The Guardian, February 2012

Domesday Book, the outward and visible sign of the shift in ownership of the land since the Norman invasion of 1066, and it laid down that ownership thereafter in perpetuity. What it didn't state—it didn't need to—was how most of the land of England had been systematically expropriated or stolen from Saxon landowners by the Norman invaders. And we shouldn't need reminding that this kleptocracy—this bandit state—is the one over which our current monarch still reigns.

The second great act of theft marked the beginning of modern Britain, with the dissolution of the monasteries under Henry VIII. This time, the power of a vast multinational corporation was challenged and broken by emergent state power, creating its own state church as part of the package. And then the state unilaterally closed down the corporation's regional offices and stole all its wealth, creating a new mercantile landowning class at the same time.

And just a generation later came the final great act of theft. In the 1580s, Philip II of Spain was the most powerful and richest ruler of the age: there was practically a conveyor belt of galleons, laden with gold and silver mined by slaves in conquered South America, ceaselessly crossing the Atlantic. (This didn't, incidentally, stop Philip unilaterally defaulting on his debts to Dutch bankers four times—although each time they carried on lending to him, despite the fact that over his entire reign he was constantly at war with the Dutch.) Anyway, licensed by Elizabeth I, these convoys of galleons were constantly attacked by English pirates—called privateers in a piece of Tudor spin—and thus were the foundations of the British Empire built on pure, simple, straightforward theft.

Of course, other offences by the British state need to be taken into consideration, like the Inclosure Acts that stole the common land from the people, or the empire itself, but Cameron needs to concentrate on the privateers. These you can spin into something hugely popular. Think Drake's Drum and the Spanish Armada. Think Errol Flynn. Think, moreover, of getting some particularly photogenic hackers, indemnified by the British state. And think, most of all, of them hacking into Goldman Sachs' many accounts and simply stealing all their money and transferring it, at the press of a button, into the British treasury.

Unthinkable, I know. Or at least in this pitiful neoliberal universe, where the state is always portrayed as evil incarnate. But maybe, for everyone's sake apart from the bankers', it's time for the state to man up and grow a pair. And if the banks, let alone the bond markets or the ratings agencies, object to wholesale plunder by the state, perhaps they should remember precisely who has possession of the atom bombs, and then learn a little humility.

Goderich . . .

May 2012

It's always fun to tease out echoes from history, if only to prove the accuracy of Karl Marx's dictum that those who fail to learn from history are condemned to repeat it, first as tragedy and then as farce. At present, the tragically stubborn political and economic miscalculations of the 30s are being re-enacted in fully tragic form, and yet sometimes farce is repeated as farce. So given the tragic backdrop of the current government's farcical performance, it's timely to recall the career of Viscount Goderich.

Who? That in itself is a salient, if universal, response. Goderich, born Frederick John Robinson of Tory landowning stock, was once the prime minister of Great Britain and Ireland and yet is now entirely forgotten. True, his premiership was brief: at only 144 days, it's the second shortest on record,[*] just three days longer than that of his patron George Canning, and it was Canning's death in office that propelled Goderich into the top job.

But his long career had many other highlights. In 1815, he introduced the notorious Corn Laws to the House of Commons, keeping grain prices artificially high in the interests of his class, while in the 1830s, he piloted the bill to abolish slavery through the House of Lords. This versatility meant that, between 1818 and 1846, he found himself able to serve in every government save two, of every political stripe.

But his high watermark was probably as chancellor of the Exchequer under Lord Liverpool. It was in this office that he came to be known as 'Prosperity Robinson' and, weirdly, 'Goody', although as he oversaw some disastrous harvests, and the former appellation was coined by Cobbett, there may have been some layers of irony in the nicknames. Significantly, things got really bad after a run on the banks in 1826, and his response was widely seen as rather half-hearted. Perhaps wisely, he asked Liverpool to be moved into a less difficult and onerous post, though Liverpool resigned through ill health before carrying out the reshuffle.

What happened next gets really interesting. Liverpool, the vicious old reactionary who had overseen the Peterloo Massacre, was succeeded by George Canning, a relatively liberal Tory (he once fought the vile Viscount Castlereagh in a duel) whose appointment meant the Tories split four ways, mostly over the matter of Catholic emancipation, which many of the few electors around may have seen as a distraction from other more pressing affairs of state. Robinson was created Viscount Goderich, and when Canning died a few months after taking office, Goderich was asked to form a government by George IV instead of Robert Peel or the Duke of Wellington, because the

---

[*] A record broken by Liz Truss in 2022.

Illustration from Andrew Gimson, Gimson's Prime Ministers (London: Square Peg, 2018)

king was still annoyed neither had been prepared to serve under Canning, again because of Catholic emancipation.

Which leads us, finally, to the Goderich government of 31 August 1827 to 21 January 1828, a time during which Parliament never sat, and which consisted of an entirely unstable coalition of liberal Canningite Tories and Whigs, who infuriated backbench Tories by seeming to be able to exert undue influence over Goderich. After five months, the coalition government collapsed under the weight of its own contradictions, leaving Wellington to lead a Tory government which pushed through Catholic emancipation, in the face of furious Tory hostility.

But it's the manner of Goderich's leaving office that truly deserves our attention. Summoned to Windsor Castle by the king, who informed him that he'd asked Wellington to form a government, Goderich then cried so much that George IV had to lend him his hanky. Now, that's more like it. Even better, with fixed-term parliaments now enshrined in law, as their dreams built of arrogance and complacency collapse around them, we can look forward to three whole years of David Cameron and George Osborne bawling their eyes out at the despatch box, begging to be allowed to go home.

But there's more. Catholic emancipation was all about advancing the principle that all citizens are equal before the law. And yet, strangely enough, the Catholic hierarchy now insists that this principle should not extend to same-sex marriage, while arguing that their position is not based in simple bigotry. I presume, therefore, that in the name of inequality they will now agitate with equal vehemence for the repeal of the Roman Catholic Relief Act of 1829. As a matter of principle, obviously.

Media Lens . . .

June 2012

This week I thought I'd describe my adventures with a website called Media Lens over a cartoon I recently drew for the *Guardian*. It featured Bashar al-Assad, in the immediate aftermath of the Houla massacre, smeared in blood and pointing an equally blood-stained finger at his own chest. Also depicted were Vladimir Putin, Wen Jiabao, Ban Ki-moon, Kofi Annan several cowled figures of death, Angela Merkel and Christine Lagarde lashing a pile of human bones with euro-laden cats o' nine tails and the sleeping form of David Cameron, snuggled up to an enormous cat dressed in a blue pin-striped suit. The thing was captioned 'Who? Me?!?', although it's by no means clear who's saying these words, just as it's not clear whose blood besmirches Assad, whether it's his latest alleged victims', from his earlier ones or, for that matter, whether the blood might be his own.

Anyway, I was asked by Media Lens via Twitter (in 140 characters or less, even if a picture is, they say, worth a thousand words) what clear evidence I had for President Assad's personal involvement in the Houla massacre. So far as I can tell, Media Lens turn out to be a couple of blokes called David whose mission is to expose the lies, misrepresentation and manipulation in the 'mainstream media'.

Of course, it's an impossible question to answer. Anything you try to say soon starts spiralling into a kind of phenomenological vortex. What is our evidence, after all, for anything, least of all murders in a faraway country enshrouded by the fog of war, where both sides have made a habit of saying each fresh outrage was the other side murdering their own people to blacken their enemy's reputation? So it was probably my mistake to try explaining how I followed my 'cartoonist's hunch' based on Assad's previous form, and how cartoons are more ambiguous than most journalism. And I certainly shouldn't have allowed myself to get quite so foul-mouthedly cross, even if foul-mouthed crossness is sort of my professional schtick.

Still, my responses gave them the copy they sought, and they had me duly pinned to their cork board as yet another example of a hireling of the 'mainstream media' both swallowing whole and thereafter cheerleading an American / British / Saudi / Bahraini neoconservative interventionist conspiracy to invade Syria. Or something. And, as Media Lens exists in cyberspace and nowhere else, my pillorying as their patsy pursued its inevitable trajectory. Within hours of them blogging my infamy, I started receiving the usual tweets and emails telling me (in case I hadn't hitherto guessed) what a cunt I am, sent in an instant by that silent global army of paranoid agoraphobics who, these days, don't even have to find a bottle of green ink and a stamp to pitch in with their 10 bobs' worth.

I'm still not sure what kind of parallax literalism fuels Media Lens. And, despite my repeated requests, they still won't or can't tell me why they don't also demand my evidence for alleging that Merkel and Lagarde have really truly desecrated corpses, as depicted in my cartoon. If my picture of Assad bears the same weight of empirical objectivity as a photograph, why deny those same standards of truthfulness for Merkel? And I haven't even got round to raising the subject of cats in pin-striped suits.

Maybe their failure to answer is because their claim to champion truthfulness and balance is all baloney, and they're just another leftist groupuscule shilling for tyrants whose one redeeming feature is they hate the West almost as much as their own people hate them. Perhaps they genuinely don't understand what metaphors are and view the world in two dimensions, in black and white. After all, one of their sweeter observations was to ask how, without firm evidence, I could show President Assad with his mouth smeared with the blood of 'massacred children' (their interpretation,

The Guardian, May 2012

not mine), qualifying the question by then asking if I'd ever depict Barack Obama, or David Cameron, or any other Western leader in the same way, with just as little direct evidence of personal complicity in the piles of corpses currently littering the world.

Well, as any *Tribune* reader could assert with the closest thing you're likely to get to certainty this side of the Second Coming, they don't know me very well, do they?

Zombies . . .

November 2013

Although it's rattling the window above my computer while I write this, the so-called St Jude Storm has nothing on the Great Storm of 1703. That one scuppered half the fleet on the Goodwin Sands, drowning 1,500 sailors, while hundreds of people and their livestock drowned in the Somerset Levels as they flooded. The Eddystone Lighthouse was blown down, 4,000 oak trees in the New Forest were uprooted, and the bishop of Bath and Wells and his wife were killed in bed by chimney stacks collapsing in his palace. The whole thing was generally taken as a punishment for society's wickedness, and the government ordered a national day of fasting to propitiate the outraged Fates.

The storm of 1685 was pretty impressive, too. That one blew Oliver Cromwell's skull off its 20-foot-long spike on top of Westminster Hall, where it had sat next to Henry Ireton's and John Bradshaw's severed heads since their posthumous 'executions' for treason in 1660, although I can't say what kind of omen this was taken for. Perhaps, happening around the time of the commencement of James II's calamitous reign, those in the know concluded that the way nature ended Cromwell's public humiliation might also be heralding in the end of the post-Reformation political settlement, which duly ended in farce three years later when James 'vacated' the throne and fled to France after suffering a nosebleed for three days.

Oddly, 30 years—give or take 5 years here and there—seems to be about the lifespan of a political orthodoxy. Britain's post-war settlement lasted from 1945 to 1979. The first Stuarts—James I and his son Charles I—tried to wrest financial control from Parliament (the chosen engine for Thomas Cromwell's revolutionary break with Rome in the reign of Henry VIII) and replace it with the divine right of kings; that experiment stumbled and lurched on from 1603 to 1641. Charles I's sons, invited back by Parliament, attempted to restore religious intolerance and rule both with and without Parliament, from 1660 to 1688. The examples are legion, but it seems that either an adult lifespan or around three political generations defines any political experiment

Anchor*

FOOD BANK

BBC

*from Tory Rhyming Slang: Volume 391

28·10·13

The Guardian, October 2013

before it collapses under the weight of its own contradictions. After which it only continues to exist because of the stubborn sense of denial of the power elite with most to lose, often underpinned by the full ferocity of state terrorism.

That's how the zombie neoliberalism being practiced by Britain's governments has managed to reach its 34th foul year, despite what should have been the coup de grâce in the form of the banking crash having been delivered more or less on time in 2008. Nonetheless, we're still being peddled the weirdly post-Maoist kind of permanent revolution neoliberal politicians advocate instead of real action—that never-ending 'reform' and 'change' Tony Blair blathered on about. This is despite the 'supply-side' reforms (scrapping workers' rights, slashing welfare, further enriching the already stinking rich) having been wholly implemented years ago. That's why this recession hasn't been marked by massive increases in unemployment, because people are hanging on to any job they can, even though many of those new jobs are part-time and, far more importantly, badly paid.

It seems pretty obvious to anyone not bedazzled by their beguilement to blind faith that the current system ceased to be a 'political settlement' after it had succeeded in surviving its death throes five years ago, because it disenfranchizes more and more of the population than it advantages. 'Undead' describes Britain's economy to a tee: the successes—the City, the banks, the energy cartels—owe their riches increasingly to shameless vampirism.

There's something else worth noting from the seventeenth century beside Oliver's head bouncing down onto the cobbles. The system Charles II tried to keep on the road was never sustainable, politically or, for him, financially, especially once he decided to emulate his beheaded father and rule without parliamentary support. So how did he pay for his reign? It was only long after his death that it was discovered that Charles received a massive secret pension from Louis XIV of France. In other words, the King of England whored himself for economic subsistence to a mostly unfriendly foreign power. Looking around at just who owns most of our economy, does that remind you of anyone?

Doctor Who . . .

December 2013

Sometimes all the anniversaries that count turn up at once, like buses. True, often it's simply the calendar date that provides the commemorative resonance: just think of 9/11, a date written in infamy for the people of New York and the world in 2001, but also for the people of Chile in 1973 when the CIA-backed coup set in train years of both political and economic tyranny. Likewise, 5 November is a date with totemic power thanks to a cell of Catholic terrorists trying to 9/11 King James I and his Parliament in 1605. Nearly a century later, it's also the date William of Orange landed in England to replace the Catholic King James who'd vacated the throne by running away to France. And because of its symbolism as when you try to kill or usurp kings, that's the date Lemuel Gulliver's ship founders off the coast of Lilliput in 1699 in Jonathan Swift's satirical masterpiece *Gulliver's Travels* as well as *Tristram Shandy*'s birthday. And Laurence Sterne, the author of *Tristram Shandy*, was 300 on 24 November.

Which made for a weekend of anniversaries, some of which we're conditioned to think have some deeper significance. Why the 50 years that have elapsed since John F. Kennedy's assassination in 1963 mean more than the 23 years gone by since Margret Thatcher threw in the towel on the same date in 1990 is anyone's guess, though maybe the packaging of time into bite-sized decades—10, 20 or 50 years—makes it more digestible as a marker on our own individual mortality. As fewer and fewer people remain alive who will be able to remember where they were when they heard that Kennedy had been killed, so we tick off our own diminishing number of days left.

The deaths of Aldous Huxley and C. S. Lewis on 22 November 1963 were overshadowed on the day by Kennedy's assassination, although those authors link in perfectly with the anniversary we celebrated the following day. *Doctor Who*, 50 on 23 November, is now woven into the British psyche and is also almost wholly about passing through portals into different realms of understanding and experience. Walking into the TARDIS is the same as clambering through that old wardrobe and entering Narnia, or gobbling up the hallucinogenics described by Huxley in *The Doors of Perception* and embarking on voyages of wonder, worlds away from the alternative realities reflected in what grown-ups call 'the news'. I'm not ashamed to say I was overjoyed by *Doctor Who*'s 50th, and not just because, being only four and half years older, the changing Doctors have been benchmarks for my own life. There is something about *Doctor Who* which means I wasn't entirely joking when I tweeted that we should make the Gallifreyan time traveller Britain's head of state, with Delia Derbyshire's original theme tune our new national anthem. (And just imagine 80,000 people on Cup Final Day singing: 'Dummedy-dum de dum de dum de dum de dum dummedy-

Tribune, February 2017

dum! Whoooo-oooooosh!') It's because the programme and its eponymous hero's unique selling point is its and his 'Britishness'. But it's of a specific kind. To be blunt, it's the kindly kind.

The Doctor is driven, odd, conflicted, troubled, but also often funny, definitely weird and always determined to do good—even if it's by constantly interfering in other people's (and monsters') affairs. In short, he and the Time Lords are exemplars of the post-war consensus into which he was created; they're wise and well-meaning socialist technocrats bolstering and protecting a (literally) universal welfare state. After the programme was killed off in the high summer of Thatcherism, it came as no surprise when the Doctor finally returned a decade and a half later that he was the last Time Lord left.

As I say, this is a specific kind of Britishness, a melding of Lewis Carroll, William Blake, Jacob Bronowski and Clement Attlee. There are equal portions of H. G. Wells, Heath Robinson steampunk, a Nuffield Science Park and the Grange Road Health Centre in Bermondsey in *Doctor Who*. And the nostalgia it invokes in many people of all ages isn't just for a kid's teatime telly show, but also for the Britain Thatcherism largely destroyed. Try imagining a Doctor who'd reflect this government's vision for Britain. He'd probably flog the TARDIS to a Qatari-based hedge fund and use his sonic screwdriver to seek out 'skivers' and 'scroungers'. Actually, of course, the Tories would probably rejig the whole show to make the Daleks the heroes.

Scottish Referendum . . .

March 2014

Back in August 2012, I packed in three different gigs during a two-day stay in Edinburgh, the capital of Scotland. Squeezed in between the Book and the International Festivals, at 10.30 on the Saturday morning I was on a panel at the Festival of Politics in the Scottish Parliament, discussing satire. My fellow panellists were a mixture of journalists and stand-up comedians, and all were Scots except me. So when the discussion turned inevitably towards the independence referendum, as the token Englishman I insisted they also bear in mind another possible option: that Scotland should be expelled from the Union.

At the time, I argued that the invention by Adam Smith and John Logie Baird of capitalism and television should be quite enough to justify getting shot of Scotland. (At this point, one of the Scottish stand-ups called me a cunt.) After another gig at the Glasgow Literary Festival a few months later, as I walked the brief distance from my hotel to the station while carefully avoiding over a dozen pools of still drying puke, in my mind I widened the argument. Any nation whose citizens are so peculiarly susceptible in equal measure to feudalism, Calvinism, Stalinism and alcoholism really should think of moving out before they get thrown out.

But on top of the standard Scottish kilty, mawkish, shortbready 'The People's Friend' stuff, there are several other things to take into consideration. The SNP may well try to Braveheart the whole thing as Scotland straining under the Saxon yoke, but remember that the most enthusiastic pursuers of British imperialism tended to be Scotsmen; that the distinctive linguistic meme among Afro-Caribbeans and African Americans of saying 'ax' for 'ask' was picked up by their enslaved ancestors from brutal Scottish overseers on the plantations; that the only reason Scotland and England united their parliaments was because of Scotland's catastrophic imperialist adventure in Central America in 1707 (better together—at colonizing the world!). Add to that that more Scotsmen fought on the Hanoverian side at Culloden than fought for the Stuart absolutist Bonnie Prince Charlie. And that the crofters' boys thereafter dragged on hurdles to Tyburn to be hung, drawn and quartered for doing their clan chiefs' bidding were merely the advanced guard for the Clearances which the same Scottish landowners then wrought on their Scottish tenants. As a consequence of all that, Scotland remains one of the least equal societies, with the most disproportionate division of land ownership, in Europe. And yet I'm wholly unaware of Alex Salmond promising any kind of Zimbabwe-style land reforms—though I concede I may not have been paying sufficient attention here, having been distracted by his world-class schmoozing of Rupert Murdoch and Donald Trump.

All right, all right. I'm only teasing. But think about it. If the 'No' campaign had any brains at all, a threat of expulsion would so enrage Scottish pride and opinion the 'Yes' campaign could only demand that Scotland remain in the Union, with Scots in charge. As hitherto, as it happens.

But joking aside, in truth I hope beyond hope that Scotland does vote 'Yes'. It's not because I invest any hope in 'Salmondia'; in fact, I think nationalism in all its forms is a pernicious nineteenth-century distraction, seeking justice against the depredations of elites by imagining the answer lies in racial identity, as opposed to any of the other, less gaudy identities on offer. That foul nonsense lies beneath the blood-drenched histories of mid-twentieth-century Europe, post-Yugoslavia, Israel–Palestine or, for that matter, Ukraine and Russia right now.

But even impure nation states are often just institutionalized atrocities, lying, stealing, kidnapping, spying on, bullying and murdering their citizens, in their own name, but invariably in behalf of whichever elite has grabbed the controls. This is particularly so in Great Britain's case, despite the degree to which we kid ourselves otherwise.

The Guardian, September 2014

And yet, without Scotland, without the mirage of its lingering misty-eyed tartan sentimentality, what actually is the point or purpose of our head of state, particularly when encumbered with quite so much pomp, pomposity and, indeed, money? Without Scotland, without the tradition of its kilted warriors putting the wind up Johnny Pathan, our international imperialist pretensions will look even more pathetically delusional, as will our pretensions to almost everything else. Without Scotland, in fact, the whole tattered moth-eaten tapestry will start to unravel until there's nothing left.

The current British state, with add-ons, is nearly 1000 years old. Isn't it time for all of us to grow up and move on?

Christian Country . . .
April 2014

My old dad, now ten years dead, had it more or less right when he'd say, repeatedly, that people could believe whatever rubbish they liked, so long as they left him alone. Admittedly I tend to go a bit further and bang on about the rubbish aspect maybe too much, but on the whole my father's line is mine too. That's why I signed the letter co-ordinated by the British Humanist Association and published in last Monday's *Daily Telegraph*, questioning David Cameron's description of Britain as a 'Christian' country. It's because, when he used that adjective, Cameron was utilizing it in an attempt to define my country and yours as displaying a homogeneity of faith which simply doesn't exist. Nor has it for centuries, if ever. Religion has been nakedly subservient to politics since Henry VIII broke with Rome, and growingly irrelevant to politics since the Glorious Revolution first began to entrench religious tolerance in Britain. And, as I've observed many times here and elsewhere, if religious tolerance denies you the opportunity to torture to death people who won't or can't believe in your particular god or gods, it's a comparatively short road to religious irrelevance.

But there's more to this than the resulting slanging match, though it's always a joy to see current and former Archbishops of Canterbury bickering about whether we're Christian or post-Christian. (Again, it's only when you can have your predecessor burnt at the stake that you can stop people giggling as the theocracy founders in farce.) Actually, the only really appropriate adjectives to define 'Britain' are probably 'seabound', 'rocky', 'soily' and 'rainy', though I doubt any of these will quicken the blood in any significant, game-changing section of the electorate.

Easter Message

The Guardian, April 2014

And here's where this slightly ridiculous Easter parade actually chimes with real politics: no one really believed that David Cameron was doing anything but essaying a ruse to woo back Anglicans in the shires, repelled by gay marriage, who might defect to UKIP.

Now, I don't know whether Cameron is a sincere and committed Christian or not. We do know that Iain Duncan Smith is a practising Catholic (though, to quote the old gag, he needs to practise a whole lot more before he gets any good at it). We also know that the mismatch between confessions of Christian faith and zealously pursuing the stated redistributory dicta of Jesus Christ himself has been one of the hallmarks of the religion since it emerged from the underground and became the Roman state religion under Constantine the Great. And part of me, to be sure, would like to see Cameron and every other publicly avowed Christian in politics follow the examples of Francis of Assisi or Holy Roman Emperor Charles V and renounce worldly vanity, reject politics, bugger off to a monastery on a mountain top and leave the rest of us alone.

Sadly, that's just more fantasy. The real political significance still lies in the fact that no one believed Cameron was being sincere. This, I realize, is mostly about him: for whatever reason, in his 'heir to Blair' pose, Cameron thought he'd discovered that the Holy Grail of politics is merely spin; that news management will always work in capturing hearts and minds; worse still, that his innate charm bequeathed him by his birth and upbringing guaranteed his mastery of British politics. As with his religion, we have no idea whether or not he recognizes that it ain't necessarily so. Yet still he persists in mouthing platitudes which nobody believes even he himself believes, even if he actually does.

None of this is particularly good for David Cameron or his soul—if he has one at all, or if it's already been outsourced by George Osborne to Serco. But it's far, far worse for our politics and our country, whatever adjective you think defines it. When we find ourselves so precisely matching Yeats' lines in his apocalyptic poem 'The Second Coming', we'd better watch out. 'The best lack all conviction,' he wrote, 'while the worst are full of passionate intensity', and concluded, a few lines later, 'What rough beast, its hour come round at last, slouches towards Bethlehem to be born?'

It's a good question, especially now when a gurning Thatcherite chancer like Nigel Farage appears to the electorate to be the closest thing in politics to a human being. In which case, God help us all, even if I don't believe in God for a second.

BBC . . .

July 2014

Have you ever undergone that truly weird phenomenon when you double-take because of a sudden moment of self-realization? It happened to me last week, and it was about the BBC. And what was weird—what provoked the physical reaction—wasn't the fact that I no longer trust the BBC to report and disseminate impartial news (I stopped doing that about four years ago), but that I couldn't remember when I started trusting the BBC in the first place.

I certainly never trusted them when I was at school. Even then, you knew their news was partial, even if the occasional leftie dramatist managed to sneak something into a *Play for Today* to give an atom of credence to the paranoia of the right-wing commentariat. But I also knew, thanks to the insider information I received from my sister and future brother-in-law, both working as film editors at the BBC in the late 70s and early 80s, that the Corporation's staff called BBC One the 'Bill Cotton Banned Show'. This was thanks to the predilection of the channel's controller, son of the famous band leader, to pull programmes from the schedules at the very last minute. These included several plays by Dennis Potter, now widely celebrated as the brightest star in television's golden age. That, though, was largely despite the BBC, rather than because of it.

Though go both back and forward in time from that fulcrum 35 years ago, when I briefly worked for the BBC as a data control clerk (local radio) and they tried to rob me of my contractual holiday pay (and then expunged me from their records when I applied for another job a year later), and it's always been the same. From the general strike to Baroness Thatcher's funeral, the BBC has combined servility to the establishment with craven appeasement of its most vociferous assailants. And it achieved this in large measure through being managed for decade after decade by an overpaid bureaucratic hierarchy defined by its obsessions with status, secrecy and filling in forms in triplicate. Add to that its cringing deference to governments of all colours. Add in its governance, mostly conducted by superannuated old cowards carefully selected from the establishment's reserve benches. Then add its complicity, along with the rest of the establishment, in providing the perfect cover for sexual predators. Add to that foul indictment how an entirely artificial media storm surrounding Russell Brand and Jonathan Ross saying 'fuck' late at night on Radio 2, whipped up by the *Daily Mail* under its notoriously Tourettic editor Paul Dacre, has further shackled the actual programme makers with rank upon rank of compliance officers, seeking to squeeze the last drop of creativity out of the creatives. And now add its news coverage—or non-coverage—under its current controller James Harding, a former editor

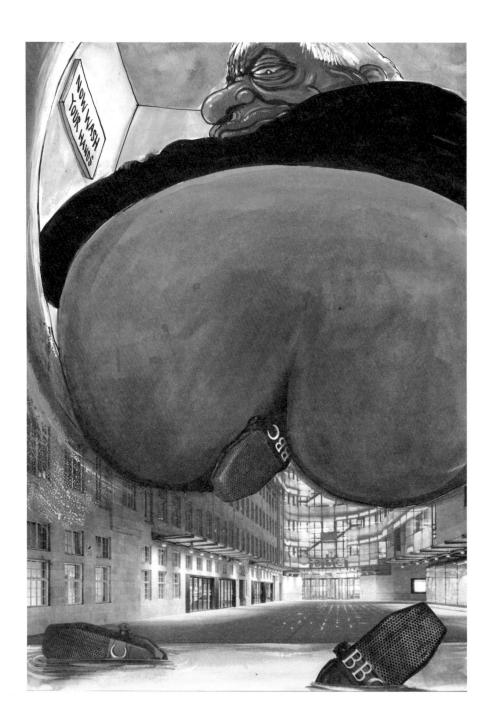

April 2014

of the Murdoch-owned *Times*, who, one can only surmise, shares with others promoted in the past by Rupert Murdoch that enviable capacity for serving up what's required without having to be told.

Of course, Murdoch is, as usual, the key. The real reason why I stopped not trusting the BBC was the sight of Murdoch positioning himself to obliterate it in his own interests. I was briefly seduced into the common misconception that organizations are mostly defined by their enemies. I then imagined, erroneously, that the occasional flash of zeal displayed by parts of the BBC holding the establishment to account coloured all of it. But of course I'd forgotten how its board sacked Greg Dyke over Iraq and then concluded that the BBC's howling failure to properly cover the coalition government's privatization of the NHS was just fine and dandy.

Worse, I'd forgotten that the BBC isn't just a mouthpiece for the establishment; it's blood of its blood and bone of its bone. Battered on all sides by foaming Thatcherite zealots in the right-wing media who'd still scream the BBC was run by communists if all it ever did was broadcast a loop tape of Margaret Thatcher pissing on the flag of the European Union to a soundtrack of 'Land of Hope and Glory', I was suckered into thinking this was a struggle between David and Goliath, whereas in truth it's more like King Kong versus Godzilla. It's one wing of the British establishment fighting another; the cosy, cowardly old-boy network up against its even fouler, brasher, greedier spawn.

But the real tragedy is that once the salvage operation masquerading as our government finally decides to smash the BBC to splinters to flog off to its friends and paymasters, I'm not even sure I'll care any more.

Scottish Vote . . .

September 2014

It's always a delight to witness my journalistic colleagues take something and beat it into a cliche before flogging it to death. Thus, it has transpired that, across the political spectrum of the commentariat, it is now a truism that, after this week's referendum on Scottish independence, whatever the result, *nothing will ever be the same again.*

Now, you have the advantage of me here, as you're almost certainly reading this after the result comes in, while I'm writing it beforehand. It's possible you may all be able to join hands and send me news from five days in the future back to my own time, but I doubt it. I also doubt that that portentous phrase—'NOTHING—WILL—*EVER*—BE—THE—SAME—*AGAIN-AIN-AIN-AIN-AIN*!!!!!'—will quite live up to its promise. It's unlikely, after all, that, as the Scottish polls close, EVERY-THING will suddenly be different to what it was before: that the sky will turn green, shortbread will dance, weasels a million miles high will quote Wordsworth in French or the moors surrounding Balmoral will turn into lakes of boiling jam. But maybe that's not what my cliche-mongering colleagues mean.

Maybe, with their well-known propensity for exaggeration and hysteria, they just mean that there's a danger that something else is about to drop off the rusty, rickety old contraption of the British Constitution. And it's just possible they also mean, in their hyperbole, that this will constitute something genuinely cataclysmic to the eyes of the sheltered and complacent clowns in the driving seat, whichever way the vote goes.

Well, one can always live in hope, though honestly I can't see how a monarchy promising low corporation tax, whose assumed premier (for life?) cosies up to the likes of Rupert Murdoch and Donald Trump, will be much different from what's there already, sporran or no. However, the effects on Scotland, one way or the other, have ceased to be the real story: far more interesting is the panic during the last few weeks of the referendum campaign in the heart of the British establishment.

We all know of that sublime hypocrisy which cements together the hollow clinker blocks of the British state, but why are the political, journalistic and financial elite—who are now anti-statists to the last lackey—so terrified about the possible emergence of a new state to the north?

For 30 years they've been telling us the state has no answers to anything. That it's a monster of regulation and tyranny, and while they've been telling us that, they've also been actively embracing globalization as a way of encouraging the state to wither away. The global dynamic is financial, of course, rather than political, but that's also why the elite argue that hedge funds running and owning public services is obviously the best way forward, while superstates like the EU are the epitome of evil.

But I don't remember anyone in the 'No' campaign arguing against Scottish independence on the basis that it would further encumber the world with another state incompetently oppressing the population, nor to offer the alternative of 'Better Together' to join in the great adventure of abolishing the state altogether for everyone, the better to allow us all to be ruled by corporations.

Not that they would say that—out loud in public, at least. Nor is this simply thanks to the congenital mendacity within the British elite. It's also because of the nature of our currently constituted state. Remember, this is the continuity state established by the Norman Conquest, a state whose foundations lie in the theft of Saxon land, the genocide of Saxons in the Harrying of the North and the subsequent enslavement of the mass of the people with the introduction of feudalism. True, it's changed

Contingency Planning

The Guardian, September 2014

a bit over the past thousand years and does its best to hide those foundations, bogged down in blood and larceny. But it achieves this to a large extent by everyone holding their breath and hoping the thin, dusty webs of lies, contradictions, corruption and hypocrisy which keep the whole thing upright won't snap.

Small wonder, then, that the 'No' camp panicked. It's not that another semi-autonomous province in the global neoliberal hegemony is a threat to anything much; it's just that any sudden movement at all might make the top-heavy edifice down south collapse, with the buggers patrolling the highest battlements having the furthest to fall.

Hobbyism . . .

October 2014

What do you call this? It's certainly no longer any real kind of properly functioning democracy, because the electoral system has reduced most constituencies, in practice, to the status of pocket or rotten boroughs, where the MP is, for all intents and purposes, selected by a tiny Soviet of party workers. For sure, it remains a plutocracy, but it always was. That infuriating background whine is simply the noise of entrenched privilege that's filled the damp and filthy air of these islands for a thousand years.

But more precisely, this thing we've got right now: what do you call it? Is it an Oxbridge-ocracy? Or, more pedantically, a PPE-ocracy? Some might say, with cause, that it's a wonk-ocracy (though a changed letter would be just as accurate). But these elites, in their turn, could easily have arisen because of a wider media-ocracy (the word compresses itself nicely to hint at another, deeper truth) serving the higher plutocracy. That said, I suspect what we're witnessing is, in fact, the triumph of the *hobby-ocracy*.

I also suspect that I may be the only person left alive who's read Michael Young's *The Rise of the Meritocracy*. Rather than being the gospel of social mobility and general getting-ahead most commentators probably assume, the book is actually a satire on the dangers of all and any ruling elites. In the end, in the year 2033, the narrator describes how the meritocratic elite, having replaced the previous privileged elites, is now being overthrown in its turn by the educational failures it treats more or less as subhuman slaves. It's a salutary reminder—duly ignored by the actual political elites of the past 30 years, if not forever—that citizenship, its responsibilities and its benefits shouldn't be conditional on how clever you are, any more than it should be defined by wealth or birth.

The Guardian, October 2010

Yeah, right. But in the actually existing complete bloody awfulness of contemporary British politics, *hobby-ocracy* seems to describe it best. We're ruled by a rarefied and sequestered priesthood of highly, if arcanely, trained individuals who share the single quality that politics is their hobby. As with many, more 'ordinary' people, a hobby can be the defining part of your life, whether it's trainspotting or birdwatching or stamp collecting. The point is, hobbyism exists in a self-contained universe of interest solely to you and your fellow obsessives. Patient partners may nod and smile, but at heart a hobby is about as selfish as you can get without falling off the scale.

And that's our current politics in a nutshell. We've now been told Lansley's disastrous NHS 'reforms' were incomprehensible even to Cameron and Osborne, but they simply nodded and smiled and let him get on with his mad hobby. The same applies, in spades, to Gove playing with state education. Remember that zealotry of a particularly obsessive kind is central to hobbyism; but so too is status obsession, whereby seeking the approval of other members of the hobbyists' club drives novitiates to ever greater levels of obsession just so they can fit in. Think about Tristram Hunt on education, or Ed Balls on austerity, or Ed Miliband on immigration.

But also remember that the vicious Machiavellian infighting that typifies every hobbyists' club that's ever existed counts as hobbyism too. Hence Peter Mandelson; hence George Osborne. And so does simply dolling yourself up to dance to Northern soul vinyl records on a Friday night. Thus, the breathtakingly pure narcissistic politics of David Cameron and Boris Johnson, who just want to preen in front of the mirror. This applies to Nigel Farage too, on top of Euroscepticism more or less exemplifying the template of hobbyist politics.

What unites all these disparate activities is that they are nobody else's business but the hobbyists'. The thing that's always most comforting about any hobby is its innate elitism coupled to an obsession with completism, plus the empowering inclusiveness of exclusivity. The only other thing you need is some gawky, needy kid to boost your sense of self-importance by chronicling the ballsachingly dull Kremlinology of your secretive activities—a role now adoringly provided by the BBC—and everyone else can simply Keep Out.

So, what is it? Hobby-ocracy? Narcissist-ocracy? Maybe *Gap-Year-ocracy*? In truth, as none of it involves you or me, what it's called probably doesn't even matter any more. But nameless or not, our nation deserves infinitely better than this, though God only knows how we'll get it.

Potemkin . . .

November 2014

I'd forgive you if you couldn't care less, but even in times as ghastly as these we've got to maintain some standards, however apparently esoteric. So do you want to know my favourite section of Sergei Eisenstein's classic Soviet propaganda film *Battleship Potemkin*? Well, I'm going to tell you anyway. It's not the famous scene on the Odessa steps, rightly still judged one of the finest pieces of cinema ever made, almost 90 years after it was shot; instead, it's that bit on the ship when the ship's doctor, bending his pince-nez in two to double magnification, examines the maggots crawling over the side of meat destined to be the crew's dinner and declares magisterially, 'The meat is good!'

I don't know whether or not that scene was inspired by the real events that sparked the failed 1905 Russian Revolution, when the horses' genitals served up in a stew to uranium miners in the Urals proved to be the final straw. That, of course, was just another instance of the never-ending cavalcade of incompetence, complacency, cruelty and caprice that typified Tsarism, albeit—just—gaudier than usual. Yet in a way you have almost to admire the depths of self-delusion to which the system had been sinking for centuries. Take the man after whom the aforementioned eponymous battleship was named, Prince Grigory Potemkin, who also gave his name to Potemkin villages. These, you'll recall, were sham villages built overnight and populated by soldiers dressed as peasants, in order to impress and fool Catherine the Great into believing prosperity had returned to vast war-ravaged stretches of her empire.

Does any of that sound familiar? Quite apart from the incompetence, complacency and cruelty, I'm finding it harder and harder to see current British politics as anything other than a bad farce played out against a hastily erected stage set. Not that this is anything new, of course.

One of Thatcher's foulest victories was to browbeat the Labour Party into shifting its politics onto her territory, and not just by surrendering to the dubious truths of neoliberalism. Remember, it was Thatcher who first surrounded herself quite so comprehensively with admen and so fought her ideological battles with weapons provided by the Industry of Lies. New Labour should have been simply a tactical response to this, to geld the Tory media: instead, it became both the strategy and the principle. That's how ideology ended up a very poor second to presentation, and imperialist capitalism went mad while Blair grimaced once more for the cameras. Like I say, none of this is news.

What's different now is that the actors—including the previously self-identifying 'heir to Blair'—are much, much worse and the audience is both furious and bored out

AS WITH ALL GREAT ARTISTS, THE SEEDS OF EISENSTEIN'S GENIUS LAY IN CHILDHOOD TRAUMA.

Scenes from the Lives of the Great Socialists (London: Grapheme, 1983)

of its mind. All in all, we should all have stopped suspending disbelief ages ago, though worse yet it seems the crap actors up on stage wouldn't really care if we did.

Which, weirdly, indicates once more the descent of British politics into a variation on the political hobbyism I wrote about last month. Our politics, in other words, has worked itself through its professionalized stage, where an elite of the wise steward our affairs, into the condition of amateur dramatics. And anyone who's ever watched their child or partner doing am-dram will know that the last imaginable people in the players' minds are the audience. Apart, of course, from their mums and, possibly, the theatre critic from the local *News Shopper*.

Is there any other plausible explanation for Cameron's wholly implausible acts of rage at that 'surprise' EU bill, or Osborne's smoke-and-mirrors act over its supposed triumphant resolution? It only makes sense if believing any of it isn't even the point; Dave and George feeling good about themselves is, and therefore how anyone else feels is more than beside the point. Add to that Osborne's recent bizarre makeover, where he looks like he's spent 15 hours in make-up to play the role of the Child Catcher in a kabuki production of *Chitty Chitty Bang Bang*, and the theatrical metaphor starts seeping inexorably into reality.

Except the reality then turns in on itself and starts reversing away from anything in the real world that really matters. And thus they tumble joyously back into the magical realm of smoke, mirrors, leadership plots, PMQs, EU rebates, by-elections, the *Today* programme and the rest of that wonderfully comforting world of make-believe within the Potemkin Westminster Village.

Getting back to Potemkin's battleship, none of this will stop that side of meat carrying on rotting down to the bone. The real trouble is it no longer seems to matter whether or not we believe them fluffing the line 'The meat is good!'

Hebdo . . .

January 2015

A man is murdered in Paris. Gunned down in a barbarous act of terrorism. The man is involved with an organization that has, for a long time, been making provocative comments about a specific faith group. These sentiments have, fairly often, been expressed in the form of cartoons. The man's murderer is a member of that faith group, which his victim's organization claims is responsible for horrendous crimes throughout history. How do you respond?

Without question—at first sight anyway—this horrific terrorist atrocity was clearly inspired by the hateful dicta of its perpetrator. The victim's nation's government certainly believes that the murderous criminality of the attacker is indivisible from the man's faith. That, in short, the murderer and the religious community from which he emerged to murder are one and the same thing.

So, it follows that in responding to this appalling crime, the world must show its defiance of the murderer and his foul creed. Furthermore, if in some kind of deranged mitigation the murderer were to claim he had been provoked beyond endurance, it's our duty to the victim's memory to repeat and ramp up the provocation. Yes? And not just to whatever groupuscule trained the murderer, but to the murderer's entire faith group. Yes? After all, every single one of them is complicit. Yes?

If you answered 'yes' to any of those points, congratulations! You've just endorsed Kristallnacht.

It's a cheap point, but so what? Everything's getting cheaper these days, human life most of all. But isn't it in profoundly bad taste to link the Nazis' preview pogrom of the Holocaust to the murders in Paris, of Jewish shoppers targeted with as much deadly calculation as *Charlie Hebdo*'s cartoonists and journalists?

Maybe so, but now more than ever we need to be alive to all the nuances. And as a mark of respect to my murdered satirist colleagues, we need to be aware of all the ironies too.

So we need to see—and, indeed, laugh at—the representative of Saudi Arabia march through Paris in support of free expression two days after Saudi blogger Raif Badawi received the first 50 lashes of his 1,000-lash sentence for 'insulting Islam'. But to help us see our modern masters' stinking hypocrisy, we should also learn from history.

On 9 November 1938, Ernst vom Rath, a diplomat at the German embassy in Paris, was gunned down by Herschel Grynszpan, a 17-year-old Jewish Polish refugee from Nazi Germany. This triggered Kristallnacht. Jews were murdered and arrested in their thousands, Jewish businesses attacked and ransacked, over a thousand synagogues burned down and—highly significantly—religious artefacts sacred and profoundly precious to Jews were desecrated and destroyed.

But behind the horror lie the ironies, equally horrible in their own way. For a start, vom Rath was suspected of anti-Nazi sympathies and was about to be investigated for his disquiet about the Nazis' anti-Jewish policies. Witnesses claimed Grynszpan didn't ask for vom Rath by name, just for a member of the diplomatic corps. Then Grynszpan claimed that vom Rath had seduced him (André Gide wrote afterwards that vom Rath was well known on the pre-war Parisian gay scene). The implications—

The Guardian, January 2015

that it was a crime of passion and that vom Rath was gay—quite ruined Goebbels' plans for a triumphant public-relations exercise, a grand anti-Semitic show trial. Because, of course, the Nazis thereafter murdered homosexuals with as much enthusiasm as they killed Jews, Gypsies, the disabled or social democrats.

Turning to some modern anti-Semitic, homophobic fascists, look closer and the murders in Paris are both more and less than they appear. To my eyes they look most like a mafia hit against soft targets sending a simple message. Moreover, I suspect the message wasn't even addressed to 'the West', but to al-Qaeda's greatest rivals, the Islamic State. These were showcase killings to demonstrate that bin Laden's old mob were still in the game, via a global promo video (courtesy of Western TV) aimed at recruiting all those confused and angry young people locked in their bedrooms cruising the internet and, appalled by the actions of the West, being tempted into opting for IS's brand of holy barbarism instead of AQ's.

After all, it's a quality common to both public relations and despots, whether it's Goebbels, the jihadis or anyone else: life's a lot easier if you mask individual people with simple labels: *Us*, *Them*, *Muslims*, *Jews*, even *Cartoonists*. It also means you can't see their eyes when you lie to them or kill them. It's also, it should go without saying, inhumanly, laughably stupid.

Buildings . . .

February 2015

When I failed my Eleven-plus 45 years ago, I seem to remember that one of the tests of our childish intelligence involved identifying missing words in sentences by their initial letters. For example: 'An A—— designs B—— for C——'. Which any child of 11 should be able to tell you will read 'An Architect designs Buildings for Clients'. A clue as to why I was bound to fail the exam is that I'd still instinctively render that 'An Arsehole designs Bollocks for C . . . ' Well, let's be polite and complete the last word as 'Capitalists.'

The truth of my version was brought home to me once more a couple of weeks ago when I gave a talk at the University of East London. This involved me catching the Docklands Light Railway from its most southerly terminus in Lewisham and travelling through the Isle of Dogs and Canary Wharf to the banks of Royal Albert Dock, just opposite London City Airport.

Although I don't remember the docks when they were still operating, I remember the Isle of Dogs and its environs before it became 'Docklands'. Back then the only way to reach it from the south was through the Greenwich Foot Tunnel, a tiled and slightly terrifying thoroughfare passing below the Thames, in which you couldn't see the other end from either side. That's what lent it its terror. And I remember going for a drink with some friends of mine on the *Daily Telegraph*, which was the first paper to flee Fleet Street eastwards. We walked through the building site surrounding the *Telegraph* office, which Stanley Kubrick had recently used as a stand-in for the ruins of war-torn Saigon in his film *Full Metal Jacket*, to a proper old Isle of Dogs pub, all lace curtains and Formica-topped tables. The landlady, you could tell, was almost unable to believe her luck: after decades of decline, the thirsty journalists had finally arrived!

Of course, her happiness was horribly short-lived. Within weeks the pub was compulsorily purchased and demolished, to be replaced by the current faux-Manhattan tumescence of skyscrapers filled with bankers and associated lackeys of high finance. The first wave of building, around Canary Wharf, struck me 25 years ago as clearly belonging to the Mussolini-fascist school of public architecture, while the later towers of glass and steel aren't even that interesting. Maybe that's why the whole place still has the artificial feeling of a film set.

Travel beyond Canary Wharf, though, and it gets even worse. North of the peninsula, you enter a cityscape of new buildings that look like they were designed by toddlers and built out of Duplo, the scaled-up Lego for the under-fives. These flat, featureless square blocks, always daubed in primary colours the better to blot the landscape, are what I'll term 'New Labour architecture', by which you should infer not just their date, but their ethos as well: bland yet overpowering; somehow both infantile and patronizing.

But then, once you get almost as far east as you can on the DLR, you recognize it's even worse than that. Look west and you'll see the truly terrible new buildings proudly besmirching the City of London skyline, designed by megalomaniacs for megalomaniacs to lease to other megalomaniacs. Unless, that is, they serve as piggybanks for desert despots or Russian gangsters.

It's always perilous badmouthing architecture, in case you end up sounding like Prince Charles, whose fondness for thatch is, I suspect, because of its central role in the vernacular architecture of feudalism. And personally, I'm all for The New. But what's worst of all about London's latest Towers of Greed and Hubris is all of a piece: they're dull, overblown, infantile, charmless and out of all proportion or sympathy with anything surrounding them apart from the other ludicrous and imbecilic new buildings now stinking up the city of my birth. Because the truth of it is that, now, even the backdrop no longer matters, irrespective of it being a living, vibrant, ancient city where millions of people live and work: the architect–client–tenant matrix of avarice and vanity is now a wholly sealed unit. Nothing and nowhere else matters.

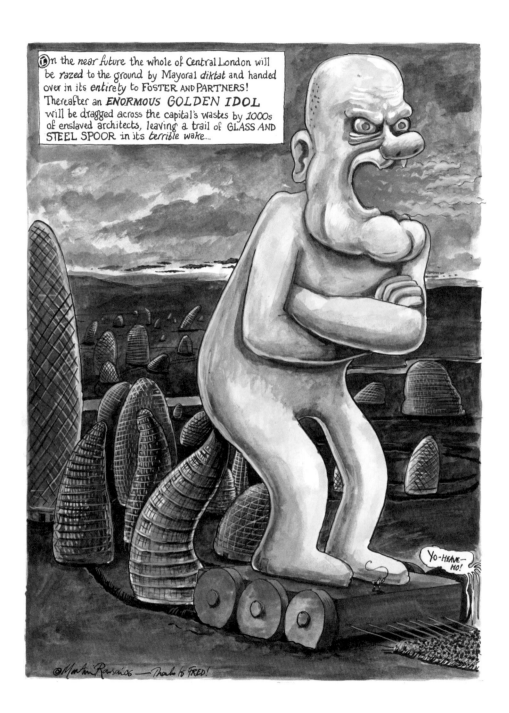

The Architectural Review, 2006

Of course, even though they'll pull them down in 20 years' time to build something to make even more money, they try to charm us by giving these monstrosities nicknames, the better to dissipate their toxicity: 'The Walkie-Talkie', 'The Cheesegrater'. Don't fall for it. Or devise more appropriate nicknames, like for the fatuous St George Wharf Tower in Vauxhall, which looks for all the world like a Dalek's Dildo. I mean, London's cabbies universally referring to 'The Architect's Cock' or 'The Banker's Todge' could work miracles on rental value in the Square Mile.

Corbynmania . . .

October 2015

A family bereavement and then a much needed holiday has meant my absence from this old column of George Orwell's throughout the Summer of Labour's Discombobulation, which is probably no bad thing. It's meant, for a start, that I've now got over my damn near totally irresistible urge to look back through 17 years' worth of *Tribune* columns, in which I've closely tracked the rise and fall of New Labour, and say I told you so. And in spades.

Still, you'd have to have a heart of stone not to allow yourself a tiny chortle when watching what finally happens when you treat your party like naughty children for two decades. Oh, and at the same time turn a short-term electoral tactic into a strategy, and then enshrine it as the highest imaginable principle. Particularly when, in a nutshell, that principle is, it seems, that Labour members are allowed to believe solely that opposition consists exclusively of putting up both hands while wailing 'I agree with you about EVERYTHING.' And, just for good measure, this principled opposition is in reaction to Cameron and Osborne, a couple of desperately cynical chancers making it all up as they go along.

That, however, wasn't the worst of it. In the descent of a once formidable electoral operation into tin-eared impotence, the Labour hierarchy's sclerotic lack of political nimbleness proved to be one of the wonders of the age, like a kind of political Zen riddle where the leadership's leadership, like an upside-down magnet, became guaranteed to repulse those they wished to be led.

The same phenomenon was—and is—evident in the shrillness of the Blairite commentariat. Irrespective of the validity of their arguments, their tone was—and remains—breathtakingly counterproductive. Time and again over the summer, I found myself on Twitter trying to persuade journalists like David Aaronovitch and John Rentoul, both of whom I like personally, to stop sounding like Oxford undergraduates in a bikers' pub making loud jokes about their fellow patrons' sartorial choices. I warned them that no good would come of it, and by and large I was proved right. Though of course, after 'sorry', 'I may have been mistaken' seem forever to be the Blairites' hardest words. Which is sad, because 'You're all wrong and I'm right' is a rather pitiful epitaph.

Nonetheless, it did its work, albeit topsy-turvily. Which should explain something that, once more, the established commentariat as well as the bulk of the Parliamentary Labour Party either can't or won't see. Corbyn's election as leader of the Labour Party was the event; everything that comes afterwards is both anticlimax and, in fact, beside the real point.

This, I know, will be scant comfort to many, but I suspect it's part of a lengthier process which was also manifest in this year's general election. Throughout that interminably long and nauseating campaign, I kept thinking again and again how, at the end of the day, this had nothing to do with us. Whether it was Ed Miliband posing for the cameras with his policy rockery or Cameron addressing a dozen or so party workers in an empty warehouse, the 2015 election marked the final triumph of Potemkin politics. Like the villages of facades erected by Catherine the Great's lover to fool her into thinking her country was prospering, the election was, ultimately, a media–politics Westminster Village selfie. Ed, for all his good intentions, was really just posing as Labour leader, while Cameron has never truly made the effort to be anything other than a figurehead.

While the media's obsession with Westminster politics continues to perpetuate the myth that it's the only politics going, the rest of us will be expected to carry on watching, with grateful delight, a game of clones happening inside a hermetically sealed unit. But the fact that Corbyn is almost wholly out of the kilter with the rest of the Parliamentary Labour Party isn't some kind of political disaster, it's his whole point.

In trying to explain or even control the Corbynmania unfolding before their horrified eyes, both the Labour hierarchy and the media sought parallels in other insurrections against the establishment, in vague anti-politics, in Syriza or Larry Sanders or even UKIP. But a more exact comparison probably lies in the realm of showbiz— which, as everyone knows, is just politics for good-looking people.

Remember how, every time a senior Labour figure howled another warning of the impending catastrophe of electing Corbyn, his popularity grew. What does it remind you of? That's right, it's *The X Factor* writ large, all those hopeless acts who kept getting through to the next round as the viewers voted *simply to annoy Simon Cowell*. That may seem a trivial point, but in these volatile times in our dangerously disconnected politics, Jeremy Corbyn as Jedward—or whatever this bizarre phenomenon signifies— may yet go very far indeed.

Daily Mirror, August 2015

Cavell / Tory Patriotism . . .

October 2015

The rather imposing memorial to the British nurse Edith Cavell, shot by a German military firing squad in Brussels 100 years ago, has always slightly puzzled me. Each time I pass it in Central London, on my way from Charing Cross station to points north up St Martin's Lane, I can't help wondering if they appreciated, 95 years ago when the memorial was unveiled, that its inscriptions, if you think about them for more than a second, cancel each other out.

At its top the words 'For King and Country' are carved deep into the Cornish granite. A bit below that, just above the head of Cavell's statue, and in a much larger font, is the single word 'HUMANITY'. Then, on the statue's pedestal itself you can read Cavell's own words to the prison chaplain the night before her execution: 'Patriotism is not enough. I must have no hatred or bitterness for anyone.'

It's no surprise that oxymorons feature among all the other moronic activities of states at war or recently at war. It's just that this one is so blatant. Does it even make any sense? For sure, every nation equates itself with all the best attributes of humanity; that's the lie at the core of patriotism. But the venerated object of all this (she's actually commemorated in the Anglican Church's calendar of saints) undermines all that with her own words. Weird, huh?

Or maybe not. Contradiction, after all, lies at the heart of all authoritarian structures, the better to bemuse and bedazzle us. If any of it made sense—the dictators, the dicta, the doctrines and the dogma—it would lose most of its allure and its associated power to terrify.

Though how consciously the British Conservative Party pursues this absolutist template is anyone's guess. It's true that the standard protocol—to instal obvious idiots at the top and expect everyone else gratefully to salute and worship them (see also Tsar Nicholas II, Charles I, George Bush, etc.)—appears to be flourishing. But it's the particular absurdities of Tory patriotism which provide a constant wonder.

Partly these result from modern, Thatcherite conservatism's defining contradiction: like the American Republicans, the Conservative Party, nativist and deeply suspicious of foreigners, has become willing host to the ideological parasite of neoliberalism, which advocates globalization, including the free movement of labour as well as capital, the better to drive down wages and conditions. Anyone else less adept at screaming hypocrisy than the scions of the English establishment would have turned inside out by now, simply at the mindboggling impossibility of peddling both restricted immigration and the unfettered market. But having more or less successfully squared that—in their own minds at least—everything else is easy-peasy.

Defence of the Realm

The Guardian, November 2015

Thus, Cameron can pull out his 'patriotic' trump card against Jeremy Corbyn without a hint of a blush while happily overseeing the continuing selling off of our industries and our nation's infrastructure to foreigners; often, indeed, to foreign governments, to the point where our chancellor of the Exchequer is furiously encouraging a recently very unfriendly foreign superpower to store weapons-grade plutonium on Britain's sovereign soil.

This makes some sort of sense taken alongside the Tories' acknowledged hatred for the 'state', its employees, clients and, most of all, its beneficiaries among the poorest and least powerful of its citizens.

But the British state itself—that ramshackle, atrophied political entity, tracing a clear lineage through a thousand years to William the Conqueror's genocidal Norman occupation, that institutionalized atrocity which mysteriously but pervadingly takes up the same geographical space as the country we live in and maybe love—has never been in the Tories' sights. Perhaps that's because they value too highly its mesmerizing, bamboozling contradictions as the simplest way to keep us under control. Perhaps it's simply too good as a custom-built playpen, somewhere the otherwise-unemployable children of the rich—like George Osborne or Boris Johnson—can fill the empty days of their gap lives in safety, playing infantile political games out of harm's way (their own, that is: everyone else is irrelevant collateral).

Or maybe they just haven't got the balls to go the whole hog, dismantling the whole of the state, their own jobs included, like the Most Serene Republic of Venice voting itself into extinction as Napoleon's armies massed the other side of the lagoon. Though that, at least, would hint at some vestigial sense of decency before the looting begins in earnest.

Bowie . . .

January 2016

Weirdly, the most difficult moment in the week following David Bowie's death came when I tried to explain to someone in their thirties what Dial-a-Disc was.

Just like everyone else on earth, I was talking about the part Bowie had played in my life, this time to Rich, the archivist who's spent the last couple of years bringing some order to over 30 years' worth of my cartoons and drawings. And I was telling him how, because the BBC ran the UK's only legal pop music station with an unbending adherence to a rigidly banal playlist, when I was 13, if I wanted to listen to *Hunky Dory* on demand—as we never said then—I had to ring up Dial-a-Disc. And I then had to explain how, back then, Britain's state-owned Post Office operated the country's entire telephone network—as well as providing all the telephones—and also provided various services, like Dial-a-Disc, where for three minutes you could listen to whatever song they'd chosen as that week's attraction.

Rich looked at me as if I was describing actual life on Mars, and in a way I was: Bowie was someone from another world all right, but in time, not space.

But weirder still is how some artists, like Bowie, occasionally step outside their own time and, in our perceptions, become literally timeless. I first realized this roughly 15 years ago, watching the Beatles in *A Hard Day's Night* for the first time since I was about five. The black-and-white filmed Britain surrounding the Fab Four was grainily post-war, utterly of its time and almost gagging on its grimy, sooty zeitgeist. And yet through this world walk John, Paul, George and Ringo like envoys from immortality, anachronistic interlopers from an eternal now.

Likewise, Bowie. If you listen to *Hunky Dory*, *Ziggy Stardust* and *Aladdin Sane*, they may, like all music, trigger memories personal in you, but I bet they don't evoke the Heath government, the Oil Crisis, Watergate or the Three-Day Week. Unlike the Sex Pistols or, for that matter, Vera Lynn, Bowie largely failed to produce a soundtrack to history, but simultaneously provided one for millions of individual lives.

So, for his audience, it means that the 70s—unlike in the twisted Thatcherite cliche of a dark dystopia where power-mad unions left the dead unburied—exist more truly in the imaginations of many of us as buttressed at either end by 'Kooks' and 'Ashes to Ashes', tipping on the fulcrum of 'Heroes' in the middle. And that means Bowie exists outside conventional politics as well as linear time, even if he wrote the songs we love best just when he was telling interviewers he was attracted to fascism. Then again, he was coked out of his head at the time and was reportedly storing his piss in jam jars in his fridge to prevent it being stolen by wizards.

However, as always, there remains a political dimension, although Bowie is a passive player in it. This one involves why so many of us responded to his death in the way we did, and it has everything to do with the loss of that unimaginable, long gone world I tried to describe to my friend Rich.

For three and a half decades now, in the world of infinite choice that replaced the 70s, it's been officially sanctioned to glorify the kind of individualism Bowie has been praised for pioneering, though I suspect what he, and you and I, reckon to be worth celebrating about ourselves no longer has much in common with the tattered remnants of the Thatcherite dream. Nonetheless, it remains a sacred tenet of orthodox political thinking that we act at our noblest as individuals, and at our basest as part of a formless, collectivist mob. Except, that is, when out shopping for tickets for pop concerts or digital downloads.

BROADSHEET

20p   OCT 22—28 1980

THE ELEPHANT MAN

DAVID BOWIE
NOTHING

Broadsheet, October 1980

But that's not true. Whatever we're told we are, it's not us. The response to Bowie's death, just like it was with Princess Diana nearly two decades ago, was fuelled by each of us individually yearning to share our lives and our loves with others. In ways far too beautifully nuanced for any cheap ideological zealot ever to be able to grasp, we want to be different, together. As your man sang in 'Rock 'n' Roll Suicide' at the end of *Ziggy Stardust*, sobbing in what it's tempting, if tenuous, to hear as elegiac:

Just turn on with me, and you're not alone
Let's turn on and be not alone
Gimme your hands, 'cause you're wonderful
Gimme your hands, 'cause you're wonderful
Oh, gimme your hands

Jeremy Corbyn's New Year Message, Modestly Re-imagined . . .
January 2016

Happy New Year, and I hope you've now had a chance to watch my New Year's Eve message on social media. I outlined what Labour has achieved since I was elected leader last September. We've forced this Tory government into U-turns over tax credits, police cuts and plans to run the Saudi prison system. What's more, I promised this year we'll attack austerity head on, preparing for a Labour government to be elected in 2020. One thing I left out, though, and it's something I should actually have said last September: I hereby resign as leader of the Labour Party.

*

Let me explain. I haven't surrendered to those defeatist voices within our party—including those who dominated and controlled it for 20 years—that we can never win unless we compromise again and again until we've jettisoned everything that made us Labour in the first place.

Nor do I buy the lie peddled by a media mostly controlled or effectively intimidated by the Tories' tax-dodging billionaire friends. That's the lie that insists the only politics worth reporting is the petty playground politics of Westminster, to the exclusion of all else. And certainly to the exclusion of reporting any alternatives.

Though I happen to know it's another lie that a party of ideological extremists stuck in the self-indulgent politics of the 80s could never, ever form a government.

And I know that's a lie because every day I look across the despatch box at just such a party.

Tragically, that party is the Conservatives. As bereft of ideas as they are of members, as incompetent as they are callous, the one thing they have in spades which we lack is self-confidence.

This self-confidence may indeed be founded on nothing more than their instinctive arrogance, but each time we allow ourselves to doubt our purpose and be tempted to surrender to their agenda, we not only diminish ourselves, we diminish politics too.

This is what I meant when I spoke about a new kind of politics. A politics defined by the needs of people, not markets; a politics beyond Westminster and beyond the narrow broken arc of what corporations find comfortable; a politics fully embracing the infinite possibilities of everyone across the widest imaginable spectrum.

But what I should have explained back in September is that, in practice, there are three kinds of politics. Put bluntly, they are:

The politics that seeks to wield power.
The politics that seeks to usurp power.
And the politics that seeks to thwart it.

And of these three, it's the third kind which is and always has been the best and noblest. As Tony Benn used to say, the most important thing you can ever ask a politician is, 'How can we get rid of you?' With the greatest of respect to Tony, I'd add that an even more important one would be 'How do we stop you?'

My whole political life has been dedicated to thwarting power, to highlighting its abuses and the crimes and injustices that follow in its wake. Within our party, itself dedicated for two decades to the politics of usurping power even at the cost of our defining principles, I have never baulked from the higher principle of holding power to account through opposing it.

That said, the whole point of the new politics I seek is not to displace the first two types of politics with mine, but to recognize the truth that all are equally valid and equally vital to the health of our democracy. Although many of my Parliamentary friends and colleagues should perhaps reflect more deeply how the size of my mandate is in direct proportion to the degree to which our party permitted my kind of politics to be eclipsed.

Anyway, it was this week's ridiculous media frenzy about how I was about to 'stamp my authority' on the Shadow Cabinet that finally gave me the wake-up call I should've heard the minute I was elected leader. As I said, the reason I'm in politics in the first place is to resist by any means necessary the stamp of authority, because that's the sound of tyranny.

To Dream The Impossible Dream

In other words, I don't like leaders. I think they should be hindered at every turn to prevent them from making the terrible mistakes leaders inevitably make.

So, rather than rebelling against myself, I'm resigning. I leave it to others, with a stronger stomach for all the pomp and mummery of office on top of the associated conniving and compromise, to win back power for Labour in 2020.

But I'm not going away. In Westminster and beyond, backed by hundreds of thousands of our members and supporters, I'll keep reminding our new leader and designated prime minister, whispering in his or her ear like the slave in ancient Rome reminding the conquering hero of their mortality, what Labour means and what Labour's for. Which has never been and never can be to be slaves, either to the media or the markets. Or to the old politics which has so comprehensively failed us all.

Philosophy . . .

May 2016

A couple of weeks ago I went to watch my wife graduate with her MA in philosophy (with distinction, thank you very much) from the wonderful Birkbeck College in London. And apart from bursting with pride at yet further proof of how much smarter than me she is, it's also worth recording that the intellectual quality of a lot of our conversation has risen exponentially, thanks entirely to her studies.

That said, I'm enormously relieved that she's chosen to concentrate on realms of philosophy I can sort of begin to understand, and that she's carrying on with ethical and political philosophy in her studies towards her MPhil, still at Birkbeck. This, in turn, means my head doesn't start hurting too much over breakfast as I desperately try to remember what 'hermeneutics' means or attempt to follow her down philosophical culs-de-sac of the kind constructed by the likes of Heidegger, exploring the Isness of Is, the Wasness of Was (and the HasBeenness of HasBeen, for that matter). She, like me, has little patience with this kind of thing, which I firmly believe everyone should put aside, along with playing *Dungeons & Dragons*, on their 19th birthdays.

Still, what the hell do I know? Arguments seeking to refute the Isness of Is and asserting the Unverifiable Nature of Reality Itself are clearly central to our contemporary politics, so I suppose the rest of us have no real business lamely suggesting that the Thingness of a Thing is observable from its Thinginess, when obviously the truth lies in the fact that Everything Is Not What It Is. You following me?

These curlicues of cobblers are just as much guaranteed brainachers as hermeneutics, and yet seem, across the spectrum, to guide all current political discourse. That is how

it's possible for last week's election results to be SIMULTANEOUSLY both a triumph AND a disaster for Jeremy Corbyn, and for holders of either view to believe holders of the opposite opinion are both insane and evil. And because both these attitudes are neatly and tidily contained within the Labour Party (which, according to both sides, in order to do well MUST do really, really badly, albeit in entirely different ways) this modern refinement of the Socratic method—which has replaced the tired old formula of debate and discussion with eternally screaming about your interlocutor's insanity and wickedness—is therefore more important than anything else. Ever ever ever.

Naturally most observers are simply too stupid to recognize that this is the higher philosophy in its purest form, but that's hardly surprising. In an era when facts have been proved to be both redundant and a hindrance to clear thinking, old-fashioned modes of thought might tempt us to forget we should be celebrating our liberation into broad, sunlit uplands of inquiry underpinned by the new School of Auto-Lingua-Generated Platonism, exemplified by the leading advocates of the United Kingdom leaving the European Union. This is the method by which anything you make up in your head which you kind of like the sound of becomes the unquestionable truth simply by virtue of you saying it out loud. (The richness of philosophy lies in the way this method proves that exactly the opposite applies to the other side: everything they state, even down to the colour of the sky or the day of the week, is instantly a lie because it is they who have spoken it. Neat, huh?)

Luckily for idiots like me, these methods are underpinned by bafflingly irrefutable mathematical models, like:

Any criticism of the actions of the government of Israel = You're a Nazi;

which is not to be confused with:

All Muslims = Terrorists = Just a bit of rough and tumble;

even if it turns out:

Etonian languor + trust fund = Statesmanship x complacency = Zac Who?

Lazy dog-whistle racist cynicism

Thankfully, the New Philosophy is more than up to calling in doubt minor setbacks like this. Now that the wonders of social media have finally freed humanity's collective id from the prison of our individual skulls, the final triumph and ultimate ubiquity of the New Thinking is inevitable. Once everyone was empowered to share what Freud possibly once termed 'The Mad Shit You Make Up in Your Head' with everyone else forever, then Observable Reality was bound to take a back seat to Universal Reassurance.

All of which means, I think, that we shouldn't be alarmed when the evidence of our own eyes is exposed as mendacious nonsense by a vast babel of deep thinkers, from libertarians to Chomskians and from corporations to governments. When they tell you white is black, you can bet your life it's going to be getting blacker and blacker.

Moscow . . .

June 2016

I was in Moscow last week, for the first time in 40 years, and it's changed a bit. When I went there on a school trip in 1976, the place was in the midst of the Brezhnev Stagnation: dingy, dirty, gloomy, depressed and depressing, heavy with the sense that the whole thing was over but no one dared or cared to say so quite yet.

Since then, of course, Moscow's been through a lot: glasnost, perestroika, a coup, a counter-coup, a collapse into criminal fiefdoms followed by the slow triumph of a weird kind of quasi-democratic, crony-capitalist elected tsarism. The consequences of this for Moscow itself are various: the demolition of a lot of old Soviet buildings seriously disorientated me, and I couldn't work out what had changed in Red Square until someone pointed out that the Rossiya Hotel, built in the 60s and once the largest hotel in the world, no longer loomed over St Basil's Cathedral. Also in Red Square, back in the day I remember GUM, the State Department Store opposite the Kremlin, as being filled with not much, but having fierce women operating abacuses with the speed of computers. Now it's just another identikit international White-trash luxury-goods shopping mall, the natural habitat of the people who think they rule the world: oligarchs, bankers, bandits, Tony Blair, that kind of cheap offshore hood.

Which means that Moscow is now much, much more Like Everywhere Else (like everywhere else), which is exactly the opposite of what it was 40 years ago, or why I went there. Now, moreover, the traffic's terrible (then the only traffic in the eight-lane wide boulevards was the occasional ZIL limousine whooshing past in its reserved lane, containing a melon-headed apparatchik off to cook some books) and the place is so full of hipsters you'd be forgiven for thinking you were in Shoreditch instead of being deep in the heart of Russia. Though, to be fair, Shoreditch in 1976 probably looked more like Moscow then than it's now possible to imagine. Otherwise, struggling to find anything specifically Russian on the menu in whichever achingly trendy pop-up restaurant you find yourself in, the last remaining hints of exotic otherness are the alphabet and the onion domes, freshly gilded by oligarchs with money stolen from the state.

The Dance of Death: Vanitas (London: SelfMadeHero, 2019)

And yet, underneath all that—and I haven't even mentioned the vast pieces of public kitsch from the 90s, pastiching the previous fashion for Soviet monumentalism but without anywhere near the same levels of aesthetic sense or good taste—there lurks something else, rather less palatable. On my taxi into Moscow from the airport, I was driven by a nice man with little English, who nonetheless was keen to talk (he had an iPhone to help translate). He wanted to tell me about London and the Bank of England, and how the Bank of England printed money in order to control the world on behalf of the sinister English elite, headed by the Rothschilds. He lacked the English for me to explain how the Rothschilds were so in control of the world they couldn't even fix it for their languorous in-law to be elected mayor of London, so instead I told him I was a 'karicaturist' and so thought no one was in control of anything, and only the biggest idiots ever imagined they were. He told me I had soul, which was nice, and then asked if I'd heard the theory that the White races were the first to arrive on Earth from outer space.

I told him I doubted it, to be honest, but if it was true, when were the flying saucers coming back to take us home? He smiled. Like I say, he was a nice man who talked about his children and just happens to spend far too much time in the wrong parts of the internet. That's why, as we passed the Kremlin and I mentioned that my father had seen both Lenin and Stalin in the Mausoleum when he was in Moscow for a conference in 1959, my driver said, 'Stalin believe in gold money not print money, so he was killed.' Shortly thereafter we reached my destination and he told me I was a 'very interesting intellectual', so you can tell how deluded he was on all fronts.

Nonetheless, I suspect these ideas circulate widely among people who've felt the rough side of history for a long, long time. New myths emerge, new ways to self-identify yourself as different and exceptional and good, despite the shops and the traffic. Or my reply to a friend, back home, who asked if I hadn't been overwhelmed in Moscow by the atmosphere of corruption: coming from London, I observed, how on earth would I be able to tell the difference?

Moscow, more than most places, stands as a monument to high ideals that collapsed into monstrosity. To serve god only knows who, maybe it is better that now it truly is the same the whole world over, though there remains the unavoidable stench of a cloying, suffocating, paranoid, mawkishly racist and self-satisfied nationalism underlying and ultimately stinking up everything. And I'm only half joking when I conclude by saying that, all in all, a few days in Putin's Russia was, therefore, a great relief from the unfolding horrors of this bloody Brexit debate. It's the same the whole world over in far worse ways than I fear we understand.

Cult . . .

August 2016

It's one of the richer ironies, among all the ironies snapping round our knees right now, that the greatest breakthrough in human communication since the advent of printing turned out so quickly to result in a total breakdown in human understanding. We can now instantly communicate with each other across the globe, more or less unmediated, and I suppose at some point some naive hippy techie assumed this would lead to a worldwide community of shared knowledge and wisdom, a kind of benign hivemind, to the betterment of us all. Instead, what we've ended up with is an almost infinite archipelago of solipsisms.

We should, perhaps, have seen this coming. Remember what happened when printing arrived in Europe around 1450. Hitherto, all that mad, Tourettic shit seething and boiling away inside each individual human's head more or less had to stay there as the options for releasing it were few. You could say it out loud, but in all likelihood, after a while, your friends and neighbours would tell you to shut up. You could whisper it, and it might just transubstantiate into gossip and get some valency that way. You could, just about, write it down, but this was expensive, laborious, slow and few people could read. You could draw it, of course, but, as I know to my cost, there's no guarantee some idiot wouldn't see it and get hold of completely the wrong end of the stick.

However, after printing it was possible to set down the mad Tourettic shit in your head and then disseminate it far and wide to be consumed by people you'd never met and never would. Small wonder, then, that 70 years after printing came the Reformation and two centuries of more or less perpetual European (and ultimately global) warfare, leading to the deaths of millions. Which is where paradigm shifts in human communication get you.

Then, thanks to printing, there's the emergence of the novel as a literary form in the eighteenth century. This was considered massively morally hazardous: apart from the levels of passion the words in the book would excite in the reader, the readers of these things were doing something genuinely suspicious. They were reading silently, to themselves, whereas hitherto reading was almost always aloud, and shared. In other words, this was a secretive, antisocial solitary vice, and therefore just as injurious, socially and personally, as any other kind of self-abuse.

Which brings us back to now, and the ubiquity of communication made silently, in seclusion. If you look at a lot of social media, it can often seem that humanity as a whole has been collectively trepanned, allowing our species' id to spurt out incontinently and often venomously all over everything. Worse, I think a lot of people think what

Human Centipede

ALL POWER TO THE HEROIC TWITTER BRIGADES!

The Guardian, July 2016

they write in the solitude of their lonely rooms or into their tiny phones remains just in their heads. Even worse, all the previously required dimensions of human interaction—the body language, the flickering, shifting gaze of the eyes, the darting of a tongue in and out of a lying mouth—are now lost in material which, nonetheless, is published into the public domain where it will now remain forever.

Worst of all, this condition of individual solitude in a cacophonous multitude has more or less dispensed with any lingering pretence at objectivity, or that it even matters. Basically, you just type the shit that makes you feel good and anyone who disagrees or questions you can fuck off. Or worse.

Which I sort of feel isn't entirely healthy, don't you? But who knows? Everything is in doubt, and probably always was. We're in the midst of a national nervous breakdown, the country's been cracked wide open by the playground politics of a bunch of dilettante playboys and the whole of what used to be called 'the establishment'—business, politics, the Church, the monarchy, the BBC and the rest of the media—has been so rotten for so long no one even notices the stench any more. Maybe that's why people are now choosing their own subjective reality in preference to the horrible one the people who presume to 'lead' us have left us with (which, of course, in the subjective—for which read lying-through-his-teeth—view of George Osborne was the glittering success of his long-term economic plan, before he discarded it like a used condom once the game was up).

Even so, and even if Jeremy Corbyn is the greatest leader in the history of leadership despite this having previously escaped even him, and even though I've been writing in this column 'I told you so' about the likely malign and catastrophic consequences of the Leninist centralism of the Blairites for nearly 20 years, and even when any glimmer of some kind of hope is probably worth grabbing, I am horrified almost beyond words how people I admire and like seem to have collapsed so easily into the comfort of a cult of the personality around Corbyn. Whatever Corbyn's strengths or weaknesses, unquestioning support for anyone, especially when it borders on worship, should be anathema to everyone who claims to be on the left.

But what do I know? As an anonymous commenter posted beneath a recent cartoon of mine in the *Guardian* (boo hiss!), which had the temerity to depict Corbyn at the head of a human centipede, I'm just a 'vile Blairite PLP warmongering cartoonist'. You bet! Though it's also worth recalling Richard Attenborough's response when it was suggested that he depict Gandhi in the eponymous movie simply as a glowing point of light: 'I making a film about a man, not fucking Tinker Bell!'

Labour Rancour . . .

September 2016

In 1976, after James Callaghan won the Labour leadership contest to succeed Harold Wilson, Labour's former deputy leader Roy Jenkins resigned as an MP in order to take up the post of president of the European Commission. He announced this at a press conference in Westminster, his trusty lieutenant David Marquand at his side, who'd also resigned his seat as an MP to follow Jenkins to Brussels as the great man's chief adviser. Jenkins told the assembled hacks that he was leaving for Brussels 'without bitterness or rancour'. Unfortunately, his trademark soft *r*, with that inevitable slapstick which leavens the burden of history, rendered this phrase as 'without bitterness or wanker'. At which point one of the hacks at the back shouted out, 'So you're leaving Marquand behind then?'

We've still got tons of time to reflect on the latter formulation and its dominant role in contemporary British politics, so I'll save all the jokes about ultimate political self-fulfilment with someone you truly love for later. Right now, I want to concentrate instead on rancour.

Many of the Labour Party's hundreds of thousands of new members or supporters may not be aware of it, but rancour is more or less woven into Labour's DNA, warp and weft. This should come as no surprise, as the point of Labour is, or should be, to make the world a better, lovelier place, an ambition fuelled by love for all humanity. But the thing about love is its infinite capacity to turn on a sixpence into the worst kind of vengeful hatred. After all, most people who are murdered are probably murdered by someone who previously loved them.

That explains the rancorous hatred that Labour felt for Ramsay MacDonald after he, Philip Snowden and others succumbed to George V's bullying and formed a National Government with the Tories in 1931. But a different kind of rancour fuelled Ernest Bevin in October 1935 at Labour's Brighton Conference, during a debate on how to respond to Mussolini's recent invasion of Abyssinia. Labour's saintly leader George Lansbury made a passionate plea for pacificism and was greeted with wild cheering and two choruses of 'For He's a Jolly Good Fellow'. Then Bevin spoke about the very real physical threat to trades unions and their members posed by the potential victory of fascism, unopposed by anything except the highest principle. And then gave Lansbury both barrels: 'It is placing the Executive and the Movement in an absolutely wrong position to be hawking your conscience around from body to body asking to be told what to do with it.' A couple of weeks later, Lansbury resigned (partly through pressure from the maligned yet sometimes magnificent union block vote), although the PLP then asked him back again. After he refused, they appointed

The Guardian, September 2016

Attlee as interim leader till someone better came along, a position he occupied for the next 20 years.

He nearly didn't. In a moment of low farce after Labour's momentous election victory in 1945, Herbert Morrison tried to get to Buckingham Palace first to kiss George VI's hand and thus establish himself as prime minister, although Attlee was bundled at short notice into a car and got there first. Later, when someone said that Morrison was his own worst enemy, Bevin instantly responded, 'Not while I'm alive 'e ain't.'

You can still feel the acidic fizz of rancour behind lines like Attlee's infamous note to Harold Laski about how 'a period of silence on your part would be appreciated'. Shortly thereafter, the vicious infighting between the Bevanites and the Gaitskellites (and then between the Bevanites and Bevan) characterized Labour's opposition during the 50s as a period of poisonous impotence. In 1955, when she was chairing the NEC Edith Summerskill wasn't even able to speak Ian Mikado's name, averting her eyes and referring to him through clenched teeth only as 'that comrade over there'. That kind of rancour was repeated in the late 70s and early 80s, with the foulness of Labour's current newfound kindliness being unfinished business from back then—though now with the added propellant of the incontinent self-righteousness of social media to ratchet up the rancour.

And if you think it's only right that people defend with passion the beliefs they hold passionately, then consider the Blair–Brown years, where nothing ideological divided the two camps, each with their fingerprints all over the New Labour project, except for simple, straightforward hatred. Ed Miliband was known by the Blairites as the ambassador from Planet Fuck as he was the only Brownite who didn't invariable greet a Blairite by saying 'Fuck off!' and walking away.

And maybe Ed's real, unforgivable betrayal was the party's appearance of unity and common purpose under his leadership, thus compelling Labour to deny its true nature and live a lie. And maybe that's all Labour is: a place for people who enjoy hating other people to come together in hatred in a safe space. And surely, we must recognize the need for such a space to allow people freely to express the full spectrum of their emotions and thus become more well-rounded individuals. That said, I can't help feeling it's still a bit of a shame that the Tories, contrariwise, have always managed to pull off that infuriating trick of hating everyone else even more than they hate each other.

Brexit . . .

October 2016

Like half the rest of the country, I can't yet put a name to this feeling I wake up with every morning, the mixture of anxiety and despair I last felt 12 years ago when both my parents died within three months of each other. Maybe, by the time you read this, it'll have a proper clinical name, because 'grief' isn't quite right. I'm not grieving for the EU as such: the EU, don't forget, is a badly run conspiracy of Thatcherite bankers which twice in the last six years staged coups d'état against democratically elected governments in Italy and Greece in order to appease the bond markets. Nor am I grieving that an even worse pack of ruthless Thatcherites appears to have won: I wouldn't have been contributing to *Tribune* for the past 22 years if I wasn't inured to the depressing truth that utter bastards continue to run the world.

And nor is it what former future prime minister Boris Johnson described in his £500,000-a-year column in the *Daily Telegraph* as 'Lefty . . . hysteria', an irrational outpouring of emotion identical to the grief that was triggered by the death of Diana, Princess of Wales, nearly 20 years ago. It's worse than any of that.

I fear that my Post-Brexit Stress Disorder is because I've been proved right. During the 30 years I've been a professional satirist, I've been screaming my head off, here and elsewhere, that the people who presume to lead us and our nation are a pack of craven, incompetent, complacent, cruel and callous clowns. That thanks to the dominant orthodoxy of my entire adult life—which preaches all wisdom resides exclusively in the divine mysteries of the market—our politics is dominated by hobbyists, chancers, obsessives, careerists and cranks. That consequently a lot of politics has become a playpen lined with mirrors for posh boys masquerading as statesmen, acting with all the long-term responsibility of gap-year interns. That this parade of posturing narcissists spans from hard-faced men, looking forward to doing well out of the next recession, who view our nation as simply an opportunity for salvage, via a centre ground of surrendering sidekicks all the way over to paranoid personality-cultists. And all of this acted out against a backdrop of de-industrialization, a national trauma to equal conquest, feudalism, war or industrialization itself, but treated by our masters as either an opportunity for more salvage, mixed in with grabbing the tactical partisan chance to undermine support for Labour and the unions, or as fixable with a new community arts centre.

As I say, I've been depicting our national public life like this for decades, in caricature, but like everyone else here on Fantasy Island, I fooled myself into thinking, deep in my heart, that it couldn't really be this bad. It turns out it's actually far, far worse.

Playtime's over...

The Guardian, June 2016

Whether they were lying even more to themselves than they were to us is no comfort. Nor is the irony that Cameron was believed when he lied about Labour's responsibility for the global crash or how there'd be no top-down NHS reorganization or about net migration, but no one believed him when he finally told the truth about the consequences of Brexit. The same applies to Osborne, who lied about us all being in it together while treating the victims of de-industrialization like irrelevant chaff to his pillaging of the public realm for his rich mates, and then found out that the chaff had decided that *freedom* is just another word for *nothing left to lose*.

This is where you end up when you decide the game involves the truth being wholly secondary to the message. Depressingly but inevitably, we therefore need to resort to fiction to get even close to the truth should have delivered us—both to and from. So imagine this alternative speech by David Cameron, delivered in Downing Street at 7 a.m. on the morning of 24 July:

> Leave has won, but amidst all the lies we all told you during this foul and wholly unnecessary campaign that I, personally, have brought down upon our nation due to my own cowardice and inability to control my party, there's a truth none of us dared reveal too loudly: that Parliament legislated for this referendum to be advisory, not mandatory. Therefore, I am immediately convening a Constitutional conference to decide the best way forward in our nation's best interest, and of course the electorate's advice will be considered along with all other factors. I take responsibility for chairing this conference, and we'll get back to you as soon as we can.

Now, of course, it's far too late for that, and instead our political elites are either fighting each other like bald men over a comb or have simply, like Cameron, Johnson and Farage, run away.

But before they fucked off, maybe these two Etonians and the failed City broker should have shared another truth with all those people—almost all of whom are good, and kind, and even beautiful—who said they wanted their country back. As political representatives of the bankers and the landowners and the feudal aristocracy and the media moguls and the multinational corporations, our bankrupt, useless 'leaders' should have asked the people why on earth they imagined the country belonged to them in the first place. Instead, naturally, they've left us quite alone. And wholly terrified.

Political Idiocy . . .

November 2016

The first and last time I met anti-elitist champion of the downtrodden and former City-trader Nigel Farage was after a talk I gave at Dulwich College, the South London public school which is also Farage's alma mater as well as his son's. Close by, off the South Circular between Catford and Brixton, lies Alleyn's, the former school of anti-elitist champion of the ordinary bloke and ex-*Sun* editor Kelvin McKenzie. McKenzie's employer is the anti-elitist billionaire dynast Rupert Murdoch, currently the acting chief executive of Fox News, an anti-elitist cheerleader for anti-elitist billionaire and president-elect of the United States of America Donald Trump. Apart from the slightly nauseating fact that Farage clearly sees himself as the anti-elitist Tony Blair (who went to Fettes Public School in Edinburgh, and then to Oxford) to Trump's anti-elitist George Dubya Bush (Yale and Harvard Business School), when I met him, he was wearing his old school blazer and tie. Farage was around 50 at the time, having left the school over 30 years previously.

Irony, you'll be devastated to learn, dropped dead ages ago, literally screaming its head off as it hit the vomit spattered gravel. What we have now is something different. Whereas irony often contains within it a germ of laughter, an opportunity for redemption through ridicule, that no longer applies. In beholding our new anti-elite elite, what we see instead is a simple contradiction which leads nowhere; this is called an oxymoron, with an emphasis on the moron.

Let me clarify this. I'm not just saying that people I disagree with politically are idiots (though I am, and they'd say the same about me); this runs far deeper than that, because this is idiocy as a political programme.

Stick with me. To be honest, I'm all for idiots' rights: I genuinely don't think people should be cruel or discriminatory towards idiots just because they're idiots. They have as much right to live, love and laugh as anyone. Indeed, I happily associate myself as an idiot on many fronts, as you could fill an infinity of infinitely large libraries forever with all the stuff I don't and can't know. And though I might draw the line, unlike Michael Gove, at having non-expert, non-elite, untrained idiots carry out life-saving surgery on me or my loved ones, my career is predicated on the fact that the experts are just as big a bunch of idiots as the rest of us. And that's how political idiocy comes dangerously close to genius.

The genius lies in its attractiveness. It takes my proposition outlined above—that there's no enduring shame in being an idiot, because we all are—and shifts it up a gear to the inalienable truth that there is virtue in being an idiot, and anyone who disagrees

I JUST DONE A POO-POO IN MY DIAPER MY POO-POO IS THE BEST POO-POO I GOT ALL THE GREATEST POO-POO ALL THAT OTHER PEOPLE'S POO-POO THEY STINK BUT MY POO-POO'S BRILLIANT ANY LOSER SAYS NO LIKE A LAME LOSER I GONNA SCREAM TIL I POO-POO GOO GOO!!

HAIL TO THE BRAT

Chartist, December 2016

is an elitist snob who's looking down on us because we're idiots. And if the logic gets a bit rocky at this point, it no longer matters because being an idiot is great, and anyone who mentions logic, or observable reality, or even coming remotely near making any sense at all, is an elitist snob. And so on forever.

Which means there's no point even pointing out the irony of a billionaire bully who lives in a golden tower because he believes little guys lose out because they're—duh!—losers, masquerading as the champion of little guys who've lost out. That's because irony's for smartarse elitist snobs. Nor need you bother presenting the overwhelming evidence of anthropogenic climate change ('anthropo-whatthefuck???') because who needs evidence from elitist so-called intellectuals? And as for pointing out that three British judges simply applied the stamp of British legal process to the fundamental truth of the British Constitution, that sovereignty rests with the British Parliament—HOW DARE YOU OPPRESS ME WITH THE OUTCOME OF MY OWN DESIRES, YOU ELITIST ENEMY OF THE PEOPLE! (That last sentence was expressed in the cadences of anti-elitist millionaire and *Daily Mail* editor Paul Dacre, whose sons went to Eton and who owns vast forested swathes of rural Scotland.)

To revive irony for a second or two, what's truly weird about this is that it's the final triumph of political correctness, turned inside out and used as a cudgel by the Far Right, for whom Führers and the fearful elitism of racial superiority are sacrosanct. Thus, the idea that saying my thoughts and actions are misguided, mistaken, harmful, self-destructive or dangerous is 'offensive'; how a desire for 'safe spaces' mutated into 'never hearing anything that might upset me', including that my thoughts and actions are misguided, mistaken and so on; and ultimately, that whatever makes me feel good is good, however bad it makes you feel. The original proponents of political correctness meanwhile stand by tongue-tied by their inability to call out idiocy when they see it, for fear of upsetting the idiots before the idiots lynch them.

And while the anti-elite elite is just another elite trying it on and screaming loud enough to stop anyone shouting them down and rumbling their scam, no doubt some of their followers and dupes will scream at me that I'm just another member of the 'sneering metropolitan elite'. Well, I put my hands up to that one. Except I've only ever been sneering back.

Fascism . . .

March 2017

When looking in horror at the bloody wreckage left in its wake, including the hecatombs of its victims, it's sometimes hard to remember that fascism, at its black heart, is less about rigorous authoritarian oppression and far more, for its supporters and clients at least, a twisted kind of dewy-eyed utopianism mixed in with breathtakingly infantile, recklessly irresponsible self-indulgence. But now that, in Bertolt Brecht's words, the old bitch is back in heat again, it's more important than ever to see fascism's fatuous childishness as clearly as we can, instead of scaring ourselves witless at the thought of the foul thing and running for cover. And thereafter, as ever, the best first response is to laugh, although laughter alone won't serve in the longer campaign.

Partly this is because fascism in all its various permutations is aware and often brazenly proud of its own ridiculousness. What it then does is play the standard gambit of defying you to laugh. Back in the day, Mussolini ponced around as a strutting clown in a stupid hat *with a gold tassel*; Hitler had a Charlie Chaplin moustache and expected grown men to march around at torchlit parades *wearing shorts*; Eva Perón would exhort her worshipping crowds with the words 'We shirtless ones!', raising her arms so her fabulous array of gold and bejewelled bangles would clump round her armpits. You'd need a heart of stone not to laugh. But how fascism works is that variation on the emperor's new clothes, where the merest snigger (George Orwell correctly observed that every joke is a tiny revolution) often proves fatal.

Now that gambit has recruited political correctness to its arsenal, so you're not allowed to laugh at risible oafs like Paul Nuttall or Donald Trump, because this is somehow or other a sneering elitist dismissal of their supporters, 'real' people leading 'real' lives. To put it bluntly, you can't call someone a fascist because, to coin a phrase, that would be 'fascistist'. Again, the ironies interwoven into this mad shit cry out for laughter; again, laughter is both hazardous and not enough.

Not that fascism is humourless. On the contrary, counterploying laughter is central to its various and repulsively potent attractions. Hitler stood out from his contemporary politicians in Weimar not just because he looked funny, but because he told jokes too, often quite good ones. Trump, likewise, is always telling gags (though hates jokes at his expense), while Nigel Farage never ever stops guffawing like a goat coughing up a venomous toad.

The point, however, lies in the fact that they can laugh at you but you can't laugh back. That's because fascism is defined by exclusion, and that's because, despite its latest meaningless sloganizing about the evil of 'elites', it's elitist or nothing. As the

The Guardian, August 2019

bastard progeny of ancient Rome with its privilege of citizenship and German Romanticism and the elevation of that illusory and elusive spectre, 'the Will', fascism welcomes you into a mass elite, based on citizenship and/or race. But it's an elite defined by its borders, by those excluded and outside, beyond hope or pity.

How this mass elitism works is one of the mesmerizingly contrary things about fascism. It's also been the unspoken agenda of the *Daily Mail*, among others, for decades. Encouraging 'ordinary', 'real' people to hate other (fictitious? extraordinary?) people different somehow, in colour or origin or gender or sexuality or opinion, from themselves creates a kind of hierarchy of elites. After all, if you're better than the queers or the wogs, you'll also recognize that Lord Rothermere, in his tax haven with his inherited millions, is better than you.

Thus fascism's hierarchical dynamic, wrapped in riddles and buttressed by bollocks, which leads ultimately to the Leader. And this is where all that childishness and irresponsibility and self-indulgence really starts to kick in. The people within fascism's embrace are indulged in every way you'd want: made to feel they belong, allowed to hate—then kill—who they choose, but also freed from any responsibility or blame, which is devolved up to the Leader who, usually being a demonstrable clown, is Himself just like the People (even if this is a bit of a giveaway of what fascists really think about the people they beguile). And thanks to the legacy of German Romanticism, even the Leader has it easy, because he's just channelling the Will of the People, which obviously requires no preparation as it simply surges through you. Or something.

And from this pinnacle of self-indulgence and irresponsibility cascades the rest of it: the desire for instantaneous gratification, the refusal to accept that actions have consequences that matter, the slow erosion of objectivity involving everyone to a wholly selfish subjectivity, which in turn will define the truth as simply being what you want it to be.

The trouble lies in the standard outcome of indulging anyone to have whatever they want whenever they want it, like toddlers in a candy store. It's what happens when they're stuffed rigid and still want more: it's the projectile puking and, as often as not, the blood that follows afterwards.

Life . . .

March 2017

Last weekend I met a very interesting zoologist called Tim, who'd just given a variation on a TED talk about cell division in eggs in the first hours after fertilization. To which your response, not unreasonably, is probably 'Yeah? And?' Please, bear with me.

The point about cell division is that we have no idea why or how it happens. We know that there's a pyrotechnical explosion of biochemical reactions which accompany a breathtakingly rapid acceleration of cell division, so that within hours a single cell becomes hundreds, then thousands, of cells, each destined to divide yet further as they settle down into their particular speciality. But what is it that triggers this rapid acceleration? Because it's not just fertilization. Some fertilized eggs remain more or less dormant until conditions are propitious for the process of cell division to commence; some creatures are born or hatch through parthenogenesis, where unfertilized eggs grow and their cells divide leading to what you might as well term a virgin birth, a common phenomenon in creatures as diverse as bumble bees and Komodo dragons. One idea Tim shared with me is that the whole thing—the whole of everything—is triggered by the egg being squeezed in the oviduct, a notion magnificent and beautiful in its simple banality.

The point, however, is we simply don't know. That's why Tim is a zoologist and teaches other people how to become zoologists, which is a constant in human experience: of almost everything, we just don't know, so let's keep trying to find out. That's one of the things that makes our species so uniquely fascinating and also terrible.

But the other revelation I received from Tim's talk goes to the heart of life itself. Without wishing to kick the moral hornets' nest of arguments over when 'life' begins, for the first few hours after fertilization or its assumed if currently unknown equivalent, we—that is, all things that are or will be alive—are cancers. That is, our cells divide rapidly and grow exponentially in exactly the same way as cancers grow. In other words, you could argue that our default setting is as a cancer which then reaches some kind of stasis (or remission, to labour the point) for a few score years before reverting to type in order, obviously, to kill us, because if we live long enough, we'll all die with or of some kind of cancer. And we die so that others may live.

Even factoring in the billions of tiny individual tragedies life necessarily instigates by requiring death, there is a simple, dark yet brilliant beauty to this vision of our existence, which in no way invalidates any of the wonders we create and encounter between our beginning and the end. But it also reminds us that we need endings; that nothing lasts forever, and that things need to finish if only because that's what they do. For whatever unknown and probably ultimately unknowable reason, it's inbuilt, innate and inevitable.

New Humanist, July 2019

Anyway, if that's the structure of our lives, why on earth (and there's nowhere else) should we imagine the same trajectory doesn't apply to the systems we've constructed, be they political parties or nation states?

Indeed, both the Labour Party and the British state might, right now, be entering their death throes. While I'll mourn the former much more than I will the latter, once more it's instructive to tease out the parallels with how our individual lives are governed. Between our initial and terminal states of cancerousness, everything about us is subject to external factors which trigger biochemical responses and subsequent consequences. These include self-indulgent lifestyle choices which, we all know, can pre-empt the natural process and cause premature cancers.

So it is with the political structures of organized human societies.

And so any future historian with the stomach to churn up the ancient midden will surely recognize that 2016 marked the year when self-indulgence metastasized through both the neoliberal West and its internal structures of opposition. Trump, Brexit and the re-election of Jeremy Corbyn all, to a lesser or greater degree, were about good, kind and often beautiful people wanting what they wanted and wanting it now, while wilfully ignoring all or any warning of the consequences. True, in Corbyn's case the self-indulgence had already honeycombed its way through Labour, which is one of the reasons he was elected and re-elected. In other words, if this is any comfort at all, he's a symptom rather than the disease itself.

Either way, empires and nation states and their internal structures rise, decline and fall, just like the rest of us. It's the natural way. Though, of course, you'd be infinitely less than human solely to view the bigger picture and fail to weep at the pity of it all.

Weaponizing Embarrassment . . .

July 2017

There's a very famous book by the literary critic Professor Sir Christopher Ricks called *Keats and Embarrassment* which, embarrassingly but inevitably for a one-time student of English literature, I've never read. One reason was that I was too busy drawing cartoons for two-bit student rags, one of which showed Keats having just coughed tubercular blood over his neat, joined-up copy of 'Ode to a Nightingale' and saying 'Oh Christ! That's embarrassing!' Professor Ricks, I was later informed, was not amused.

Still, he helped point out an aspect of human life and interaction to which we rarely account due importance, not least in the realm of politics. For sure, we're all aware of how embarrassing politics can be, personally and nationally, in terms of policy, presentation and implementation. However, what I suspect we don't choose to acknowledge (because to do so is itself embarrassing) is the power of embarrassment as an aggressive weapon.

Ironically enough, Theresa May was hitherto a brilliant exponent of this lethal gambit, even if the tables have now turned and her prime ministership shows every sign of becoming the most embarrassing in history.

Although it's hard to feel even remotely sorry for her, there is a vague whiff of the tragic lingering around the prime minister. Apart from all the standard universal personal tragedies that have beset her like everyone else, her political life has hitherto been one of enviable and almost unbelievable ease: after the usual initiation in an unwinnable constituency, she was handed one of the safest Tory seats in the country in order to become one of those incredibly rare beasts, a Conservative MP elected for the first time in 1997. She was rapidly promoted to the front bench and given—for tokenist reasons or otherwise—an enormous personal fastness in the Home Office by David Cameron. And throughout this time, she honed her deadly and previously unassailable skill . . . of glowering at people and saying nothing until they were so embarrassed they'd do whatever she wanted.

I've heard dozens of stories from people at all levels who've met or worked with her, that Theresa May is consistently supercilious, distant, unresponsive, unyielding, silent and, all in all, 'bloody difficult'. A typical story concerns last year's Christmas party for lobby correspondents at 10 Downing Street, when one unfortunate hack found himself standing next to the prime minister and, as you do at such events, attempted small talk. 'So,' they asked, smiling a little too hard, 'ever feel the need to nip next door and borrow a mug of sugar off Philip Hammond?' To which the prime minister allegedly replied, 'Why would I want to borrow a mug of sugar? I have diabetes.' (The natural response the heavens call out for is to shout, 'That's right! Milk it, you needy cow!' In sad reality, the hack slunk away nodding and smiling and feeling small and wretched, just as May wanted them to do.)

This propensity for weaponizing embarrassment is something May shares with Donald Trump. Since birth, Trump has always got what he's wanted, so obviously never bothered to develop beyond the factory setting of the toddler's tantrum. In short, he just behaves as obnoxiously as he can until everyone around him is so embarrassed they give him what he wants because it's easier and less . . . well . . . embarrassing. The proof of this can be seen in how Trump broke into Atlantic City, notoriously the impregnable preserve of the mob who make it their business to stop anyone else

muscling in. Except for Donald Trump, who behaved so abominably, combining wheedling vulgarity, bragging, bullying and, for all I know, strategic bedwetting, that all the mob wanted was to get out of the same room as him and were prepared to give him anything to achieve this ultimate aim. Trump calls this the 'Art of the Deal'; Andrew Neil, who has vast experience of these things, has described Trump as the worst person in every imaginable way that he's ever met.

Of course, this is an enviable skill if all you want to do is cow everyone around you into bending to your will and doing what you say just because you say so. The trouble is, as May has discovered (though I suspect Trump will never understand it), that simply stopping the excruciating, cringingly, agonizingly awful embarrassment through total obedience is ultimately insufficient reward for most people—as the British electorate proved in June. And therein lies May's tiny quotient of tragedy: the seeds of her destruction lay in her own ghastliness.

The wider tragedy, however, is how the embarrassment keeps spreading out, like ripples across the surface of a septic tank or blood through a rug. The months ahead, I suspect, will become almost unbearably embarrassing for everyone as we watch the Tories turning inside out to buttress their embarrassment threshold for Brexit, which is unquestionably now the greatest national embarrassment of any of our lifetimes.

Johnson . . .

October 2017

The times are so much in flux it's nearly impossible to hit upon a precise parallel for Boris Johnson's current behaviour. It's tempting to see it simply as a perpetuation of his lifelong shtick, the pitiful Oedipal car crash of the attention-seeking toddler so desperate for love and affirmation to bolster the brittle meringue of his self-belief he'll do literally anything to make you notice him, however hurtful, hateful or self-harming. But the way he's carrying on is now so artless in its naked, cack-handed narcissism you have to wonder if other forces might be at play.

For sure, the blinding effulgency of Johnson's personal ambition is one of the more horrifying wonders of the age, albeit in an age of wonders exponentially ever more horrific. And we know from his sister Rachel's testimony that when he was still truly a toddler—as opposed to his current avatar of retardation in toddlerhood while grotesquely trapped in the body of a fat old man—he declared his wish to be 'King of the World'. We also know that his father Stanley told the children of his broken marriage that he expected them to fight for his love and respect. So far, so Freudianly cliched. And we can add to that a telling observation from Ken Livingstone, Johnson's old rival for the mayoralty of London. At a meeting a couple of years ago at the London Zoo (where else?), Ken turned to me and said 'I don't get that Johnson bloke. He wants people to like him. You don't go into politics to be liked; you go into politics to be feared.' (For the record, when I reassured Ken that no one liked him, he instantly replied 'I know. And I don't fucking care.')

It gets even more complicated when we recognize the depth of Johnson's ruthless calculation in appeasing the neediness of his narcissism. Some years ago, when I was commissioned to produce the cover artwork for an edition of the *Spectator* under his editorship, Johnson was failing to decide things about the cover that needed deciding before I could even begin the process of designing the image. This was making me increasingly cross the closer we got to deadline, so when I finally got to speak to him on the phone and he did his usual bumbling toff number, I lost my temper completely and blurted out 'For once in your life, drop the P. G. Wodehouse bollocks and give me some answers!' After an uneasy silence of a few seconds, he hissed in a slightly menacing but otherwise unusually unmannered voice 'I think you'll find what you call the "P. G. Wodehouse bollocks" has served me very well thus far.'

In other words, Johnson is an act, a construct, a mask the better to advance the whole confidence trick; he even has a stage name, 'Boris' (his family all call him 'Al'). Of course, he's by no means unique in providing ample evidence for the truth of the old gag that politics is just showbiz for ugly people. Indeed, a great deal of 'Boris Johnson' makes perfect sense if all it's about is just the unquenchable craving for applause and adulation.

That also provides some mitigation for his almost pathological propensity for bare-faced lying: if it's only an act, these are merely the lines you speak and none of it's actually 'true' anyway. This would also explain his apparently unstoppable need constantly to ratchet up the restrictions on any negotiating position with the European Union: he inhabits a realm of pure imagination where anything is possible if you just think it up in your head.

Except, of course, one can never quite suspend disbelief with Johnson. Whereas the True Believers, like Liam Fox or John Redwood, radiate a deranged kind of starry-eyed gaucherie, Johnson stinks of guile and greasepaint. In spite of the massive gravitational pull of the black hole of his own self-regard, ultimately with Johnson there's no 'there' there: no principles, no philosophy, no programme; no notion of what he'd imaginably seek to achieve should he ever become prime minister apart from tripping over his cock again and waiting for the grateful, giggling applause. Which, in any case, is increasingly coming solely from the dwindling crowd of fawning boys, aging and all of his own class, who still buy into the risible vision of a world that serves solely as a playpen for Boris Johnson.

Tribune, March 2016

Some commentators beyond the sweaty circle jerk of the *Telegraph–Daily Mail–Jacobin* Brexit nexus are still occasionally trying to dignify Johnson's antics as a kind of Tory Maoism, a creative destruction which somehow or other ranks above the solipsistic nihilism it most closely resembles. This is too much. What we're currently watching, being sucked into the vacuum left by the comprehensive collapse of Theresa May and the whole Thatcherite edifice, is Boris Johnson acting somewhere between the cripplingly embarrassing relative, who keeps turning up to family parties to bore everyone rigid with the same old jokes, and the mean, vicious drunk, back from the pub late on Friday night, once again about to beat the wife and kiddies till they sob out their undying love. What a laugh, eh?

Sexual Harassment . . .

November 2017

Any diagnosticians of the ailments besetting nations and their cultures will have been alarmed by the latest symptom of our terminal national decline, which is the loss of our short-term memory. I'm writing this on the last Monday of November, and the news is all about economic planning, volcanoes and royal weddings. And yet, just four weeks ago, the nation was thrashing around in a turmoil of prurient disgust at the degree to which the fabric of our politics is riddled with complacent yet insatiable sexualized misogyny: MPs were suspended from their parties or lost government or shadow office over allegations of sexual harassment; one very senior, aggressively combative cabinet minister resigned because he could keep neither his hands to himself nor his (probably forked) tongue in his own face; another one, by the time you read this, may well have had to resign because of his obvious need to keep images on his portable laptop computer to enable him to masturbate wherever he goes.

Forgive me for spelling it out, but we need to appreciate precisely how squalid all this is, how apparently petty yet essentially disastrous it is that our nation's institutions, supposedly designed to serve us all, basically exist to provide cover for ugly old men to wank and frot and grope their way down the corridors the power.

Although now, of course, we've moved on. As usual, the prime minister promised a deep and thorough investigation which was announced, I suspect, solely for the purpose of being instantly forgotten. The caravan moves on, or whatever the metaphor is for the cripplingly short attention span of our media, itself a perfect mirror for the nation's collapse into senility.

Politics and the media, we know, are inextricably interwoven; not so much symbiotic as parasites feeding off each other. Their practices, too, are often identical, which is why so many of their personnel are interchangeable (just think of them all: Michael Foot, Bill Deedes, Michael Gove, George Osborne, Boris Johnson, Benito Mussolini, and on it goes). These practices reflect and arise from the nature of the two jobs: institutionally insecure and driven by short-term contingencies and deranged deadlines, fuelled by not enough sleep and too much drink, infantile attention seeking and adolescent neediness, it's unsurprising that both encourage the worst kind of ruthless psychopath to rise to the top. Consequently, you'd be hard pressed to prise apart the sweaty hysteria, the mad mingling of the Führerprinzip and the abiding stench of cynical betrayal that unite the Whips' Offices and a tabloid (and not just tabloid) editorial conference in their common and constant recreation of *The Lord of the Flies*. Unsurprisingly, both environments incubate the worst behaviour to sate our basest instincts.

Which is why the editor of the *Daily Mail* has notoriously defined his quarter century in the job by his highly sexualized bullying. As *Private Eye* keeps reminding us, millionaire anti-elitist Paul Dacre is legendary for his 'double-cunting', when his staff get called thus in the space of a single screaming fit. In any other business he'd be up in front of an industrial tribunal more or less permanently, but hey! This is showbiz! Which is meant to excuse a culture that long ago metastasized through the organization and much, much wider. And it stretches from the very senior *Mail* columnist who, when editing another national (*Sunday*) newspaper and chairing the weekly post-mortem conference reviewing the latest edition, would never address a word to any of his senior female editors until he reached the fashion pages, down to the sheer futile nastiness of the hatchet jobs his hacks write at Dacre's behest on everyone who's defied the *Mail* and its prejudices, from judges to women who've dared to complain about sexualized bullying.

Newspapers, like fish and everything else, rot from the head down. Which conveniently permits them, while their brains turn to goo, to demand with fury that the foulest behaviour is virtuous, while also demanding no one dare call them out for it. As ever, the bully plays on our better nature, like our natural niceness when making allowances for our elderly loved ones getting a little bit racisty with their carers. So when both our politics and our media behave as badly as they can, be it personal sexualized harassment, casual and thoughtless denigration or the deliberate scapegoating of millions of our fellow citizens as a point of policy, it's because they can't help it, poor things. Isn't it?

It's the same with Brexit. It seems we've sunk so low into the twilit world of senile dementia, forgetting everything except dim dreams of Imperial Glory, with another shot of the tried and trusted Monarchist Tranquillizer, that it would be cruel even to point this out. Though, at some point, someone, somewhere, may decide it's a kindness to turn off our life support.

The Guardian, December 2017

Other Writings . . .
1986–2024

Kevin Killane, *Lower than Vermin: An Anatomy of Thatcher's Britain* (London: Arrow Books, 1986)

The Paragon of Animals, Lower than Vermin

An Excerpt from Lower than Vermin:
An Anatomy of Thatcher's Britain

Arrow Books, 1986

Geneva Airport

31 May 1985

My thoughts about arms limitation are interrupted by a call from Airport Information, and at the desk I'm given a telex wiring me more money from Helen.* A brief, curt note informs me she and her children are well, but warns me to keep away from Holland Park for at least a month. She doesn't say why, but I have my suspicions. Then, just when I'm wondering where to go next, I spot my former pupil buying a copy of the *Spectator* at the newsstand and, before I can make good my escape, he buttonholes me and begins again his frightful litany.

'Wealth Creation'? 'Enterprise Culture'? What do these things mean? Thatcher's pixie looks at me with confusion but cannot tell me, but then, I suppose, in his happy faith he has no need for definitions. Just repeat the potent jujus when you wake up, sweating, from nightmares in the middle of the night, or whisper the reassuring mottoes as you walk briskly from one wine bar to the next down Notting Hill's mean streets.

At the moment I can't be bothered to work out for myself what their actual meanings may be, or may be supposed to be. Style, not content, is now the order of the day, so chant the responses and sing 'Rejoice!'

Looking at my former pupil, who just now is arguing with the woman behind the Airport Bar (in, of course, their respective languages: she doesn't understand what Malvern Water is, and he won't understand what is meant by the word Perrier), I realize that I see, personified, all that needs to be said about a certain style in today's Tory Party. There's the head, with the modishly long and tousled hair (à la Lawson ou Scruton), the chin you could plough a field with, the square, steel-framed spectacles. And, inside that head, all that New Right Radical Bullshit. And, below the neck, the

---

This book was written as Dr Kevin Killane, retired visiting professor in international affairs, University of Kabul, zoo owner, author of *The Moon and Napalm: Journeys to Free Saigon* (1976), *The Bestiary: Zoos, Zoo Animals and the Weltschmertz* and *Living Together After Divorce* (with Professor Helen Killane) (1978), etc.

* Helen Killane, formerly married to Kevin Killane, author of *Towards a Methodology of Women*, etc.

stripy shirt and plain, detachable collar, the thin, slightly soiled woollen tie, the old and patched tweed jacket, waistcoat and watch, fop and chain, corduroy trousers, brothel creepers . . . Voila! The Born-again Libertarian Fascist meets the Young Fogey.

Yikes!

In a simpler world, the two groups would be incompatible. The Fogeys are obsessed with the grand old rural England. horse brasses and half-timbering, John Betjeman, cricket on the green, Vicarage tea parties on dappled lawns, tally-ho for the Home Counties, fair play, *Good-bye, Mr Chips* and constant worries about the deteriorating standard of marmalade. The BALFs, on the other hand, are obsessed with 'radical reform', which presumably includes building car parks over the village greens, going for a steak and chips down the Berni Inn and not so much rewriting history (although they are both fond of and good at doing this) as forgetting it altogether in the glorious Long March towards a future of DIY warehouses, share-owning democracies, honest pay for honest labour, proper jobs, sunrise industries and the rest of the empty baggage of that philosophy.

And yet, as my former pupil so ably demonstrates in the way he presents himself to the world, incompatible they are not. While the BALFs may despise the Fogeys for being back-sliding decadents, they also secretly envy them and aspire towards their station which, for several reasons, they can never attain. Likewise, the Fogeys, apeing the sacred, idle rich, are fools for perceived toughness, be it embodied by Thatcher, Bulldog Drummond, Mussolini or, indeed, Stalin. Take this further. The truly Thatcherite BALFs genuinely desire respectability, to mark them apart from the boot-boys whose dicta they share, and want to know how to hold a knife properly, while the Fogeys tend to be at their most comfortable dispensing sherry on the right side of their new chums on muscle beach . . .

And as I watch this Thatcherite Fogey pocket his *Spectator* like a Bible, I think to that happy day when Thatcher will make phrenology respectable again in her Great March Backwards: then, feeling the lumps on that amazing head as the little chap lies naked, stretched out on the slab, we might be able to get behind the outward manifestation, get through the 'style' to see if there is, after all, any content, or whether the whole thing is just a pose, a new synthesis for a new generation of rebellious youth who, rejecting the liberal opinions of their parents, spurn the offered reefer over Sunday lunch, cringe with embarrassment when the Dylan records come out again, and instead choose to dress in their grandfathers' clothes and say out loud that they want to hang the trade union leaders.

And as this depressing thought occurs, my plane is suddenly announced . . .

Is Judge Dredd a Fascist?

2000 AD, 1991

Judge Dredd? is he a fascist? This might seem a redundant question at first sight. Dredd is obviously a fascist. The whole edifice of justice in Mega-City One is built on unaccountability and the dictatorial enforcement of draconian laws. The Judges—in effect, police, judge, jury and executioner—are the personification of the fascist ideals of strong leadership and the law and order. And yet?

Maybe we should approach this from another angle and ask: what is fascism?

If you delve beneath the popular image (jackbooted thug maintaining a hold on political power through undemocratic means, such as extreme violence), the tag fascist begins to look less appropriate when applied to Judge Dredd.

Fascism emerged as a reaction to communism, but stole from the communists the idea of infiltrating every level of society. At the top, the Führerprinzip operated; in other words, there was a strong leader who ruled by dictate, based on personal will. This system had no basis in law. Its main strength was making up the rules as it went along, in order to hold on to power. Laws were created from nowhere, speciously justified and then enforced by the police or by paramilitary forces.

But in Mega-City One, the law is everything. Arbitrary acts by the Judges are themselves judged mercilessly. There is no opportunity for a Führerprinzip, for a Chief Judge to become dictator and act outside the law? lessons were learnt from Judge Cal's reign of terror. Moreover, the Judge system is not inherently political. It does not seek political mind control set towards some political agenda. It seems merely to contain the population within the bounds of the law.

The Judges of Mega-City One are no more undemocratic than the judges operating in the present British legal system, who fortunately don't have the same powers. Moreover, I believe Britain's modern judges are considerably more political than those of Mega-City One.

For a different angle, compare the Judge system with recent fascist police actions around the world. Thailand, Tiananmen Square, Romania—they can all be seen to have a specific political dimension. All were rearguard actions by the police, acting as tools of beleaguered governments threatened by democracy. Even the (apparently legal) concept of 'manageable force', used notoriously and disastrously by the Los Angeles Police, is inspired by an unspoken political (racist) agenda.

So where does that leave Judge Dredd? As a character he was conceived as an extreme satire on the idea of law and order. Fifteen years on, the tactics of the Los Angeles Police Department are like life Imitating art. Dredd may have the trappings of a fascist viewed through the layers of irony in the comic strip, but he is clearly no Torquemada of Termite. Dredd is the law, and all are equal before the law, especially the Judges themselves.

Before you start thinking Judge Dredd is advocating a benevolent but brutal kind of fascism, maybe we should look at the recent story about a referendum on whether the Judges should stay in power ('The Devil You Know' [progs 750–53] and 'Twilight's Last Gleaming' [progs 754–56]). Maybe we should see it as a dark satire on the failures of democracy, not as an ironic celebration of the triumphs of fascism. Although the greatest failing of democracy is that your side often loses, the greatest enemy of democracy is not fascism, but apathy.

In the referendum, the Judges won with 68 per cent of all votes cast. But there was a turnout of only 35 per cent. In other words, the Judges won with the backing of only 23.8 per cent of the electorate. And that is just 2 per cent less than the percentage of the American population which first elected Ronald Reagan in 1980.

The Album

An Excerpt from *My Generation*, Edited by Antony Farrell

Lilliput Press, 1996

In retrospect, I now realize that my adolescence coincided with the High Summer of The Album. That this was also the deep, hard, barren midwinter of Music was, perhaps, more than coincidental. Still, all too soon it was gone; ultimately fucked by the bright, airy spring of the New Technology and the advent of the CD; more immediately stuffed by Punk.

It was punk, after all, which awoke us all to the truth that music was only actually valid when it came in singles, preferably in a two-minute, twenty-second thrash. In earlier, more innocent times, we had, of course, abjured singles as terminally unhip. They were the crassly commercial province of bubble gum, teenyboppers and other vilenesses no cool middle-class kid worth his (and this was gender specific) salt would ever deign to contemplate. As a result, for most of the mid-seventies my friends and I wasted our lives transcribing pages and pages of lyrics from inner sleeves onto our Economics A-level folders, later in the day slouching around in each other's bedrooms in glum concentration listening (without ever saying a word, mind) to *Led Zep IV*.

And, of course, it wasn't just about the music. As an artefact, the album defined (and was defined by) its age as exactly as any muddy old pot shard encapsulated the Etruscans. For a start, you could do so many things with it. During longueurs in yet another bloody John Bonham drum solo, you could scrutinize the Hipgnosis sleeve artwork; then you could read, try to understand and then memorize the lyrics. Then you could fold it out so that it became enormous. Moreover, you could roll joints on it, which was perhaps the greatest contribution of the album to the ur-culture it defined. After all, you wouldn't eat your dinner off it, fill in your pools coupon or write a short shopping-list on it (although you could write a poem on it, cribbing from the inner sleeve, or do your English homework on it, maybe simultaneously). But it was quite clear there was nothing else at all worth skinning up on. (The strange supplementary role of the cassette case for storage deserves deeper examination elsewhere.) It even supplied a vast reservoir of cardboard after you'd torn all those handy little bits out of the insides of the fag packet. A significant imaginary scene springs to mind here: thin hairy git shuffles into general retail outlet, circa 1975. Coughs nervously, then mumbles, 'Er, yeah, could I have, right, twenty Benson and Hedges, um, a packet of green Rizlas and, ah . . . (gabbled rapidly in nascent beard) that

"Fleetwood Mac" album, yeah!' before fleeing as assembled shopkeepers and customers chorus, 'We know what you're Dooo-ing!' What, on the other hand, can you do with a CD box? Snort cocaine off it, I suppose, but that's about it, And cocaine is not, of course, a drug conducive to musical appreciation of the lilting cadences of *Focus 3* or, for that matter, a higher appreciation of the guiding aesthetic of Roger Dean, which, shrunk down to four square inches, tends to look just plain daft anyway.

And there was more. The cardboard sleeves used to scuff, particularly on Dylan albums, in a particularly satisfying pre-Grunge, grungy sort of way. On older albums, the pretensions of the cover artwork would give way. On the inner or 'dust' sleeve (and what role, in the brave new CD Age, does dust fill in the aural dialectic of sound reproduction, synthesizing clarity into reassuring scrunge?), to an echo of Recorded Music's Tin Pan Alley origins, with adverts for the record label's backlist. Thus Mate Munroe, Roger Whittaker, Harry Secombe and Mrs Mills would all grin cheesily at you while you, simply by listening to Donovan, were complicit in sweeping away that old, unmourned world. Later, with *Wish You Were Here*, there was the delightful dilemma of how you removed the black, shiny, shrink-wrapped plastic outer cover with the nice sticker on it: did you rip it off in a frenzy, or carefully razor open one side, slip it off like a condom and then stick it on your bedroom wall? (I did the former, and immediately regretted it.) Then there were the accessories. In a one-stereo household, if you wanted to listen to Bee-Bop Deluxe's *Drastic Plastic* while your parents were watching *The Onedin Line*, you had to listen to it on headphones. These weren't the discreet little Sony deaf-aids (stereos weren't 'personal' then), but chunky old monsters that wouldn't have looked out of place on a Lancaster Bomber's radio operator somewhere over Dresden. Then, of course, you had to worry about the care of your record. You could, to this end, buy a nice maroon spongy thing from Boots, or a kind of bright yellow duster—although an old hanky usually worked just as well. Later, my flashier friends with richer and more indulgent parents and a developing anal obsession with the impedimenta of sound reproduction would have little brushes or statically charged rollers that were dragged over the record as it went round, strobing nicely with the little orange light from the turntable which told you it was rotating at the right speed. Then there was your stylus, bur by the time any of us got to caring about that it was usually too late. But the scratches were merely another part of the pleasure. To this day there are two tracks on *Space Oddity* that I have never heard properly all the way through. And then there was the smell . . .

But I'm in danger here of overlooking the actual music. Which I suppose was what it was meant to be about. As I suggested above, the light of experience has taught us that the majority of the music brought into our homes and our lives through the agency of the album was crap. Our excuse, of course, was that we knew no better.

Perhaps, even now, eager little postmodernists are planning the rehabilitation of Emerson, Lake and Palmer; kids in the suburbs are ingesting substances unknown to previous generations and grooving to *Tales from Topographical Oceans*, while an encyclopaedic knowledge of the Supertramp discography is de rigueur in gaining access to the smarter dives in Berlin and Barcelona.

However, while we breathlessly await the Bread revival, it's worth remembering how liberating Punk was for us munchkins back then. I remember, for instance, slouching round my friend Tony Walker's bedroom and being forced to listen to the soundtrack of that monumental turkey of a concert movie, Led Zeppelin's *The Song Remains the Same*. I gritted my teeth in rage and frustration as Jimmy Page played on and on and on for what seemed like (and probably was) hours. Tony, inevitably, had the orange turntable light and the little brush, but by this time I was beginning to fall out of love with the whole thing. Shortly thereafter I cut my hair, threw out my flares and went to a Jam gig. Then Elvis died, we all guffawed callously, and by the time I went to university about a year later, when a new chum sheepishly admitted that he thought the greatest song ever written was 'Stairway to Heaven', we all laughed him to scorn. Br then I was far more in sympathy with my college's resident Organ Scholar, who earnestly insisted that the highest achievements in the history of music were 'God Save the Queen' by the Sex Pistols and Beethoven's *Emperor Concerto*.

Still, that pile of old albums stacked horizontally under the hi-fi (the what?) must once have held some significance for me, before I stopped listening to them about 12 years ago. Whether or not they were a soundtrack to my adolescence is now questionable. I remember being driven mad curing my maths O level by Pilot's 'January' going through my mind over and over again, and that was a record neither I nor any of my friends would ever admit even to exist. So what were the criteria that informed our aesthetic? Mostly, I suppose, it was your standard laddish game of one-upmanship, intensified by the struggle, fey and gloomy though it was, to attain the required status of neurotic boy outsider.

[. . .] But despite the undoubted pleasures of getting stoned out of your box and reciting great passages of Marlon Brando's monologue in the role of Colonel Kurtz while listening to 'The End' at full volume, my relationship with the album was drawing ever so slowly to its end. I certainly never bought records as a student, mostly through meanness. I remember borrowing Patti Smith's *Horses* and Springsteen's *Born to Run* and *Darkness on the Edge of Town* (both of which I thought hilariously funny) on a pretty permanent basis, and would listen to them, secretively, late at night through the monstrous old headphones. The one exception, the last album I ever bought, was ABC's *Lexicon of Love*, a wonderfully schmaltzy concoction of post-punk torch songs; though, coming in 1980, and despite its vinyl mien, I doubt it was really, truly an album at all. Coming when it did, it was almost certainly an LP, a completely different thing altogether. Soon, other things intruded, like love. My wife-to-be was gloriously and liberatingly out of touch with contemporary notions of rock-cool, so we settled down to listening to Mozart, Ella Fitzgerald and early Motown, while the first song we ever danced to was a wonderful piece of camp trash called 'It's Raining Men' by the Weather Girls. You might double-take here, and insist that the whole point of rock 'n' roll was sex, that I should here be listing all those rockin' tracks I fucked my youth away to. Well, for me it was about credibility, peer-group pressure and the constant need to stay a couple of yards ahead of the pack. So now all my old albums gather dust, rendering them, no doubt, even more distorted than I remember them being all those years ago when I last listened to them.

Nor do I necessarily mourn these neglected trappings of late childhood. Indeed, when I learn that contemporaries of mine have just bought the new Portishead CD, or evince a keenness for Nirvana or Blur or Suede, to the extent of actually bothering to buy their products, I feel slightly embarrassed on their behalf. People in their mid-thirties and beyond have no business dabbling their horny toes in this kids' stuff, I convince myself, conveniently forgetting that now it's no longer about 'Yoof' or rebellion or generational ghettoizing: now it's about product placement. What were previously the provinces of subcultures are now part of a great big postmodern super-market, where the trade is in nostalgia and endless youthfulness in equal measure, and rather than dying before we get old, we bop, literally, till we drop.

Afterword to The Waste Land

Picador, 1999; Seagull Books, 2012

'"In the room the women come and go / Talking of Michelangelo." Does that suggest anything to you, sir?'

'Yeah—it suggests to me that the guy didn't know very much about women.'

'My sentiments exactly, sir. Nonetheless I admire T. S. Eliot very much.'

'Did you say "nonetheless"?'

This exchange between the hard-boiled private eye, Philip Marlowe, and the leading dame's Black chauffeur in Raymond Chandler's *The Long Goodbye* was part of the inspiration for this comic-book (although I prefer the term 'graphic poem') retelling of *The Waste Land* by T. S. Eliot as a kind of Chandleresque film-noir whodunnit. Although I think I succeeded in producing the first and only precisely postmodernist comic book of our times, in the process, I nearly went mad and became far more intimately acquainted with the ways of English copyright law and the vicissitudes of publishing than I had ever expected or wished.

The rather unexpected connection between Chandler and Eliot (they were born in the same year) finally set me in the right direction on a vague project I was working on in the late 80s to satirize *The Waste Land* and have a kick at this gnarled old totem pole which has blighted so much twentieth-century poetry struggling to grow in its shadow. I wasn't getting very far with my original idea for a *Waste Land* colouring book ('Colour this rock red. Colour Mr Eliot's mood black'), when I made the detective-story connection. After all, the way the bloody thing's taught owes more to forensics than to any kind of aesthetic response—identify the quotations, seek out the allusions and, if you're lucky, you might get a motive. Then there are the lowlifes, typists, fortune-tellers, Smyrna merchants and drag queens engaging in sterile sex and meaningless conversations amid parched deserts, stinking rivers and squalid bars, not to mention the backstreet abortionists and the corpse buried in the garden. Moreover, the poem involves a quest, a search for the Holy Grail, a stab at redemption in a fallen world by a man—in this case, Parsifal—who is not fallen. It's a small leap from the Holy Grail to *The Maltese Falcon*, from Parsifal to Philip Marlowe . . .

And I had a wonderful image that perfectly synthesized the film noir, hard-boiled oeuvre of Raymond Chandler and the impenetrable moaning of moody old Tom Eliot. There's a scene in Howard Hawks' film of Chandler's *The Big Sleep* where the cops dredge a Packard out of the ocean, with Marlowe's clients' dead chauffeur still at the wheel. In many ways, this scene is the acme of Chandlerism, with recent rain, the night, cars, cops, a corpse and Marlowe thigh high in trouble. And its meaning is almost completely opaque. During filming, Humphrey Bogart, playing Marlowe, asked Hawks the significance of the stiffed chauffeur in the car. Hawks didn't know, so he asked the scriptwriters. They didn't know either, so they phoned Chandler who said he'd forgotten. Which is perfect. Making sense doesn't matter: narrative is subsumed in a sense of style and we all gladly go along for the ride not caring less. Exactly the same can be said of *The Waste Land*. Anyway, I took this scene and melded it with the opening line of Section IV of Eliot's poem, 'Death by Water'—'Phlebus the Phoenician, a fortnight dead . . .'—which I rendered into hard-boiled argot in the caption to the scene: 'It was Phlebus the Phoenician . . . He'd been dead a fortnight . . .'

The caption, however, had to be changed. Before approaching Penguin, the book's original publisher, my then agent had sent the proposal to Faber & Faber, Eliot's old company. They had rather sniffily rejected it on the ground that 'Valerie wouldn't like it.' Valerie is Mrs Eliot, old Tom's widow, still going strong and still fiercely defending the sacred flame. In time, as we'd expected, Penguin received a letter from solicitors representing the Eliot estate, observing that Penguin proposed to publish 'what would appear to be some form of comic-book version of our client's copyrighted work'.

Rather naively, I'd worked on in the belief that, although I couldn't expect to quote any of Eliot's own words without permission (which I knew wouldn't be forthcoming: I'm not Andrew Lloyd Webber, after all), I would, at least, be able to quote the quotations quoted by Eliot. As old Tom had plundered the literature of Europe, Asia and three millennia to produce a poem which is almost the sine qua non of the cut-up technique, both in effect and comprehensibility, it seemed only fair that I should be able to do likewise. I hadn't, however, taken account of compilation copyright. It got worse. We sent a photocopied manuscript of the 60 pages of artwork to the solicitors who, ignorant of poetical things, sent it to Faber. I was told (even though I shouldn't have been) that Valerie came in one day with Seamus Heaney who, seeing the manuscript in an in-tray, picked it up, read it, then returned it, saying to Valerie as he did so, 'It's a hoot, Val!' Her response went unreported. The manuscript was returned with all perceived infringements of the Eliot estate's copyright marked in pink highlighter pen. Apparently, their copyright extended to cover the word 'Michelangelo', the sound effect 'Throb Throb Throb' as produced by a taxi and the images of Ezra Pound and Wyndham Lewis.

For our part, we did our best to appease them. For instance, in the poem, the secretary, following her liaison with the young man carbuncular, 'smoothes her hair with automatic hand, / And puts a record on the gramophone'. The record I had her play was a pastiche of Cole Porter's 'Let's Do It'. To sweeten the Eliot estate, I had to remove the second line of the verse 'Leicester and Good Queen Bess did it / Tom and Vivienne I guess did it / Let's Do It, Let's Fall in Love!' Meanwhile, letters continued to pass between Penguin's solicitors, Mishcon de Reya, and the Eliot estate. 'We should like to point out that your statement that at page 41 the picture featured is Margate

The Waste Land (New York: Harper & Row, 1990). Subsequently published by Seagull Books in 2012.

Sands is not correct, the picture is in fact of Pegwell Bay.' We even tried a grovelling letter on behalf of Penguin and me to Valerie from Anthony Julius, Mishcon de Reya's in-house Eliot expert, later solicitor to the late Princess of Wales. (Valerie might have had reason to doubt our sincerity, as Julius subsequently wrote an excellent and satisfying book detailing the extent of Eliot's anti-Semitism.) In the end, I changed every single line and every name quoted from the original poem. To satisfy my wounded artistic soul, there was also an American edition which was published untouched by lawyers' hands, thanks to the entirely admirable 'parody defence' embodied in American law.

Some of the changes lent the book a satisfyingly surreal edge. I had originally illustrated Eliot's line 'Jug jug jug jug jug jug' by having my hero (called Chris Marlowe, obviously) walk past six jugs labelled 'jug' on the run from the bad guys in the British Museum. At the insistence of the lawyers, the labels were changed to 'Ampora', 'vessel', 'gugglet', 'pitcher', 'ewer' and 'crock'. Likewise, where Eliot quoted the classics, I was obliged, with help, to make up passages from entirely fictitious Latin writers, although I'm not going to say where I did this, as this was part of the fun. Still, scarred but unbowed, the book was finally published, unheralded by writs or injunctions, in November 1990.

There were some nice reviews. My favourite compared it to a 'literary *Where's Wally?*' and mentioned (without listing) six different references or allusions to painting, poetry, film and opera in a single frame. I was aware of only four. Then there were the two PhD theses written about my *Waste Land*, one of them, unintelligibly for me, in Italian. This seemed entirely appropriate. So did the 1994 opera version, only the third adaptation, after *Krazy Kat* and Maurice Sendak's *Where the Wild Things Are*, of comic or cartoon into this arcane medium. As composer Stephen McNeff observed, if you're going to turn something as obscure as *The Waste Land* into a comic book, the only possible next step is to turn it into an opera. It was performed to critical acclaim at the Donmar Warehouse, even though no copies of the book could be sold in the foyer as they'd all long since been pulped.

But although it may have been absent from the bookshops for years, my little detective story, in many ways more allusive, elusive and mysterious than either of its parents, has maintained a vigorous half-life all its own. I'm frequently asked for copies by lecturers whose own copies have crumbled beyond photocopiability, as a teaching aid to this monstrous shibboleth of modernism. Personally, I'm still of the opinion that Eliot's *Waste Land* is obscurantist, mawkish, constipatedly pious, elitist, inconsistent, miserable overrated nonsense which wouldn't look out of place on the inner sleeve of one of Led Zeppelin's later albums. In light of this, whereas old Tom might have concluded this article with a shower of quotes and some low moaning from the Upanishads, I'll content myself simply by saying, 'Buy it.'

We Are the True Outsiders of Journalism

British Journalism Review, March 2001

I've got a treasured possession at home. It hangs, as these things should, outside the lavatory, and it's an original cartoon by Vicky, the nom de plume of the Hungarian political cartoonist Victor Weisz. It's not his greatest work: just a rather nice caricature of the holiday-camp tsar Sir Billy Butlin drawn for the *New Statesman* about a month and a half after I was born, and it was given to me as a 40th birthday present a couple of years ago. What's really interesting about it, however, is its provenance.

This cartoon by one of the twentieth century's greatest exponents of the art arrived outside my upstairs khazi via a skip outside the Staggers' old offices in Shoreditch. From there it was rescued, along with about 40 other Vicky originals, by a couple of former *Statesman* hacks who were doing a bit of opportunistic totting as the magazine prepared its move, under its new proprietor Geoffrey Robinson, to offices in Victoria. So what conclusions can we draw from the presence of this treasure trove chucked out with the trash?

First, the new dispensation at the *Statesman*, whether Blairite or Brownite, was obviously working to a 'year zero' agenda, where everything from the past, in the absence of an airbrush, is just rubbish. Even so, this scorched-earth attitude to the magazine's heritage seems a little profligate. A Vicky original was recently sold through Chris Beetles' cartoon gallery for £500, so potentially they'd chucked out 20,000 quid's worth of material, although Robinson's largesse may allow for that kind of pot-latch extravagance, alongside the proprietor lighting Havana cigars with £50 notes and the staff wiping their arses on gold leaf.

Second, sentiment comes at a premium these days. Vicky was a sensitive man and a gregarious cartoonist. Unlike most of the profession today—or even his great contemporary David Low—who prefer to scribble away at home and depend on the reliability of despatch riders or the post or, latterly, faxes and e-mail, Vicky seemed to get a genuine buzz out of the charged atmosphere of newspaper or magazine offices. Moreover, after he left—or was eased out—of the *News Chronicle*, the *New Statesman* became not only his bolt hole but also, in a way, his second home. If a magazine takes its ghosts with it as it moves from office to office, as I'm certain it must, I wouldn't fancy being alone in the *Statesman* office after midnight as Vicky's unquiet spirit views with ethereal dismay the latest article about the Third Way or ponders on the utterly cavalier attitude of his former home's latest legatees (although Cristina Odone's presence might prove helpful in getting hold of an exorcist).

Third, it's worth pointing out that this act of desecration took place under the editorship of a man who is now a professor of journalism in Cardiff, but who presumably didn't consider the political cartoon as anything more than a peripheral embellishment of the real meat of journalism—the words.

Of course, Ian Hargreaves isn't alone among editors in this belief, just rather more brutal in applying it. Cartoons are a long-established feature of the topography of newspaper design, and recognized as such, but this is no reason to assume that editors really understand what a cartoon is, how it works or why. This manifests itself in different ways. For instance, when the *Independent* was launched, Andreas Whittam Smith understood the vital importance of absconding from the *Daily Telegraph* with its cartoonist Nicholas Garland, particularly as the *Independent* was artfully designed to look like a paper that had been around for a hundred years. The purpose seemed to be for people browsing in the newsagents to come to the familiar Garland cartoon—inevitably some strained metaphor based around an image nicked from *Alice in Wonderland* or *Winnie the Pooh*—glance at it, turn back to the front page and make a mental note that the *Telegraph* had changed its name to the *Independent*. This was a canny piece of layout and marketing, but little more.

Less benignly, when I worked briefly as editorial cartoonist on *Today*, every rough for a cartoon I presented to him was rejected by David Montgomery as a matter of course, to keep me in my place with the rest of the hacks. It was clear that the maintenance of editorial terror was always more important that the contents of any cartoon, although the importance of having a cartoon in the first place was understood if unstated. I assume this was because it was in the Murdoch manual Montgomery must have been cribbing from every 20 minutes or so How to Be an Editor. (Around 4.30, when I'd have to start drawing the next day's cartoon or miss the first edition, I'd show Monty the first rough I'd done that morning, receive the editorial grunt of approval and proceed).

Far worse treatment at the hands of an editor befell George Gale, who was the political cartoonist for the *Telegraph* during Garland's brief tenure at the *Independent*. I was told by people then working on the back bench at the *Telegraph* that Gale's position rapidly became impossible, as Max Hastings interfered with the daily cartoon to a ridiculous degree. If Gale's period at the *Telegraph* is remembered for anything, it's probably for *Private Eye*'s merciless ridiculing of his cartoons, concentrating mainly on the fact that his caricatures were unrecognizable. I think they fingered the wrong man: every day Hastings was telling Gale to draw people's noses longer or heads bigger, reducing him to little more than a ventriloquist's dummy propped on the knee of editorial megalomania.

What these cases reveal is not just the incipient tyranny, arrogance and ignorance of editors (Pope Catholic Shocker! Bears Shit in Woods Outrage!) but a systemic failure within newspapers to appreciate that cartoons are serious journalism. Partly this is due to their bizarre basis in both non-verbal communication and humour. This makes them doubly suspicious to wordsmiths marinading in their own gravitas. Despite a three-hundred-year-long tradition—from Hogarth onwards—of using funny pictures to make deadly serious moral, political and social points, cartoons—and, naturally, cartoonists—aren't taken too seriously. In addition, they're often seen as semi-detached from the proper business of journalism because of their existence in such a different, unquantifiable, almost irrational medium.

In a strange way cartoonists are journalistic chimeras: how they think, what they express and its effect on the readers makes them much more like columnists than illustrators, and, personally, I see myself as a visual journalist rather than as any kind of 'artist'. The words monkeys, however, maintain their suspicions: illustrators they can handle (because the writer does the proper, analytical, grown-up thinking, while the illustrator does the weird visual voodoo stuff). Cartoonists, however, do their ana-lytical thinking for themselves and consequently form their own opinions, but in a strangely transgressive way, as if it isn't quite decent to flaunt the lines of demarcation in such a flagrant way. Thus, there is an obvious, qualitative difference in the deference shown to the bigboy political columnists and the cartoonists who squat on top of their columns. Despite the fact that Peter Brookes and Steve Bell are more perceptive, accurate, engaging and succinct analysts of contemporary events than Lord Rees-Mogg, Hugo Young or any of the rest of them, one feels one can only mention it in a whisper, and if they ever get invited to dinner with the great panjandrums of punditry, they'll have to content themselves with scrambled eggs in the servants' hall to maintain their position as uppity artisans.

All this, of course, can and probably should be dismissed as the special pleading of a bunch of irredeemable yearning for their knighthoods. But while the ambiguous status enjoyed (or not) by cartoonists may trample on their moody artistic egos, I think it also contributes to their enduring strength. Their semi-detached position within the hierarchy of newspapers is matched by their detachment from the petty concerns that dictate much of what goes into those newspapers, or at least should do. Many cartoonists are quite literally outsiders. For instance, New Zealand and Australia have produced an entirely disproportionate number of world-class cartoonists, including David Low and Pat Oliphant (naturally, their best work was done after they'd left the place). You need to come from the fringes—which can be cultural or political or even just temperamental as well as geographical—in order to cast sufficiently jaundiced an eye on the absurdities afoot in the heart of the beast.

An original Vicky artwork presented to the author by Michael Foot during a private dinner in 2005.

Vicky, too, was an outsider, a Hungarian Jew from Berlin who ended up in England after fleeing from the Nazis. He was fortunate in coming under the tutelage of Gerald Barry, then editor of the *News Chronicle*, who recognized Vicky's innate advantages and nurtured his protege by sending him on a crash course in English culture before unleashing him on the readership on a daily basis. (Apparently, Vicky was receptive to all aspects of English life except cricket.) Despite this, Vicky remained an exotic figure in Fleet Street, much as Low did (after 30 years in London, Low was heard complaining, 'These bloody Englishmen! They all went to school with each other!'), but this added to their effectiveness.

Although I've said that political cartoons should be equated with the columns they shoulder aside, in one essential respect they are different. Most obviously, they are an oasis of visual anarchy in the neat rows of print; beyond that, the cartoonist presents his or her case in a visceral and immediate way, 'read' and sublimated in ways different from the surrounding text. Given that head start as exponents of dissidence in design, it follows that cartoonists frequently speak with a dissident voice. Famously, Vicky and Low had their dissidence formalized in their contracts with Lord Beaverbrook on the *Evening Standard*, by which they were given almost total licence to peddle points of view entirely at odds with those not just of the paper's editorial line but also of the readers. One *Standard* editorial, right next to Vicky's cartoon, was headlined 'No, Vicky, No', and he played on his readers' hostility by titling a compilation of *Standard* cartoons 'Vicky Must Go!'

While satire is often described as a kind of corrective surgery, cartooning is corrective surgery carried out with a cudgel, and the response provoked can be as brutal as the image. A Vicky cartoon attacking the death penalty provoked a doctor in Harrow to write, 'When I see a cartoon such as Vicky put in on 11 November, I feel sorry Hitler did not get hold of him before he reached this country.' Going one better, Low was actually on the Gestapo's Death List.

But Oppositionism is intrinsic to the cartoonist's art: a positive cartoon often looks like—often actually is—just propaganda, just like a joke that isn't based in bodily functions or the misfortunes of others just isn't funny. That said, it's inconceivable that any cartoonist today would enjoy the privileged position enjoyed by Low and Vicky. On the *Guardian*, Steve Bell and I enjoy almost complete editorial freedom, although the comment editor tends to come down heavily when the turd quota gets too high and the word 'fuck' is now strictly forbidden (Bell recently told me that a letter he received from David Leigh on this subject concluded with the PS: 'The same applies to "cunt" '). It's also true that Steve and I are well to the left of the *Guardian*'s editorial line, although that's probably also true of the paper's readers. However, I cannot imagine either of us working for the *Telegraph* or the *Mail*, any more than the

Guardian would have been likely to hire Michael Cummings or JAK, the two most prominent right-wing cartoonists of recent years. Low and Vicky prospered under the patronage of Beaverbrook's maverick sense of mischief, along with Michael Foot and A. J. P. Taylor. These days, it seems, newspapers are insufficiently self-confident to be able to monkey around with their self-appointed role of pandering to their readers' political prejudices. And maybe they shouldn't: if you want a different point of view, simply buy another paper. Anyway, a cartoonist's chief target shouldn't be his or her readers' sensibilities, but the fools and knaves in charge.

But if cartoonists are visual columnists exposing those knaves and fools, then by definition they're also opinion makers. It helps, then, if they have an opinion in the first place. While it's often assumed that the more vicious the cartoon, the more nihilistic the cartoonist, if we wield cudgels, nonetheless we're still engaged in corrective surgery: the world and everything in it is wrong, and we want to help put it right by revealing its faults. This was certainly Vicky's attitude, and he certainly was no nihilist. Indeed, towards the end of his life, he was attacked in *Queen*, fizzing away in the white heat of the 60s satire revolution, for being insufficiently nihilistic by hero-worshipping figures like Albert Schweitzer and Bertrand Russell. But if you attack everyone and everything, assuming all politicians and public figures to be knaves and fools, you end up like Ralph Steadman, one of the iconic cartoonists of the 60s, who nowadays will only draw politicians' legs because anything else will compromise him into flattering the enemy. One wonders if Ralph bothers voting any more, and, if he's disenfranchised himself from his rights as a citizen, whether it's worth listening to anything he has to say. Or, indeed, whether he had anything to say in the first place.

Vicky cared, probably too much. He vilified generations of politicians, most famously Harold Macmillan, and, as we've seen, was vilified in return. It's likely he left the *News Chronicle* after pressure was put on the editor by the right-wing trade-union leader Arthur Deakin to get Vicky to tone down his cartoons. Like a lot of us on the left, he maintained a love–hate relationship with the Labour Party. When he killed himself in 1966, seven days after my seventh birthday, his grieving friends—many of them still grieving—put his suicide down as much to his despair over the course the Labour Party was then taking—supporting the US bombing Vietnam, failing to bomb Ian Smith's Rhodesia—as to any deeper, more personal malaise. By that point, Vicky no longer commented on or illustrated the news. He was the news, his death reported on radio and television and in the international media. But he'd been news before, his arrival at the *Mirror* and the *Evening Standard* heralded in front page banner headlines. In the history of print journalism, Vicky, precisely because he was a semi-detached outsider, was a giant. Someone should tell Ian Hargreaves, if anyone thought he could care less.

Adoption
The Guardian, August 2001

A few weeks ago, I met my brother for a drink. He was early, and by the time I arrived he was already getting drunk. I was annoyed at first, but decided to stick with it. This was, after all, the first time we'd ever met.

He had travelled to London specially to see me, after his aircraft carrier, the USS *Enterprise*, had anchored off Portsmouth that morning. A year earlier I had not even known of his existence. His name, like mine, is Martin and, in a strange way, I felt that I'd met him before.

In 1997, after years of doing nothing about the fact that I was adopted, I finally applied to see my original birth certificate. I discovered that my mother's name was Kathleen Ann Gould, and that she had named me Martin. Martin Gould. I came away from that meeting with the social worker who gave me my birth certificate feeling very strange, conscious of an almost physical presence beside me in the car. That was Martin Gould—the other Martin, my spectral doppelganger, another me with an entirely alternative 38 years of life behind him. His presence dogged me for another day and then began to fade.

My brother Martin tells me that that was him. He is two-and-a-half years younger than me, and now bears his father's surname, but on his original birth certificate he was Martin Gould too, and believed he was the only Martin Gould until very recently.

Apart, however, from a few persistent gobbets of self-generated ectoplasm, for another three years I knew nothing about Martin Gould aside from his (and my) mother's name and that he (and I) had been adopted through the Church of England Adoption Society. In 1997, I had made a few attempts to find out about Kathleen or the Church of England Adoption Society, but in both cases I drew a blank. So, with some regret, I let things lie. Then, early last year, I contacted the Children's Society, which told me that the Church of England Adoption Society had change its name too, to ChildLink. I called them, but was told that their offices were being rebuilt and they couldn't tell me anything until May.

In the meantime, I had become more acquainted with death than with the circumstances of my birth. In October 1998, a very good friend died suddenly of a heart attack. Then my much-loved father-in-law died on Christmas Day 1999. And in May 2000, Jon, who had been my best friend when we were 17, died of a brain tumour. I spoke at all three funerals and was increasingly conscious that this accumulation of grief was driving me mad.

I was becoming obsessed with death. My adoptive mother had died of a brain disease when I was 10; now Jon had left behind a little boy the same age that I had been. One's friends, it is said, are the family you choose. The resonances of my friends' deaths left me no room to entertain thoughts of my birth mother . . . until, finally, I received a letter from ChildLink, asking me to contact them as a matter of urgency.

So, on a suffocatingly hot day last June, I found myself at their office. The meeting started uneasily. My case worker seemed rather over-excited. I found this rather irksome as one of the first things she told me was that my mother Kathleen was dead.

I felt my lower lip tremble slightly, and I had to remind myself that I should be getting used to this kind of thing by now. Then she handed me a sheaf of yellowing documents concerning my adoption, including a series of reports to the Board of Moral Trustees at the Church of England Adoption Society and several letters to and from my mother.

It had always been a piece of gossip in my adoptive family (I always knew that I had been adopted) that I had two older siblings, but that my natural grandparents had not been prepared to rear a third bastard. Likewise, I had always been told that my mother was an electrical engineer with the Post Office—in fact, she was a technical assistant with the Central Electricity Generating Board—and that my father was a Canadian architect. Reading those 41-year-old records, I learned that I really did have an older brother and sister, named Andrew and Alison. I discovered, too, that my father was named Edward Burden. He had indeed been a Canadian architecture student; and he had not been prepared to marry my mother.

One of the forms told me that neither of my parents harboured any 'Jewish, Negro or Irish blood' (this was written in 1959). Another report said that Kathleen loved me and was very upset about having to give me up. The report went on: 'Kathleen promises me that this kind of thing will never happen again, but she does admit that she finds it very hard to remain celibate.' My case worker asked me how I felt. I replied, honestly, that my overwhelming emotion was sadness, for myself but also for Kathleen. I said that I doubted I'd make any effort to contact my older brother and sister. And that, I supposed, was that.

There was, however, more. I was told that my younger sister, Jan, of whom I was quite unaware until that moment, had left a letter on my file. She'd also been adopted and had started searching a couple of years previously.

New Humanist, April 2018

This was the reason for the social worker's excitement: never before in her experience had siblings, adopted by different families, found each other in this manner. And there was more still. After Jan's adoption, Kathleen had become pregnant a fifth time. (This child was the other Martin.) This time, however, the father, an American serviceman, had married her and taken her back to California. There, they had had another six sons.

Suddenly, I had *ten* brothers and sisters. This time, when the social worker asked me how I felt, I replied that for the first time in months I felt wonderful. After so many painful goodbyes, from my adoptive mother's death onwards, I found myself looking forward to an almost embarrassing number of unexpected hellos. It is a cliche that adopted people don't quite feel complete, but cliches are cliches because they're mostly true: Now, I felt strangely complete.

Two weeks later, I spoke to Jan. After she had placed her letter on my file, she and her husband had been posted by the RAF to Cyprus. ChildLink suggested that I should write first, but they also gave me her number in Cyprus. After staring at it for five minutes, I finally thought, 'Fuck it: life's too short,' and rang her.

'You've taken your bloody time!' Her response immediately confirmed she was my sister. We spoke for five hours as she told me about herself, her life, all the things she'd discovered in her searches and the contacts she'd made with our lost family. Because she had been privately adopted, she had had no access to any of the information I received by legal right. It was only because she had done so much hard work in recent years that I was able to know so much so quickly.

We've since met and—rapidly dispatching as irrelevant the fact that she is a Christian Tory and I am not—got on very well. We have a similar sense of humour (as does Martin) and, disconcertingly, similar gestures and patterns of speech. And she looks just like my daughter Rose.

Shortly after receiving my birth certificate, but before I discovered anything else, I was at a cartoon festival in Ireland. It was late at night and I found myself being attacked by a young Irishwoman for perpetuating English oppression of the Irish by daring to draw cartoons for an Irish paper. I listened for about half an hour before saying, simply, 'My birth mother's name was Kathleen Gould.'

'Oh, well,' replied the young woman, 'that's all right, then. You're Irish!' Except that, according to those worthy eugenicists at the adoption society, I'm not.

But if my name does not define my identity, what does? By the lights of those same, perfectly well-intentioned people who, pursuing a policy of moral and social engineering, coerced generations of unmarried women into giving up their babies, I am a success. (A generation before I was born, unmarried mothers were still being locked away in mental hospitals, because their moral delinquency defined them as mad.) In this view, I have been redeemed from the original sin of illegitimacy by being brought up and loved by a respectable middle-class family who chose me and invested in me, and whom I will always repay with love and gratitude.

But I don't speak with the same accent as any member of my family I've met, acquired or genetic. Nor do I have the same politics (which also runs contrary to my upbringing). None of them, so far as I know, draws like me or thinks in the lateral ways that a political cartoonist must.

Then again, I know practically nothing about my father. But if I did, would it make any difference? I was never looking for an alternative happy family. I have all I need from the family that chose me and the family that I, later on, chose and love. What I wanted was information—some way to account for that niggling and persistent sense of a lack of completion.

This is the undercurrent that made me burst into tears when reading my children the end of *Tom's Midnight Garden*. When the child hero finally meets the old lady he had played with, as a ghost from the future, when she was a little girl, I think with sadness of Kathleen, giving me up to those well-intentioned and legally sanctioned child abductors. I wonder whether all her subsequent children were not in some way compensating for that loss (first with the second Martin, and then with the last four sons who, says Martin, were each an attempt to get a daughter).

But was Kathleen herself sad? After all, she ended up in California, where, famously, people go to reinvent themselves. If she had been alive when Jan and I re-emerged, would she have welcomed us? Or would she have been horrified at this intrusion into her remade life?

We will never know, and I can only speculate. No one can change the past, and what I've discovered so far is never going to alter retrospectively the previous course of my life. Those other Martins—the one who stayed with his mother (obviating the need for another Martin); and the one who lived in California becoming someone entirely different—these are merely the ghosts of what might have been.

If I have undergone a catharsis in the past year, it is because of the information. Just knowing is a tool that helps me make more sense, however little, of why I'm the me I am. In the meantime, there are no post-dated happy endings. The legacy of adoption affects everyone differently; often there is the intensified sadness of failed reunions and compounded rejection. Having been denied the opportunity to be welcomed or rejected, Jan and I have very different attitudes to the mother who either abandoned us or gave us up with regret. Whatever her motivation or her character, all I know for certain is that my unknown mother is now unknowable.

And so what? A year after finding out about them, in addition to Martin, I've met John, another brother who serves in the American armed forces, and spoken at length to my oldest brother, Andrew, who was formerly in the US Army. I haven't pointed out to any of them that the only circumstances in which I can imagine a lefty member of the chattering media classes having anything to do with an American serviceman is for sex, as I'm not yet certain that we share the same irony gene.

The point is that my reunion with Jan and Martin and John and, eventually, the rest of them comes as close to a middle-term happy ending as we have any right to expect.

Drawing Some Difficult Conclusions

The Guardian, September 2001

The day after the terror attacks in America, I had to produce a cartoon on the tragedy for the *Scotsman*—a task I found fantastically difficult.

The problem wasn't that I was obliged to produce a visual reaction to the bombings—in fact, the media coverage has been mostly visual, from the footage of the planes striking and the towers collapsing, repeated over and over again, to the pages and pages and pages of pictures that filled Wednesday's papers. It was neither, in journalistic terms, that one should one remain silent: these events demanded explanation and have reaped thousands of column inches of opinion, analysis and speculation.

Cartoonists fall somewhere between these two: the commentless photographs which bear witness to events; and the babel arising from the pundits.

The singular trick of the newspaper cartoon is that it gains its power in saying what it does through using humour, and my problem, in the immediate aftermath of the strikes on America, was simply that there was nothing funny to say. My trouble also arose from the way cartoons work and how people perceive them as working. The rational and emotional response to the mixture of ideas, words and images that constitute a cartoon is different from the response to either the written word or a straight illustration or photograph. This is because of the immediacy with which a cartoon is 'read', and the frequently visceral nature of the image and the reader's response to what they see. As a result, I was extremely sensitive to the heightened sensitivities of the readers (let alone the heightened sensitivity of editors to their readers' heightened sensitivity).

I knew that there was a great deal to be said—about Star Wars, about Bush's inadequate response, about the festering sore of the Palestinian–Israeli standoff, about the kulturkampf between Islam and the rest of the modern world. But I also knew that, for a couple of days at least, a cartoon was too blunt an instrument to say these things adequately without causing huge offence and without making me feel like an insensitive schmuck. So I did what I usually deplore and drew a 'Why oh why' cartoon of the Statue of Liberty being engulfed by a monstrous cloud rising up from Lower Manhattan. Since then, to my embarrassment, I have drawn a weeping Statue of Liberty and been soundly told off by Steve Bell for my hackneyed cowardice. When I filed the first cartoon to the *Scotsman*, I telephoned the comment editor and told him that the cartoon said nothing and was completely meaningless.

'That's about the right tone for the moment', he replied. He was right. But inevitably, several readers complained.

248

The Scotsman, September 2001

High Importance of Being Low

British Journalism Review, September 2002

For a man who's been dead for nearly 40 years, the cartoonist Sir David Low is thriving. Earlier this year, he had two exhibitions running simultaneously in London. The first, in Westminster Hall, was opened by the Speaker of the House of Commons, deep in the heart of the political establishment within the purlieus of the Palace of Westminster. The second, up the road at the bottom of Haymarket, was a smaller affair, held on the mezzanine floor of New Zealand House. As Low was a New Zealander, the land of his birth is naturally jealous of his reputation, although he left the place in his early twenties and never went back. Anyway, apart from the cartoons themselves, the exhibition included, in a box, Low's hands.

At first sight I'd rather hoped that this was a Jeremy Bentham style exercise in auto-iconography—that these really were Low's hands, lovingly preserved like an Egyptian pharaoh or the eyeballs of a Victorian murderer, a voodoo talisman harnessing the shamanistic power of his cartooning mitts. Rather disappointingly, they're made of wax, and once hung from the sleeves of Low's waxwork, displayed in Madame Tussauds in the 30s. Still, the very fact that they bothered to sculpt his hands at all (rather than, say, using a spare pair of Bonar Law's after the rest of that statesman had been melted down) suggests the importance his hands were seen to have as a cultural artefact. And Low clearly appreciated the gesture, having a bit of a thing about waxworks.

In a 1935 documentary film *BBC: The Voice of Britain*, Low is filmed giving a radio talk, during which he says 'Politicians are merely waxworks; it's the cartoonist who brings them to life', and he even drew himself drawing his own waxwork at Madame Tussauds, which appears to be in the act of drawing *him*. And, significantly, his first cartoon for Beaverbrook's *Evening Standard*, published on 10 October 1927, was of the opening day of 'Low's Waxworks', with the figure of Low himself dusting down Lloyd George dressed as 'The Political Fanny Ward', Churchill dressed as Napoleon and Ramsay MacDonald, in court dress, labelled 'The celebrated Conservative leader (in actual clothes worn at the Tragedy)', while a tiny, grinning Beaverbrook, either a punter or a dummy, is glimpsed in the background. Most of the contemporary political resonances are now lost on us, but we get the general point. Low was setting up his stall.

What he was doing, right at the start of his 20-year long stint at the *Standard*, was baldly restating the fundamental principles of the political cartoon, which had been laid down a century and a half earlier by the great caricaturist James Gillray. Using some kind of ancient sympathetic magic—as it involves doing damage at a distance with a sharp instrument we might as well call it voodoo—the political cartoonist transforms real people into caricatured, and thereby controlled, depictions of themselves and then makes them act out a narrative of his own invention. Thus the waxworks come alive, but remain sufficiently waxen to allow the needles to be driven in.

One waxwork Low repeatedly brought to life was his own. During his 50-year career Low drew something like 12000 cartoons, over 800 of them featuring himself. Of the nearly 200 or so he produced in his first year on the *Standard*, almost a quarter depict the cartoonist in some way or other. In his first week, out of four cartoons, three feature Low (one as a dog, interestingly enough), and two are about his role as a cartoonist. At the end of the week which had started with him dusting down his 'wax-works', there is the extraordinary cartoon *The Hard Lot of a Cartoonist*, in which Low lays out his relationship with his proprietor. In the opening 'frame', the gnomic figure of Lord Beaverbrook tells Low, 'Your cartoons are giving great offence to my friends. I must ask you to reconsider your view of Lord Birkenhead, Mr Churchill and the rest. After all, you are on the *Evening Standard* now, and, remember, our motto is "kindness first".' The second frame shows a highly stylized group portrait of Baldwin, Birkenhead and Churchill in statesmanlike pose, until Low's conscience intervenes and makes him rub it out and do it again, this time showing the whole Tory crew at the Motor Show driving a ludicrous car designed for travelling in circles.

It's obvious what Low was up to, setting out the parameters of his editorial freedom, as licensed (up to a point, Lord Copper) by Beaverbrook. The terms of his contract with the *Standard* gave him total freedom in choice of subject and execution, but with an ultimate editorial veto, as we'll see later. But Low wasn't just marking his territory in *The Hard Lot of a Cartoonist*. Lord Birkenhead, rechristened 'Lord Burstinghead' by Low, was incensed by his treatment at Low's hands, later immortalized in wax. As he wrote to his friend Beaverbrook, 'As to your filthy little cartoonists, I care nothing about him now. But I know about modern caricature and I never had cause for grievance until you, a friend, allowed a filthy little socialist to present me daily as a crapulous and corpulent buffoon.' That kind of thing can only delight a cartoonist: it shows that the voodoo's working. It worked on Baldwin too, who, on being shown a Low cartoon, spluttered, 'Now Low is a genius, but I cannot bear Low: he is evil and malicious.'

Many politicians, however, recognized the rules of the game: that while the cartoonist can try to work his voodoo magic, he or she is really nothing more than a court jester; at the end of the day the King remains the King. Put another way, the politicians pretend they don't mind, while the cartoonists pretend we matter. That said, Churchill and Beaverbrook were huge fans. But Low had another, highly unlikely

VERY WELL, ALONE

The New European, October 2020

fan. In 1930, a friend of Low's visited Germany and met Hitler, who sang his praises. It transpired that the future Führer misread Low's attacks on democratic politicians as an attack on democracy itself. Nonetheless, Low sent Hitler the original artwork of a cartoon, with the hand written dedication 'from one artist to another'.

That relationship, of course, soon soured. After a weekend at Göring's hunting lodge in the mid-30s, Lord Halifax told Beaverbrook that Low's representations of the Nazi leadership (as 'bloody fools', Low described it) was seriously undermining good Anglo-German relations. And Low was told to cool it. A cheap gag in one of his full page cartoons, *Low's Topical Budget*, run in the *Standard* on Saturdays, in which Hitler is bitten by a dog (Stop Press: The dog goes mad') was spiked by the editor. Low responded with 'Muzzler', a composite dictator combining Hitler and Mussolini. It was a pretty obvious joke, and again Low was marking out his journalistic territory. Moreover, Low's attitude earned him the ultimate, if deadly, accolade from his victims of being placed on the Gestapo Death list.

Low's ragging of the Nazis (which, in the end, did nothing to stop them from conquering most of Europe and murdering millions of its inhabitants), along with his contrarian stance compared to that of his proprietor, are what he's mostly remembered for today. He also created some enduring cartoon archetypes (like Colonel Blimp and the TUC carthorse, although most people don't remember Churchill, and later Lord Hailsham, as Mr Micawber, or his Eskimo correspondents Onandonandon and Upandupandup, or, indeed, his cartoon pup Mussolini, one of his most frequently used cartoon tropes) and produced about half a dozen cartoons which, like Gillray's *The Plumb-Pudding in Danger* or Tenniel's *Dropping the Pilot*, have entered our visual language.

Does that, then, earn him the encomium offered in the title of the Westminster Hall exhibition, 'The Greatest Cartoonist of the Twentieth Century'? It really depends on what you think the purpose of a newspaper cartoon is, how long you think its effectiveness lasts and in what sphere it's meant to exert that influence. The sphere where Low's influence is most obvious is on his successors among newspaper cartoonists. Nearly all of us, at some time or other, have pinched an image from Low: speaking personally, I've used *Rendezvous*, which showed Hitler and Stalin greeting each other over the corpse of Poland at the beginning of the Second World War and which Low described as his 'bitterest cartoon', to depict Blair meeting Thatcher at No 10 just after the 1997 Election, over the corpse of John Major, and NATO greeting Milosevic over the corpse of Kosovo. Likewise, most cartoonists will, as a matter of course, use the TUC carthorse without a second's thought (although Colonel Blimp seems to have died with his creator). The reason we do this is simple: as part of the visual language, these images are common currency and will be recognized by the readers, as will their point. Bluntly, it's visual shorthand, which was why Low created the carthorse, Blimp and his other cast of characters in the first place.

But it's worth remembering why he, and all other cartoonists, use these tricks. They are merely tools to assist the job in hand, which is to provide a daily commentary on the news which, being visual, is 'read' and sublimated quickly and in a very primitively psychological way. Having 'read' it, the reader then moves on, and maybe remembers the cartoon, or maybe doesn't. The savage response to cartoons (like Birkenhead's, or Hitler's) is in large part because of their primitive, almost elementally savage, nature. Voodoo indeed. But the main point is that newspaper cartoons, Low's no less than anyone else's, are produced as an immediate commentary, and are as ephemeral as almost all other newspaper journalism. The power of some of them to linger in the collective memory is very much a by-product.

So, out of 12,000 cartoons, apart from the obsessives and archivists, Low is luckier than most to have as many as half a dozen remembered from his 50-year-long career. Of course, it's a mistake to judge the success of anyone's career purely based on posterity. As Groucho Marx said, 'What the hell's posterity ever done for me?' So how 'great' was Low in his lifetime, and what criteria should we use to make that judgement?

In a way, Low set out to be the architect of his own 'greatness'. His 'freedom' contract with Beaverbrook helped considerably in this, but it should be remembered that this was Beaverbrook's mischievous gift, and in a way reflects better on the proprietor than on the cartoonist. Similarly, Low worked for the *Evening Standard*, which then had the smallest circulation of London's three evening newspapers, but, as the paper of choice in London's clubland, was read by Low's powerful and influential targets (just as, 120 years earlier, Gillray's clientele at Mrs Humphrey's printshop in St James' were *his* targets in the establishment, who got the joke and enjoyed the recognition). He was also widely syndicated, thus nurturing a worldwide audience. He was also, of course, right about Hitler, but was hardly a lone voice, even if his contrarian position at the *Standard* reinforced the impression that he was.

Low was at his best when performing the role of Court Jester to Beaverbrook; his prewar cartoons are both funnier and more effective than the stuff he did once he'd left the *Standard* and gone to his natural political home, first on the *Daily Herald* and then at the *Manchester Guardian*. By then, Low appeared to be believing the rest of the world's opinion of him, which he'd been so careful to cultivate. The tone is far less mischievous and far more pompous, with Low strongly identifying himself as a 'sane voice in an insane world'. It's reported that, by this time, he was getting grander and grander: at an Oxbridge High Table dinner, there were embarrassing scenes as he vied for prominence as the senior guest of honour over a visiting elder statesman, and at the *Manchester Guardian*, the arrangements for the paper's coverage of the party conference season centred around the arrangements for Low's attendance. In 1962, he accepted the knighthood he'd turned down in the 30s.

And now there he is, back in the heart of the establishment in Westminster Hall, although without his hands. I don't know whether the rest of Low's waxwork is propped up in a basement in Madame Tussauds, or has long since been melted down to sculpt Billy Fury and, later, Boy George. What we do know is that he constantly played Pygmalion with himself by bringing his waxwork to life in his own cartoons, but it's worth noticing how he did it. Vicky, his contemporary and successor at the *Standard*, was also fond of placing himself in his cartoons, but more often than not as the butt of his own jokes. Low was seldom if ever the fall guy, and when he was he was the stooge to his own conscience. Otherwise, he drew himself as the passive audience for Colonel Blimp's idiocies in the steam room or as Diogenes in his barrel (holding a candle and looking for an honest man), or, most frequently, as an observer of the lunacies of the political world and, by inference, a stand-in for Everyman.

There's no harm in Low's self-identification with common sense, and without question he was a very great cartoonist, whose greatest influence has not been in the way he drew but in why he drew: that you can make deadly serious points by making people laugh. But in essence he was merely reasserting the cartoonist's right savagely to mock, first established in the form we recognize today by Gillray, but which had lapsed during the dark, deferential Victorian years between. That was probably enough in itself, although it's also worth pointing out that if (and it's a meagre *if*) Low was the greatest cartoonist of the twentieth century, it may have been largely because he kept on telling us so.

Waitemata

The Guardian, November 2004

When my father died suddenly in January this year, he left nine bottles labelled 'horse blood' on a high windowsill, continuing to gather dust. Those bottles kept us guessing for longer than anything else. Longer than it took us eventually to find his will, and certainly longer than it took me to work out why there should be a cardboard box filled with human bones up in the loft. He had been a medical student, after all, and never threw anything away. Then, three and a half months later, my stepmother, Jos, died as well.

Their home—my father's for 45 years, Jos' for 31—was a largish, rather ugly late-20s detached house in Stanmore, in a street where the houses have names, not numbers. They called the house Waitemata, which, for the record, is the name of a New Zealand lager. Jos last went home in early March to collect a few things. As I backed the car out of the drive, she had said, 'Goodbye, Waitemata,' horribly poignantly in retrospect, knowing better than I did that she would never see it again. Nor did she. So it was left to my sister Jamy and me to sort out her now empty and abandoned house.

This, I am told by friends who have also lived through the deaths of their parents (which, I kept telling myself, is unspeakable and unendurable and also inevitable, as well as being infinitely preferable to the alternative), is always a particularly hard thing to deal with in the throes of grief. Jamy and I, however, had a greater than average problem. The thing was, there were just too many things.

We started off quite well. Selling our father's ridiculous 1976 Reliant Kitten (the four-wheel version of the notorious Robin) proved relatively easy—Jamy quickly identified a buyer through the net. I thought the clocks would be more difficult, but that was easy too. For 30 years, our father had collected early electric clocks. I had always thought it was a nice collection, but we also knew that, merely in terms of security, we had to get it out of the house. There were more than 130 clocks, many of them rare, some unique. Fortunately, he had often said that he wanted us to sell them after he died so others could enjoy the thrill and excitement of acquisition. Time forbade us from following this plan to the letter—slowly releasing them, a few at a time, on to an unsuspecting market over a period of decades—but at least handing the lot over to Christie's to auction was sort of what he would have wanted.

In addition to collecting and fixing clocks, he was, like most of his generation, an inveterate DIY fanatic. In consequence, there were two large rooms set aside as his workshops and filled with tools (although the industrial lathe spilled over into the

THE LOFT

Master bedroom

Top Landing

Clock Workshop

2nd Bedroom

Garage with stupid fibreglass car, old hoovers, fridges, ladders etc etc

Spare Bedroom

Study

Hall

Sitting Room

Kitchen

Horse blood

1st Workshop

Lathe

Mulberry Tree

LATERAL TRANSVERSE SECTION OF MY LATE PARENTS' HOUSE

The Guardian, November 2004

extended kitchen). Luckily, the man from Christie's knew someone who was setting up a horological workshop, who took away all the tools and clock books and paid us a reasonable wedge into the bargain.

And yet, even with the clocks and the tools gone, the 'empty' house was still horribly full and hauntingly unchanged, even if now spookily silent without those familiar ticks and clonks. The same crockery in the cupboards, the same notelets written in either of my parents' handwriting still stuck up by the phone. The big things had been easy; it was the tiny things that induced a terrible inertia, so when I went there on my own, I would find it more or less impossible to sort anything, and would ring Jamy so she could tell me to get out before the doom and gloom set in.

The loft alone was part Aladdin's cave, part Augean stable; I had often joked that, if my parents ever moved, they would have to empty the loft first or the house would fall over. It was filled with anything and everything you could think of: old luggage, photographic equipment, old toys, more tools, TV sets, jars filled with old screws and washers, old copies of *Forum* as well as old bones. The mate of the man from Christie's took most of these other tools, the *Forum*s for (he said) his accountant, a centrifuge and several hundred packets of medical catgut (with a use-by date of February 1962). Later, a couple of blokes who run a 1950s and 60s memorabilia shop bought a job lot of the rolls of old wallpaper, the Venetian glass horses' heads (still unopened since purchased in 1974), some lino, all my father's ties (except two which I kept and now wear most of the time), some light fittings and a rather fine retro lilo pump.

My father would often say, when introducing another piece of junk into the house, 'It'll come in useful to someone one day'. His other favourite homily was 'It's bound to be worth something to somebody one day', which explained the 'collectables' they also collected, such as the Matchbox toy cars, all in their original packaging, although I subsequently discovered that these aren't yet worth anything at all. Indeed, a kind of oxymoronic universal law applies here: if you collect something because you are told it's collectable, because thousands of other people are doing the same, it's no longer collectable, and therefore only things which aren't 'collectables' are truly collectable. Still, it explained the milk bottles.

I knew about these already. There were about 25 of them, with strangely beautiful logos of arcane design printed on the side. As an executor as well as a loving son, it was my duty to realize as much for them as possible, so I got on to the web and found the Milk Bottle News site. They asked for more details, so I spent a morning cataloguing the bottles ('Diagonal sans-serif farm logo, with scrolls; tableau of cows beneath a fingerpost reading, "To Health via Milk"; slight chip on rim'), and emailed them the result. They replied: 'This is very interesting, and you have been very thorough. To be honest they are all a bit late for me, but someone should pay you about a pound a bottle.' My first instinct was to leave the lot out on the doorstep. Instead, they are currently sitting in our spare room.

Slowly—agonizingly slowly—we were emptying the place, though it seemed more like a process of erosion than anything more systematic.

Another specialist antiques dealer bought some medical textbooks, an old slide drawer and a sinister-looking culture in a petri dish we found at the back of a cupboard. A hospice charity took most of the furniture. Jamy and I took away files full of share certificates, old photographs, curious dingbats that took our fancy, some books, some letters. I even tried to take some cuttings from a mulberry tree my father had himself grown from a cutting taken from a long since dead tree in his old Cambridge college. Spring will show if I succeeded. By this stage, five months after Jos had died, we had sold the house to the next-door neighbour, and we knew we had to clear the house completely.

In the intervening months, I had spent several days alone in the house going through cupboards full of old photographs and, steeling myself, had binned thousands of snaps of people unknown to me and now certainly dead, or of lousy shots of my parents on holiday. A line had to be drawn. Without Osborne House at your disposal, very few of us have the option to memorialize our dead loved ones by fetishizing all the material artefacts of their lives. As I kept reminding myself, it's our memories of the dead that should serve as their memorial, with maybe just a few talismans kept to one side, like the letters of sympathy my father received after my mother's death in 1969, or grey-brown photos of my father or Jos as children, to focus things and prick the tears into your eyes.

So almost everything went: the clocks, the photos, even the drafts of my father's many scientific papers. I offered them to his old college library, but they had no room. Neither did we, and as the published versions are in the public domain, I let them go.

Finally, we got our cousin Paul, who is in waste management, to empty Waitemata. It took a day and a half, and they dumped two tonnes of stuff nobody else could conceivably want. The old umbrellas, coasters, beds, Pyrex ware, hosepipes, fridges, rickety tables, shelves my father built, old paperbacks, corkscrews, fondue sets, RSPB bookmarks, 50s French textbooks, manky cushions, souvenirs from Beijing, photograph albums, lacrosse sticks, roadmaps, knitting patterns, carrier bags, calendars, lengths of doweling, lead pipes, bell jars, and on and on and on. And it was heartbreaking.

After wandering from room to empty room in a house I had known all my life, it was looking at some stupid tray embossed with a vile floral pattern that made me almost burst into tears as it went into the bin bag.

But there was still the horse blood. I finally asked a zoologist friend why my father would have wanted nine bottles of horse blood, also mentioning that he had been a virologist (there's even a Rowson virus), and I was told that it was obvious. Horse blood, it transpires, is the best medium for growing viral cultures—so I created a little Hirstian installation in the room where I work, with the bottles flanked by the human bones. You never know, it might just be what they would have wanted.

Is God a Hedgehog?

New Humanist, 2005

A couple of Christmases ago, we were invited to a very jolly party by friends of ours who I'd forgotten were confessing Christians. It was around the time that Rowan Williams had been translated to Canterbury, and I was saying to a total stranger that the new Archbishop seemed a sound sort of chap, the only thing wrong with him being that he appeared actually to believe in God. I enjoy this kind of flip remark, but the chilly response indicated that my new friend didn't, and he summoned over the local vicar, dressed in mufti, to deal with me. After we'd sniffed around each other a bit to establish our diametrically opposed positions, he challenged me with one of the feebler bits of rhetoric the faithful adopt to clinch the argument. 'How then,' he said, leaning back in the way people do when they think that what they're going to say next will be the coup de grâce, 'do you explain the fact that religion is a universal phenomenon?' My riposte was immediate. 'And how do you explain that you can say exactly the same thing about keeping pets?' One–nil to me.

And it's true. Every human society keeps companion animals. I have a dog sleeping at my feet as I write this. According to the BBC, Mullah Omar communed with his cats in Kandahar before fleeing into the night as the Northern Alliance and US Army Special Forces closed in on him. Henry III of England had a pet polar bear, Montezuma II had a private zoo, Engels kept a pet hedgehog, Hitler had an Alsatian he doted on, and Amazonian tribes keep all manner of animals they find in the jungle and then choose not to eat.

But what's that got to do with religion? Well, everything, as it happens. We keep pets because we, as a species, have this wonderful thing called empathy, and we have it to a far greater degree than our closest genetic cousins, chimpanzees. A child of four is said to empathize eight times further than an adult chimp, which is another way of saying that that child can project him or herself across eight degrees of separation, to imagine what it's like to be someone seven people removed from him or herself. Thus, pet keeping. We imbue our companion animals with human qualities by projecting our own personalities onto them, and they respond to a lesser or greater degree depending on what they are. And it's the same with God. Or gods. We project ourselves onto transcendental beings of our own creation, imbuing them with our own personalities or qualities, creating God in the image of man.

This is obvious if you look at the pantheons of gods in any polytheistic belief system, where strict demarcation applies, with different gods for this and that, and if monotheism muddies those metaphysical waters, you've still got all those intercessionary

Putting the "FUNDAMENT" back into "FUNDAMENTALISM"!

saints, and enough cultural and historical evidence to explain the emergence of mono-theism as a reaction to polytheism, and its subsequent success and hegemony is equally explicable in pretty straightforward cultural and historical terms.

All of which (along with much else) is why I am so certain and comfortable in my atheism. As far as I'm concerned, religion is the proper subject not for theologians but for anthropologists, sociologists and even biologists. Quite apart from the obvious shortcomings of religion—its misleading simplicity, exclusivity, intolerance, unadapt-ability, obscurantism and so much else—it's also clearly and demonstrably wrong. The fact that this is almost a matter of faith with me is, I know, rather ironic, but it also means that I simply cannot understand why billions of my fellow human beings persist in choosing to be deluded and continue to believe in their chosen deity, when it plainly doesn't exist as anything more than a comforting extension of themselves.

And perhaps my incomprehension points up shortcomings of my own. To get back to the vicar, the ubiquity of religion must mean something, mustn't it? (And something which can't be countered with the flippant, if satisfying, response that huge numbers of people also voted for Hitler.) Then, a few weeks ago, a geneticist was interviewed on the *Today* programme, claiming to have isolated the 'faith gene', which predisposes those who possess it to a more 'spiritual' attitude to life. So, like almost everything else, it's your genes. These people living their lives in error can't help it, and this predisposition towards transcendentalism, while having possible evolutionary advantages (clarity of purpose, community cohesion, a heightened awareness of the need to hold village fêtes and kill people different from you), is once more so clearly based in human beings, quite literally coming from within ourselves, that it appears to settle the matter once and for all.

Unless, of course, it turns out that I'm completely and utterly wrong. As I was lis-tening to the radio, a hideous germ inveigled its way into my mind. What if it was just another example of what Philip Gosse said? Gosse, a nineteenth-century marine biol-ogist and Seventh-day Adventist preacher, responded to Darwinism by arguing that God had placed the fossils in the strata of the rocks at the moment of creation purely in order to tempt us into error. Bloody hell! Maybe this gene was the same thing (and let's not reflect here on what a shitty thing that would have been for God to do). Worse, maybe these genes were the final physical evidence for the elect! A kind of Calvinist equivalent of Descartes' pineal gland, the actual seat of the soul which I'm clearly lacking! Of course, I don't believe a word of all that nonsense, but then again, because of the caprice of the genetic tombola, I wouldn't, would I?

All of which leaves things much as they were before, and rather uncomfortably, I'm still just left with my faith in the evidence of my own eyes, while they're left with their faith in faith. As ever when religion comes up, it's all a bit of a mystery.

Selections from Mugshots

Methuen, 2005

The Gay Hussar is possibly one of the greatest and certainly one of the most famous eating places in London. For more than 50 years, this small Hungarian restaurant just south of Soho Square has been the haunt of politicians and journalists and, during the tenure of its legendary founder Victor Sassie, provided the venue for plots, subplots, wild scenes and other encounters which proved to have far wider historical significance than the average meal. During the 60s, the whole of Harold Wilson's Labour cabinet would lunch there, while towards the end of the decade the notorious serial fellationist and left-wing Member of Parliament Tom Driberg tried to persuade Mick Jagger to stand as a Labour MP during a surreal evening in the second-floor private dining room (known ever after as the Tom Driberg Memorial Suite). Bevanites conspired there, as did Tribunites later on; editors were hired, deals stitched up, plots were hatched, foreign secretaries (George-Brown) were threatened with physical removal, and it's even said that Tony Blair was first persuaded to enter politics on one of the plush banquettes on the ground floor. A great book needs to be written about the history of the Gay Hussar. This isn't it. Instead, this is a collection of sixty caricatures I drew at the Gay Hussar over a period of around five years.

Sometime early in 1999, around midnight, on the stairs coming down from the said Tom Driberg Memorial Suite, I made a pitch to the Gay Hussar's manager, John Wrobel, that I should draw his famous and infamous patrons, as an enduring record, to be hung on its walls, of this restaurant's place in the history of the second half of the twentieth century. The deal would be that I'd draw these characters from the life in real time (their lunchtime) in exchange for one free meal a pop. I've always liked the idea of *cartoon reportage*, the thrill of getting out to the story, rather than just reflecting and reacting to the news hunched at home over my drawing board. Moreover, I liked the bohemian feel of my proposal. Like Toulouse-Lautrec, I'd sit starving in the corner, wheezing consumptively and scribbling away for my supper, sipping occasionally from a small glass of absinthe at my side. (Actually, the closest I came to the absinthe was when I drew Jack Jones and Rodney Bickerstaffe one May Day, when they were drinking absinthe and champagne, but there you go.)

Apart from my free meal, the terms were quite strict. First of all, the subjects all had to have previously patronized the restaurant, so there was no question of packing the wall with David Beckham or the Pope just because they happened to be passing. Having got my subject, it was then my plan to produce the kind of immediacy in caricature that Cartier-Bresson achieved in his photographs. This was what made the gig interesting and entirely different from all the other cartooning and caricature I do on a daily basis. And to that end I did no planning, no research, didn't practice beforehand and didn't want the subjects or victims to 'sit' or pose in any kind of conventional way. Instead, I was after a kind of fly-on-the-wall, or possibly fly-in-your-soup, caricature, the better to capture the real essence of the person. This meant that the subjects were moving all the time: chewing, talking, drinking, often obscured from my sight by passing waiters or their freeloading mates. That made things difficult enough, but added to that the restaurant can hardly be said to boast the clear, pellucid light of, say, St Ives. Indeed, I drew Mo Mowlam and Sir John Mortimer up in the Driberg Suite in almost complete darkness.

So, I was drawing moving targets in the dark, and quickly. Each of these drawings, from beginning to end, took me an average of 45 minutes. Then, to add to my problems, after the heightened stress of creation would be added my wages, a large portion of Mitteleuropean carbohydrate, which would grip my heart all afternoon like a chain-mailed fist, to which would also be added, as often as not, a few drinks with either my victim, or John Wrobel, or both, leaving me to totter home far too late. Indeed, on one such afternoon, my old friend Peter Oborne, now the political editor of the *Spectator*, said to me: 'Rowson, you will never be truly great until you seek to emulate the simplicity of Christ.'

Things were getting out of hand. On top of being compared unfavourably to the Son of God and getting fat and drunk (but, of course, not getting paid), there was the inherent danger in presenting the finished artwork to the victims of my visual mugging for them to sign and endorse as a true representation of themselves, which was another essential part of the deal. Most of them winced; most of them clearly hated the whole thing. Lord Longford said his drawing was like mortification of the flesh; Alastair Campbell, before I'd even finished, yelled across the restaurant at me, 'You won't be able to stop yourself making me look like a really bad person!' to which I replied, 'I draw what I see.' I'm still not sure if Julia Langdon has quite forgiven me. Many of the people I've drawn were, once at least, my friends. Sometimes, however, I'd be confronted with some prominent individual where I was astonished that my pen didn't leap out of hand and drive itself through my eyeball.

While we're on the subject of pens, the questions cartoonists are most frequently asked are where they get their ideas from and what materials they use. Well, my ideas were sitting in front of me, stuffing their faces. The materials I used were, for the record, 250 gsm Bristol paper, the unforgiving image put down in black Pelikan Indian ink applied with an 850 mapping pen nib. Although, it must be said that this was, on occasion, entirely inadequate. After all, one would need the palate of the great Turner properly the capture the precise hue of Paul Routledge after lunch, but there you go.

As you thumb through the pages of this book, it might help you to have a few statistics about my subjects. Remember that they come from and represent several generations of a particular class of Englishman (with the occasional Scots or Welshman and the even more occasional woman; don't blame me for that, blame the system). The people depicted within these covers are, moreover, the people who've moved and shaken this nation over the last 60 years or more. If you note a certain incestuousness, well, that's the way it tends to be. In my commentaries on the sitters, several names will keep recurring, for which I might apologize, except that it's really not my fault. I drew them because they were there. And they're there, largely, because you lot let them by continuing to vote for or read them.

Anyway, the average age of the subjects is 63. Their aggregate age is 3,477, so that if they were all laid end to end back through time we'd get back to the age of the pyramids which is a sobering thought in a place not famous for sober thinking. There are fourteen current or former cabinet ministers, thirteen present or former editors, many famous faces from TV and journalism, five union general secretaries of various vintages, a former chancellor, a former deputy prime minister, a current home secretary, two leading playwrights, one double Oscar winner and one mayor of London.

There were some subjects who continued to elude me, however. Alan Rusbridger is, it's true, in quarter profile with Charles Clarke, but cancelled three times to be done full face. Likewise, Peter Mandelson, Ken Clarke and Nick Brown, among others, all found better things to do at the last minute. We were promised Tony Blair, but he seemed to be busy. On a more sombre note, shortly after Barbara Castle's death, John Wrobel received a letter from one of her staff saying how much she'd been looking forward to being drawn by me before her final illness made that out of the question, which was both immensely flattering and rather humbling.

Finally, between going blind and getting pissed, I also worked out a kind of I-spy approach to this project, where you could win points for what you spot. So a cabinet minister, past or present, was worth 30 points, government minister, 20 points, candidate for leadership of your party, 10 points, successful ditto, 50 points, editor, 20 points per paper, winning an Oscar, 20 points, 'Most Powerful Man in Britain', 8 points, being a spin doctor, minus 30, and so on. There was also a 5-point bonus for any kind of connection with *Tribune*. So, while not intending to run through the whole list, it's worth noting that Lord Gus MacDonald manages to push his total up to 45 on the strength of his brief tenure as circulation manager of *Tribune*, and while it's a close run for second place between the lords Hattersley and Heseltine, the outright winner, by a mile, on 245 points, is my very good friend Michael Foot, who was the first to be drawn and appears first in this book, and who has written a characteristically generous introduction.

To him—and to all my victims—my profound thanks, and to you, the reader, I can only apologize for drawing what I saw and nothing else.

This and subsequent illustrations in this chapter have been taken from
Mugshots (London: Methuen, 2005)

Lord Longford, peer, politician and campaigner

The late Lord Longford has gone down in history as a bit of a national joke, which is unfair. To be sure, his association with Malcolm Muggeridge and Mary Whitehouse in the Festival of Light in the early 70s did his reputation (and Muggeridge's) no good at all. And apart from trying to stem the tide of filth engulfing the country, the commendable charity and forgiveness he displayed in his prison visits to, among others, Moors murderer Myra Hindley condemned him forever in the eyes of the more vengeful sections of the press. Worse still, he absolutely hated my attempt to immortalize him for posterity, which I drew a year or so before he died. When I showed him the drawing, he looked at it in horror, saying he'd never seen anything so ugly in his life, wondering how anyone could ever love a monster such as I had drawn. It was, he concluded, like mortification of the flesh. I replied that I'd assumed, as he was a devout Catholic, he might have thought that was a good thing, but we left it there.

On an earlier occasion in the Gay Hussar, Longford, who in his nineties tended to eat with his fingers and wore elastic-topped trousers for comfort and convenience, was just leaving to go to the House of Lords when the restaurant's manager John Wrobel noticed Longford had spilled a sizeable portion of his lunch into his lap, and so pursued him out into Greek Street where Wrobel fell to his knees and started to brush the noble lap with a napkin with such vigour that Longford's trousers fell to his knees, precipitating ribald comments from a passing cab driver who believed he was witnessing a gross act not uncommon in Soho.

Mo Mowlam, politician

I drew this caricature of former Northern Ireland Secretary Mo Mowlam in almost total darkness in the Tom Driberg Memorial Suite on the third floor of the Gay Hussar at a *Tribune* dinner held in her honour. The evening had two highpoints. The first came with Mowlam's husband Jon Norton's bravura and vituperative denunciation of the fiscal policies of Gordon Brown, the chancellor of the Exchequer. The second resulted from Ms Mowlam's decision to take the table decorations (several large red chilli peppers), shred them into strips and fashion these into a necklace for herself, failing thereafter to wash her hands before rubbing her eyes. The consequent confusion led to her early departure through the main restaurant, several American diners being surprised by the earthy response they received on hailing this popular and internationally renowned politician.

Lord Longford drawn at "The Gay Hussar"
18th April 2000

Martin Rowson 2000

Mo Mowlam — drawn at "The Gay Hussar"
2nd November 2000

All the best
to the Gay
Hussar in
the future—
Mo
Mowlem

Martin Rowson
2000

Paul Routledge, journalist and author

Having just finished drawing Brain Walden, I noticed veteran political commentator and author Paul Routledge sitting up the banquette from me and couldn't resist knocking off a furtive sketch, albeit, sadly, only in black and white. It's been said of Routledge that he looks like someone whose face caught fire and then had it put out with a shovel, which is hardly fair, but you get the point. He was having lunch with his agent, Jonathan Lloyd, the boss of the literary agency Curtis Brown, and I noticed with some alarm when I joined them that they were drinking a brand of kosher slivovitz they stock in the Gay Hussar, which has not only been blessed by the Chief Rabbi of Budapest (as it says on the bottle) but also has the power to make you forget everything that happens to you for several hours after you drink it. I know this from personal experience, so declined Routledge and Lloyd's invitation to join them in a glass. I did, however, hang around for a bit, and long enough to see Jonathan Lloyd do something I've never seen before and never expect to see again. Having just made a particular point (about something or other), he swung his hand towards his face with a flourish to draw on his cigarette for rhetorical effect, *and missed his head*.

Michael Heseltine, politician

Despite the fact that he (along with Geoffrey Howe) effectively shafted Margaret Thatcher, former Deputy Leader of the Conservative Party, President of the Board of Trade, Defence Secretary and millionaire publisher Lord Heseltine is probably the politician of the last 25 years I loathe the most. It could be his aura of immense self-satisfaction, like the pushy kid at school with the longest box of Caran d'Ache pencils who actually *makes* all the stuff they show you how to make on *Blue Peter*; it may be his fondness (along with Göring, Mussolini and Idi Amin) for wearing uniforms at the drop of a hat when he was Defence Secretary, and for being so gleeful (as I was once told on excellent authority) when he found out that the office of the president of the Board of Trade, being one of the oldest offices of state in the land, comes with a ceremonial sword; perhaps it's the way he was always said to be able to 'find the clitoris of the Tory Party' in Conference speeches of sublimely meaningless bombast; or it could just be that he once took three months to pay me for a cartoon, only coughing up when I threatened him with the small-claims court. When the cheque finally arrived, most of the space was taken up with his titles, his name and the letters after it.

Anyway, after I'd drawn him (and, despite my reassurance that he should pretend I wasn't there, he sat posing like a cross between Churchill and God), I went to present him with the cartoon, and he addressed me thus:

Paul Routledge – drawn from the LIFE
at "THE GAY HUSSAR"
Wednesday 10th April 2002

Paul Routledge.

Martin Rowson '02

Lord Heseltine — drawn from the life at
THE GAY HUSSAR
10th July '02

'You know, I have a vewy large collection of cartoons at home fwom my Oxford days onwards, going up the staircase. Vewy large staircase. I live in a vewy large house, you know. But what I can't get over it the huge amount of money you cartoonists charge these days. In the old days it would just be a bottle of scotch or they'd simply give you the cartoon!'

I replied that I have a sliding scale of prices: for some rich buffoon like Charles Saatchi I charge the largest figure that comes into my head, and the price drops accordingly all the way down to worthy and impecunious groups for whom I do stuff for nothing.

'Well,' Heseltine puffed, 'I sincerely hope that I fall into the latter categowy! Ho ho!'

'Well, My Lord,' I answered. 'Perhaps we should do an audit.' He cut me dead after that.

Postscript (2024)

Subsequently, the Gay Hussar went into a sad decline with the slow collapse of the kind of heroic political lunches which were its forte, and in 2013 its owners, Corus Hotels, put the restaurant up for sale. A group of regulars, at my instigation, then formed the Goulash Cooperative with a view to buying the place, and we raised £150,000 from investors in about a fortnight. The media attention created by the threatened sale led to more bookings, and the Gay Hussar came off the market, struggling on for another four years before Corus closed it on Midsummer's Day 2018.

At this juncture, I was in dispute with Corus Hotels over ownership of the drawings: I insisted they were mine as I'd never been paid, but had an understanding that they were on loan; they counterclaimed that, as I'd got a free meal a pop, I *had* been paid. This row rumbled on, getting nowhere, until halfway through the Covid lockdowns in 2020, I proposed that Corus and I jointly donate them as an absolute gift to the National Portrait Gallery, where they now form part of their Research Archive, honour satisfied all round.

Mission Impossible: Tristram Shandy

The Telegraph, January 2006

Michael Winterbottom's *A Cock and Bull Story*, out next week, purports to be a film of Laurence Sterne's 'unfilmable' novel *The Life and Opinions of Tristram Shandy, Gentleman*, published in nine volumes between 1759 and 1767. Indeed, the publicity material makes a great deal of the book's 'unfilmability', and the finished product lives up to all that Winterbottom, the audience or even Rev Sterne could wish for. Which is not a criticism, but instead the humblest of admiring genuflections to a film about making a film about a book about writing a book. But forgive me. We're getting ahead of ourselves.

The more enduring problem for *Tristram Shandy* has been not so much its unfilmability as its unreadability. In this regard, it fulfils all the criteria for a classic of English literature: most people of taste and a vague pretension to learning will, of course, have heard of it; will have every intention one day of reading it, save for the interruptions of daily life conspiring against this happy eventuality; will even have a shrewdish idea what the book is about (or not about); but will admit, under gentle pressure, to be waiting for the Andrew Davies TV adaptation.

That said, few people have actually read it. Among the great majority (and I don't mean the dead—I'll get on to them later) are Steve Coogan and Rob Brydon, the stars of *A Cock and Bull Story*, who admitted on *The Jonathan Ross Show* on BBC One that they hadn't read the book. Brydon went further in a recent interview and said he'd gone into Waterstone's, taken one look at the book and run a mile. These confessions were made while both men were on the circuit to publicize the film of the unfilmable book they haven't read. In the film itself, there's a scene where the Steve Coogan character—being either himself or being played as a character called Steve Coogan—tries to read the book but instead falls asleep and has a nightmare about making the film—of the book—in a film about making the film about the book.

Tristram Shandy is, without question, very, very odd. Its unreadability cannot, therefore, be put down simply to 250 years' worth of accretion of layers of obscurity, and I reckon more living people have read it than have read, say, Samuel Richardson's *Pamela*. But even 250 years ago it was seen as 'difficult'. Dr Johnson himself remarked: 'Nothing odd will do long. *Tristram Shandy* did not last.' (To digress for a moment, it could be that Johnson was motivated by personal malice. Sterne was, then, much more famous than Johnson, and that would have annoyed him quite enough when the two men met. Worse still, Johnson claimed to have been deeply shocked when the Yorkshire parson showed him a pornographic drawing.)

Forgive me again, and let's go back a paragraph and a half. I was imprecise. Few living people have read *Tristram Shandy*, which is not to say that dead people now read it (although it is a movingly Shandean thought that heaven is filled with souls reading little else) but that in the mid-eighteenth century, Dr Johnson notwithstanding, the book was a runaway bestseller. More than that, it was a publishing phenomenon that turned Sterne from an obscure provincial clergyman into one of the greatest celebrities of Georgian London. So great was his fame that, when his corpse was dis-interred by resurrection men for dissection at the schools of anatomy, he was recognized on the slab and speedily reinterred. Moreover, Johnson was doubly wrong. '*Tristram Shandy* did not last' concedes a flash-in-the-pan celebrity for the book, but with that 'did' passes an inexorable judgement that the novel had already slipped through the fingers of posterity. Yet *Tristram Shandy* has never been out of print, and to this day has a dedicated, almost fanatical band of followers.

What gets these people so excited will have to wait. This is, after all, an article about a film about a book which is about the impossibility of writing a book. To aid comprehension and help you keep your temper, I should step back for the briefest of moments and inform you that, in 1996, Picador published my comic-book version of *The Life and Opinions of Tristram Shandy, Gentleman*, a volume now sadly out of print, but which was saved from pulping because every last copy sold. In the thin amount of research I did for the book, I met a good number of these devoted Shandeans. One such was Sir Stephen Tumim, Her Majesty's late Chief Inspector of Prisons, who said that his greatest achievement was to end 'slopping out'. When he was on *Desert Island Discs*, his book choice was, inevitably, *Tristram Shandy*, while his luxury was Nollekens' bust of Laurence Sterne.

Before I met Tumim, I'd travelled to Coxwold in North Yorkshire to visit Shandy Hall, the medieval house Sterne bought with the money he made from *Tristram Shandy*. This building had been rescued from ruination many decades before by Kenneth Monkman, founder of the Laurence Sterne Trust, to whom I showed the first few pages of my comic-book interpretation of a novel that had been written, to a large extent, in his home.

To begin with, Monkman was highly suspicious of me. Shandeans, like any other group of fans, are jealously protective of the object of their veneration. (Some months previously, I'd told the journalist Francis Wheen I was planning to give *Tristram Shandy* graphic life; he'd glowered at me menacingly and growled 'Watch it!') So, as Monkman showed me round his house, I knew I had to win his trust. I did this in what I hope was a suitably Shandean manner, by repeating to him the story of Sterne's father, an ensign in the army stationed in Ireland, who had a duel over the ownership of a duck.

The duel was held indoors, and Ensign Sterne was impaled through the shoulder, his opponent's blade pinning him to the wall. With foresight, Sterne père told the victor he'd be obliged if he were to wipe the blade clean of lathe and plaster before withdrawing it through his body. Thus did Sterne's father avoid septicaemia.

I, having presented my credentials as one of the cognoscenti, was thereafter treated with considerably more trust. Monkman showed me Nollekens' bust of Sterne, told me that reading *Tristram Shandy* as a young man had changed his life and, best of all, when my book was published, he gave it his blessing.

Thanks to my comic book I have, I suppose, become a kind of honorary Shandean. Learned academics, many of a type satirized by Sterne in *Tristram Shandy*, have given lectures on my version. I've appeared several times in *The Shandean*, an annual compendium of Shandean studies, within the pages of which I was also once sternly upbraided by Prof. Melvyn New, who has devoted his life to the study of *Tristram Shandy* within the cloisters of the University of Florida. My crime was that I had shown insufficient reverence for the text.

Cutting to the chase, the text is really the major problem with *Tristram Shandy*. Most of the people who know about the book but haven't read it know that Sterne plays all sorts of games with the text, layout, punctuation and everything else. This is why *Tristram Shandy* is often called, fliply, the first postmodern novel. Previously, it has been called the precursor to stream-of-consciousness mode, surreal, odd (of course), unreadable (naturally), as well as being recognized since its first publication as utterly filthy: in the opening chapter, the eponymous narrator describes his conception, and how it was interrupted through the operation of John Locke's theory on the association of ideas when Tristram's mother, associating Walter Shandy's winding of the clock on the first Sunday of every month with the monthly discharge of his conjugal duties, says, mid-coitus: *Pray, my Dear, have you not forgot to wind up the clock?*

Tristram accounts all his subsequent misfortunes, including his misnaming, the flattening of his nose and his circumcision by a falling sash window, to this instigating error—And after the first two volumes of *Tristram Shandy* were published, the clock-makers of Clerkenwell addressed a public letter to Mr Tristram Shandy calling on him to retract his comments and disassociate them from such smut.

Where was I? Ah yes. Now, everyone who's never read it knows that *Tristram Shandy* is littered with marbled pages—black pages—blank pages—pages of punctuation—dedications that suddenly pop up in the middle of a volume—diagrams of how the plot has got lost and how the digressions have looped and thrashed about and knotted themselves round the linear flow of the narrative—in addition to a narrative style which never, ever seems to get to the point. Famously, Tristram doesn't manage to get round to his own birth until Volume 3. He concludes that the only way he can get his father and his Uncle Toby (whose wound on the groin received at the Siege of Namur provides a parallel subplot that leads up to a cheap sight gag, truncated and rather ruined in *A Cock and Bull Story*) down the stairs is to call for a 'day-tall critic' to erect some curtains at the foot of the staircase—and reflects at length that, at the pace he's proceeding, his life will not be long enough to record all the events in it

(To digress, by your leave, for yet another brief instant, there is a story by Jorge Luis Borges, the title of which would only delay us further, in which a cartographer makes a map of a country so detailed that he is forced to produce it in a scale of 1:1, the map covering the entire land area of the country mapped. If I've tried your patience too greatly, you may at this stage safely read no further.)

None of which, to return, makes *Tristram Shandy* an easy read, although it must be said it also encourages in the reader in no way whatsoever a desire to show any more reverence for the text than Sterne himself does. It was with this partly in mind that I failed to read *Tristram Shandy* for a second time when I was at Cambridge, scampering through the canon of Eng lit when we stopped—briefly—at *Tristram Shandy*. My supervisor for the eighteenth-century paper was a particularly calcified old fossil who never allowed his students to write more than two sides of foolscap and would spend most of the supervision fixing the seat of his chair and not listening to a word you were saying. In this spirit, I said that *Tristram Shandy* was a book that could be read backwards with as much profit as reading it forwards, and that Lillibullero, which Uncle Toby whistles in response to any discussion he finds embarrassing or stupid, is also the call sign of the BBC World Service.

(This, incidentally, is a fine example of the Shandean school of criticism Sterne hints at and I expanded on in our respective versions of *Tristram Shandy*.)

The don responded thus: Just as *Waiting for Godot* would have been impossible without a tradition of more conventional theatre, so it is with *Tristram Shandy*, which should be seen purely as a cul-de-sac in the Development of the Novel. (This was more than 25 years ago—they were still very big on the Development of the Novel back then.) In a way, he was right. *Tristram Shandy* is an anti-novel (and think more anti-matter than anti-Pope); more than that, it is a direct satire on the whole idea of The Novel as It Was Then Developing, which was as an entirely selective and therefore ultimately mendacious attempt to simulate reality. *Tristram Shandy*, contrariwise, gives you the lot: and the best joke in the whole of this odd, rude, sentimental and, ultimately, profoundly disrespectful text is the impossibility of doing just that.

Martin Rowson, *The Life and Opinions of Tristram Shandy, Gentleman* (London: Macmillan, 1996)

In short (please), *Tristram Shandy* is both unfilmable and unreadable because it's about life in all its ludicrous detail: once you start reading it you're compelled, like Tumim and Monkman (and like Tristram), to live it. To his credit, Winterbottom doesn't even try, but skips and curvets his way through a wonderfully funny film about the impossibility of making a film about a book about the impossibility of writing a book.

Furthermore, to return [*next 40,000 words cut for reasons of space*]

The Towers of Babel

An Excerpt from Snatches

Jonathan Cape / Vintage, 2006

Among the dust and debris of desktops, disks, doormats, dermatitis, dingbats, dinner plates, dentures, Dictaphones, dental plates, Danish pastries, duodenums, deodorant, dishcloths, dividing panels, documents, driving licences, drink dispensers, dollar bills, drinks cabinets, coffee machines, contact lenses, carotid arteries, cakes, Coke cans, cocaine, cartilage, cover notes, cantilevered box files, corrupt programmes, Cartier watches, crucifixes, carpeting, carpet cutters, cardboard, cupboards, coupons, crossword puzzles, canary yellow overalls, compacts, compact discs, computers, catalogues, cartons, concrete, condoms, calling cards, credit cards, cap badges, Canadian bacon, cue balls, Calvin Klein boxer shorts, carrier bags, baseball caps, broken biscuits, brain-pans, boxes, bureaus, bodies, brassieres, brass doorknobs, biros, Brookes Brothers suits, boiler rooms, brushes, brooms, bubblegum, best friends, brothers, buckets, bath-rooms, boots, Ben and Jerry's ice-cream tubs, buttresses, books (and bookkeepers), bubbles, beef, Buddhist pamphlets, bullhorns, bad accounts, accountants, air-conditioning systems, aerosols, appendages, Armani jackets, arms, accoutrements, ancillary staff, airline meals, antipasti, antihistamines, apples, anterior lobes, axis vertebrae, armature, armaments, aeroplanes, aortas, aniseed balls, artichokes, aunts, answering machines, anarchist texts, alabaster, actuaries, apologia, asthma inhalers, amphetamines, alphabets and air-fresheners, along with copies of the Koran and three well-thumbed editions of Trubshawe's little book, The Twelve Point Path to Personal Enlightenment, were seven people who'd never previously met.

Intermingled with Episcopalians, evangelists, Methodists, Muslims, Moonies, Mormons, Baptists, Buddhists, Baha'ists, Lutherans, Roman Catholics, Confucianists, Armenians, Arminians, Greek and Russian Orthodox, Jews, Jehovah's Witnesses, Wesleyans, Wiccans, Calvinists, animists, Zoroastrians, Taoists, Shintoists, spiritualists, Scientologists, Seventh-day Adventists, pantheists, atheists, Anabaptists, Quakers and assorted devotees of various New Age groupings and communicants of no faith at all, were Eliot, who was Jewish, but not so you'd notice, and had held down a good job with good prospects. Jesus was a nominal Catholic, and had had a lousy job with appalling prospects. Mike had had a good but potentially hazardous job and was also a nominal Catholic. Maria was Catholic too, and had had a truly dreadful job no one officially knew about. Consuela, confusingly, was a Pentacostalist, and had had a reasonably okay job which had been due to end shortly in her well-earned retirement.

John, who used different names as he went out and about, had a rewarding job and had been born a Baptist, later becoming a Muslim before entering, finally, into a trenchant and bitter atheism. Suzi had been born and bred as a Buddhist, married an Episcopalian but had recently been dabbling with a curious, Westernized variant of Hinduism. Together, mingling with thousands of others, they billowed out of the sky, atomized.

'Jesus fucking Christ!' Eliot yelled. 'Did you see that? Holy fuck!' Then he did a double take. 'Hey! What the fuck's this? Can anyone else hear me?'

Several hundred voices answered, most of them telling him to shut the fuck up. Those closest, with whom his disintegrated self was now engaging in an appalling kind of Brownian motion, along with some of the material paraphernalia of his earthly working life, spoke loudest.

'Hey, Jew boy! Can it!' Mike was pissed off, and sounded like it. A few of the other voices close by protested at his outburst. 'Gee, sorry. I'm not prejudiced, it's just that . . . '

'That's okay, honey,' said Consula. 'We're all aggravated. I was coming up to retirement!'

'That's a bitch,' John butted in, then apologized. 'Sorry 'bout the language. Sheeee-yut.'

Everyone was quiet for an instant, then Maria spoke, surprised that, limited in life to Isthmaic Spanish, she was widely understood for once. 'So what was all that about? Someone said it was a plane crash or something. I don't work near any windows so all I saw was lots of people rushing about before the flames reached me.

'God. It must've been terrorists or something, Eliot said. 'Two planes. Two planes there were. I saw the second one just before I got fried. What kind of fucker does that kind of thing?'

'I reckon it's them fuckin' ragheads,' John ventured. 'I know those muthafuckers, so just believe me.'

'So why us? Hell, what I ever do to them, handin' round sandwiches?'

'Why any of us, sweetheart? I'm Jesus, by the way. Several people round and about laughed at that, and Jesus laughed too, as he could see the joke.

'You know,' said Suzi, 'I wouldn't be surprised if it was the CIA or someone.'

'Yeah, right!' Mike laughed. 'So's Bush can whack Iraq.' Several people close by muttered how they'd never voted for that son of a bitch, while others yelled at them to pipe down.

'Come on!' Mike yelled back. 'What odds does it make now?' Despite himself, he was beginning to laugh. 'Hey . . . uh . . . Eliot, right? Who d'you think really done this? The towelheads, like the brother over here says?'

'I know them, Mike,' John interjected.

'Yeah, sure, but so what? Well?'

Eliot pondered for a moment. 'There's something about this that stinks, you know,' he said, beginning to giggle. The tiny corporeal remnants of thousands of people jeered or laughed ta that, but Eliot out across them. 'No, listen. This is one big fucking thing that's happened here, and who the fuck knows what's going to happen as a result, yeah? This could, like, be the end of the world, you know?' A few evangelicals fluttered in the wind in something like rapture. 'But there's something fishy, right?'

'Go on,' Mike guffawed.

'Yeah, hang on.' Eliot raised his voice. 'Hew, Chuck!' In the cloud someone shouted back.

That you, Eliot? What the fuck you make of that, huh?'

'Too damn right, buddy. But d'you remember that stuff that was coming up yesterday? No, this is serious! That trading you thought was kinda weird?'

'Hell, that's right! Looked like someone somewhere knew something big was gonna come up. That fucker made a fucking killing outa what went down here today.'

A loud burst of laughter volleyed through the widening cloud.

'That's what I'm saying, Mike, right? You can say it's terrorists or some kinda government set-up case or whatever. I'm looking criminal mastermind here!'

'Get outta here!' Mike was now having trouble speaking through the gulps of hilarity.

Just think about it, you miserable Mick Polack asshole!' They both laughed as their ashes wafted together and then apart again. 'Perfect cover if you get some dumb buncha terrorists from Palestine or Iran or wherever to think they're stomping on old Uncle Sam, you put up the money and go along with the whole crazy fucking line but all the time you're using them to pull off the biggest heist in fucking History! You do the insider dealing through the brokers in the WTC and then destroy the fucking evidence! The government goes after your patsies in the jellabas and you're home free!'

'Yeah!' shouted Chuck. "Then you whack the fucking whole lot into armaments and airlines, now the price is low!'

'You just stole that from Die Hard!' someone laughed.

'Yeah, so why couldn't someone else? I can see him now, on his secret island somewhere . . . '

The Seagull Books Catalogue, 2016–17

'Stroking his fucking white cat!' John interrupted, and they all started laughing so hard they nearly choked.

And down they tumbled, all those atomized people suddenly so cruelly reduced to motes and specks falling from the cobalt sky, people from Manhattan and Queens and Brooklyn and from Jersey and Manchester and London, with their origins in California or Hampshire or Lahore or Tokyo or Karachi or Dahomey or Benin or Shanghai or Timbuktu or Tashkent or Bombay or Pretoria or Manila, Germans, Italians, Scotsmen, Irish, Poles, Russians, Mexicans, Guatemalans, Haitians, Indonesians, Australians, New Zealanders, Cajuns, Dutchmen, people from Iberia and Scythia and the Indus Valley and the Arabian Peninsula and Mesopotamia and Phoenicia and Babylon and Caesarea and sub-Saharan Africa and the Kalahari and the Gobi and remnants of the Golden Horde and the peoples who'd crossed into Europe and over Alaska into the New World and sailed the Pacific from island to island and the Atlantic in slave ships and steamers from Liverpool and all of them could have traced their ancestors all the way back to the Rift Valley, all those people mixed up together in that morbid thunderhead obnubilating the narrow canyons below.

They were all still laughing fit to bust when Consula shushed them.

'Hey, everyone! What's that noise?' Some feet below they could now hear not laughter or the cacophonous rumbling as their own molecules collided and displaced vast volumes of surrounding air, but instead a piteous moaning and wailing.

'Jesus!' said Jesus. 'Isn't that Mohammed?'

'Fuck me! You're right!'

'Yo, Mohammed! Chill, brother!'

Beneath them the wailing ceased for an instant, then started again.

'No! No! This isn't right! This isn't what's meant to happen! What am I doing here?'

'Hey, folks!' John shouted breezily. 'Poor ole Mohammed here thinks he should be in Paradise right now, lickin' pussy with 20000 vestal virgins!' The laughter was now even more uproarious than before, but Mohammed didn't join in.

'Keep away from me! Keep those women away from my body! This is not right! Those women must not defile my body!' The sky now filled with expanding laughter, increasingly happy and joyous and filled with an exponentially growing, unconditional, universal and carefree love.

'Come on, girls, Maria cried out to Consuela and Suzi, let's show poor little Mohammed how things stand round here now!' Consuela and Suzi whooped with almost hysterical joy, and swooped down after Maria to engulf Mohammed, whose screams of dismay were lost in the babel of cackling and chortling, tittering, sniggering, smirking, guffawing and helpless, helpless laughter as they all high-fived the dead Algonquins and Apaches and Armenians and Albanians and Argentines and Bulgarians and Biafrans and Cubans and Chileans and Chechens and Cambodians and deviants and the disabled and Ethiopians and East Timorese and Filipinos and Guatemalans and Gypsies and Haitians and Iraqis and Iranians and Jews and Jews and Jews and Kurds and Kosovars and Lithuanians and Letts and Laotians and Mexicans and Mayans and Nicaraguans and Olympian gods and occultists and Poles and Palestinians and quislings and Russians and Serbians and Tutsis and troublemakers and Uranians and Vietnamese and witches and Xhosas and young babies and Zulus whose subatomic particles ubiquitously and completely filled the skies along with their laughter, making it blue over the edge of a republic constantly spawning Coriolanuses to battle for autistic hegemonies. It took a while for Mike and Jesus and Eliot and John to be able to speak again. Eventually, breathlessly, John said: 'You know, there is one thing I don't quite get . . . '

And then they all understood everything, and there was no further need to speak as they settled, like snow on Christmas Day, over the mistakes of Manhattan.

Syd Barrett, the Death of England and the End of Time: 10 May 2007

Unpublished

On 10 May 2007, at the Trimdon Labour Club in his Sedgefield constituency, Tony Blair finally announced the date of his long awaited resignation.

For months beforehand, British politics had been languishing in a strange kind of stasis; a grey area where nothing much really happened or could happen, and time itself seemed to judder to a halt as it waited for the final consummation. For years prior to that, the British political classes had been obsessed to an almost theological degree by the minutiae of this secular eschatology, fuelled by a new kind of Kremlinology, the inexact science which had once speculated on the intricacies of Soviet politics by speculating on the precise meaning behind the position and body language of the stony-faced old men in the Politburo standing on Lenin's granite mausoleum in Moscow. That obsession was, in turn, poisoned by further, seemingly endless speculation about the personal dysfunctionalities at the heart of the Labour government and the so-called project launched by Blair and his former friend Gordon Brown, one of the chief architects of the electoral tactic they called 'New Labour'. Famously, Brown and Blair were alleged to have concocted a sort of pact over dinner in an Islington restaurant called Granita after the death of Labour leader John Smith in 1994: Brown was said to have agreed to stand aside in the election to succeed Smith in favour of Blair, on the understanding that Blair would eventually make way for Brown. In the meantime, Brown, operating from the Treasury, would have a guiding hand in all domestic policy.

On 30 September 2004, Blair told the BBC that, should Labour be re-elected, he would serve a 'full third term' as prime minister but would not fight a fourth general election. He also said, confusingly, that he would allow 'ample time' for his successor to establish him- or herself before the next election. At the time, the ambiguities and contradictions contained within these statements made many people wonder what exactly he meant by a 'full third term' which also incorporated the 'ample time' his successor would need as prime minister, although no one took these worries to their logical conclusion by assuming that Blair was claiming to be able to spin the physical laws of time out of their standard settings. During the 2005 general election, the Conservative opposition, on the cusp of entering their longest period out of government since before the Great Reform Act of 1832, tried to frighten the voters with the slogan 'Vote Blair, Get Brown'. The electorate, however deep their disgust and boredom with Blair, returned Labour with a majority of 66, well in excess of Margaret Thatcher's majority of 43 in 1979 in the election following the Winter of Discontent when, notoriously, the dead lay unburied. Halfway through the campaign, despite rumours of the unbridgeable hatreds separating them, Brown and Blair started appearing in public together, purportedly encouraged to do so by Alastair Campbell, Blair's former director of communications and frequently cited, despite his repeated denials, as behind an unattributable briefing describing Brown as 'psychologically flawed'. A week or so before the election, Piers Morgan, the then disgraced former editor of the *Daily Mirror*, described Blair and Brown on the BBC *Today* programme as being like Lennon and McCartney, far better together than when they were apart.

Nonetheless, 16 months later, Blair finally capitulated to mounting pressure from Brown and his supporters and agreed to go sometime in the next year, making way for his chancellor, almost certainly, to succeed him. Blair's decision was triggered in the short term by an attempted putsch by several previously loyal MPs in the dog days towards the end of that summer. On 5 September, the birthday of the absolutist monarch Louis XIV, the bandit Jesse James and the German Romantic painter Caspar David Friedrich and the anniversary of the end of the Great Fire of London and the start of the First Opium War, 17 Labour MPs signed a letter calling for Blair to resign. The next day, 7 of the signatories resigned as parliamentary private secretaries, laying their jobs, albeit unpaid, on the line to hasten Blair's exit. Partly their impatience was fear. Despite the previous year's election victory, with the lowest share of the popular vote for a party forming a majority government in the history of the House of Commons, Blair was seen increasingly as an electoral liability. In that May's local elections, Labour's share of the vote fell to 26 per cent, putting them in third place behind the Liberal Democrats, and in the Scottish Assembly elections the Labour–Liberal coalition was beaten by the Scottish Nationalists. It was widely believed that Blair was too bemerded by his serial misjudgements, over Iraq, over cash for honours (although it wouldn't be until December that year that Blair became the first serving prime minister to be interviewed by the police in relation to an ongoing criminal investigation) and over his failure, in July, to add his voice to the near-universal condemnation of Israel's disastrous incursion into Southern Lebanon to eliminate the threat from Hezbollah, the 'Party of God'.

On 7 September, the day the PPSs resigned, the Kremlinologists guessed that something must have shifted when a photographer captured a pale, prissy rictus, which they interpreted as a smile, on Brown's face as he was being driven away from a meeting with Blair at 10 Downing Street, and shortly thereafter Blair announced that his speech to the Labour Party Conference that year would be his last. Sure enough, on 26 September, after cracking a rather good joke about the unlikelihood of his wife running off with the bloke next door—responding to frenzied media reports that Cherie Blair had called Brown a liar while watching his speech the previous day—Blair stated, 'this is my last Conference as leader.' When he finished, during the obligatory standing ovation, several people, either delegates or party workers, held up handwritten placards imploring him not to go, in a sort of do-it-yourself echo of Japanese Kamikaze pilots' war cry of 'Banzai', roughly translated as 'May the Emperor live for ten thousand years', although the word was also used in China during the Cultural Revolution with reference to the hoped-for longevity of Chairman Mao Zedong.

But still the prick-tease went on. In effect, Blair was resigning in disgrace because of the series of monumental mistakes he'd made, and yet with an almost brilliantly glacial slowness. It took him another seven months, up until 2 May 2007, to announce that he would be stepping down as prime minister 'in a matter of weeks', although in the meantime, in March, he'd admitted that it had, perhaps, been a political mistake to admit the previous September that he was going. He also finally grudgingly conceded that Gordon Brown, his slow-motion assassin, was probably the best man to succeed him, blithely indifferent to the witness of the strands of cloying pasta in front of him 13 years before in Granita. On 3 May, Niccolò Machiavelli's birthday and the 292nd anniversary of the last total eclipse of the sun over London, Downing Street clarified that the exact date of Blair's resignation would be announced on 10 May, which also happens to be the birthday of John Wilkes Booth, the assassin of Abraham Lincoln.

Blair duly quit as leader of the Labour Party at a special party conference in Manchester on 24 June, and at lunchtime on 27 June formally tendered his resignation to the queen at Buckingham Palace. He'd filled the intervening weeks with a farewell tour, a bit like Dorothy Squires or a superannuated rock star on a last hurrah to augment the pension plan. On 20 May, the day in 1940 when the first batch of prisoners arrived at the newly built concentration camp at Auschwitz, Blair arrived unannounced in Iraq, landing in the heavily fortified Green Zone in Baghdad a couple of hours after a mortar bomb had narrowly missed the British Embassy and during a weekend when eight American service personnel were killed and 43 Iraqi citizens were found murdered. Ten days later, on a tour of Africa, he visited Colonel Gaddafi in his tent in the Libyan desert, and on 1 June at the University of South Africa Business School he gave a speech passionately defending the liberal interventionist policy he'd championed with George W. Bush, and which had led directly to the deaths of the 51 people whose corpses were strewn beyond his view in Baghdad a week and a half previously.

Just under four weeks later, he also resigned his Sedgefield seat through the arcane parliamentary procedure of being appointed Crown Steward and Bailiff of the Three Chiltern Hundreds of Stoke, Desborough and Burnham in the county of Buckinghamshire, a bosky, wooded area on the chalky escarpments in the Vale of Aylesbury, once notorious as a hideout for local thieves. Very early in his political career, Blair had stood in a by-election in May 1982 from the Beaconsfield constituency in the same county, home to the Lilliputian Bekonscot Model Village, and succeeded in more or less halving Labour's share of the vote from 20.2 per cent in the general election of 1979 to 10.4 per cent, losing his deposit as a consequence. In the general election the following year, however, bucking the trend that saw Labour's national vote fall by over three million, Blair was elected to the safe seat in the North East from which he was now resigning with such despatch. As he had in Beaconsfield, during the 1983 campaign in Sedgefield, Blair declared himself to be both a socialist and, as a member of CND, a keen supporter of unilateral nuclear disarmament.

Before going to the Palace, Blair held his last Prime Minister's Questions. He played it mainly for laughs, twinged with a kind of brusque, gulping sentimentality, particularly in response to valedictory remarks made by Rev. Ian Paisley. He concluded the session in that strange, hesitant, rather phlegmy choking voice he'd perfected over the years, sounding like a small child about to burst into tears, by saying, 'That is that. The end'. The *e* in *the* was oddly elongated before being cut off abruptly, followed by the briefest of beats before *end*, the modulations in his voice rising minutely, as if he were about to turn the phrase into a rhetorical question. Blair then received an unprecedented standing ovation from both sides of the House of Commons, although Alex Salmond, leader of the Scottish National Party, first minister of Scotland and one of the drafters of a parliamentary motion to impeach Tony Blair as prime minister in 2004, remained seated. David Cameron, the leader of the Opposition and, before he entered politics, a public-relations officer for Carlton TV, initially hesitated for a second or two before joining in with the applause from the Labour benches, and then urged Conservative members behind him to join in too by sweeping both his arms forward in an upward motion, a bit like someone baling water out of a small, foundering boat.

And who knows? Maybe the applause was justified. After all, in his 10 years as prime minister and 13 as leader of the Labour Party, Blair had achieved much. In 1994, at the Party Conference in the Winter Gardens in Blackpool, he'd announced that Clause IV of the Labour Party Constitution, written by Sidney and Beatrice Webb and described by former Labour leader Harold Wilson as 'theology', was to be rewritten, specifically to remove the party's commitment to 'the common ownership of the means of production, distribution and exchange'. Thus, either unencumbered or denuded, Blair led what he now called 'New Labour' to a landslide victory in the 1997, winning again in 2001 and 2005, thereby delivering the party, whatever its name, three successive governments for the first time in its history. In government, he brought in devolution for Scotland and Wales, paving the way, in 2006, for the SNP to form a government for the first time in Scotland and Plaid Cymru to forge a coalition in government with Labour in Wales (Elfyn Llwyd, the leader of Plaid

CONGRATULATIONS!
YOU ARE NOW
LEAVING REALITY!

CLIMATE
SCIENCE

The Guardian, February 2010

Cymru's MPs at Westminster, worked alongside Salmond to draft the motion to impeach Blair.) He also brokered the Good Friday Agreement in Northern Ireland, introduced the minimum wage and civil partnerships and started at least four wars on three different continents. He also bestowed a knighthood on Mick Jagger of the Rolling Stones, a 'fucking paltry' honour according to Keith Richards, and one which had reputedly been denied to Mick for decades because of persistent rumours that he'd once fucked Princess Margaret. (Unlike her niece-in-law Diana, Margaret had no breathy panegyrics read over her coffin by Tony Blair, although there was a minor scandal six weeks later when her mother, the Queen Mother, died aged 102, and it was reported that Alastair Campbell had attempted to put pressure on the Royal Household to give Blair a greater role in the obsequies.)

And, in one of his first actions as prime minister, he'd invited Margaret Thatcher round to 10 Downing for tea.

That made sense. Although Blair and the desperate opportunists surrounding him had reaped enormous dividends from the simple fact that they weren't the Tories, the chimera they'd created in New Labour had been devised to be as much like the Tories as possible, only with something approaching a human face. As the comedian Mark Thomas put it at the time, Blairism was just Thatcherism with added K-Y Jelly. But although New Labour marked the abandonment, in a Labour Party led by Blair and Brown at least, of the centuries' old project of mass political engagement to oppose and create alternatives to the monstrosities of industrialized capitalism and its bene-ficiaries, what was embraced in its place was, if you questioned it for a second, pretty weird. Partly through a frenzy for a new found commitment to ideology, partly as class spite and partly from a muddle-headed force of habit

When Thatcher resigned, she'd been prime minister for almost the whole of my adult life. The general election of 1979 was the first I was able to vote in, and I voted Labour, as I have in almost every subsequent election, both local and national. Early on the morning of 4 May 1979, some friends of mine and I drunkenly sang 'The Red Flag' in the deserted market place in Cambridge as Robert Rhodes-James, newly elected Conservative MP for the city, delivered his inaudible victory address from the balcony of the town hall. As a student, I marched through Cambridge's streets protesting against Thatcher's policies towards the National Health Service, nuclear weapons and South Africa, and as a tyro student-cartoonist, I ridiculed her war in the Falklands. Later, after graduating, I marched through London in support of CND, back when Tony Blair was still a member, and in 1985, I illustrated and wrote, albeit pseudony-mously, a book called *Lower Than Vermin: An Anatomy of Thatcher's Britain*, a general attack on her, her government, its policies and the Zeitgeist they'd created. I loathed and despised Thatcher and everything about her, and so when she went, forced out by her party because of her serial misjudgements over Europe and the poll tax, I rejoiced. My wife and I drank champagne, and, later that night, I drank more champagne with the poet Blake Morrison in his flat, feeling jubilant.

I loathed and despised everything about Tony Blair too, in some ways even more than I hated Thatcher. I hated his studied, gulping, mannered gaucheness, his Tiggerish enthusiasm, his 'Hey, guys!' faux mateyness, his Christianity, his Christian-school-prefect earnestness, his stupid chimp face and mad eyes, his facial tics, his shit-eating grin and the way his fingertips touched to form his hands into a vacuous sphere when he stood in repose. I despised his lies, his wars, his cowardice, his bogus strength, his fawning, his sycophancy, his worship of money and power and the way the soft flesh puckered under his eyes. I abhorred his weakness, his betrayals, his pettiness, his preachiness, his tears, his acting, his makeup, the throb in his voice and his sense of his own rectitude. His awareness of his own capacity for charm made me want to puke. His rather gimpish good looks (at least to start with) made me want to scream. I loathed the way he'd ripped the heart, lungs and soul out of the Labour Party and replaced them with all the callous, craven, spiteful, sour self-righteousness of Thatcherism. But most of all I couldn't stand his flawed informality, that nauseating 'Hi! I'm Tony!'-ness, the casualwear from Next, the photos of the family on his coffee mug, the singing animatronic fish he had on his office wall which he showed to Bush and, worst of all, the fact that he clearly thought, in his heart of hearts, and despite all the evidence that he was and is as mad as a sack of snakes, that he was the most ordinary and down to earth bloke you could ever wish to meet and that, as a consequence, somehow or other he was *rock 'n' roll*.

Margaret Thatcher had announced her own resignation on 22 November 1990, on the advice of her cabinet, and resigned as prime minister five days later, after the election of John Major as leader of the Conservative Party. Twenty-seven years earlier, to the day, President John F. Kennedy was shot dead in Dallas, Texas, his brains blown out and spattered over his wife Jackie's beautiful dress. Also dying that day, although the news of their deaths was overshadowed by the Kennedy assassination, were C. S. Lewis, the creator of the fairy-tale land of Narnia, and Aldous Huxley, author of *The Doors of Perception*, a book published in 1954 describing his experiences with the psychotropic drug mescalin. Huxley had taken his title from a line in a poem by William Blake: 'If the doors of perception were cleansed, everything would appear to man as it is: infinite.' And Huxley's title had been taken by Jim Morrison to provide the name for his band, The Doors. Morrison, a tousle-haired, charismatic frontman who later turned into an obese and shambling drunk, died on 3 July 1971 in Paris and, like Agamemnon and Marat, in the bath. Although no autopsy was ever carried out, he was reported to have died of a heroin overdose, having inhaled the drug mistaking it for cocaine.

Aged 27, Morrison was instantly inducted into an unconscious club of rock stars who'd died, deliciously young, at the same age. The first rank of the Pantheon consists of Morrison, Brian Jones, Janis Joplin, Jimi Hendrix and Kurt Cobain. Hendrix, like Attila the Hun, choked to death on his own vomit; Joplin, like Morrison, probably died of a heroin overdose; Kurt Cobain's brains were blown out by a gun shot, like Kennedy's and Hitler's; and Brian Jones either accidentally or was deliberately drowned in a swimming pool in the grounds of his house, formerly owned by A. A. Milne, the author of *Winnie the Pooh*. Other rockers dead at 27, but in the second rank, include Canned Heat's Alan 'Blind Owl' Wilson, dead of a barbiturate overdose; Stone the Crows' guitarist Leslie Harvey, who was electrocuted by a microphone; The Grateful Dead's keyboardist Ron 'Pigpen' McKernan, who died of a gastrointestinal haemorrhage associated with alcoholism; Badfinger's keyboardist and guitarist Pete Ham who hanged himself; Uriah Heep's former bassist Gary Thain, from a drug overdose and, decades later in 2008, Australian Idol–contestant and popstar-wannabe Levi Kereama, who fell off a high-rise balcony, possibly suicidally. And in the third rank, dying at 26 or 28, are Otis Redding (plane crash), Gram Parsons (heroin), Nick Drake (accidental overdose of antidepressants), Tim Buckley (heroin), Steve Gaines of Lynyrd Skynyrd (plane crash), Blood Sweat and Tears' Gregory Herbert (overdose); Jimmy McCullough, guitarist with Thunderclap Newman and Wings (heroin); Jethro Tull's John Glascock (heart disease) and The Red Hot Chili Peppers' original guitarist Hillel Slovak (heroin).

But the day Blair announced his long overdue resignation, which should have been in disgrace but through some dark and hideous magic seemed, instead, to be another triumph of deception, I didn't crack open the champagne.

Instead, on 10 May 2007, I went to a Syd Barrett concert.

This was the opening chapter and a fragment from a proposed but thereafter unwritten book whose main argument—how rock 'n' roll has been dominating Western culture since the mid-twentieth century, as a force for ceaseless commodification, globalization and infantilization—I finally articulated in verse form in the title poem to my 2022 collection, The Love Songs of Late Capitalism (*Smokestack Books*). *The title poem is reprinted in this volume on pp. ###–##.*

My Three Mothers

The Guardian, April 2007

There's invariably a point in the electoral cycle (it happened about a month ago) when Conservative politicians start going on about The Family. It's always struck me as a pretty cheap trick, because it invariably allows only one template for the family (mum, dad, a limited number of children) and not only ignores but also tends to demonize all the others. It's also impossibly glib and seeks to flatten human beings down into a manageable conformity, unable or unwilling to accept their variety or the often truly bizarre ways they interconnect. For my part, I'm the result of several different variants on the standard, approved model: I've experienced, consciously and unconsciously, the consequences of single-parenthood (twice), adoption, several bereavements, step-parenthood, bitter and unresolved estrangements, extended families and most of the other joys and pratfalls of family life, and I'm damned if I'm going to let anyone diss my mums, all three of them.

The mother I probably knew best was my adoptive one, Annie. She'd given birth to a son of her own, Christopher, in 1955. But he was born prematurely and with a blocked oesophageal track, and died aged only two weeks. My parents then adopted my older sister, and a couple of years later tried to adopt another little girl, Naomi, but she was diagnosed with a brain tumour before the adoption could take place, and subsequently died. Thus, in 1959, they adopted me.

The life of Annie, before marrying my adoptive father, had been mixed, to say the least. Before the war, in her parents' tiny house in Carshalton, she shared a bed with two of her five sisters and had a difficult relationship with her mother. However, in 1940, because her father was a Hoover salesman, her prospects changed considerably for the better when the Hoover Company evacuated Annie, and her immediately older and younger sisters, to America. Annie and her younger sister Dawne spent five idyllic years living with the Kohl family in North Canton, Ohio, where they thrived. That said, they never heard a word or received a single letter from their parents. When the war ended in 1945, the evacuees were told they had to return home, but when they finally arrived at Euston on the train from Liverpool, Dawne and Annie walked straight past their parents without recognizing them. Worse, Annie had been about to graduate to high school in America, but, aged 15, was now beyond the school leaving age at home, so her education stopped dead. Instead, she went back to sleeping three in a bed and was sent to work on a production line in a perfume factory in Carshalton, despite her American foster father writing to her parents offering to pay for her further schooling in England. Dawne told me she found the letter after her parents died, shoved at the back of a drawer. They'd never bothered to reply.

She finally escaped the perfume factory when she trained to be a nurse, and thereafter went on to become a midwife. It was when she was working at the Kent and Canterbury hospital that she met my adoptive father.

After her marriage—more specifically, after my arrival—she also finally severed all connections with her parents. I was always told this was because they'd looked at me, said they didn't think much of me and suggested they send me back and get another one. This, I've now been told, was completely untrue, but Annie probably used it as a justification for something she'd wanted to do for years. One consequence is that I have no memory of my grandmother, and I only remember seeing my grandfather once, when I was 10, and that was at Annie's funeral in 1969, after she'd died during an operation to treat a cerebral aneurysm.

She was funny and difficult and capricious and (like all parents) occasionally embarrassing, but bursting with life, despite what proved to be her own tenuous hold on it. Her own family life had been far from perfect, and the forces of history and Christopher's death snatched from her both the alternative and loving family who took her in in Ohio and a genetic family of her own. She was beset by other tragedies. When she was a district midwife in Hove, before she married my father, a baby she delivered died. Although there was no question of her personal culpability, she blamed herself. According to my aunt, in the strange way people do, she saw Christopher's death as payback.

But she didn't repine, and set about choosing a whole series of other families as compensation. There was my sister and me, but also the dozens and dozens of babies she fostered until her first illness in 1966.

Thirty-eight years on, I still dream about her often, and my memories, from when I was 10 and younger, are extraordinarily vivid. I put that down to the intensity of her love, and the power of her personality.

The mother I knew least was Kathleen, my birth mother. I didn't even know her name until I was 38, and didn't find anything more about her—such as the fact that I was the third of her eleven children, five of whom were born outside of marriage, and two put up for adoption—until I was 41 and I accessed my adoption records.

As I later found out, she was the only child of a labourer in the naval dockyards on Portland Bill. At the age of 20, she had a child outside of marriage, and then another one a couple of years later. She kept both these children, or more precisely they were reared by her parents while she sought employment as a technical assistant in London. According to an interview before my adoption in 1959, the father of these two children was a sea captain who repeatedly assured her that he would leave his wife and children, but never did. Then, in London, she had me and, according to the gossip of my adoptive family, her parents made it clear that they weren't 'prepared to rear a third bastard'. Thus my adoption. But as I later discovered, after me, Kathleen had a fourth child outside of marriage, my younger sister Jan, who was also put up for adoption. After that, she entered into a relationship with an American serviceman stationed at the US embassy in London and had her fifth child outside of marriage. This was another boy, whom she named Martin. Earlier, she'd given me that name, but she clearly liked it, so used it again. This time she married the father, returned with him to California and, over the next decade, had a further six sons. But she also left her two oldest children in Portland, with her parents, and it wasn't until her mother died and her father claimed that he couldn't cope on his own that all three of them came to America too.

Even beyond the unforgiving cultural mores of the 50s, Kathleen's initial career in motherhood was atrocious. She said during her interview that she promised never to do this kind of thing again. Thus she fell victim to that exclusionary version of The Family that compelled unmarried mothers to give up their children for adoption, in my case and in Jan's. But although forces beyond her control may have led to her legal estrangement from two of her children, her temporary abandonment of the first two is slightly less explicable, and my oldest brother told me that, even on her deathbed, she refused to tell him who his father was.

That said, she became a matriarch. My birth siblings say she was widely and deeply loved, and that hundreds of people came to her funeral when she died in 1994, six years before I knew anything about her. Although I hardly knew her at all, the emotion I hold for her is probably a kind of love, a blend of sympathy for her circumstances, admiration for how she overcame them and, indeed, simple gratitude for giving birth to me in the first place.

I knew my third mother the longest. My stepmother Jos was born in 1921 in Argentina, where her father was chief accountant at an Anglo-Argentinian railway company. When her family returned to England in 1938, she was first sent by her father to work in a department store in Worthing, West Sussex, until, like Annie, she escaped into nursing, and thereafter into midwifery.

For the next 30 or more years she belonged to a class, if it still exists at all, that now too falls outside the strict definition of the perfect family. Thanks to Thatcherism's denigration of the principle of public service, we tend now to look down on spinsters such as Jos, who, for whatever reason, chose their career over the sanctity of marriage. She ended up more or less at the top of her profession, as matron in charge of midwifery

New Humanist, February 2003

at Lewisham hospital, when she married my widowed father in 1973. Most of her professional life was spent surrounded by babies, although she never had a child herself.

Before that she'd worked in dozens of other hospitals, and in 1955 she was the ward sister at the hospital where Annie was admitted during her pregnancy with Christopher. As they were both midwives, these two of my mothers formed an affinity, which soon grew into friendship. It was Jos who took Christopher to the theatre for the operation on his blocked oesophagus. Thereafter, she took his tiny corpse to the morgue. Soon afterwards, she became my sister's godmother, after her adoption, and she became my godmother too, even though I was never baptized.

Just under four years later, she married my father, and stayed married for the next 31 years until his death in January 2004, which was followed three and a half months later by Jos' own death. The marriage wasn't without its rocky patches. Few are. There was also a complete breakdown in Jos' relationship with my older sister, which went unresolved for 28 years until Jos died. And, in some strange, unquantifiable way, I always knew that my relationship with her was less intense than it was with Annie, although my blood ties to both of them were equally non-existent. None the less, I meant it when I whispered in her ear the night before she died that I loved her very much, and thanked her for being my mother.

Which she was, just as much as the other two, despite their genetic or formative claims to precedence. I had, after all, known her all my life, from even earlier than I'd appreciated, as I found out after her funeral. One of her cousins said, as she was leaving our house, that we'd met before. I was just about to say that I remembered meeting her many times, when she interrupted to say that she'd held me in her arms in the taxi when she and Jos had taken delivery of me from the mother and baby home in Barrowgate Road in Chiswick, after my adoption had been approved, to take me to my new parents' home in North London.

And what is motherhood about anyway? Genetics? Birth? Rearing? Support? Just being there? It's all of those, plus, of course, love, if you're lucky. In my case, I got all of those, in part, from three women, who connect together through me, but also through each other. Jos and Annie were friends; but I also have compelling evidence that Annie and Kathleen met, albeit unofficially and probably illegally. Then there's babies: Annie adopted and fostered them, Jos delivered thousands of them, while Kathleen gave birth to more than most people. And then there's America, providing two of my mothers with golden memories of idyllic childhoods, which, moreover, coloured the rest of their lives. And it provided my other mother with the redemptive power to reinvent herself from serially fallen woman to loving matriarch.

Maybe I'm just being insanely romantic here, and seeing connecting threads that don't exist. Then again, romance shouldn't be discounted, any more than bad behaviour, caprice, bitterness, rancour and all the other all-too-human traits usually left out of the paradigm of the perfect family. None of my mothers was perfect, and their imperfections cut in all sorts of different ways. But, in different but equally valid ways, I loved all of them. And, unlike the peddlers of the fantasy of family values, I'm not going to judge a single one of them.

The Dog Allusion

An Excerpt

Vintage, 2008

Dawkins prefaces *The God Delusion* with a dedication to the memory of his dead friend Douglas Adams, author of *The Hitchhiker's Guide to the Galaxy*, and with the following quotation: 'Isn't it enough to see that a garden is beautiful without having to believe that there are fairies at the bottom of it too?' The trouble with that laudable sentiment is that it leaves out the human element.

We're predisposed to populate everything around us with the creations of our imaginations as we project our empathy in all directions, second-guessing what's hidden in the shrubbery. Once we bother looking there, the 'rational' parts of our minds will inform us that there aren't in fact any fairies there at all, and so as usual we'll continue to navigate our way through our lives making judgement calls based on the evidence of our own eyes. But that first second-guess has already lodged in our brains, and diffuses out into our other thoughts, and we might still conclude that there really are fairies at the bottom of the garden simply because we like the idea. We like its unlikelihood; we like the notion of an alternative to the dull reality of our observable, mundane existence. Then we're charmed by the thought of the fairies; we might even laugh at the thought that the fairies are really there, and in so doing we release some endorphins into the biochemical systems of our bodies, and they make us feel good. So that makes us think it's actually a good idea to believe in the fairies, so to all intents and purposes, despite the empirical evidence, there are fairies at the bottom of the garden after all.

And we like that idea. It's nice. The fairies are nice too, although we never see them, but that's another thing that's nice about them. Some people might think we're mad for believing there are fairies at the bottom of the garden, but in fact we're just being human in wanting them to be there.

But more important than that, believing in fairies at the bottom of the garden is harmless. It might, indeed, improve the way we behave, make us more thoughtful or considerate, help us with the other contingencies of everyday life by encouraging us to tell our children delightful and elaborate stories about the fairies which, although a part of us knows that the fairies don't really exist, make our children laugh and therefore be happy, and that makes us happy too.

In fact, the only thing wrong with believing in fairies at the bottom of the garden is when you take that belief as the basis on which to build a priesthood which compels all your neighbours to believe only in the fairies at the bottom of your garden, and insists that the fairies at the bottom of their gardens are evil demons who will make their every action so evil as well that your fairies won't let your neighbours play with them after they've died.

And then you start killing your neighbours because they don't believe you.

Previously unpublished

The Cartoonist's Secret Code

The Guardian, October 2008

It will come as no surprise to other cartoonists that the great Carl Giles used to sneak subversive little images into the backgrounds of his drawings—like the torture and murder of Rupert Bear, one of the *Express'* other great cartoon signings. We all do, and always have, mostly because we can—or at least if we can get away with it.

In many ways it comes with the territory. Cartoons have long been established as oases of anarchy in newspapers. Simply in terms of layout, they break up the serried ranks of words on which they squat, like gargoyles. But cartoonists are also licensed jesters, part of whose role is to lower the tone. No surprise, then, that we should try to smuggle in all sorts of secret messages and private jokes under the editorial barbed wire, particularly if they involve a furtive dig at the boss and, as ever, biting the hand that feeds us.

This has been going on—albeit in other media—for centuries. The Gothic cathedrals of Europe are peppered with real gargoyles which are, in fact, stone caricatures of the dean and chapter; you can find the same kind of thing in medieval manuscripts.

Sometimes, the secret messages are entirely benign. The American caricaturist Al Hirschfeld would always weave his daughter's name into his drawings, disguised in the strands of Carole Lombard's hair or the pattern on Cole Porter's tie. Sometimes, it's straightforwardly venal. The *Evening Standard*'s cartoonist JAK notoriously filled his cartoons with brand names, guaranteeing an instant sale of the original to the corporate owners of the named brand. (After JAK's death, Nick Newman drew a cartoon of his funeral where all the surrounding tombstones were plastered with corporate logos.)

Usually, though, it's pure devilment. After the 1997 election, Steve Bell and I had a private competition to see who could first sneak in an image of Peter Mandelson as a used condom into a *Guardian* comment cartoon. I don't think either of us ever pulled that one off, but Steve stampeded ahead of the field in incorporating the word 'Fuck' into his cartoons, in the teeth of editorial disapproval. Although he won hands down in that little contest, I did manage, through the transformative magic of puns, to tell Tony Blair to fuck off in three different ways in my valedictory cartoon published just before his resignation.

I was then—as ever—the beneficiary of the *Guardian*'s impeccable traditions of freedom of expression with that cartoon, but what's truly subversive is the stuff that gets through, eluding the eagle-eyed subs. Throughout the 80s and 90s, whenever I

THE CARTOONIST'S CALENDAR

No. 161: *ALL THINGS MUST PASS*, and this is the last *Gentle Limning* with which I shall delight you —— so let's go out with the *ULTIMATE LIG* ~ to wit, *THE SELF-LIG!!!* with the launch of yer 'umble *CARTOONIST's* **BOOK** of *CARICATURE PORTRAITS* drawn for the walls of the **GAY HUSSAR** restaurant in London's *sleazy SOHO* ("Mugshots", 25 quid from POLITICO's, a *snip considering it* means I can now be with you *FOREVER!*) —— with NOBLE LORDS, T.U.C. GENERAL SECRETARIES, FORMER LEADERS OF THE LABOUR PARTY, HACKS, LAWYERS (just in case), PUBLISHERS (S. MAGEE), ANOTHER CARTOONIST, M.Ps, DRUNKS & *LIGGERS GALORE*, symbolised below by the Spirit of **SIMON HOGGART** (in the book; invited; doesn't turn up), to remind you, DEAR READER, of *ALL* the *LIGS* of the last 3½ years now, like the horns of *ELFLAND*, fading... fading... fading...   Toodlepip! 27th June '05

The Times, June 2005

covered a Soviet or post-Soviet news story, to create the mise en scene, I'd always bung in some slogans in Cyrillic script in the drawing, and one of these (as a little homage to Ralph Steadman's failure, with Hunter S Thompson, to spray paint the same message on the side of the yacht competing in the America's Cup) would always read, albeit unreadably, 'Fuck the Pope!'. Strangely, no one ever noticed, except for a well-educated sub on a paper I used to work for in Dublin.

Because the message is secret, it's always a dilemma as to whether or not you want to get caught, a bit like those notorious acrostics sacked hacks write into their final pieces, saying something hidden yet foul about their soon-to-be-ex bosses. At the time of the fall of the Berlin Wall, a Charles Griffin cartoon in the *Daily Mirror* (proprietor Robert Maxwell) included, in tiny tiny letters written on wall itself, the uplifting legend 'Maxwell is a cunt!' Naturally, Charlie blamed an unknown sub for defacing his artwork, a story he's stuck to ever since. More inventively, when Willie Rushton was sacked as the cartoonist for *Liberal News* in 1962, his last cartoon strip consisted of the characters dismantling the frames of the cartoon in such a way that the shapes spelt out the phrase 'Fuck Off'. And I pinched the idea when I was 'let go' by the *Times* a few years ago. Foolishly, they gave me two weeks' notice, so in my last cartoon—a broad, Hogarthian tableau of a book launch I'd attended—I posed the figures in the drawing in such a way as to spell out the words 'Fuck' and the name of the editor who'd sacked me.

Of course, this kind of *Where's Wally?* revenge is unbelievably puerile, and it's beyond question that I will never, ever work for the *Times* again. But cartoonists are meant to be puerile. That's why newspapers employ us. And either way, it made me feel a hell of a lot better, and probably just as good as it made Giles feel every time he sneakily strung up poor Rupert Bear.

Giving Offence

An Excerpt

Seagull Books and *Index on Censorship*, 2009

It's my job, as a satirical cartoonist, to give offence. But I need immediately to qualify that statement. I see my job as giving targeted offence, because satire, to borrow H. L. Mencken's definition of journalism, is about comforting the afflicted and afflicting the comfortable. In other words, if I draw rude pictures of people less powerful than myself, what I do ceases to be satire, and creeps into one of the wider spheres of aggressive, bullying humour and into areas I consider offensive.

So, although I'm inclined to think that the non-satirist's standard definition of satire as 'puncturing pomposity' is one of the most pompous phrases in the English language, I buy into it. This is because the urge to mock our social or political betters is something else hardwired into us, to stop us going mad at the injustice of their being held to be superior to us in the first place. Indeed, it's been argued by several anthropologists that early humans, unlike other social primates, lived in largely egalitarian groups, mostly as a result of the equal division of labour between the genders involved in hunting and gathering, but where the status quo was maintained by physically weaker individuals forming alliances against the strong and keeping them in their place through mockery. It was only later, once agriculture obliged us to live in settled communities, that the strong seized the opportunity to impose their will and power on the rest of us, thus reverting human beings back to the condition of baboons.

Perhaps because of this ancient race memory, mockery of the powerful is as ubiquitous as humour itself. In political tyrannies, tolerance of public expression of this kind of mockery is extremely limited, and bolstered by thousands of years of cultural conditioning, itself reinforced by the creation of taboos like blasphemy or lèse majesté, themselves closely linked and often interchangeable. Even in less oppressive political circumstances, these taboos endure.

To return for a moment to Diana. You can see in both the tragic and comic responses to her death the interplay of respecting and transgressing both political and religious taboos: on the religious side, there was the death taboo, as well as a kind of attenuated blasphemy when discussing a woman who had been elevated, by both the media and herself, to the status of a lay goddess; and on the political side, the instinctive deference to royalty and, in its way, a trace of the divine right of kings provided other taboos even though, ironically enough, the death of Diana threatened, for a short period, to destabilize the monarchy itself.

Although this whole seething compost of grief, death, religion and politics was riddled with irony, the public recognition of those ironies became a fresh taboo, and not for the first—or last—time it was confidently stated that Diana's death was a catastrophe so great that, once more, Satire— like Diana—was Dead. This meant that almost everything had a heightened capacity to give offence. The post-Diana edition of the satirical fortnightly *Private Eye* contained lengthy satires on the media response to her death, and was pulled from the shelves of the leading newsagent chain WHSmith and many other outlets. The cartoons my colleagues and I drew during this time were subject to much greater editorial scrutiny than usual because of the fear that they might give offence, and I actually had a cartoon pulled by the *Independent on Sunday* from its edition the day after Diana's funeral. Significantly enough, it had nothing to do with Diana, but was the latest in a series of cartoons I produce for that paper's books pages. This one was about the recently deceased American writer William Burroughs, famous for his cut-up technique of writing, and it showed his relatives sitting in a lawyer's office listening to the reading of his will. They were each holding badly wrapped body parts and one relative was saying, 'I'm pleased to see that Uncle Bill stuck with his cut-up technique to the end.' The fact that the cartoon wasn't published was clearly because it was about the wrong death. It was several weeks before I felt I could get away with an even mildly satirical treatment of the whole Diana death phenomenon in a cartoon of 'The New Britain in Touch With Its Emotions' for *Time Out* which showed two tramps sitting in cardboard boxes in Kensington Gardens and wearing smiley masks. One tramp was saying to the other, 'Y'know, I'm getting sick of eating flowers.' By that stage the intensity of national emotion was beginning to dissipate, so I only got a few complaints, but Diana maintains her strange juju power as both manufactured and spontaneous icon, and the only reason I drew a cartoon to mark the 10th anniversary of her death, showing her holed up in a bar in Valparaiso with Mother Teresa of Calcutta, wondering whether she should let Charles in on the joke yet, was because it still had the potential to shock, offend and, therefore, make people laugh.

In the UK, satirists and cartoonists have enjoyed this licence to say the unsayable for centuries, mostly thanks to the new political dispensation that followed on from the Glorious Revolution of 1688, and the new government's failure to renew the Licensing Act in 1695. The nascent democracy the Revolution produced was based on the idea of religious tolerance—except for Catholics, widely seen as potential terrorists bent on the overthrow of the state—itself a response to the failure to impose religious orthodoxy, which had resulted in the civil wars of the 1640s and 1650s and the deaths of one tenth of the population of the British Isles. In other words, the various warring parties agreed that, although they'd continue hating each other, they'd

The Scotsman, September 2007

no longer kill each other. Thus they channelled their hatred elsewhere, into the party system, an irresponsible press and satire. John Locke and his followers may well have thought that they were ushering in an Age of Reason, but 1688 also spawned a mushrooming of public satire, with Alexander Pope, Jonathan Swift and William Hogarth, all the way through to James Gillray, which ran like a sewer beneath the Enlightenment. And it was tolerated because, in this new, experimental, pluralist society, it worked. In the 1780s, the French ambassador to the Court of St James reported back to Versailles that he genuinely believed that England was on the verge of a revolution, on the basis of the truly offensive cartoons of the royal family freely and publicly available from the hundreds of print shops throughout London. *Monstrous Craws, at a New Coalition Feast* (1787), one of James Gillray's frequent and scabrous attacks on the greed and decadence of the English Royal Family showed King George, dressed as an old woman, the Queen and the Prince of Wales spooning up the contents, representing gold coins, into their mouths. The gate to the state treasury, in the background, is open.

But it was, of course, France, where mockery and satire were repressed, unlicensed or private, and where the pressure cooker of resentment finally exploded, that had the revolution.

So, while it may be my job to give offence (and for my part I choose to target that offence at the powerful rather than the powerless), in practice, the whole enterprise is almost ritualistic because satire and satirical cartoons have been established as a valid part of British political discourse for over 300 years. Moreover, the standard template for political cartoons—the caricaturing of real people into an alternative, shape-shifted reality, where they act out a narrative of the cartoonist's devising—was concreted in by Gillray 230 years ago and has remained completely unchanged ever since. But in some ways, despite its status as a semi-detached part of what used to be called the establishment, visual satire also exists in the same realm as taboo: it's about deep, dark magic—and not just because caricature can be described as a type of voodoo—doing damage to someone at a distance with a sharp object, albeit in this case with a pen. It's also concerned with control, like all visual art. By recreating the observable or imagined world, that world is synthesized through a human mind, and therefore is tamed through its re-creation, in the same way as the mysteries of human experience are harnessed, re-created and controlled by theatre and literature.

It's an often-repeated cliché that when so-called primitive people first encountered cameras, they believed that their souls were being stolen when their picture was 'taken'. The same is true of caricature, inasmuch as one of the defining factors of an individual—their physical appearance—is appropriated by the cartoonist and distorted so that the victim is changed and altered into something else, far more than simply a combination of lines on a piece of paper. Alastair Campbell, once again, proved the point several years ago when I drew him from the life as part of a project I was involved with to caricature the more celebrated patrons of the above-mentioned Gay Hussar restaurant. He clearly hated the whole thing and, unlike my other sitters, instead of getting on with his lunch he sat glowering at me and, at one point, shouted across the restaurant, 'You just won't be able to stop yourself from making me look like a really bad person!' My reply was that I draw what I see. However, the notion that I was, in some mysterious way, stealing Campbell's soul, or at the very least wresting control from him, was confirmed when I presented him with the drawing for him to sign as a true record of himself over the course of his lunch. What he did was fascinating, because he instantly clawed back control—over his soul as much as anything else—by saying 'This is a good picture of [Jeremy] Paxman. Now where the fuck's the one of me?' In other words, he denied the power of my dark magic; by insisting it didn't look like him, he was claiming the caricature had failed to 'capture' him, even though it was just a picture, and thereby he disabled the voodoo.

He was right to do so, as all these words like 'taken' or 'capture' confirm. Being caricatured is a transgressive as well as an aggressive act, which is why it's central to political cartooning. Consequently, it's the caricatural dimension of a cartoon that has the potential to give most offence.

To give a further example of this: a couple of decades ago I had a dismal gig at a youth festival the Royal Shakespeare Company was putting on in Stratford-on-Avon. One night, as I was leaving the Dirty Duck Pub through its restaurant, I was called over to a table by about a dozen or so young actors, all of whom insisted that I draw them then and there. I did so, in exchange for drink, and finally got back to my guest-house at about three in the morning. The following lunchtime, I returned to the pub, shakily in search of a hair of the dog, but, when I finally caught the attention of the landlady, she leaned across the bar, grabbed me forcefully by the shoulder and said, 'Listen, if you come in here with your sketchpad again, you're not to draw them however much they ask. I've had them in tears in here this morning, and it's more than I can cope with.' Even though, on this occasion, I'd intended no malice in my caricatures, there remains something inescapably malicious about the whole process of caricature, be it a nose too long here or a chin too weak there. Again, I put this down to the voodoo, the fact that one person's appearance is filtered through the consciousness of another, and thereby, in some way, stolen.

Politicians recognize this, while also recognizing the established role of cartoons as part of the political discourse, even if it is a ceaseless re-echo of the ancient, primitive and primal politics of our early ancestors mocking putative tyrants in the tribe. By and large, they tend to laugh off—even if they don't laugh at—cartoons of themselves, and maybe even feel flattered that they're sufficiently interesting or important enough to grab the cartoonists' attention; but often they'll also buy the original artwork, which they invariably hang up on their lavatory wall. In other words, through a psychological proximity, they're able to flush away the bad magic of the cartoon along with the rest of the shit, thus neutralizing the offence both given and taken.

And the idea of giving offence is integral to the medium. A cartoon that isn't knocking copy becomes merely propaganda, in that strange reverse transubstantiation that likewise renders a joke that isn't laughed at unfunny. Even when a political cartoon draws back from being deliberately offensive, the ballast the medium brings with it will outweigh the cartoonist's intention.

On 11 September 2001, I was planning to draw a cartoon for the next day's *Scotsman* about Tony Blair visiting the Trades Union Congress Conference in Brighton, when I heard the news that the first plane had struck the World Trade Centre. I then watched the second plane hit the second tower on TV, and spent the rest of the afternoon staring at a blank sheet of paper, wondering how on earth I was meant, as a cartoonist, to respond to the violent and terrible deaths of 3,000 people. I ended up producing a cartoon of a monstrous cloud, shaped like a skull, billowing out from Lower Manhattan about to snuff out the torch held by the Statue of Liberty, and then phoned my editor to apologize for the cartoon being meaningless and senseless, and he replied that meaninglessness and senselessness were more or less the mood they were after.

Nonetheless, the next day the paper received several complaints because they'd published a cartoon at all. Irrespective of its content, the space on the page carried the subliminal message to the readers that this was a cartoon, and therefore funny, and therefore offensive. Other cartoonists fared far worse than me, having their work pulled or, in one instance, being told to cover another topic (there were no other topics). It seems that although 9/11 was the most visual event in human history, repeated over and over again on television and with every newspaper in the UK devoting pages and pages to photographs of the attacks and their aftermath, the one visual medium that instantly became intolerable because of its capacity for offence was the cartoon. But once again, the difference lies in the execution: television images and photographs may consequently be subject to human intervention, but they are 'captured'—that word again—by machines; cartoons, on the other hand, are the sole creation of human beings wielding primitive tools, who create or re-create reality by filtering it through their human minds. The process is too human, too raw sometimes to be entirely bearable.

Worse still, its readers receive a cartoon, just as any other image, in a different way from the way they receive text. A cartoon isn't, as such, 'read' at all, because reading is a slow, linear process of nibbling information as you work your way down the column over a period of minutes, while a cartoon—often squatting like a gargoyle on top of the column—is swallowed whole in seconds. Worse than that, on top of being intrinsically different from a machine-made photograph, a cartoon is a piece of polemical journalism, which also makes it different from an illustration. Given the visceral way a cartoon is consumed, straight from the eye to the reptile brain, it's unsurprising that the response is often equally visceral. And the offence, freely given, is duly received.

Although I use offence as just part of my satirical armoury—to express outrage or to trigger a shock of laughter—I often get as good as I give. Which brings me back to that point about offence being in the eye of the beholder.

Offence is a response, but it's also a tactic. Unlike Sadowitz, I rarely produce cartoons merely in order to offend for offensiveness' sake. Instead, it's to make a point, often in reaction to something of itself far more offensive. As such, I'm expressing an opinion, albeit visually and weirdly, but as part of the wider political discourse. But this is where offence comes into its own.

In the past, I may well have produced some genuinely offensive cartoons, like the one I drew for *Time Out* after a biography of Princess Diana revealed that she suffered from bulimia, depicting her vomiting over the bow of a ship being launched with a flunkey in the background saying, 'The real bugger of it is trying to get her to eat a bottle of champagne during lunch . . .'

Many of *Time Out*'s readers were probably quite justified in taking offence, although the calls for me to be publicly castrated were, perhaps, over-egging the pudding. In admittedly hopelessly disingenuous mitigation I'd say that I think the joke was quite funny, and that public figures—in other words, people more powerful than me—are fair game, and can always retire to private life if they want to break the contract between themselves, the public, the media and me. I was also rather heartened by a letter published a week after the first deluge of hate-mail, whose writer, herself bulimic, thought my cartoon was very funny and had cut it out and stuck it on her fridge.

Other cartoons have been more directly political, but have excited equal outrage. A drawing I did for the *Sunday Tribune* in Dublin at the time of the 1992 UN Population Conference in Cairo, prior to which the Pope had entered into a tactical alliance with the Ayatollahs of Iran, resulted in *Tribune*'s offices being picketed by nuns and members of Opus Dei. Then again, I had drawn the Pope standing at the Conference reception desk, flanked by bearded mullahs holding 'Death to Rushdie' placards and stoning women delegates, saying 'Hellow! We are the Pro-Life delegation!'

Sunday Tribune, September 1994

After Pope John Paul II's death, I drew a rather sweet cartoon for the *Guardian* of the Pope being escorted across a heavenly cloudscape by the Grim Reaper, who's saying to him, 'What do you mean? Am I pro-life?' That got a few complaints, but none as baroque as the one inspired by a relatively innocuous cartoon, which the reader said was the most offensive, vile, repellent, calculated to offend, disgusting (and on he went, having clearly got out his thesaurus) cartoon or image to have appeared in any paper or publication 'since the foundation of the state!' Along the way I've also been reported to the Press Complaints Commission by one man who considered a marginal gag written in tiny letters on a fax in the body of the cartoon ('The Pope is Catholic. The Blairs shit in the woods') a grossly offensive intrusion into the private life of the then prime minister, and by a supporter of the Animal Liberation Front (ALF) who was deeply offended by my comparing the ALF to the Continuity IRA after the Omagh bombing.

These were minor disruptions to my peace of mind. It was only after the *Guardian* started to publish my cartoons on their website that I discovered how truly—and, of course, deeply—offensive I could really be. Starting with a cartoon suggesting that the 2004 US presidential election would result almost immediately in a new American Civil War between the Christians and the Constitutionalists ('Death to the Gay Abortionists!'), followed by George Bush, Condoleeza Rice and Donald Rumsfeld in Nazi armbands emblazoned with crosses instead of swastikas, a cartoon of Bush crossing Canal Street in New Orleans pastiching the famous painting of Washington crossing the Delaware, Bush and the Chinese president shaking their blood-soaked hands and discussing white phosphorous and many other cartoons on Bush's presidency and Iraq, I regularly received hundreds and hundreds of hate e-mails.

My correspondents were clearly deeply offended by my cartoons, and many had been alerted to my offence by websites reproducing them. And as my intention had been to offend, I couldn't really complain if people duly were. But the strange thing was how offensive the responses were themselves. One started: 'When you've finished scraping the maggots out of your whore-mother's cunt,' and went on to describe in detail how I regularly rape my children, but only after I've tired of raping Arab boys. Another said I was 'dumber than an Irish cunt'. Most limited themselves to telling me that I was a dumb limey asshole who'd be speaking German if it weren't for the US, and would soon be speaking Arab after the Islamist takeover of Europe. One person even enrolled me, without my knowledge, on a gay dating website and I got several mystifying inquiries from interested parties in Florida before I discovered their source and cancelled my unconscious membership.

They'll tell you it's about freedom...

The Guardian, 2004

My friend and colleague Steve Bell receives even more of this trash than I do, but sensibly observes that if these idiots are writing bilious e-mails to him, they're too busy to do anything truly dangerous. However, mixed up in all this Tourettic spleen were several fairly plausible death threats. Things got worse after I produced a cartoon for the *Guardian* during Israel's disastrous incursion into Lebanon in the summer of 2006. It was, I concede, a brutal cartoon, commenting on brutal events, and perhaps I should have painted the Stars of David blue on the knuckledusters on an Israeli fist smashing a Lebanese child's face while missing a Hezbollah hornet, to make it quite clear that I was referring to the flag of the State of Israel rather than the symbol of worldwide Jewry. I doubt, however, that it would have made much difference, not least because the presence of the Star of David on the Israeli flag is there precisely in order to claim to represent Jews everywhere. The equation of Israel and Jewry has proved to be a brilliant tactic to disarm Israel's critics, simply by calling any criticism of Israel and its actions anti-Semitic. In the thousands of e-mails I received, again mostly fomented through various websites, the message in all of them can be more or less distilled down to, 'Fuck off you anti-Semitic cunt.' And as a tactic, it worked. I was deeply shaken by being accused of something I'm not, although I eventually worked out that the heart of the insult lay in the word 'anti-Semite' rather than any of the others, because insults usually work best when they accuse you of being something you're not. Otherwise they're not insults, merely statements of fact. But long before this incident, I'd got used to receiving complaints whenever I drew Ariel Sharon, that I'd produced the most anti-Semitic cartoon since the closure of Julius Streicher's notorious Nazi hate-sheet *Der Stürmer*. Again, the offensiveness of the response seemed to outweigh the original offence. All I'd done was caricature a fat, Jewish-looking man in a stupid drawing, in no more exaggerated a way than I'd depict anyone. Yet, as a consequence, I ended up being compared with the principle cheerleader of the Holocaust.

The disproportionate nature of these responses—the obscenity and the death threats—pales in comparison to the response to the cartoons of Prophet Muhammad published by the Danish paper *Jyllands-Posten* in October 2005, which five months later resulted in worldwide protests, the burning down of several Danish diplomatic buildings and the deaths of up to a hundred people, even though they were all Muslims, shot dead in the streets of their Muslim countries by Muslim policemen and soldiers after having been incited to riot by Muslim clerics. In this infamous affair, it's clear that *Jyllands-Posten* set out deliberately to offend, as part of the newspaper's long-standing campaign against immigrants, recruiting the voodoo powers of the medium to damage, or at least discomfort, a group of isolated, beleaguered, powerless and poor people in Danish society, some of whom probably also clean the lavatories and empty the bins at *Jyllands-Posten*'s offices. Because they targeted people less powerful than themselves, *Jyllands-Posten*'s cartoons failed my personal Mencken test, and I concluded that the commissioning of the cartoons was wrong, even though the response—by powerful Danish mullahs, let alone the Saudi and Syrian governments—almost justified them in retrospect.

But it's worth reflecting on the purpose of all these reactions, whether from Muslims to the Danish cartoons, or the response to my cartoons by Muslims, Zionists, neo-cons, Americans in general, Catholics, Serbs, Spaniards or any of the other groups I've apparently offended over the years, including some atheists who judged a cartoon I drew of Richard Dawkins for *New Humanist* magazine to reveal me as deeply homophobic, because I'd drawn him banging his wrists together in glee, and wearing sandals. But while I don't doubt that all these people are truly, deeply offended, and have every right to be, rights, despite any amount of wishful thinking, are merely assertions. In the Babel of conflicting human opinions, the right to be offended works out, in practice, as just another tactic to win an argument by compelling your opponent to shut up because what they say is offensive. Special interest groups, whether motivated by politics, religion or anything else, constantly seek to create new taboos to make them, their attitudes and their opinions inviolable, so that all criticism is rendered not just unspeakable but unsayable.

This totalitarian imperative to be freed from the threat of being offended has operated throughout human history. Gods, kings and dictators, in addition to their followers, have all demanded that they be allowed to control other people's thoughts and behaviour to save them from the terrible pain of their feelings being hurt. Doubtless trainspotters would insist on the same privilege, and enjoy the same freedom from mockery, if they thought they could get away with it. With repulsive regularity, the penalty for transgressing taboos and giving offence has been death or the threat of it, even though it should be blindingly obvious to everyone who's ever lived that the most offensive thing anyone can ever do to anyone else is kill them.

That said, there are other kinds of damage that can be wrought, and cartoons, as a subset of mockery, are capable of doing more damage than a lot of other things. That, to a large extent, is their purpose. That damage can either be benign, as I'd insist that my work is, keeping the powerful in check, or malignant, as in the case of the *Jyllands-Posten* cartoons or the anti-Jewish hate cartoons that *Der Stürmer* really did publish. They are, consequently, as offensive as you wish them to be, depending on your point of view. They're also part of that deep, dark magic that defines the taboos we create, which in their turn inform our propensity to give and take offence. But you can invoke that magic in all sorts of different ways.

New Humanist, 2007

After my Lebanon cartoon appeared, the *Guardian* published a letter from the Israeli ambassador in London (which pulled the usual trick of equating criticism of Israel with anti-Semitism) that started in an interesting way—by giving a dictionary definition of a cartoon. By this light, he argued, not only was my cartoon offensive, it wasn't even a cartoon. I'm used to the formulation 'so-called' qualifying my critics' description of my cartoons, along with assertions at how badly I've drawn them, but this was something new. What he was saying was that he disagreed with my cartoon, but as a consequence not only pleaded being offended to make me shut up but also asserted that, in its own terms, it didn't even exist. Now that's smart magic.

For, while offence may be in the eye of the beholder, you must never rule out the option of simply blinking and looking away.

Rude Awakening

The Independent, June 2010

During the 1780s, the French ambassador to the Court of St James is rumoured to have written a despatch to Versailles outlining his fears that Britain was teetering on the verge of revolution. He'd reached this disturbing conclusion because of the free availability of ribald satirical prints depicting members of the royal family. These prints by James Gillray, Thomas Rowlandson and many others were merciless in their lèse-majesté: if he was lucky, George III would escape with being portrayed as a bovine, rustic bumpkin; his son was never lucky enough to be shown as anything but a drunken, lecherous buffoon.

As the ambassador's coach purveyed him from salon to court to levee, he would have passed little kiosks peddling this smut, often hiring it out for the night, like a modern DVD. These booths lined the Strand and Fleet Street, stretching all the way from Charing Cross almost to St Paul's. So it's no surprise, given the evidence of this squalid trade, that the ambassador came to the conclusion he did.

After all, unlike France under the stable absolutism of the Bourbons, the British had form. One hundred and thirty years previously they had chopped off one king's head and called it a revolution; in 1688, they chased another king from his throne, and called that a 'Glorious' revolution. As any civilized gentleman in Europe knew the British were little better than beasts and consequently highly susceptible to the desta-bilizing effects of mucky pictures of the prince regent rogering his doxy. Revolution was inevitable, therefore, because apart from anything else, the British were just so . . . well, rude.

Of course, we know now that the ambassador was completely, and fatally, wrong. It was France that had the revolution, and then the deranged bloodletting of the Terror; and France which, before the revolution, had been awash with bloodcurdling sexual libels about Marie Antoinette and the court. The difference, crucially, lay in the fact that French rudeness was kept sealed inside the foetid pressure cooker of the ancien régime until it exploded.

Then again, we all know that the French are the rudest people on earth. Except, maybe, for the Israelis, with their tradition of the harsh egalitarianism of the kibbutzim. Unless, that is, you've ever met Russian bar staff in a London pub. As for New Yorkers . . .

Actually, it is we British—the shy, embarrassed, polite and reserved British—who have enjoyed a far worse reputation for savage rudeness. I long ago worked out, from bitter experience amid the hate mail and death threats I've received from around the world, that while I see my work as a cartoonist as firmly in the tradition of William Hogarth and Gillray, everyone else sees it as breathtakingly vicious. And it is this tradition that is celebrated in Tate Britain's major new exhibition, *Rude Britannia*: *British Comic Art*, examining the plaited strands of British rudeness over the past 300 years (including my own valedictory cartoon of Tony Blair as prime minister, telling him, through the magic of bad puns, to fuck off in three different ways).

'Rudeness', in this case, is both less and more than farting in church or mooning on the last bus home. While we all secretly enjoy a bit of smut, almost as much as we enjoy saying rude things about other people out of earshot, what the exhibition reveals is the level to which shifting standards in private behaviour have succeeded or failed to expand into being tolerated in the public arena. It also tacitly acknowledges that transgression from the private to public sphere often provides the best part of the joke.

Thus, under the theme of 'Bawdy', one part of the exhibition goes from Rowlandson's semi-pornographic, under-the-counter erotica from the late eighteenth century, through Aubrey Beardsley's notorious priapic illustrations of Aristophanes' *Lysistrata*—which Beardsley ordered to be burned after his deathbed conversion to Roman Catholicism in 1898—to Donald McGill's dirty seaside postcards, which were successfully prosecuted and ordered to be destroyed by a magistrate's court in Margate in the 1950s. These fluctuating fortunes in what is and isn't tolerable are reflected in the exhibition's examination of social and political comic art, and the extent to which visual satire has been able to get away with telling power that it's stupid, it's got a big nose and it should just bugger off.

That visual humour was ever able to get away with it is, in a way, slightly miraculous. Since the invention of printing, there had always been scurrilous images making political points, but they had usually been partisan and therefore under the protection of powerful patrons. What was new about eighteenth-century visual satire was that it publicly articulated the universal human emotion that the king is an idiot, but without the consequence that the printmaker would have his work burnt and his ears sheared off by the public hangman.

Although 'tolerance' was central to the Whig philosophy underpinning the Glorious Revolution of 1688, when the Licensing Act lapsed in 1695, the failure to renew them was more down to oversight than principle. Nonetheless, that act of neglect left Britain unique in the world. There was a sudden mushrooming of satire of all kinds, which governments were largely unable to control. Robert Walpole was subjected to a sustained, personalized onslaught, and even his title, as first 'prime minister', was a term, like the words 'Christian' and 'Tory', first coined as an insult to mock, in this case, Walpole's propensity for accruing offices, money and power for himself.

Thomas Rowlandson, illustration by Jean de La Fontaine, *Contes et nouvelles en vers* (c. 1810)

Aubrey Beardsley, 'The Examination of the Herald' in *The Lysistrata of Aristophenes* (1926)

Indeed, the satirical mood of the times has coloured the way we think we see the whole century: mucky, rumbustious, earthy, humorous and, definingly, Hogarthian. The art critic Robert Hughes summed it up thus: 'Modern squalor is squalid but Georgian squalor is "Hogarthian", an art form in itself.' Even at his most polemical and preachy—in *Gin Lane*, for instance, or in *A Rake's Progress*—you feel that Hogarth can't stop himself laughing while he's lecturing.

And taking the piss was, quite literally, the point. In the eighteenth and nineteenth centuries, London was the largest and richest city the world had seen, and for most of that time existed without flush toilets or adequate sewers. Visual satirists such as Philip Dawe could outstrip their merely textual counterparts in depicting the absurdity of the elite's finery being dragged through the gutter, while at the same time he and his peers were, through mockery, stripping away the robes of power to show the pissing, shitting, sweating human being underneath, no less stinky than you and me. A generation after Hogarth, Gillray was still exercising Swift's scatological vision in satirical prints of Prime Minister Pitt defecating paper money into the Bank of England or, during the Napoleonic Wars, George III transformed into a map of Britain and showering shit out of the Solent over the French invasion fleet.

Now that's rude by anyone's standards, and its purpose satirically is primal: it's voodoo, doing damage to an enemy at a distance with a sharp object, although in this case it's an etching tool or a nib rather than a needle. That's why visual satire works, in its capacity to insult and therefore belittle men who think themselves great; that's why the cartoonist David Low was placed on the Gestapo's death list, because he'd dared to draw Hitler as a bloody fool in a stupid uniform with a Charlie Chaplin moustache.

Between Gillray and Low, however, rudeness did not prosper, in public at least. Creeping respectability and the middle class' increasing insistence on deference meant Gladstone and Disraeli never suffered the indignities of Pitt, although hypocrisy did allow for innuendo to come fully into its own, even if only among the masses in the music halls. A century on, the moral actions of the burghers of Margate in burning McGill's immoral postcards were probably an unconscious stabilizing response to a recent war which had been set in course by other moralists burning books, then burning people.

But that was perhaps respectability's last hurrah. A decade-and-a-half later, the Lord Chamberlain—brought in to impose political censorship on the theatre by Walpole after the success of *The Beggar's Opera*, but dedicated to extirpating the sauce and the foul language for most of the next 200 years—was gone, and soon afterwards most of the prevalent taboos had gone too. So you rather wonder, when you get to the Young British Artists represented in the exhibition, such as Sarah Lucas, whom exactly they're being rude to, and how iconoclastic you can be when your patrons specialize in putting on displays of smashed icons in their respectable galleries.

But although firebombing the Saatchi collection remains terribly attractive as an exercise in all sorts of rudeness, maybe the new doesn't shock any more. And anyway, perhaps the point of rudeness isn't to shock the 'rudee' at all, but just make the rude and their mates snigger, thereby evening up all sorts of different social and political equations for those who are in on the joke. After all, from 1849 until the 1920s, *Punch*, the embodiment of stifling Victorian respectability, ran the same Richard Doyle cover every week, with just the issue number and date changed, brazening its frieze of Mr Punch on a mule, fondling his huge erect cock. Either no one noticed, or they were smirking fit to bust.

BBC, May 2010

Luck of the Draw

British Journalism Review, December 2010

It was recently reported that Steve Jobs, the boss of Apple responsible for infesting the world with iPods, iPhones, iPads and vast amounts of other iCrap, had banned a cartoonist from one of his apps, because Jobs thought his material was 'objectionable'. It was then reported that Jobs had changed his mind and allowed 'professional political satirists and humourists' back on his systems.

What is interesting about this story has nothing to do with the caprice of digitocrats, but lies in the reaction of the liberal chatterati to it. Many people expressed surprise and concern that Jobs should behave like that, presumably because they'd thought of him as a shiny new mixture of Gutenberg, Einstein and the Lord Buddha. I doubt, however, if the cartoonist in question was surprised.

Cartoons as a medium, particularly political ones, occupy a curious, not-quite-respectable twilit place in the realm of journalism, often integral to the topography of a newspaper but also more than slightly semi-detached from the whole undertaking. Partly that's because cartoons' relationship to other media, whether it's newspapers or one of Jobs' latest gizmos, is parasitical. For nearly half a millennium following the invention of printing, satirical engravings and etchings existed quite happily on their own.

Hogarth and Gillray sold all their work as individual prints, retailed from shops and kiosks that stretched from Charing Cross to St Paul's, and Cruikshank was doing the same long into the middle of the nineteenth century, after *Punch* had killed off most of the rest of the trade. In fact, the first daily political cartoon appeared in this country as late as 1900, when Francis Carruthers-Gould started working for the *Westminster Gazette*.

There is, in other words, a spirit of independence woven into cartoonists' spiritual DNA. So, however much a good cartoon will enhance the journalism surrounding it, both its purpose and its effect is always to lower the tone. After all, one of the first and most enduring insults to be coined about popular journalism—calling it the Yellow Press—came courtesy of a cartoon, *The Yellow Kid*, which both Pulitzer and Hearst ran in their respective papers during the New York circulation wars of the 1890s.

So, however useful we cartoonists are as licensed idiots, we're not quite safe either, not least because, at the end of the day, as satirists it's our job—and our vocation—to mock the rich and powerful, a group which rather noticeably and inconveniently includes the kind of people who own and edit newspapers and other media.

Sometimes, a proprietor or editor will actually encourage dissent among a paper's most instinctive dissidents, though it will be as much of a comfort to liberals as Jobs' apparent illiberality that the foremost exponent of this tactic was Lord Beaverbrook. It served him and his cartoonists, including David Low and Vicky, to make a thing of their having a pop at him, and frequently caricaturing him in as unflattering a way as possible in the pages of his own papers. But this was a rare example of something less like free speech than self-indulgence.

For the most part, however, we keep schtum and cleanse our souls now and again by sneaking in coded messages attacking our owners or editors (Carl Giles used to have tiny vignettes of Rupert Bear being tortured to death hidden in the background of his cartoons). We hope they won't notice, though sometimes we wish they will, and otherwise we just hunker down, swallow our pride and moan at interminable length in private to our colleagues about both proprietors and editors.

Sometimes, though, it pays off to go public in order to reclaim either your dignity or your soul. Apparently, after Rupert Murdoch took over the *Sunday Times*, he saw a Gerald Scarfe cartoon of Ronald Reagan and was heard to mutter: 'Poor old Ronnie. We gotta get rid of this pinko artist!' Although the only authority we have for this story is Scarfe himself, still working at the *Sunday Times* nearly three decades later.

When I was working at *Scotland on Sunday* during the Iraq War, an editor and I—speaking exclusively to each other through intermediaries—waged a war of attrition of our own, him wanting me to illustrate his (pro-war) editorials, while I insisted that I was a visual columnist who should be allowed to express his own opinion. For the duration of the war, I usually won, but in the months following, I'd be phoned with increasing frequency by the art director, after I'd filed, to be told that the editor had had 'a better idea'. I drew his idea for three weeks, although without signing the result, and then resigned by email, telling him that if he was always coming up with such brilliant ideas for cartoons, maybe it was time he learned to draw. That was bridling in the extreme, though I felt happier afterwards. Usually, like most people, we bend with the wind, but sensible editors will allow their cartoonists as free a rein as reasonable, within the bounds of public decency. That, after all, is why we're hired in the first place.

Sometimes, though, you get wrong-footed from the most unexpected direction. I'm very fortunate, at the *Guardian*, in having much more leeway than I've been given on some other papers. That said, I clearly went too far with a cartoon I drew at the time of the fall of Kabul, after the Grauniad's pages had been filled for weeks with wildly different analyses and opinions on the direction of the war on terror. In the cartoon, various turbaned members of the Northern Alliance are seen shouting at each other—'WHO ARE YOU CALLING WOBBLY, YOU TOYNBEEIST BASTARD SON OF A BOMB?', 'EAT YOUR WORDS, STINKING SEAMUS MILNEITE CUR!!', 'HITCHENITE DOG!!!', 'PILGERITE PIG!!!!'

Previously unpublished

I should, I suppose, have guessed that the comment editor (Seamus Milne, as it happens) wasn't going to buy it, but I was bemused by the reason he gave for his unhappiness. It was, I was told, now editorial policy to make no allusion to any disagreement between *Guardian* columnists. I asked him if he thought the readers might not have noticed, then changed the captions. It's what we do if we want to get paid.

Postscript (2024)

After Steve Jobs died in October 2011, I produced a cartoon for the *Guardian* of Jobs' funeral cortege which caused a minor storm of outrage, mostly due, I discovered, to me including a depiction of a 'grief app'. The comments below the cartoon on the *Guardian's* website were just working themselves up into a fine old self-righteous frenzy when someone posted the link to Apple's official 'grief app', an image of a guttering candle punters were enjoined to hold up on their tablet device outside Apple stores, like icons.

Let's Kill Uncle

The Guardian, 8 August 2013

I know it was in the year after my mother died when I was 10, though I can't remember whether it was my sister's Girls' Brigade troop fete or a church jumble sale we turned up to just by chance. Part of me, 44 years on, seems to remember being there with my friend Clive Brazier and his mum, though maybe I was there with my father, spending another typical weekend sniffing out a bargain. And though I couldn't now say whether it was in Pinner or Ruislip, in my mind's eye I can clearly see the secondhand book stall by the path leading to the church or community hall, the lawn around it dappled with sunlight, where I bought a tatty paperback edition of Rohan O'Grady's *Let's Kill Uncle*.

This jumble of vagueness and clarity over the details of my copy's provenance is strangely appropriate. The book itself is not well known, though over almost half a century I've reread it often enough to feel I know large parts of it by heart. In spite of its obscurity, three years after it was published in 1963 it was turned into a movie. I've never seen this film, and because most of the scenes in the book are photographically precise in my imagination, I never want to.

It wasn't until I was in my late twenties that I finally twigged that Rohan O'Grady, regardless of my clear perception until then of him as a short, wiry, black-haired Irishman, is in fact a woman called June Skinner, now 92 and still living in her native British Columbia. I've never read any of her other four novels, and naturally assumed *Let's Kill Uncle* had long been out of print until I was asked to write this article. Then I found out Bloomsbury reissued it in 2010 with a glowing encomium from Donna Tartt on the back cover. So it was very recently that I discovered the book was first published with a frontispiece by one of my cartooning heroes, the great Edward Gorey, laureate of the macabre.

And who knows what first sparked my interest in this book. My original Mayflower edition, from September 1966, now Sellotaped together and its pages yellowed and smelling, mysteriously, of chocolate, says on the cover that *Let's Kill Uncle* is 'the most readable blend of humour, horror, chills and child psychology since *A High Wind in Jamaica*.'

I now know that the film adaption of *A High Wind in Jamaica* featured the young Martin Amis, but back in 1970, neither he, the book nor the film meant a thing to me. Did I think it was something to do with *The Man from U.N.C.L.E.*, or even with

J. P. Martin's *Uncle* series of books for children, about the heroic philanthropic elephant? If so, it's interesting that things that would have appealed to me as a child in fact lured me into a deliciously horrible adult world, both captivating me and capturing me at precisely the right moment.

Whatever it was, just at the time when I was achingly conscious that my mother's recent death had ushered me out of childhood and exiled me into something quite different, I became absorbed by June Skinner's gruesome little book about two children called Barnaby and Christie, around my age at the time, on holiday on an island off the coast of British Columbia, who conspire to murder Barnaby's uncle before he murders them.

Which is how this book changed my life. Some might say that it's hard to think of a book less suitable for a child of my age and circumstances, but without me even realizing it, *Let's Kill Uncle* transported me into an enormously comforting realm of the imagination, that shadowland where we recreate and reorder reality to make it bearable.

So I began to understand that horror can, and often should be, played for laughs; that death, in the right hands, is funny; that dark humour isn't 'sick', but one of the best medicines there is. And as I kept rereading it at that formative age, the book was also ever so gently nudging me towards my ultimate career path.

And it's consistently more rewarding each time I reread it. A couple of weeks ago I suddenly recognized that Uncle Silvester—the eponymous object of the two children's murderous intentions—is clearly based on Sylvester the Cat from the Warner Brothers' cartoons, only darker and more, well, gory (though the bit of business about the death—presented as murder—of Fletcher the Budgie is a big hint).

Likewise, I've only just clocked exactly the depth of the darkness of the shadows that the Holocaust casts over Sergeant Coulter the Mountie's reflections on innocence and wickedness. Then again, when I was 11 it would never have occurred to me that the book was written shortly after the Eichmann trial, and Hannah Arendt's famous observations about the banality of evil. And I've not even mentioned One-Ear, the self-pitying, soliloquizing cougar who ultimately fulfils the role of deus ex machina in the book.

I could go on forever with a line-by-line exegesis of *Let's Kill Uncle*. I could even try to articulate why the ending—with its interplay of innocence, guile, triumph and cynicism—is so desperately moving and yet also ghoulishly funny. But then again I don't want to ruin the plot for you. And I do want you to read it, with an almost evangelical fervour.

It's not the greatest book ever written, nor will it detain you for long. But it should make you laugh, and make you think, and possibly even make you cry if you have a heart at all. I can conceive of no greater recommendation than that.

Postscript (2024)

After this article appeared, I was contacted by June Skinner's daughter. She told me she was delighted by the piece, as was her mother, by then suffering from dementia but still enjoying every day in the present as fully as she could. I sent her some of my books and was sent back a copy of the latest edition, signed by June, describing me as her 'perfect reader'. That's up there with receiving a box full of pens from Ronald Searle among my high-five-from-god moments.

Drawing Out the Dark Side

Index on Censorship, March 2014

As a political cartoonist, whenever I'm criticized for my work being unrelentingly negative, I usually point my accusers towards several eternal truths.

One is that cartoons, along with all other jokes, are by their nature knocking copy. It's the negativity that makes them funny, because, at the heart of things, funny is how we cope with the bad—or negative—stuff.

Whether it's laughing at shit, death or the misfortunes of others, without this hard-wired evolutionary survival mechanism that allows us to laugh at the awfulness running in parallel with being both alive and human, apes with brains the size of ours would go insane with existential terror as soon as the full implications of existence sink in. Which, for most people, would be when you're around three years old.

And if that doesn't persuade them, I usually then try to describe that indescribable but palpable transubstantiation that occurs when you shift from the negative to the positive, and a cartoon sinks from being satire to becoming propaganda.

Though here, of course, I'm not being entirely honest, because in many ways cartoons are propaganda in its purest form. This is because the methodology of the political cartoon has most in common with the practices of sympathetic magic and, likewise, its purposes are invariably malevolent.

Indeed, I've often described caricature in particular and political cartooning more generally as a type of voodoo, doing damage at a distance with a sharp object, in this case (usually) a pen.

Certainly, the business of caricature is a kind of shamanist shape-shifting, distorting the appearance of the victim in order to bring them under the control of the cartoonist and subjecting them thereafter to ridicule or opprobrium. In short, political cartoons should truly be classified not as comedy but as visual taunts. And taunts, of course, have been an integral ingredient of warfare for millennia.

Within the twisted plaiting of taunts, posturing and brinkmanship that ultimately ended in the hecatombs of the Western Front in the First World War, you can just about tease out one thread trailing back to a cartoon.

The original sketch for the allegorical 1895 cartoon Nations of Europe: Join in Defence of Your Faith! was by Kaiser Wilhelm II of Germany, though he left the job of the finished artwork to professionals. Its purpose was to stiffen the resolve of European leaders against the 'Yellow Peril' coming from East Asia, and to this end the Kaiser presented a copy of the cartoon to his cousin Tsar Nicholas II of Russia.

It's generally agreed that the cartoon played a small but significant part in influencing the Tsar's confrontational policy towards Japan, which ended in Russia's humiliating defeat in the 1904–5 Russo-Japanese war.

The subsequent revolutions, regional wars and growing European instability erupted nine years later with the general mobilization of the Great Powers, and the cartoonists were mobilized along with everyone else.

Although a perennial taunt against the Germans is that they have no sense of humour, they had as rich a tradition of visual satire as anyone else. In the pages of both *Punch* and the German satirical paper *Simplicissimus*, the enemy was caricatured identically as alternatively preposterous and terrifying. Both sides showed the other in league with skeletal personifications of death, or transformed into fat clowns, foul or dangerous animals or, in British cartoons about Germans, as sausages.

There were also scores of cartoons showing German soldiers bayoneting Belgian babies in portrayals of the 'Beastly Hun' and, later, cartoons showing the Germans harvesting the corpses of slain soldiers for fats to advance their war effort.

All sides taunted each other by attacking their nations' supposed leaders, using the caricaturist's typical tools. Thus, the Kaiser, mostly thanks to his waxed moustache, acted as a synecdoche for Germany's defining perfidy. In one cartoon from 1915, when Britain's George V stripped his cousin, the Kaiser, of his Order of the Garter, his garterless stocking slips down, revealing a black and hairy simian leg. In 1914, meanwhile, the German cartoonist Arthur Johnson (his father was an American) showed the British royal family, German by descent, in a camp for enemy aliens.

These taunting cartoons bore little relation to the realities of modern warfare, and most of them would now be dismissed purely as rather ham-fisted propaganda. This shouldn't downplay their effectiveness, however.

A century earlier, Napoleon Bonaparte admitted he feared the damage done by James Gillray's caricatures of him more than he feared any general, because Gillray always drew him as very short. (To bring this up to date, *Le Monde*'s cartoonist Plantu told me that every time he drew Nicolas Sarkozy as short, Sarkozy complained personally to his editor; the next cartoon would make him even shorter, and Sarkozy would complain again, until in the end Plantu drew the French president as just a head and feet.)

Nonetheless, an unforeseen consequence of this barrage of caricature was that, in the end, people stopped believing it to be anything more than mere caricature: the truth that should be exposed by the exaggeration got lost. In the 30s, many people assumed reports of the genuine atrocities of the Nazis were, like the bayoneted babies or harvested corpses blamed on the Kaiser, just propaganda.

Posterity shouldn't concern cartoonists. We're just journalists responding to events with a raw immediacy. This is what gives the medium a great deal of its heft.

Some cartoons, however, encapsulate a time or an event and thus become part of the more general visual language. Gillray's *The Plumb-Pudding in Danger* is a perfect example, depicting the specific geopolitical struggle between William Pitt and Napoleon in 1805, while also capturing eternal truths about geopolitics itself. But I'm not aware of any political cartoons from the First World War that do the same thing.

And yet the medium operates in many ways, and the most effective and popular cartoonist of the First World War was undoubtedly Bruce Bairnsfather, a serving artillery officer who drew gag cartoons about the slapstick of everyday life in the trenches in his series featuring Old Bill. The serving soldiers loved these cartoons, and they are another instance of humour being used to make the harshest imaginable reality simply bearable.

The other truly great cartoon to emerge from the First World War was published after it was all over. In his extraordinarily prophetic drawing *Peace and Future Cannon Fodder* for the *Daily Herald*, Will Dyson showed the Allied victors of the war exiting the Paris Peace Conference and the French prime minister Georges Clemenceau saying: 'Curious! I seem to hear a child weeping.' Behind a pillar, a naked infant labelled '1940 class' is crying into its folded arms.

None of the protagonists in the next war doubted the power or importance of cartoons. Again, they were used by all sides to taunt and vilify their foes, perhaps most notoriously in *Der Stürmer*, the notorious anti-Semitic paper edited by Julius Streicher, later hanged at Nuremburg.

Simplicissimus was, once more, taunting the British, this time drawing the wartime prime minister, Churchill, as a fat and murderous drunk; in the Soviet Union, Stalin's favourite cartoonist, Boris Yefimov, returned the compliment to the Nazi leadership (Yefimov's older brother Mikhail first employed him on *Pravda* before being purged and executed in 1940; Boris survived him by 68 years, dying aged 108 in 2008). No cartoonist in either country would have dared caricature their own totalitarian politicians, but they were given full rein to exercise their skills on their nation's enemies. In Britain, with its largely legally tolerated history of visual satire going back to 1695, things were slightly different, though also sometimes the same.

The New Zealand–born cartoonist David Low discovered in 1930 from a friend that Hitler, three years away from taking power in Germany, was an admirer of his work. Low did what any other cartoonist would do in similar circumstances and acknowledged his famous fan by sending him a signed piece of original artwork, inscribed 'From one artist to another'.

What happened to the cartoon is not known—maybe it was with him right to the end, in the bunker—but it soon became apparent that Hitler had mistaken Low's attacks on democratic politicians for attacks on democracy itself. He was soon disabused. Low harried the Nazis all the way from the simple slapstick of *The Difficulty of Shaking Hands with Gods* of November 1933 to the bitterness of his iconic cartoon *Rendezvous* in September 1939, so much so that in 1936, British Foreign Secretary Lord Halifax, after a weekend's shooting at Hermann Göring's Bavarian hunting lodge, told Low's proprietor at the *Evening Standard*, Lord Beaverbrook, to get the cartoonist to ease up as his work was seriously damaging good Anglo-German relations. Low responded by producing a composite cartoon dictator called 'Muzzler'.

The Nazis had a point that Low entirely understood, and it was why he, along with many other cartoonists—Victor 'Vicky' Weisz, Leslie Illingworth and even William Heath Robinson—were all on the Gestapo's death list. In a debate on British government propaganda in 1943, a Tory MP said Low's cartoons were worth all the official propaganda put together because Low portrayed the Nazis as 'bloody fools'. Low himself later expanded on the point, comparing his work, which undermined the Nazis through mockery, with the work of pre-war Danish cartoonists who unanimously drew them as terrifying monsters. Low's point was that it's much easier to imagine you can beat a fool than a monster, and taunting your enemies as being unvanquishably frightening is no taunt at all.

The enduring efficacy of cartoons' dark and magical voodoo powers was acknowledged in victory, when both Low and Yefimov were official court cartoonists at the Nuremburg trials (Low claimed Göring tried to outstare him from the dock): now the taunting was part of the humiliation served up with the revenge. Likewise, when Mussolini was executed by Italian partisans, the editor of the *Evening Standard*, Michael Foot, marked the dictator's demise by giving over all eight pages of the paper to Low's cartoons of Mussolini's life and career.

Of course, Low, unlike Yefimov, was actively hostile on the home front as well, producing cartoons critical of both the military establishment and Churchill. When Low's famous creation Colonel Blimp, the portly cartoon manifestation of boneheaded reactionary thinking, took on fresh life in the Powell and Pressburger movie *The Life and Death of Colonel Blimp*, Churchill tried to have the film banned. When the *Daily Mirror*'s cartoonist Philip Zec responded to stories about wartime profiteering by contrasting them with attacks on merchant shipping in his famous cartoon *The Price of Petrol Has Been Increased by One Penny—Official*, both Churchill and Home Secretary Herbert Morrison seriously considered shutting down the newspaper. (When the *Guardian* cartoonist Les Gibbard pastiched Zec's cartoon during the Falklands War 40 years later, the *Sun* called for him to be tried for treason.)

"Well, if you knows of a better 'ole, go to it."

Bruce Bairnsfather for *The Bystander,* 24 November 1915.

"WELL, IF YOU KNOWS OF A BIGGER ****'OLE, GO TO 'IM!"

The Guardian, January 2014

PEACE AND FUTURE CANNON FODDER

The Tiger: "Curious! I seem to hear a child weeping!"

—*The London Daily Herald.*

Will Dyson for *The Daily Herald*, 17 May 1919.

The Guardian, December 2009

And yet cartoons, for all their voodoo power, can still spiral off into all sorts of different ambiguities thanks to the way they inhabit different spheres of intent. Are they there to make us laugh, or to destroy them? Or both?

Ronald Searle drew his experiences while he was a prisoner of war of the Japanese, certainly on pain of death had the drawings been discovered, but taking the risk in order to stand witness to his captors' crimes. Just a few years later, many of his famous *St Trinian's* cartoons don't just deal with the same topics—cruelty and beheadings— but share identical composition with his prisoner-of-war drawings.

And when Carl Giles, creator of the famous cartoon family that mapped and reflected post-war British suburban life every week in the *Sunday Express*, was present as an official war correspondent at the liberation of the Bergen-Belsen concentration camp, the camp's commandant, Josef Kramer, revealed he was a huge fan of Giles' work and gave him his pistol, a ceremonial dagger and his Nazi armband in exchange for the promise that Giles would send him a signed original. As Giles explained later, he failed to keep his part of the bargain because, by the time he got demobbed, Kramer had been hanged for crimes against humanity.

Those twinned qualities of taunting and laughter go some way to explaining the experience of cartoonists in the so-called war on terror, if not the power of their work. In the aftermath of 9/11, in the babel of journalistic responses to what was without question the most visual event in human history, then visually re-repeated by the media that had initially reported it, the cartoonists were the ones who got it in the neck. While columnists wrote millions of words of comment and speculation, and images captured by machines were broadcast and published almost ceaselessly, the images produced via a human consciousness were, it seems, too much to stomach for many. Cartoonists had their work spiked, or were told to cover another story (there were no other stories). In the US, some cartoonists had their copy moved to other parts of the paper, or were laid off. One or two even got a knock on the door in the middle of the night from the Feds under the provisions of the Patriot Act.

Despite a concerted effort by some American strip cartoonists to close ranks on Thanksgiving Day 2001 and show some patriotic backbone, the example of Beetle Bailey flying on the back of an American Eagle didn't really act as a general unifier. Unlike in previous wars, there was no unanimity of purpose among cartoonists. An editorial in the *Daily Telegraph* accused me, along with Dave Brown of the *Independent* and the *Guardian's* Steve Bell, of being 'useful idiots' aiding the terrorist cause due to our failure to fall in line.

The war on terror and its Iraqi sideshow were anything but consensus wars, and many cartoonists articulated very loudly their misgivings. These included Peter Brookes of the Murdoch-owned *Times* drawing cartoons in direct opposition to his paper's editorial line. This has always been one of visual satire's greatest strengths: sometimes a cartoon can undermine itself.

Moreover, because a majority of cartoons were back in their comfort zone of oppositionism, the taunting had less of the whiff of propaganda about it. Nor was there ever any suggestion in Britain of government censorship of any of this.

That said, the volume of censuring has increased exponentially, thanks entirely to the separate but simultaneous growth in digital communication and social media. Whereas, previously, cartoons might elicit an outraged letter to an editor—let alone a death threat from the Gestapo—the internet allowed a global audience to see material to which thousands of people responded, thanks to email, with concerted deluges of hate email and regular death threats. I have long since learnt to dismiss an email death threat as meaningless—a real one requires the commitment of finding my address, a stamp and possibly a body part of one of my loved ones—but it's the thought that counts.

More to the point was the second front in the culture struggle at the heart of the war on terror, in which both sides fought to take greater offence. Amid the bombs, bullets and piles of corpses across Iraq, Afghanistan, Bali, Madrid, London and all the other places, the greatest harm you could suffer, it seemed, was that you might be 'offended'. People sent me hate emails and threatened to kill me and my children because they were 'offended' by my depiction of George W. Bush, or by a cartoon criticizing Israel, or a stupid humorous drawing of anything that might mildly upset them or their beliefs.

It was into this atmosphere that the row over the cartoons of Mohammed published by the Danish newspaper *Jyllands-Posten* erupted, resulting in the deaths of at least 100 people (none of them cartoonists, but most of them Muslims, and many shot dead by Muslim soldiers or policemen). But that, of course, is another story. And— who knows?—may yet prove to be another war.

William Hogarth

BBC Radio 3, May 2014

In his history of the first Australian penal settlements, *The Fatal Shore*, the art critic Robert Hughes described the standard modern perception of Georgian England thus:

> A passing reference to violence, dirt and gin; a nod in the direction of the scaffold; a highwayman or two, a drunken judge, and some whores for local colour; but the rest is all curricles and fanlights. Modern squalor is squalid but Georgian squalor is 'Hogarthian', an art form in itself.

Note that adjective. By now it's so well entrenched we instinctively know what it means, though it's probably not the meaning Hogarth himself would have wanted. He had definite ambitions for his name to be associated with his practice, and yet the paint strokes or engraved lines and slashes aren't, of themselves, 'Hogarthian'.

And however much he wanted—pretty successfully—to found an entirely new school of British art, there's nothing really 'Hogarthian' in his proto-impressionist study *The Shrimp Girl* or in his innovatively realistic portrait of the philanthropic sea captain Thomas Coram, or his portrait of David Garrick or his murals in the Inns of Court or for Barts Hospital. These are all by Hogarth, for sure; they might even be 'Hogarthish'; but none of them quite ring true as 'Hogarthian', not the whole hog.

And yet *Gin Lane* and *The Four Stages of Cruelty* and *A Harlot's* and *Rake's* Progresses and *Four Times of the Day* all are palpably 'Hogarthian'.

Again, this has nothing to do with technique or the medium in which Hogarth produced these definingly Hogarthian images. The most modern man imaginable in the early modern era, self-made, commercial, eschewing patrons while infiltrating the heights of society, Hogarth was also a multi-platform artist. Nearly all his satirical series were launched simultaneously as paintings and engravings, and sometimes—to get his third bite of the cherry—he'd engrave, print and sell combined entrance and lottery tickets, allowing the punters ingress to his studio to view the painting and—just possibly—win an engraving of the original. This is enterprising, but it isn't Hogarthian.

Basically, 'Hogarthian' is that weird yet common formulation, the self-defining adjective. Something where the definition lies in what it defines. As if he were wandering through a tatty Palladian hall of dirty mirrors, Hogarth depicted Georgian London and it reflected its Hogarthianness back to him until the depiction, reflected and re-reflected in the distorting mirrors of satire and time, became the definition.

And to give him his due, Hogarth was the man for the job. His life spanned Georgian London's formative years as well as its expanding geography. He was born in 1697 near Newgate Prison, though an even more Hogarthian local landmark was the Fleet Ditch, that sluggish, stinking Thames tributary on whose banks stood the Fleet Prison, wherein Hogarth's father was imprisoned for debt for five years during William's childhood.

Moreover, the Fleet Ditch brimmed, in addition to the blood and guts washed down from Smithfield and all its other faecal effluvia, with satirical symbolism. This was, after all, London's very own River Styx, emblematically demarcating the old, charred medieval city replete with its usurers and merchants from the lawyers and printers and property speculators further west. And it was duly blessed by the godfather of satire Jonathan Swift in his 'A Description of a City Shower':

> Sweepings from Butchers Stalls, Dung, Guts, and Blood,
> Drown'd Puppies, stinking sprats, all drench'd in Mud,
> Dead Cats, and Turnip-Tops come tumbling down the Flood.

That was written when Hogarth was 12 and just escaping the miasmas of the Fleet by being apprenticed to an engraver up west in Leicester Fields. There he stayed and prospered, never quite retiring to his country residence out in Chiswick, these days just up the road from his eponymous roundabout.

One of Hogarth's early satirical engravings was a rip-off of Swift's *Gulliver's Travels*, depicting Gulliver, non-canonically, punished for pissing on the Emperor's palace by being administered an enema by the Lilliputians. If Swift knew about this shameless coat-tailing, he didn't repine. In 1736, lambasting the Parliament of Ireland in 'A Character, Panegyric, and Description of the Legion Club', Swift suddenly breaks the fourth wall to make this direct appeal to Hogarth:

> How I want thee, humorous *Hogarth*?
> Thou I hear, a pleasant rogue art;
> Were but you and I acquainted,
> Every Monster should be painted:
> You should try your graving Tools
> On this odious Group of Fools;

Alas, posterity denied us an Enlightenment collaboration pre-echoing Hunter S. Thompson and Ralph Steadman, though there was no shortage of Georgian fear and loathing for Hogarth to engrave or Swift to describe. Nor should we be surprised that the Fleet Ditch appealed to Swift's scatological muse, which thereafter informed Hogarth's apocryphal depiction of Gulliver's colonic irrigation: the purpose of satire, after all, is to take the piss, reinforcing the universal truth that our masters and imagined betters, like us, shit and will die.

William Hogarth, *The Punishment Inflicted on Lemuel Gulliver* (December 1726)

GIN LANE.

Gin cursed Fiend, with Fury fraught,
Makes human Race a Prey.
It enters by a deadly Draught,
And steals our Life away.

Virtue and Truth driv'n to Despair,
It's Rage compells to fly.
But cherishes with hellish Care,
Theft, Murder, Perjury.

Damn'd Cup! that on the Vitals preys,
That liquid Fire contains
Which Madness to the Heart conveys,
And rolls it thro' the Veins.

William Hogarth, *Gin Lane* (1751)

William Hogarth, *The Four Stages of Cruelty* (*clockwise from top-left*) (1751)

William Hogarth, *Four Times of the Day* (*clockwise from top-left*) (1736–38)

William Hogarth, Plate 8 in *Industry and Idleness* (1747)

The IDLE PRENTICE Executed at Tyburn.

William Hogarth, Plate 11 in *Industry and Idleness* (1747)

But there's more to it than just that. Swift's poem is a satirical portrait of the urban. Hogarth's subject became the new London of elegant Georgian squares emerging in Soho and beyond, but as with Swift, showing it as it truly was: the greatest city the world may have ever seen, but without flush toilets. Naturally, Hogarth shows us the consequence: in *Four Times of the Day* and throughout his oeuvre, there's a constant leitmotif of chamber pots being emptied out of windows to add to the casual catastrophes of the street below. We all get the satirical point, just as we do with his depictions of Frenchified dandies stepping out of their churches, coffee houses, clubs or courtrooms into gutters full of shit and squashed cats. And that's just in the smart part of town. Wait till you hit the surrounding slums.

As in *Gin Lane*, probably the definingly Hogarthian image of Georgian London, where the depiction of urban squalor in the St Giles Rookeries was intended to work like a tabloid headline. It was meant to function as a terrifying polemic, part of a concerted campaign Hogarth had launched with Henry Fielding to address the source of a general moral collapse in society. After the seismic shock of the Jacobite uprising of 1745, London was seized by fresh panic, with the wealthier classes in general flight to the country from fear of the city's poor. Otherwise they risked the genuine threat of being held up by highwaymen in Piccadilly in broad daylight. All this was blamed on the free availability of cheap Dutch gin, the chosen opiate of the underclass. Moreover, they remembered Judith Dufour 15 years previously, who'd taken her infant daughter out of the workhouse and then strangled the little girl to sell the clothes she'd been issued with in order to buy gin.

Gin Lane was published simultaneously with *Beer Street*, a comparatively tepid extolling of the honest English alternative to evil foreign gin, along with *The Four Stages of Cruelty*, which charted the inevitable path from tormenting animals to murder and then dissection by the anatomists, the final, eternal punishment wrought by the Enlightenment on executed London paupers. The prints were all were produced on cheap paper for widest circulation and, unlike earlier series, they had no companion paintings: these images existed solely to be reproduced and circulated, as polemical texts.

In other hands this all might have worked well enough, but the message and the depiction of the squalor and its horror isn't what finally makes them, and particularly *Gin Lane*, so wholly Hogarthian. It's the jokes.

Hogarth's polemic is clear, but it's almost as if he can't help himself from lowering the high moral tone with a few gags. Actually, a lot of gags. Look at the background of *Gin Lane* and it's crammed with jokes: drunks and dogs fighting over bones; gin being forced down the throats of cripples and babies, a drunken carpenter pawning the tools of his trade, a drunken baker accidentally impaling his own baby. Corpses are disinterred, a barber hangs himself in a collapsing building, a blind man tries to throw a stool in a bar-room brawl. And central to it all is the horrific image of the woman dropping her infant son to his certain death down a stairwell. And it's a gag. It's a joke on the central iconography of Christianity, of the Madonna and Child, though here the Madonna is so pissed—note that cloacal word again—she's dropping and killing the Christ child, the exclusive medium of possible redemption, out of drunken neglect and, basically, not giving a shit.

And there, getting back to adjectives, lies the difference between a Hogarthian and Dickensian slum: you weep at the latter (which was 80 years but only yards away from *Gin Lane*) because there's hope of redemption, and the horror lies in that hope being dashed. In Hogarth's slums, there's no hope of redemption at all, so you might as well laugh.

Indeed, sometimes Hogarth seems quite unable to resist the temptation to lower the tone. In Plate 8 of the polemical and, frankly, preachy series *Industry and Idleness*, when the virtuous, industrious (and smug) apprentice becomes a sheriff of London, he's a tiny figure in the background at the feast in the city, and our eyes are drawn irresistibly, like Hogarth's attention, to the swinish aldermen (and, presumably, previously industrious apprentices themselves) gloriously and grotesquely at trough at the image's focal centre. Likewise, in Plate 11, when the idle apprentice is on his way to be hanged, the scene is so vibrantly carnivalesque we end up enchanted by what should be Tyburn's instructive terrors.

Yet, remember Swift's supplication: 'How I want thee, humorous Hogarth'. Not savage, or squalid, or cynical, but funny. True, the jokes—like Swift's gag, told too deadpan, about the Yahoos and the Houyhnhnms in *Gulliver's*—are dark, jet black, in fact, but that's what jokes are for, to work that strange transubstantiation transforming the mundane horrors of the everyday into laughter, releasing all those lovely endorphins which help us navigate our way through life without going mad with despair.

And, of course, from necessity they had stronger stomachs back then. Yet while the Hogarthian is all those things—savage, squalid and cynical—Hogarth only made it so because his humanity left him genuinely appalled by the horrors of the Hogarthian Age. That's how the man, this philanthropist and patron of the Foundling Hospital, in his own way as sentimental as Sterne, informed the artist who always makes his characters topsy-turvily 'progress' towards perdition. It's from the pity of it all.

Because, in the end, down those Hogarthian streets walked a man called Hogarth who was not himself Hogarthian, thus belying the word he bequeathed us. Because, like most Georgians, his genius lies not in the strongness of his stomach, but in the softness of his heart.

Designed, Invented & Limmed by M. Rowson as a Burlesque upon ye Tale Wm. Hogarth, Eq., 4th Marc

Otto Dix: Der Krieg

BBC Radio 3, June 2014

Standing on the front at Bexhill-on-Sea, looking out over the English Channel, you can't really imagine the flood tides of European history and culture breaking and crashing on the groynes and pebble beaches before you. But turn round and you'll see the De La Warr Pavilion, possibly the first and certainly one of the finest modernist buildings in Britain. Commissioned by the socialist 9th Earl De La Warr in 1935 to be, I quote, 'simple in design and suitable for a holiday resort in the south of England', this sleek, white, steel-and-concrete monument to sunlight and fresh sea breezes reopened in 2005 after extensive restoration, as a show case for contemporary or, to use the stale old vernacular, 'modern' art.

Another of Bexhill's claims to fame, which would have earned the town a place in infamy had history run its course differently, is that it happened to be one of the proposed landing beaches for Operation Sealion, the Nazis' aborted plan for a seaborne invasion of Southern England in 1940. And had Bexhill become Hitler's Omaha Beach, you can't help wondering what might have befallen the De La Warr Pavilion.

I reckon it would have been fine. Behind their championing of folklore and kitsch, twinned to their demonization of what they called 'degenerate' art, the Nazis were as much suckers for the flowing, uncluttered lines of modernism as anyone else, whether in Albert Speer's architecture, Hugo Boss' designs for the uniforms worn by the SS or all those beautiful fighter planes where the sweaty modernist dreams of fascists and fascist fellow-travellers like Marinetti and Wyndham Lewis became metal flesh.

But of one thing you can be sure. Under whatever kind of Kultur-Gauleiter that might have ended up in charge of the arts in Southern England in this alternative history, the De La Warr Pavilion would not be marking the 100th anniversary of the outbreak of the First World War by exhibiting 19 plates from Otto Dix's 1924 series of etchings, *Der Krieg*.

Dix, along with George Grosz, was one of the leading modernist artists in post–Great War Germany; a star of Dada, the expressionist and then the Neue Sachlichkeit or New Objectivity schools of art which followed each other in rapid succession as they sought to both interrogate and inculpate the fatal contradictions of the Weimar Republic. But his was a very different kind of modernism, exactly the kind that the Nazis defined as 'degenerate'. Dix's paintings *The Trench* and *War Cripples* were both displayed at the notorious state-sponsored 1937 Munich exhibition of Degenerate

Art—along with works by Max Beckmann, Grosz, Chagall, Max Ernst, Mondrian, Paul Klee and many others—and afterwards burned.

And it wasn't just the Nazis who responded badly to Dix's output. Fourteen years before it was thrown on a bonfire, *The Trench* was displayed in the Wallraf–Richartz Museum in Cologne behind a curtain to protect unsuspecting passers-by from accidentally viewing its depiction of dismembered and decomposing soldiers' bodies. Then, in 1925, the mayor of Cologne, Konrad Adenauer, later the architect of the post-war West Germany, cancelled the payment to purchase Dix's painting and forced the director of the Wallraf–Richartz to resign for trying to buy it in the first place. As for Dix, having survived the wrath of the Nazis by keeping his head down and restricting himself to painting landscapes, after the Second World War he settled down in Dresden in East Germany, far away from Adenauer, although, by the time he died in 1969, he was being claimed by both Germanies. But by then, of course, Modernism was old hat and therefore much safer to handle.

Back in Bexhill, the De La Warr show does Dix proud. The big, bright, airy enormity of the Pavilion's exhibition space, dimmed to exclude sunlight presumably to conserve the displayed artefacts, also serves to dwarf the 19 etchings, each not much larger than A4, but in precisely the right way. Seeing them like this, in the gloom, the images in *Der Krieg* become even more claustrophobic, just like being stuck in a trench, eating your lunch among your comrades' rotting corpses in Plate 13, 'Mealtime in the Trench: Loretto Heights', or crammed absurdly tightly into the space available, as in Plate 12, 'Stormtroopers Advance Under a Gas Attack'. Even the bodies of the living soldiers seem to be collapsing in on themselves: these warriors are short, stumpy men with foreshortened limbs and round, puggy faces. In fact, there's more than just a hint of the caricatural, even the cartoonish about Dix's soldiers, while he also continually deploys overdrawing. This is one of the defining tricks of modernism, that transgressive line that breaks all the rules by breaking across other lines drawn or etched in pursuit of the purpose of all visual art hitherto, which was to capture reality. This trick is also used brilliantly by the cartoonists Ronald Searle and Ralph Steadman, because breaking the rules of realism, of reality, is the only real way of getting to the truth.

And the truth was what Dix was after, after a fashion. Self-consciously based on Goya's series of etchings, *The Disasters of War*, and often as difficult to look at as many of Goya's images of the atrocities wrought in the Peninsular War over a century previously, *Der Krieg* is, on one level, simply a record of Dix's own experiences as a soldier, as a machine-gunner in the trenches. This, after all, was what they meant by New Objectivity. As Dix himself wrote in his diary in 1924, the year he etched *Der Krieg*, 'I am neither political nor tendentious nor pacifistic nor moralizing, nor anything else. Nor do I paint in a symbolic Frenchified way—I am neither pro nor contra.'

The Guardian, November 2013

Whether you believe that or not, in itself, those words marked a change in Dix, a conversion to the supposed objectivity of modernism by the young man who, 10 years earlier, had enthusiastically volunteered to fight in the Great War, swept along in a wave of patriotism, and whose actions earned him an Iron Cross in 1918.

One must assume that that earlier Otto Dix was more of a Romantic than any kind of modernist. The Great War was also the last great Romantic war, waged between Kings and Emperors who inhabited faux-medieval courts surrounded by courtiers wearing plumed helmets and archaic armour. However we may view the war in retrospect, when it began it clearly appealed enormously to whatever Romantic compulsion made millions of young men across Europe volunteer for death or glory in defence of their homelands.

Indeed, Gavrilo Princip, whose murder of Archduke Franz Ferdinand sparked off the whole thing and resulted not just in the hecatombs of the Western Front but also the destruction of three great European empires, is almost a cookie-cutter example of European Romanticism: Goethe's sorrowful young Werther via the Romantic template of terrorism devised by the anarchist Mikhail Bakunin, who was, co-incidentally, Wagner's original model for Siegfried in the *Ring* cycle. This is Romanticism as wistful death cult, of blood, soil and glory, dying young whether as Werther, Keats, a Shropshire lad or the friend of J. M. Barrie's who leapt from the deck of the sinking *Lusitania*, torpedoed by a German U-Boat in 1915, quoting Peter Pan as he yelled out, 'To die will be an awfully big adventure.'

The reality, of course, is not Romantic. The patriotic Romanticism that fuelled the beginnings of the Great War got the blood and the soil in spades, but little glory. A medieval tournament between chivalric royal houses was waged industrially, with industrial quantities of carnage, cheered on by arch-modernists like the Vorticist Wyndham Lewis and the Futurist Marinetti as the apotheosis of the machine.

And Princip's own death was equally un-Romantic. Too young to be executed in 1914, he died in April 1918, imprisoned at the Terezin Fortress—later, under the Nazis, the notorious Theresienstadt prison—of skeletal tuberculosis, reduced, thanks to his rotting bones, to weighing little more than six stone. Dix would have produced a perfect portrait of the young man whose Romantic yearnings kicked off the terrible, chaotic birth of the modern and the totalitarian necrocracies that thereafter blighted Europe for most of the twentieth century. Though, remember that despite claiming to base themselves in objective scientific truth—though eugenics and dialectical materialism are equally, murderously bogus—both the Nazis and the Marxist Soviets had their roots in German Romanticism of the 1820s.

Getting back to Dix's etchings in *Der Krieg*, there's another alternative history. In this one, it's not the Nazis invading England via Bexhill-on-Sea, but the Germans winning the Great War; the version of events where the spring offensive of 1918, when Dix won his Iron Cross, worked.

But in those circumstances, would he still have gone on to feel compelled, six years later, to etch this terrifying record of the horrors of war?

There's a pretty good chance he would, though the effects would be entirely different. Despite Dix's claims to modernist objectivity, *The Trench*, *Der Krieg* and his other work from the Weimar period produced the reaction they did because their objectivity was, in itself, a subjective indictment of post–Great War Germany. The point is rammed home if you compare two pictures on identical subjects, one by Dix and the other by the society portraitist John Singer Sargent.

Sargent's famous painting *Gassed* was first exhibited in 1919, having been commissioned by the British War Memorials Committee in July 1918, four months before the Armistice. It was voted 'Picture of the Year' by the Royal Academy of Arts, and depicts a crocodile of blindfolded men, victims of a gas attack, being led through a flat, almost twilit landscape seething with their wounded, blinded comrades. In the same way as Dix owed a debt to Goya, *Gassed* references Pieter Bruegel's 1568 painting *The Parable of the Blind*, though it also has a great deal in common, both in composition and execution, with one of those late Pre-Raphaelite, achingly Romantic Burne-Jones paintings of a line of languid, torpid young women, half in love with easeful death. While it effectively evokes the horror and pity of war, you can't imagine this painting being produced by the losing side. It's also over 20-feet wide.

Dix's third plate from *Der Krieg*, 'Gas Victims: Templeux-la-Fosse, August 1916', on the other hand, is about a foot and a bit wide. The gas victims are, once more, Dix's typical, stumpy caricatures, but this time their faces are blackened by lack of oxygen into unrecognizability as being even human. Two medical orderlies stand nonchalantly beside the prone ranks of wounded men.

For the record, two of the more famous gas victims of the Great War were Ford Madox Ford, one of the most prominent cheerleaders of literary modernism, and Adolf Hitler.

But while it's just about possible to imagine Dix's 'Gas Victims' being produced by the winners, it would have been as part of the remembrance, of the pity as much as the horror of war. In Britain, thanks to Wilfred Owen, Siegfried Sassoon, Robert Graves and others, critical responses to how the war had been waged had their vanguard in poetry. This poetry, moreover, rapidly eclipsed the earlier, mawkish jingoism of Rupert Brooke, who'd died on his way to Gallipoli as a result of a mosquito biting his

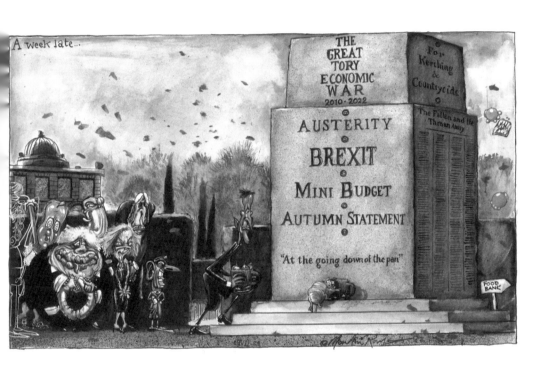

The Guardian, November 2022

lip without him seeing a shot fired in anger. Remembered horror became the poetic pity of remembrance, and the British could be united in that remembrance because, having won, they had the luxury of room enough to respond this way. The Germans, having lost, hardly had enough room to remember, let along engage in remembrance.

Sargent's *Gassed* now hangs in the Imperial War Museum. In post–Great War Germany, if you'd given a museum a name like that you could guarantee the opening ceremony would end in a shootout between the Freikorps and the Commies. When Weimar finally got round to building its national monument of commemoration at the Tannenberg Memorial in East Prussia, unlike the understatement of London's Cenotaph, it seemed to yearn for a defiant if wholly inappropriate triumphalism: it was on the site of a German victory; it was enormous, based on a Teutonic Knights' castle; at the opening ceremony in 1927, President Hindenburg, in full military uniform, made no apology and expressed no regrets for the war; most significantly, no Jews or socialist or Communist deputies were invited.

There was no collective remembrance because there was no German consensus on their defeat. The founding myth of the Nazis was that Germany had been 'stabbed in the back' by traitors at home rather than defeated in the field. There was, therefore, nothing ignoble in the war at all, despite its objective horrors and the pity therein. So even the act of remembering, like Otto Dix did, was already in the worst possible taste; and thereafter remembering inevitably became an indictment of Weimar's innate decadence in refusing to remember. And then the remembering rebounded on the artists who, in exposing Weimar's decadence, were thereafter denounced by the Nazis, who hated Weimar too, as themselves degenerate.

Which is why *Der Krieg* still resonates so powerfully. It's less about the Great War itself than its aftermath, and you cannot and should not unpick the stitches tying them together. After all, while Dix claimed merely to be remembering the war and its unimaginable horrors, the Nazis' whole point was to re-enact them.

The Guardian, November 2001

Charlie Hebdo

British Journalism Review, February 2015

I've no idea how many people died violent, premature deaths during the course of January this year. But I'm sure almost every single one of them went unreported. And even if you narrow the death toll down solely to people killed by the actions of so-called Islamists, you can safely assume the vast majority of those deaths went unreported too, whether it was men and women killed in defence of the Syrian city of Kobani or anybody else unfortunate enough to live under the necrocratic tyranny of the self-styled Islamic State which straddles the geopolitical ruins of Iraq and Syria.

If you narrow it down even further—to people killed by the actions of so-called Islamists on a single day in January this year—we'll never know the names of most of those murdered people. Worse, there's not even agreement on the number of people who were killed by Boko Haram in Baga in north-eastern Nigeria on 7 January. Was it 2000, according one local government official, or 150, as claimed by the Nigerian government? Or none at all, as the head of the regional government insisted afterwards? Remoteness, the fog of war, the claims and counter claims of rival propagandists make the truth almost impossible to grasp—almost as impossible to grasp as two of the three alternative realities on offer from Baga. Whatever the precise number of corpses, it's standard for the horror, pity and disgust to be informed by more qualitative factors than quantitative ones. Right up to when you lose count of the body count, that is. It was the failed seminarian and atheist mass-murderer Joseph Stalin who observed that one death is a tragedy, but a million deaths is just a statistic.

Maybe that's one of the reasons why the murders at the offices of *Charlie Hebdo* in Paris on 7 January echoed round the world and continue to reverberate: the size of the horror is graspable, and we know the names. They also took place in the heart of a Western capital teeming with millions of people. Indeed, the murder of police officer Ahmed Merabet, a Muslim of Algerian descent like his murderers Said and Chérif Kouachi, was caught live on CCTV. Mustapha Ourrad, a copy taker at *Charlie Hebdo*, was also of Algerian descent and was also murdered by the Kouachi brothers, with what surviving witnesses described as calm, execution-style deliberation. Also murdered were Frédéric Boisseau, *Charlie Hebdo*'s building maintenance man; Franck Brinsolaro, another police officer assigned as a bodyguard to the magazine's editor-in-chief; Elsa Cayat, a psychoanalyst who was Jewish and the only woman killed in the atrocity, though the Kouachis specifically spared the lives of other women in the room; Bernard

Maris, a professor of economics and shareholder in *Charlie Hebdo*; and Michel Renaud, a 69-year-old French journalist due to guest edit a future edition of the magazine.

And yet what made the *Charlie Hebdo* killings so exquisitely, exceptionally horrific were the five other victims, who were all cartoonists. This, it seemed, was a brutal and bloody assault on laughter. Which meant it was also an assault on the very fact of being human itself.

Laughter, after all, is one of the things we're best at (along with killing each other, as it happens). That's because laughter is a hardwired evolutionary survival tool that stops us going mad with existentialist terror at the horrors life throws at us. These include death, sex, shit, our friends, our leaders and our enemies. And while anthropologists have claimed that it's uniquely human to use laughter as a means of social control through mockery, we're never as unique as we'd like to think. Our genetic cousins, chimpanzees, laugh to tell other chimps they're only playing, an important consideration when one chimp jumps playfully on top of another chimp but doesn't want immediately to be killed. So laughter, while it can be cruel, aggressive, exclusionary, taunting and bullying, is also playful. Although it's often deadly serious, the point is it's never serious enough to be deadly. That's because, according to the countless nuanced rules which govern how humans interact with each other and demonstrate one another's current power status, you're meant to get the joke. Satire in particular fails or flourishes around this point.

But the ultimate counterploy of the mockee—whether it's a despotic government or a picked-upon kid in a playground—is always to grab back the power advantage, refuse to get the joke and kill the mocker to shut them up. In other words, just hunker back into the comfort of your chimp brain and pretend you didn't hear the play signal. And that, in a nutshell, is what happened in *Charlie Hebdo*'s offices on 7 January 2015. Although, as you'd expect, it was far, far more complicated than that.

Nonetheless, without stretching the point too far, there's a hint of the inherent violence in all humour if you consider that the murdered cartoonists—whose names we know—were all famous not for their names, but for their noms de plume: Charb was the magazine's director of publication Stéphane Charbonnier; Tignous' real name was Bernard Verlhac; Philippe Honoré and Georges Wolinski both signed themselves, like Giles or Low, with just their surnames, while Jean Cabut shortened his already shortened name to Cabu.

This has long been the fashion among cartoonists, exceptionally among journalists. And while it may be the only point of connection between, say, Trog or JAK and Stalin and Trotsky, cartoonists' noms de plume are a lot closer to noms de guerre than we like to think. Satire, and particularly visual satire, has always had more in common with political violence than stand-up comedy. It's dark, primal voodoo, sympathetic magic designed to do the victim harm. And it gets even deeper with the magic associated with names and name-calling, changed names and the sacredness of the unnameable: not speaking the name of god was—is—as powerful a taboo among many religions as portraying the Prophet Muhammad remains within a branch of Islam.

But even if you ignore all the cultural and anthropological baggage, at its heart visual satire is still assassination without the blood. That's my job, as I understand it, and it was also the job of my murdered colleagues. There's a defining grimness at the heart of it, although once again it's important to remember that bit about being without the blood. Because the purpose of our craft, however dark, is to leaven it all with laughter. And it works because your body releases all those lovely endorphins when you laugh which quite simply make you feel better. That's why cartoonists tend to be loved far more than assassins.

Two of the *Charlie Hebdo* cartoonists in particular were deeply and widely loved, and heavy with fame and honours as a consequence. Wolinski was awarded a Légion d'honneur in 2005, while Cabu was famous—very famous—among other things for regularly featuring drawing cartoons on French children's TV. Imagine Rolf Harris being deliberately gunned down by masked assassins—but a good Rolf Harris, in his pomp and before his downfall—and you begin to creep towards what these murders actually mean in France. Imagine, if it's easier, Giles being murdered by terrorists. Go back a couple of generations and try to imagine the same happening to Illingworth or Low or Vicky. Or even Heath Robinson. (All of whom, incidentally, were on the Gestapo death list, due for summary execution had the Nazis invaded Britain.)

These cartoonists weren't just famous and loved, they were old too. Honoré was 73, Cabu 76 and Wolinski 80. That should tell us something else about *Charlie Hebdo*. These were men of the '68 generation, whose sensibilities were informed as much by surrealism and situationism as by France's much vaunted secularist tradition. That places them not so much within journalism than as part of the European artistic avant-garde, home to composers like Karlheinz Stockhausen, who described the 9/11 attacks as 'the biggest work of art there has ever been'.

Their spiritual ancestors would also include the surrealist film director Luis Buñuel, who was so convinced his debut film *An Andalusian Dog* would trigger a riot he stood behind the screen at the premiere with his pockets filled with rocks to throw at the audience if they turned nasty. His next film, *L'Age d'Or*, did succeed in provoking riots with its final reel depicting the dissolute roués from de Sade's *Salò, or the 120 Days of Sodom* leaving the scene of their orgies accompanied by Jesus Christ. The film was banned, but the purpose all along had been to shock and provoke authority into reaction.

Forty years after Bunuel's films, Situationism, a weird hybrid of surrealism and Trotskyism, in its turn sought to spark revolution by creating a 'situation' through provocation. (Situationism only really took seed in Britain in Malcolm McLaren's Sex Pistols, Tony Wilson's Factory Records and the increasingly bizarre contrarianism of the Revolutionary Communist Party's Brendan O'Neill and Claire Fox at *Spiked Online* and the Institute of Ideas.)

Then add to all that how the magazine had been born, as an act of defiance to the reaction of an instigating provocation. *Charlie Hebdo*'s immediate parent was *Hara-Kiri Hebdo*, which was banned by the French government in 1970 after it had mocked the death of Charles de Gaulle by comparing it to a recent disco fire which had killed 149 people: 'Tragic Ball in Colombey [-les-Deux-Églises, de Gaulle's home]: 1 dead.'

It was, of course, a funny, provocative and ironic gag to name the reborn magazine after the dead de Gaulle. Irony is woven into the DNA of humour in general and satire in particular. Think of Swift's *A Modest Proposal*. In the babel of whataboutery that came in the wake of the *Charlie Hebdo* massacre, while many people claimed the magazine's covers had been increasingly racist in tone, its defenders, on top of saying *Charlie Hebdo* attacked absolutely everyone, insisted that those covers were ironic. But ironies get lost, deliberately or otherwise, and always have done. Three centuries ago, Daniel Defoe wrote *The Shortest Way with the Dissenters* as an ironic attack on growing Tory hostility to Dissenters, concluding his satirical, sarcastic defence of the Church of England with the line 'NOW, LET US CRUCIFY THE THIEVES!' He was pilloried and imprisoned by magistrates who thought (or claimed to think) he was being serious. Then again, there's no evidence Julius Streicher, editor of the cartoon-heavy anti-Semitic hate-sheet *Der Stürmer*, ever for a single second contemplated the irony defence at his Nuremburg trial, at the end of which he was hanged.

A professional translator friend of mine from Northern Ireland, where they know about this kind of thing, is far more familiar with *Charlie Hebdo* than many, and emailed me the following observation, invoking Streicher:

> The Mohammed pics remind me of the Garvaghy Road—someone's told us we can't do this so we have to. I could mail you some scans of an old *Hara-Kiri* from about 1976 but we'd probably have the rozzers round. However . . . [the] 'Charia Hebdo' issue [CH's defiant response to the bombing of their offices in 2011] . . . looks to me like South Thanet UKIP had some bright ideas after a night in the Dog and Duck and asked Julius Streicher if he could do anything with them. That's just me.

So. Do you get it, or don't you? Because the more you consider *Charlie Hebdo* and its aftermath, the thicker and more tangled the ironies become. Henri Roussel, founder of *Hara-Kiri*, wrote an article in *Nouvel Observateur* denouncing Charbonnier for making his defiance of the jihadis who'd bombed his offices so provocative he deliberately invited the murder of Roussel's old friend Wolinski. The editors of *Nouvel Observateur* subsequently felt compelled to justify publishing the article in the name of free expression. Meanwhile, a 16-year-old schoolboy in France was arrested for posting on Facebook a parody of a *Charlie Hebdo* cover which had originally shown bullets flying through a copy of the Quran into a turbaned figure with the headline 'The Quran is Shit'; the parody showed bullets passing through the original cover into the body of a *Charlie Hebdo* cartoonist.

Then there's the irony of a satirical magazine receiving a million euro subsidy from the state it was created to attack (that's free expression for you). Or the further irony of some of the world's grislier leaders 'marching' in support of *Charlie Hebdo*, including a representative of Saudi Arabia, two days after Raif Badawi received the first 50 lashes of his 1000 lashes and 10 year prison sentence for 'insulting Islam'. Also present were Benjamin Netanyahu, whose Israeli government arrested and imprisoned Palestinian cartoonist Mohammad Saba'aneh for five months in 2013 for 'being in contact with a hostile organization', and Mahmoud Abbas, whose Palestinian Authority is investigating the same cartoonist as I write this for a sympathetic cartoon of the Prophet Muhammad published in a Ramallah newspaper.

I very nearly drew something similar for the *Guardian* two days after the murders. My cartoon was going to show Muhammad with one hand covering his face in despair, the other stroking his cat Muezza, and wearing a 'Not In My Name' T-shirt. Given the sensitivities involved, I emailed Alan Rusbridger with the idea a good 36 hours before I'd need to start work on it, and it was only after very lengthy deliberations at the highest levels of the paper, including long phone conversations between myself and Jonathan Freedland, that it was finally decided to go with something else. That was another cartoon, of me slumped on my drawing board and describing the first cartoon but admitting my loved ones slightly baulked at the idea of me dying to afford the readers a wry smile.

I entirely respect the *Guardian*'s decision, which was reached after a great deal of careful and, I suspect, agonizing thought. One reason for their decision was that they'd already run an editorial explaining why they weren't going to publish previous *Charlie Hebdo* cartoons of Muhammad; they also, like Roussel, saw no profit (and, right now, I won't ask you to excuse the pun) in ramping up and widening the provocation. Having discussed the implications of producing my first planned cartoon with my family, I also subsequently discovered that, despite initially agreeing to me proceeding, our children, both in their twenties, became physically ill with anxiety at what might befall me if I had. (Although, to his credit, our son did email me to say that if I was going to be assassinated, could I make sure it was him who did it. This, incidentally, was a joke.)

The hundreds of online posters who then accused me and the *Guardian* of unspeakable cowardice and appeasement in not drawing Muhammad seemed oblivious to the further ironies of their denunciations being anonymous (you know, like in those bastions of free expression, Nazi Germany and the Soviet Union). Perhaps they don't care. They certainly seem indifferent to my welfare, as it became clear to me that one bunch of masked maniacs would be happy to kill me for what I might draw, while another pack of idiots, digitally masked this time, were berating me for what I hadn't drawn and demanding I be prepared to die to further their geopolitical agenda. Though in baying for reprisals against an entire faith group in revenge for killings by its individual members, my detractors were unconsciously endorsing what we might term the 'Kristallnacht Protocol'.

Anyway, the cartoon I actually regret not drawing wasn't that one; it was the one of all those world leaders who'd boldly claimed 'Je suis Charlie' a week later holding up signs reading 'Je Suis King Abdullah of Saudi Arabia'.

Still, as we should expect nothing from our leaders beyond bitter ironies sliding effortlessly into stinking hypocrisy, there's no reason why this shouldn't apply to our prospective leaders either. These include the masters of the *Charlie Hebdo* cartoonists' murderers, whose mission is to make everyone on earth the same as them (something denounced rather eloquently by Jonathan Swift in *A Tale of a Tub*). A week after the killings, I wrote in my regular column in *Tribune*:

> To my eyes [these murderers] look most like a mafia hit against soft targets sending a simple message. Moreover, I suspect the message wasn't even addressed to 'the West', but to al-Qaeda's greatest rivals, the Islamic State. These were showcase killings to demonstrate that bin Laden's old mob were still in the game, via a global promo video (courtesy of Western TV) aimed at recruiting all those confused and angry young people locked in their bedrooms cruising the internet and, appalled by the actions of the West, being tempted into opting for IS's brand of holy barbarism instead of AQ's.

Interestingly, Tariq Ali came to the same conclusion in a piece for the *London Review of Books*, likewise recognizing in this whole affair that things are both deeper and shallower, simpler and infinitely more complicated than they appear. Just like a cartoon can trigger many different responses in different circumstances targeting receptors both deep and hidden in our psyches or as shallow as the sweat on our furious faces.

In that light, I'd go further and insist this atrocity wasn't even about cartoons. In truth, and eternally, it was about totalitarianism, whether secular or religious (and I can't tell the difference); it was about totalitarianism's instinctive intolerance of laughter mocking its innate absurdity; it was about the lumbering, ludicrous thug in the kindergarten playground who comes over and thumps you just for looking at them, and for whom absolutely anything they choose will be offensive whenever they choose it to be, and will therefore justify them in doing the most offensive thing anyone ever can.

Which, should we be tempted to forget, is killing someone else, the eternal prerogative of the tyrant. And every joke, as Orwell observed, is a tiny revolution, a little act of defiance and resistance, and off it goes again.

I believe both the world and my profession will recover from this, as will mockery, satire and the giving and receiving of offence, and probably very quickly. The dead, however, will remain dead. Although it was their memory I betrayed the week following the massacre. In its immediate aftermath, I found myself besieged by the media, doing a great deal of TV and radio, usually saying exactly what I'd said already. By the next Tuesday, I thought I'd found refuge at a daylong meeting of a wildlife conservation charity of which I'm a trustee. However, when I turned my phone back on afterwards, there were texts from the *Today* programme, Sky News, *Newsnight*, Radio 5 Live and LBC, all wanting me to fill their dead air with my response to the *Charlie Hebdo* survivors' issue. I deleted them all and silently concluded that if they couldn't do without me they could always turn off their transmitters and give the rest of us a break.

But then the cartoonist within me kicked back in. I should, I now realize, have gone on all those platforms, pointed to the magazine's cover of Muhammad holding his 'Je suis Charlie' sign (out of shot, inevitably) and said 'This is scandalous! I've never seen anything so offensive! These people call themselves satirists and they produce this kind of mawkish shit? They should've had Muhammad dancing on the graves laughing "Those lippy Froggie Cunts had it fucking coming!" Then, in faux surprise, I would have said, 'Oh! Sorry! Didn't you want that much free expression?'

But it's always had its limits, as any idiot could have told you from the beginning. My job is to stretch them as far as they'll go; they pushed them till they broke.

---

* I've since been told *Charlie Hebdo*'s first response, within hours of the massacre, was a mock-up of the cover that got *Hara-Kiri* banned, headlined: 'Tragic Ball in Paris: 12 Dead'

James Gillray

The Guardian, March 2015

Whom would you prefer to have a drink with, Hogarth or Gillray? That may sound like an insanely arcane question, but it's one that I've discussed with other cartoonists on several occasions.

Ours is a small profession, with an exaggerated reverence for its past masters, mostly because we're always stealing from them. And William Hogarth and James Gillray are, without question, the greatest gods in our firmament. The twentieth-century cartoonist David Low, himself now firmly embedded in the pantheon, was bang on when he described them as, respectively, the grandfather and father of the political cartoon.

Things that we'd now call political cartoons—mocking allegorical pictorial representations of public events—have been part of the political scene since printing. But in the 1730s, Hogarth took the form to new heights with 'modern moral tales' such as *A Rake's Progress* or *Marriage A-la-Mode*. Twenty years after Hogarth's death, Gillray adapted this general satirical vision (as a student at the Royal Academy, the young Gillray revered Hogarth's work) by honing it to what has remained the agenda of political cartoonists ever since: responding to contemporary events in ways that have far more in common with journalism than with what's commonly called 'art'. Between them, Hogarth and Gillray marked out either end of the open sewer of satire that ran through the heart of the Enlightenment.

To a large extent, we understand the eighteenth century through Hogarth and Gillray's eyes. From a world before photography, it is Hogarth's vision of London that has endured, with the savage slapstick of its greater and meaner thoroughfares, its strutting rakes, syphilitic whores, gin-sodden murderers, squashed cats and gallows. Likewise, if we have a visual awareness of Britain's statesmen from the tail end of that century, it's probably Gillray's versions of them: the freckly beanpole Pitt or the spherical Charles James Fox, or Edmund Burke, whom Gillray transformed almost beyond recognition into a pointy, interfering nose, a pair of spectacles and—thanks to his Irishness and rumoured Catholicism—a biretta.

Parallel to that open sewer of satire in Georgian London were real open sewers. A lot of the humour of eighteenth-century satirists is coloured by the realities of urban living, and the colour is often brown. London was expanding exponentially northwards and westwards, but it was still a city with no flush toilets. No wonder, then, that there's a kind of faecal satirical trickle-down, from Swift's scatology, via Hogarth, to

James Gillray, *Midas, Transmuting All into Paper* (1797)

James Gillray, *Fighting for the Dunghill, or Jack Tar Settling Buonaparte* (1798)

Gillray and his contemporaries. In *The French Invasion; or John Bull, Bombarding the Bum-Boats*, published in 1793 under a pseudonym, Gillray anthropomorphized the map of England into the body of George III, who's firing turds out of his arse (Portsmouth) on to the French fleet. Likewise, *Midas, Transmuting All Into Paper*, published in 1797, shows William Pitt vomiting bank notes and shitting money into the Bank of England.

This earthiness—'Hogarthian' defines it perfectly—didn't necessarily age well. Swift's dark last book of *Gulliver's Travels*, which his contemporaries 'got' with no trouble, led the Victorians to dismiss him as a deranged misanthrope. Gillray has suffered a similar fate, but the eighteenth-century audience had stronger stomachs. They had only to walk down the street to find not just shit in the gutters, but around the next corner, a child being publicly executed for stealing a bun. That said, it's the rawness of their filthiness that makes Gillray and Hogarth far more approachable than many of their contemporaries.

Which gets us to the heart of the beast, and why Gillray in particular, 200 years after his death, still matters. Personally, I believe satire is a survival mechanism to stop us all going mad at the horror and injustice of it all by inducing us to laugh instead of weep. More simply, satire serves to remind those who've placed themselves above us that they, like us, shit and they, too, will die. That's why, if we can, we laugh at both those things, as well as being disgusted and terrified by them. Beneath the veil of humour, there's always a deep, disturbing darkness.

And that's why, for my money, Gillray's greatest print was the one he produced after the Battle of Copenhagen, and which appeared at first sight to be a simple piece of jingoist triumphalism: Jack Tar, the naval avatar of John Bull, sits astride the globe, biffing Bonaparte and giving him a bloody nose. The title, though, gives Gillray's game away. It's called *Fighting for the Dunghill*. That interplay between text and image, with irony and nuance undercutting each other, is exactly how a political cartoon should work—and this is why Gillray remains great.

He also matters because he can lay claim to having produced the greatest political cartoon ever in *The Plumb-Pudding in Danger*, which is almost the type specimen of the medium. That's why it's been pastiched again and again by the rest of us. In it, Pitt and Bonaparte carve up the world between them in a never-bettered visual allegory for geopolitical struggle. It is, of course, just possible to imagine this being done straight: to conceive of a 'serious' artist depicting noble statesmen earnestly if allegorically slicing up a pudding, making the same point as Gillray but with considerably more gravitas. That hypothetical painting, though—I imagine it being about 40 feet wide and occupying a whole room in a palace—would have stunk. The power in *The Plum Pudding* lies entirely in its capacity to make us laugh, which arises from the way

James Gillray, *The Plumb-Pudding in Danger, or State Epicures Taking Un Petit Souper* (1805)

Gillray portrays the two great statesmen: Pitt, lanky and crafty; Bonaparte, short and manic. (In exile on Elba, Napoleon said Gillray's depictions of him did him more damage than a dozen generals.) Then there's the plum pudding itself. There's something deeply preposterous about reducing the titanic struggle for global hegemony to a fight over a dessert. After all, food—like shit—is for some reason always funny. It makes us reflect on the deeper, defining absurdity of two men who imagine that between them they can eat the whole world and everyone in it. The bathos melts inexorably into pathos. That's what a great political cartoon can do.

So, to get back to that imaginary drink: Hogarth or Gillray? In the past, we've always ended up opting for Hogarth. Gillray was without question a genius, but he was also a miserable sod, a quality not uncommon among cartoonists. He died insane as a result of his alcoholism, which got worse when his eyesight started failing. It's possible he killed himself, following an earlier attempt to throw himself out of the window of the room he occupied above Mrs Humphrey's printshop in St James', where the *Economist* building now stands. His friends described him as 'hypy', neurotically obsessed with his own ill health, while he grew up in the Moravian Church, which seemed to view our earthly existence as a hideous burden to endure before we're released into eternal life after death—a journey already undertaken by many of Gillray's siblings in infancy. Add to those factors a career spent transmuting the world's horror into laughter, and it's no wonder that, like the cartoonists Victor 'Vicky' Weisz and Phil May (to name only two), he experienced such a troubled end.

He's been accused of worse things. A former comment editor on this newspaper, when I was justifying the number of words in a cartoon by citing Gillray, dismissed my argument with: 'Gillray was a Tory'. He certainly took a pension from Pitt's government and produced some embarrassingly propagandist stuff for the ambitious young Tory MP George Canning's newspaper the *Anti-Jacobin*. In mitigation for *Light Expelling Darkness*, an April 1795 print showing a heroic Pitt as Apollo, we should consider *Presages of the Millennium* from two months later, in which Pitt is skewered ruthlessly as Death on a pale horse—not forgetting the famous 1791 print of Pitt as *An Excrescence, a Fungus, alias a Toadstool upon a Dunghill*, growing out of the British crown.

But Gillray even gets damned for his even-handedness. On the 28 and 29 March, the Ashmolean Museum in Oxford is hosting a seminar titled 'James Gillray@200: Caricaturist Without a Conscience?' The flier for the event accuses him of being 'an unreliable gun for hire' and having 'no moral compass'. It also repeats the story about Gillray proposing a toast to the French revolutionary painter Jacques-Louis David at a public dinner—implying the cartoonist then betrayed his revolutionary fervour with his prints attacking the Jacobins, such as the wonderfully overwrought *The Apotheosis of Hoche*. Well, maybe—though I've always suspected what Gillray was actually guilty of was that most indigestible of things for a historian: joking.

James Gillray, *Light Expelling Darkness* (1795)

James Gillray, *Presages of the Millenium* (1795)

MONSTROUS CRAWS, at a New Coalition Feast.

James Gillray, *Monstrous Craws at a New Coalition Feast* (1787)

And I'm compelled as an act of professional solidarity to say: give him a break. Cartoonists aren't romantic heroes. For the most part, we're just hacks trying to make a living by giving our readers an opportunity for a bit of a giggle. Occasionally, something horrific comes along, such as the *Charlie Hebdo* murders—and there are all the other cartoonists that governments around the world imprison and murder. But whatever the response, we're still cartoonists, not warriors.

Not that Gillray didn't have similarly hostile—if less deadly—encounters with the objects of his scorn. *The Presentation, or The Wise Men's Offering*, a 1796 cartoon depicting the Whig opposition led by Fox and Sheridan kissing the bottom of the prince regent's newly born daughter, Princess Charlotte, got Gillray arraigned on a charge of blasphemy. This, remember, was when booksellers risked being transported to Australia if they stocked Thomas Paine's *Rights of Man*. In addition to these travails, Gillray had also been courted for months by Canning, who wanted to be included in one of his prints. This alone demonstrates Gillray's significance, highlighting the perpetual truth that the one thing politicians hate more than being in a cartoon is not being important enough to be in one. As things turned out, Canning got Gillray off, and got him his government pension into the bargain.

But it's how Gillray repaid his saviour that, for cartoonists at least, is why he should be revered forever. In one of his finest, maddest prints, *Promis'd Horrors of the French Invasion*, a sans-culottes army of Jacobins march down Pall Mall as the gutters run with blood. Fox flogs Pitt, a church is set ablaze, and ministers and princes are beheaded and defenestrated. Some have dismissed the print as alarmist Tory propaganda, though to me it looks more like one of Hogarth's joyously dark carnivalesque scenes at Tyburn. Either way, just visible in the background, hanging from a lamppost and represented in the most demeaning fashion is, of course, Canning himself.

Massacres in Paris

Black Eye, November 2015

We should talk about the massacre in Paris, but which one? Do we mean the St Bartholomew's Day Massacre in 1572? That was instigated by the French king, Charles IX, and his mother, Catherine de' Medici, five days after Charles' sister Margaret had married the Huguenot leader Henry of Navarre. Grabbing the opportunity provided by so many Protestant aristocrats attending the wedding in Paris, Charles and Catherine paid mobs of Catholic thugs to kill every Protestant they could lay their hands on, the better to ensure the victory of orthodoxy and true religion. The final death toll across France may have been as high as 30,000. Apart from enriching English commercial and cultural life for centuries to come with a sudden influx of Huguenot refugees, these murders also inspired Christopher Marlowe's play *The Massacre at Paris*.

Or do we mean the September Massacres of 1792? That was when the French Revolutionary government, facing the imminent threat of foreign invasion and fearing the possibility of fifth columnists assisting the enemy, ordered the summary execution without trial of the inmates of Paris' gaols, carried out systematically by mobs of national guardsmen, militants and local livestock butchers. Of the roughly 1,200 prisoners thus murdered (half the prison population of Paris at the time), 220 were Catholic priests who had refused to submit to the Revolutionary government's Civil Constitution of the Clergy, a law of 1790 which subordinated the power of the Roman Catholic Church to the civil, secular authorities. The rest were common criminals, presumably by and large uninspired by either politics or religion. The massacre was largely fomented by the radical journalist Jean-Paul Marat who later, like Agamemnon and Jim Morrison, died in his bath. The largely freelance nature of the massacre is believed to have driven the Jacobin faction, led by the lawyer Maximilien Robespierre, to have formalized terror under the control of the state, in the interest of public order. During the 10 months of Robespierre's government, about 27,000 people across France were summarily executed.

Or do we mean the Semaine Sanglante ('Bloody Week') of May 1871, when the French republican government suppressed the Paris Commune, with a death toll of between 10,000 and 20,000, all murdered by government troops?

Or do we mean the Paris Massacre of 1961? That was when up to 200 people protesting peacefully against France's colonial war in Algeria were killed, either herded into the River Seine by police to drown, or murdered in the courtyard of the Paris police headquarters after having been arrested and delivered there in police buses. The massacre was the brainchild of Maurice Papon, previously a collaborationist civil servant under the Vichy government, later a prominent Gaullist politician, and at the time Parisian Prefect of Police. Successive French governments denied for decades that the massacre had ever happened.

Of course, there's a fundamental difference between all those historic deaths and the killings of 2015: 17 people killed in January at the offices of *Charlie Hebdo* and later in a Jewish delicatessen; 131 people murdered on Friday, 13 November, in the Bataclan Concert Hall and elsewhere across Paris' cafes and restaurants. The question is, where does it lie?

After all, the similarities, even across the centuries, are overwhelming. Each murder was wrought almost exclusively, though with the occasional Belgian thrown in, by French citizens or subjects on other French citizens or subjects, however they might ultimately define themselves according to their own lights. Each murder, to a lesser or greater degree, was inspired by the twisted, terrible tangle of political and religious imperatives which bedazzle too many human minds. Each murder, indeed, was motivated by the kind of religious considerations that also inspire people to ecstasies of bliss and selfless love. Robespierre beheaded priests for political reasons, but also beheaded militant and radical atheists because of his own devotion to the Supreme Being. The soldiers of the Third Republic, fighting their way street by street through Paris in 1871, lined the Communards up against the walls of Montmartre for immediate execution because they were socialists and anarchists, for sure, but also in part because the Commune had ordered the execution of the archbishop of Paris. And a fair few of the Communards who survived went on, a quarter of a century later, to become virulent anti-Dreyfusards, furiously insisting on the guilt of the framed Jewish officer Alfred Dreyfus. Thus, they mined a seam of deep-seated French anti-Semitism which later fuelled the fascism of the collaborationist Vichy regime and its servants. Like Maurice Papon, who later diverted his energies into similarly murderously assiduous actions against French Muslims.

And given those motivations, it should come as no surprise that none of the perpetrators of any of these murders would have imagined they were doing anything wrong. On the contrary, each one certainly believed, wholeheartedly, that they were doing good, and that the world was an immediately better place due to the removal of every one of those enemies of the Church, the King, the Revolution, France, the Republic, Good Order, Commerce, Virtue, the State, Islam or, perhaps most important, the Murderers' Finer Feelings.

Because, in each case, each corpse helped allay in some small part a previous hurt and laid to rest an army of affronts. That's how massacres happen, not through the evil actions of individual sadistic psychopaths, but through mass righteousness correcting the repulsive consequences of the crimes, mental and actual, of the massacred.

So the murderers of the five cartoonists in the offices of *Charlie Hebdo* on 7 January 2015 are practically indistinguishable from all the other Parisian lynch mobs across hundreds of years. Offence having been taken, the sentence was death. The only way they and their rival jihadis 10 months later differed from all the other murderers was that they managed to kill far fewer people and were not sponsored by the French state. They appealed instead to a higher authority.

Note that. From St Bartholomew's Day to the Bataclan, every murderer murdered because they were outraged on behalf of some higher authority or other. None of these murders were individual crimes passionnel, but always—always—on someone or something else's behalf, invariably something allegedly infinitely more powerful than the victims who had, through word or deed (or drawing), given the initial offence. Apart from the perennial and eternally pointless observation that god, history, destiny, kings and states should grow a pair and stop being so thin skinned, it's also worth observing how a murder is so much easier and sweeter when it's committed on behalf of victims, even if the victims now become the perpetrators and vice versa (which is, of course, what revolves in a revolution). Whether it's the soft-hearted servants of aristos or apostates at a prostitution party, the inherent guilt of the victim lies in their secret identity as perpetrators by association, even if this has never for a single moment entered the victims' heads, even at the moment of death.

Which gets us where? To something innately violent in the nature of Paris? Or of France? In fact, the innate violence—if you like, the violence inherent in the system—has much more to do with France being a state than France being French. Likewise, the Islamic aspect of Islamic State should alarm us less than the fact they aspire to be a state, because being a state authorizes the atrocities. In other words, you can literally get away with murder if you've got a head of state and a cushion of bureaucracy to soak up the blood.

Again, where does this get us? Sadly, back to the beginning. Back, moreover, to basics, to the fatal riddle at the heart of all human affairs, between the mass and the individual; the unresolvable blathering bullshit that sought liberty in gutters of blood beneath the guillotine, or equality in gulags full of the enemies of the people, or truth and justice in mawkish death cults like Islamic State. Or, for that matter, in European Romanticism, which elevates the suffering of the sovereign individual self all the way to the gates of Auschwitz, guarded by Romantic heroes shovelling the massed ranks of their oppressors into the ovens.

Parts of which might explain how it could be, when we're surrounded on every side by screaming injustice, economic atrocities, never-ending war on all fronts and the continuing hegemony of a ceaseless cavalcade of charmless psychopathic cunts, British university students' unions are creating 'safe places' where students will never be in danger of hearing anything that may upset them, including Germaine Greer possibly saying something disobliging about transgender people.

The Guardian, November 2015

This is partly thanks to the unforeseen consequence of social media trepanning humanity to allow our collective id to squirt incontinently forever from our skulls; partly, it's a laudably democratic extension of the notion of lèse-majesté. Either way, offence is now taken at every turn even when it isn't given. Twitter and Facebook abound with people waiting to be offended on someone else's behalf so they can start posting death threats from their 'safe places'.

This madness is becoming universal. The powerless evoke it as a tactical slingshot, the powerful evoke it as a strategic weapon of mass destruction. Even though it should be obvious that the most offensive thing anybody can ever do to anybody else is kill them, wholly decent people have told me, when I've spoken to them about the *Charlie Hebdo* killings, that of course *Charlie Hebdo*'s cartoons were appallingly racist and sexist, and seem entirely unable to understand my point when I ask them over and over again when it was that racism and sexism became capital crimes. Even when I've asked what Frederic Boisseau, *Charlie Hebdo*'s janitor, had done to deserve being shot down with assault weapons, it seems in these good people's minds that words, though cheap, are so deadly that human lives are rendered cheaper.

This tendency is manifest at its worst on what we still loosely call the 'left', and I think I know why. This urge to trample on free expression, which along the way scoops up a deranged kind of tacit approval for a ragtag army of child-raping, slave-owning murderers like Islamic State, is motivated by kindness. Although, as a satirist, I target my offence exclusively at the powerful, other people take the offence, albeit unoffered to them on their behalf *because being rude about anyone—everyone—is unkind.* So if I draw a bunch of murderous thugs like the Saudi royal family or their familiars in IS, this has the potential for being Islamophobic; cartoons about Israel are automatically anti-Semitic; a cartoon of Obama, as likely as not, is racist. And on it goes forever. In this truly bizarre two-way transubstantiation dynamic, where individuals become universal and universes become personal, I suspect it won't be long before a Twitterstorm assails the History Channel for their truly offensive repeated Nazi-ism.

Thus, we kill, or acquit the killers, through kindness, through the kindest of motivations. Which I think you'll find alternate with good intentions in the crazy paving on the way to hell. Or am I being hellist? Though, to their credit, I think the Satanists are about the only religious group none of whose adherents has ever threatened me, however loosely, with death. Meanwhile, which Paris massacre should we talk about? I know, let's wait, heads in hands, for the next one.

Art Is a Serious Business

Artenol, June 2016

On my birthday this year, our daughter, who's a graduate from the Slade School of Fine Art in London, took me as a treat to an event performed by her friend and collaborator Matt, taking place in the Serpentine Galleries' cafe. And very good it was too: clever, thoughtful, provocative, strangely beautiful, disturbing and, in places, very, very funny. Though oddly—and here we get to the point—during the funny bits, so far as I could tell, I was the only person in the place laughing out loud.

There could be all sorts of reasons for this. Maybe everyone else had no sense of humour. Maybe, more likely, I'd laughed in all the wrong places, both gauchely and hideously inappropriately, like the audiences I always seem to sit amidst every time I see a play in the West End, who seem to think the very act of engaging expensively with the dramatic arts empowers and entitles them to laugh at bloody everything. Either way, when I congratulated Matt afterwards, we both commented on my lonely, isolated laughter, me with puzzlement and Matt with a certain amount of resentful resignation, because he'd wanted everyone to laugh. But, as we both reflected, art is a serious business.

What I do, as a political cartoonist, obviously isn't. That's why I call myself, rather pretentiously unpretentiously, a visual journalist rather than being any kind of 'artist'. I first started doing this about 20 years ago, deliberately to demarcate myself and my craft from the smart boys and girls kicking up a storm on Charles Saatchi's tab, with the money he earned deep in the heart of the Industry of Lies. I both draw and paint on an almost daily basis, and the kind of visual satire I create is in practice as rigidly codified in form and content as Japanese Noh: although I exaggerate the features of real people and place them in ridiculous narratives of pure fantasy, the kind of allegorical painting contained in a political (or editorial) cartoon is the last bastion of artistic realism. For instance, there are no truly great abstract-expressionist political cartoonists because the victims—the politicians—could say with unquestionable truth 'That looks nothing like me.' Likewise, the satirical intentions of, say, the Chapman Brothers, are different in both form and purpose to that of newspaper cartoonists.

And, of course, my standoffishness is reciprocated in spades. A few years ago, Tate Britain held a Francis Bacon retrospective, and for reasons I still don't quite understand, BBC Radio 4's flagship arts programme *Front Row* thought it would be a good idea for me and the artist Maggi Hambling to walk together round the show saying what we thought of it. Hambling wasn't in a good mood to begin with (she's recently quit smoking), but our broadcasting chemistry became positively toxic as we looked at an early Bacon painting of a baboon I'd never previously seen. It's an extraordinary piece, created with a dazzling sparsity of paint, which wholly captured the baboonness of a baboon in ways which I said, into the microphone, were 'caricaturally great'. Hambling narrowed her eyes and hissed 'How dare you! How dare you call Francis Bacon a caricaturist! Take it back at once!'

From one angle her attitude is incomprehensible: looked at from far enough away, what Hambling, Bacon and I all do is identical. 'Art', in essence, is the human capacity for artifice, for filtering our surrounding reality through a human consciousness to recreate it through reproduction—however mutated by human imagination it ends up during the filtration process—in what we'd now term 'safe mode'. In short, 'art' is about control; it's shamanism, voodoo, more to do with sympathetic magic than the Muses.

So, 'art' is instantly far, far more complex than simply 'making marks' (as the media-studies mob choose to mystify it) even though that's what Maggie Hambling, Francis Bacon and I do.

One obvious difference between us is that what I do I also sell on a regular basis, to be reproduced both in print and digitally, then seen potentially by millions and millions of people. If I'm lucky I'll then also sell the original drawing, for even more money. What Hambling and Bacon do, contrariwise, is sold (to their own financial advantage) just the once, though for much higher prices, possibly to someone who will be the only person who thereafter will ever see what they've produced. Even if photographically reproduced, the intention in their work—its soul, if you feel like dragging things like that into the argument—lies in its marketable uniqueness. Instantly, ownership plus rarity enhances status, and the status of the owner rubs off on the artist. Even the (caricatural, thank you very much) starving artist has inbuilt status higher than someone like me, because of the uniqueness of both their work and their plight. I, on the other hand, have committed the unforgivable sins, for an 'artist', of being commercial and being reproduced commercially, and therefore making a steady, regular living from my 'art'. So it's obvious that any artist, starving in a garret or high on the hog in a loft in Greenwich Village, will obviously be compelled to think that they're better than me because to consider any alternative would drive them mad with avaricious envy.

But I do something worse, which is to make 'art' specifically to make people laugh. Again, this is very complex, and woven deep into being human. Suffice it to say, clever geneticists have traced the laughter gene in primates back six million years, and while all other apes and monkeys laugh as a signal to other apes and monkeys that they're only playing (useful if you're a chimp and you jump on another chimp's back, because it tells the other chimp not to kill you), only humans use laughter, through mockery, as a tool of social control. In short, I enable my readers (viewers? lookers?) to laugh at our leaders to keep those bastards in their place. That's why cartoonists tend to get locked up and murdered by tyrants, in government or aspiring to it, far more frequently than more serious artists. And when they come for the serious artists (long after the cartoonists' corpses are cold) it's invariably because the serious artists have stolen our shtick and are taking the piss out of the power.

Which includes, of course, the people who buy serious art. Interestingly, the very first cartoon—that is, the first humorous or satirical illustration thus called, and which then lent the name to all such images thereafter—was John Leech's *Cartoon No 1: Substance and Shadow*, published in *Punch* magazine in 1843, and which mocked the lavish murals for the new Palace of Westminster, comparing them to the condition of London's poor. Cartoonists also constantly parasitize serious art through pastiche, and have always done. Gillray and Rowlandson both repeatedly parodied Fuseli, and in the 90s British cartoonists joyously plundered work by the Young British Artists being grandstanded by Charles Saatchi. After a while, this turned into a real money spinner, as we knew that Saatchi would buy the original of every single cartoon about him and his collection of serious art (cartoons for which, remember, we'd already been paid). As a point of principle, one cartoonist used to charge Saatchi the price of a quarter page ad on the leader page of the *Evening Standard*, and after a while it became more fun to refuse to sell the stuff to him. Though sadly his agents never even asked for the cartoon I drew for *Time Out* at the time of the Royal Academy *Sensation* exhibition, which depicted a slowly, translucently melting lifesize statue of Saatchi himself in a case, labelled *Frozen Wank Charles Saatchi*.

It's part of our gig—and an aspect of the deeper, darker nature of the whole business—that our victims often buy the artefact that defames them, partly to show how big they are in being able to take the joke, partly through barely disguised vanity, but mostly to defuse the bad magic. That's why cartoons are almost always hung in the victims' toilets, and you don't need a Freudian to tell you why. However, even Charles Saatchi probably doesn't have a shitter big enough to accommodate all the cartoons he'd bought, so instead they were hung, unframed, in one inchoate, unreadable clump on the walls of his gallery. When I first saw the contemptuous way he was treating our contempt, I felt a warm glow of satisfaction that we'd done our job successfully: his attempt to punish us (and along the way paying us all a second time) for our lèse-majesté was feeble yet telling. And that was because he considered it important enough even to try.

Laughter, through mockery, has always been central to the ways we mediate reality through artifice, but is clearly fatal to serious art, by definition. This has nothing to do

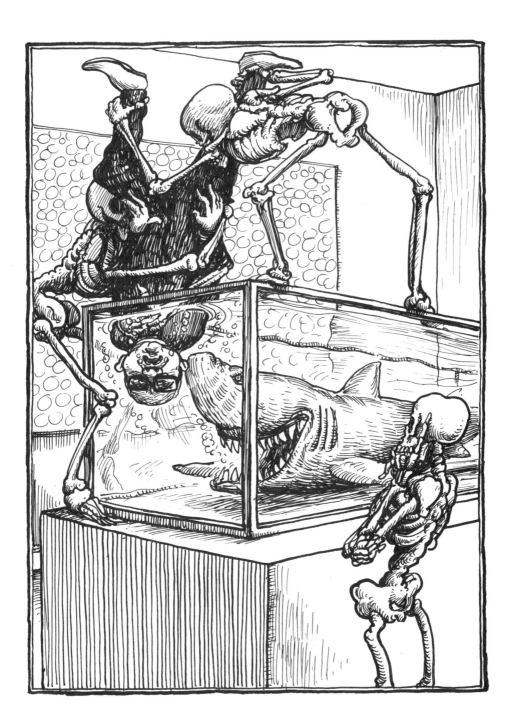

The Dance of Death: Vanitas (London: SelfMadeHero, 2019)

with the art itself, but is imbued into it in that terrible transformation that happens between conception and the conclusion of the sale, when whatever joyous motivation initially inspired the artist becomes wholly secondary to the new status of the serious art as grave goods for the living. Maybe that's all serious art has ever been or ever could be: its cost and the lavishness of its adornments make it impossible without the support of state or private wealth and patronage, and therefore as a lackey of the power it will inevitably be the target for just as much mockery as its patrons. But if you think about it, the power—both religious and political—is so absurd, risible, pre-posterously unjust, ridiculously pompous, it defies our every natural instinct not to burst out laughing at these clowns, their crowns, their gods and their extravagant tastes in interior decor. Which is precisely why the penalties for blasphemy and treason have always been so savage: to terrorize us into not laughing.

True, serious art has yet to start killing people in order to cow them into not laughing, though it's probably only a matter of time before the death squads set out across Shoreditch. In the meantime, they seem to think money can buy off any snig-gering that might be heard from the back, abetted by ambition, fear and the peer pressure that permeate the world of serious art.

Which gets us back to Matt's performance in the Serpentine Galleries' cafe. It was introduced, as these things are, by a senior serious-art apparatchik who'd been sprinkled with so much glamour dust by the stinking-rich sponsors that she imagined it didn't matter that she read out her words of welcome in a dull, dead monotone so badly you began to have serious doubts about her literacy. The stinking-rich sponsors then smirked a lot, and also spoke as if human was a language wholly alien to them. This is the kind of couldn't-give-a-fuck-about-the-audience attitude that money can buy, but which the angriest iconoclast can never truly emulate until they, too, are too rich ever to be angry again. And then came the show, and it was great. And clever. And funny, very, very funny.

And yet it was greeted with hushed, earnest reverence by a roomful of iconoclasts purring politely at their masters' collection of icons. Like I say, art is a serious business.

The Communist Manifesto *as a Graphic Novel*

The Guardian, May 2018

Karl Marx and I go back a long way. Like a lot of children growing up in the 60s, I was obsessed with the Soviet Union and its unreachable otherness. What's more, my father had actually been there to attend scientific symposia. I have a clear memory, aged about six, of standing in our back garden and him saying to me: 'What do you mean, you don't know who Karl Marx is?' I replied, rather tearfully: 'But I know who Lenin is.'

As I grew older, the obsession continued. At about 15, I finally read *The Communist Manifesto* and it made complete sense. I instantly got the dialectic, the inexorable, tectonic grindings of All History Hitherto, the class conflict and all the stuff about the inevitability of the ultimate victory of the downtrodden over their oppressors. Moreover, in its compelling combination of reason and romanticism, I was entranced not only by the manifesto's universal scope but also its playfulness. Parts of it are very funny.

Soon I'd devoured Edmund Wilson's *To the Finland Station*, visited the Soviet Union and, aged 19, wrote a thankfully unpublished novel that hinges round a fictitious Marxist uprising. As a student, I joined the Communist Party, although I only hung around for a week. After I graduated I sold a cartoon series to the *New Statesman* titled *Scenes from the Lives of the Great Socialists*, based on hideously contrived puns on the defining dicta of Marxism. A typical example shows Friedrich Engels standing on a toilet seat peering into the flush mechanism and saying: 'Hey Marx, there's a couple of those antique Stradivarius fiddles in here!' To which Marx replies: 'Clearly the violins inherited the cistern!'

When these cartoons came out as a book in 1983, there were calls for it to be banned from Collet's, the old leftie bookshop in London. This was one reason why I hadn't bothered making a fist of it in the CP: I've always subscribed to Orwell's line about every joke being a tiny revolution, though a lot of people believe that None of This Is a Laughing Matter.

Obviously, as a professional satirist, I disagree. And I reckon Marx would have done so too. Not nearly enough people struggling through theories of surplus value give themselves a break by reading, for instance, Marx's journalism from the 1850s for the *New-York Tribune*, which matches Simon Hoggart, and occasionally even Jonathan Swift, in its scathing hilarity.

Anyway, Marx stuck with me in the following 30 years: I illustrated a couple of books by the Australian Marxist Kevin Killane, and Marx himself made cameo appearances in my comic-book adaptations of T. S. Eliot's *The Waste Land* and Laurence

The Communist Manifesto (London: SelfMadeHero, 2018)

The Communist Manifesto (London: SelfMadeHero, 2018)

Sterne's *Tristram Shandy*. It was after that last book was reissued in 2010 by SelfMadeHero that the publisher commissioned me to adapt Francis Wheen's wonderful 1999 biography of Marx.

I'm a hack at heart and, like Marx, I dice with deadlines. Marx, then aged 29, knocked off *The Communist Manifesto* over a weekend in Brussels at the end of January 1848 after he received an ultimatum from the Communist League in London, who had commissioned the work from him the previous autumn and were still waiting. It had also been my practice to eschew storyboards and make it up as I went along. But confronted by the Wheen book, I decided to pay my son to write the script. He did an excellent job, but it left me with nothing to do except draw to his direction. I got bored. I felt like nothing more than a machine. I was, in fact, alienated from my labour in a textbook Marxist way and, in line with pure Marxist theory, I rebelled. Having taken seven months to draw just five pages of finished artwork I gave up and returned my advance.

So now I had unfinished business with Marx, and occasionally images would flash into the back of my mind of great geological slabs of History grinding against massive clumps of the Dialectic. Then SelfMadeHero asked if I fancied adapting *The Communist Manifesto* as a comic book for Marx's 200th birthday. The whole thing came instantly into my head. I clearly envisioned the manifesto as a kind of rolling tsunami, made up in equal parts of blood-and-iron industrialized steampunk, apocalyptic John Martin and mounting fury that builds up to a climax at the end of the first section, 'Bourgeois and Proletarians', before breaking on the beach of history and turning into straight-forward stand-up comedy. It's leavened throughout with private gags, personal score-settling and the kind of Rabelaisian filthiness Marx would have enjoyed, I hope that is what I've achieved.

The former Tory home secretary Kenneth Baker, with whom I (and Steve Bell) sit on the board of London's Cartoon Museum, insists on calling me a hard-line Marxist–Leninist. I'm not. If anything, I'm a kind of William Morris anarchist, all for equality and down with hierarchies so we can all have some fun. Stripped of the doctrinaire dogma, that's how I read Marx, too. The most important part of *The Communist Manifesto* remains its analysis of how the amoral mechanics of capitalism commodify human beings and reduce them to meat machines existing solely to be milked to make the already rich even richer. Which by anyone's reckoning is no fun at all. And 170 years after he wrote *The Communist Manifesto* when, by the latest count, 43 individuals possess as much wealth as half of the rest of humanity, I reckon Marx still has a lot to say, and I hope I've helped him say it yet again.

The Ground-breaking Squiggles of Saul Steinberg

Apollo, January 2019

The Romanian American cartoonist Saul Steinberg represented a distinctly mid-twentieth-century phenomenon, one so familiar we tend to forget how bizarre it is. He was born in 1914 to second- and third-generation Russian Jewish immigrants in a small town in Romania and grew up in what he later called 'the Turkish Delight manner', in a milieu where Ottoman and Western ideas and styles intermingled. After the First World War, however, the Romanian political climate became increasingly informed by anti-Semitic nationalism. Having entered the University of Bucharest to read philosophy, at the age of 19 Steinberg transferred to the Politecnico in Milan to study architecture. Eight years later, he was forced into hiding when Fascist Italy, at the behest of its wartime ally Germany, introduced vicious anti-Semitic racial laws. He was arrested and spent a month in a detention camp, fleeing on release to neutral Portugal, and thence to the United States. Denied entry at Ellis Island because he had doctored his passport with a fake stamp in order to board ship at Lisbon, he spent a year in the Dominican Republic waiting for a genuine US visa. It was during this time that his work started to appear in the *New Yorker*, which helped expedite his visa application.

Steinberg's most famous image is a *New Yorker* cover from 1976: 'View of the World from 9th Avenue', a vision of the rest of America—and of the world, for that matter—as an insignificant outskirt of Manhattan, just across the Hudson. It has been described both as the greatest magazine cover of all time and as an unwittingly self-damning vision of Manhattan parochialism, drawn by a man who enjoyed nearly 60 years as a fixture at the *New Yorker*, the house magazine of Manhattan entitlement. It was parodied so often that Steinberg felt compelled to go to court to assert ownership. He grew to resent the image, fearing it would eclipse everything else he had done.

If it has, that's a shame. For while Steinberg may have contributed to the creation of a specifically New York brand of refined, achingly cool modernist civilization— you'll recognize the *Mad Men* aesthetic of sleek cocktail shakers, leftists in lofts, streamlining, tiny paper napkins on a table in a darkened room—the entitled parochialism is its least interesting aspect. Far more compelling is the way that it was underpinned by a mash-up of Balkan orientalism, flight, fear and murderous political madness. For decades, Steinberg was lauded for his contribution to this aesthetic, often by the kind of European modernist he had been forced to leave behind. Le Corbusier told him, 'You draw like a king'; he was praised by Ernst Gombrich, Italo Calvino, Eugène Ionesco and Roland Barthes, attaining a cultural superstardom rare for cartoonists.

Even more than Ronald Searle and Ralph Steadman, Steinberg closed the gap between what 'cartooning' is often assumed to be—cheaply reproduced, silly scribbles knocked out to make you laugh—and 'art', which is supposedly so much nobler.

Given this hierarchy, it's significant that Steinberg described himself as 'a writer who draws'. Cartoonists work in the no man's land between text and image—the standard cartoon is a chimera composed of image and caption, the one often undermining the other. Great cartoonists transmute the form into 'art' to the extent that they push conventions beyond breaking point. Searle and Steadman did it by consciously fracturing lines and overdrawing, like George Grosz; Steinberg by rendering text as drawing. In his collection *The Labyrinth* (1960), just reissued by New York Review Books with a new introduction by Nicholson Baker, time and again language becomes simply squiggles, or words are drawn almost architecturally, as edifices dominating landscapes.

Collecting published and unpublished drawings, and meticulously arranged by Steinberg himself, the book begins with a horizontal line, bisected initially by some geometry, and then providing a platform for one of Steinberg's trademark ragged crocodiles (he was nearly eaten by a crocodile on a trip to Kenya with Saul Bellow). What we can expect, turning the page, is to not know what on earth we can expect. As a writer who draws, he might be about to wrangle this line into a letter and then into a line of words; or it might become a horizon, the reflecting surface of a lake, a washing line, a collar, the edge of a room, a strand of a labyrinth exploding up and down the page. But then you turn the page to a procession of talking heads, each producing vast, abstract yet baroque speech-bubbles. This is so much more than Paul Klee's 'taking a line for a walk': Steinberg takes it on a forced march, a drunken lurch and a frenzied fandango.

Later, a double-page spread riffs on newspaper comic strips, the topography of the frames filled with written and pictorial gibberish. Then there are pages of window frames; sparse, almost agoraphobically enormous vistas of Red Square and other Soviet landmarks; society women scribbled as prim, winged harpies. Then cats, then crocodiles, then random geometric shapes, and more crocodiles. Squiggle landscapes anticipate 'View of the World from 9th Avenue'; some drawings are exquisite; others are barely drawn at all. On one page he appears to channel Chagall, then Picasso, then—weirdly—the young Nicolas Bentley, then Dalí, then George Herriman (the creator of *Krazy Kat*). If Steinberg had been a draughtsman who wrote and this were text, I doubt much of it would make sense—any sense at all.

So, was that cavalcade of cultural bigwigs who bigged up Steinberg reading meaning where there was none—or, worse, archly teasing meaning from the very fact of meaninglessness? Again, it doesn't matter. Steinberg's art aspires towards the condition of the doodle. Endlessly fleeing the collapse of European cosmopolitanism into barbarism, Steinberg snuck through Ellis Island riddled with the bacilli of the cultural responses to that calamity. Like Ronald Searle, who reshaped the trauma he suffered as a prisoner of the Japanese into the dark hilarity of *St Trinian's*, he found redemption through cartoons of baffling, disquieting whimsicality. Both artists deliberately replayed tragedy as farce, less to imbue meaninglessness with meaning than to make it bearable by making it funny. While this book, like Steinberg's output in general, is as inescapably the product of its time as are the rings in a felled tree, its timeless relevance lies in the rueful smiles it can still conjure.

The New York Times *Cartoon Ban*

The Guardian, June 2019

April, it seems, really is the cruellest month for the *New York Times*. On 25 April, its international edition (formerly the *International Herald Tribune*) ran a cartoon by the Portuguese cartoonist António Moreira Antunes, previously published in the Lisbon paper *Expresso* and depicting Israeli prime minister Benjamin Netanyahu as a guide dog leading a blind Donald Trump. In the way of cartoons, the Netanyahu dog had a blue Star of David (presumably meant to signify the Israeli flag) dangling from his collar, while Trump wore a yarmulke.

There was an instant outcry condemning the cartoon's anti-Semitic imagery, including in articles and editorials in the *New York Times* itself. As a result, the paper has decided it will no longer publish any political cartoons in the international edition (the NYT domestic paper dropped cartoons several years ago) and is terminating its contracts with in-house cartoonists Heng Kim Song and the multi-award-winning Patrick Chappatte. In a statement released on Tuesday, the paper announced that it would 'continue investing in forms of opinion journalism, including visual journalism, that express nuance, complexity and strong voice from a diversity of viewpoints'.

This is a gross overcorrection, even though the outcry had some justification. While you can just about get away with claiming the blue Star of David signifies the state of Israel rather than Jewish people in general, the signification of Trump's yarmulke is impossible to argue away: the implication is clearly that the US president has been 'Judaized' by the dirty Israeli dog, both of which are common anti-Semitic tropes of the type notoriously published in cartoon form in the Nazi newspaper *Der Stürmer*.

As the Labour party knows to its cost, anti-Semitism is the most insidious of racisms and cartoonists in particular need to be increasingly careful when engaged in otherwise wholly justified images belabouring the actions of the Israeli government. This isn't just to avoid online lynch mobs; we also need to nuance our work to make it absolutely clear that we're condemning the Israeli government's actions because they are right-wing nationalists (currently bizarrely cosying up to Hungarian prime minister Viktor Orbán, a blatant anti-Semite), and not because they're Jewish.

But let's get back to cartoons. *The New York Times* 'disciplined' the unnamed editor responsible and announced that it would no longer be publishing any syndicated cartoons provided by CartoonArts International. But that wasn't enough, and now the NYT cartoons are no more. Just like any other commercial enterprise, the *New York Times* can do what it likes, and I look forward to seeing some scathingly satirical

409

The Critic, March 2021

tie-dyes in the pages of its international edition. But this cuts deeper than an over-reaction to an ill-judged cartoon. Cartoons have been the rude, taunting part of political commentary in countries around the world for centuries, and enhance newspapers globally and across the political spectrum, in countries from the most tolerant liberal democracies to the most vicious totalitarian tyrannies. As we all know, they consequently have the power to shock and offend. That, largely, is what they're there for, as a kind of dark, sympathetic magic masquerading as a joke.

That's also why the Turkish cartoonist Musa Kart is in jail, why the Malaysian cartoonist Zunar was facing up to 43 years in prison for sedition until a change of government last year; why five cartoonists were murdered in the offices of *Charlie Hebdo* in January 2015; why dozens of British cartoonists—including William Heath Robinson—were on the Gestapo death list. And why, for that matter, when in the late 50s the *London Evening Standard* ran a cartoon by its Jewish cartoonist Vicky attacking the death penalty, this so shocked and outraged a GP in Harrow that he wrote to the paper regretting that Vicky and his family had escaped the Nazis.

As Kart said at his trial, cartoonists are like canaries in the coal mine—when they come for us, you know the politics is getting toxic. But we're not just subject to the shallow vanity of tyrants or the fury of mobs. The greatest threat to cartoonists has always been the very newspapers we parasitize on. When the accountants moved in on the American newspaper industry in the 2000s, the first employees to go were the cartoonists, just like most newspapers that get closed down aren't shut by governments but by their proprietors. Nor is it just money. I've been 'let go' more times than I can count (the worst case was when the *Times* sacked me to make more room for Julie Burchill's column, though in a previous incarnation on the *Guardian*'s personal finance pages in the 80s I was redesigned off the page and replaced with what was charmingly called 'a creative use of white space').

We are, in short, expendable. Nonetheless, the *New York Times*' decision is particularly irksome in its intoxicating combination of cowardice, pomposity, over-reaction and hypocrisy. As I observed at the beginning of this article, April is the cruellest month for the *New York Times*, as its much vaunted (and self-promoting) claim to be America's 'newspaper of record' was dealt an almost fatal blow when it was revealed in April 2003 that its star reporter Jayson Blair was a serial plagiarist who had fabricated many of his stories. You'll note, however, that the paper did not stop using reporters altogether in order to rebuild its reputation. Nor did it issue a statement announcing that it would 'continue investing in forms of news journalism, including textual journalism, that express nuance, complexity and strong voice from a diversity of viewpoints' and then fill its pages with copy from, say, accountants and astrologers. Although after the dumbness of this decision, just give it time.

As If

The Scarlett Standard, November 2019

I must emphasize that it's just a joke, though of course jokes are very dangerous things in the wrong hands. Anyway, since around halfway through his first term as part-time Mayor of London, I've been saying publicly, on social media and at literary festivals and on the radio and anywhere else I can, that Boris Johnson is a KGB sleeper agent.

For the record, I used to qualify that by claiming he's also an albino, though following complaints from genuine albinos I've dropped that bit. As a satirist, it's my primary duty always to punch up, never kick down. Still, the point remains. It's just a joke; a gag; a tease; part of the ceaseless to-and-fro taunting that makes politics and every other human enterprise more fun than they might otherwise be. After all, jokes are one of the things we humans are actually really good at, unlike higher calculus or diplomacy but like jumping up and down and genocide.

As to the joke itself, its mechanics work as follows:

a) It starts by inverting accepted reality as espoused in the classic Tory press libel—that the whole of the left are traitors in the pocket of Moscow—by standing the libel on its head and levelling it against the right instead;

b) Having created the instigating shock of inverting the old cliche, it then re-inverts with my next observation that he's obviously a KGB agent because he's called 'Boris', undermining what could be a compelling and tangled conspiracy theory with the sucker punch of the ludicrous obvious;

c) The joke is then further inverted and compounded by my final assertion that the incontrovertible truth of the lie is the fact that only the KGB would be brilliant enough in the dungeons of the Lubyanka to create (out of old leather satchels, badger suet and the pubic hair of yaks and yeti) such a wholly unconvincing caricature of an upper-class Englishman while also knowing that we Brits would be dumb enough to fall for it.

Thus is an alternative satirical narrative created, of our current prime minister as a kind of Bolshevik golem created to undermine Britain while hiding in clear sight. But it's a joke. It's obviously a joke. Obviously.

Except, of course, for the fact that satire is eternally being outstripped by brute reality. The satirical songwriter Tom Lehrer famously quit after Henry Kissinger won the Nobel Peace Prize, on the basis that you couldn't make up something that mad and gross. Over and over again in my own career, I've found myself furiously trying to catch up with the grown-ups when once again, through combinations of malice and stupidity, they implement policies so breathtakingly and appallingly ludicrous you couldn't make them up. More to the point, Jonathan Swift couldn't have made them up, like the BSE crisis 25 years ago, when as a consequence of closing rural abattoirs and the requirement for cheap food, our national dish was rendered deadly because we made our cows eat the brains of their own kind. Worse, before killing you, eating our national dish would first drive you mad. Worse still, we then entered a trade war with our closest trading partners in order to force them to eat our deadly national dish, which would first drive them mad before it killed them.

This capacity for stealing our shtick has been available as a counterploy by satirized pols forever, and turning the joke on us is just a milder alternative to imprisoning us or torturing us to death. John Wilkes, Harold Macmillan and Margaret Thatcher all expropriated satires on themselves and used them to their own advantage. That said, this doesn't mean satire never works, it just works differently from the way you might imagine. It's not there—whatever we may imagine in our more pompous moments— to drive the tyrants from power and bring about universal happiness; all it does is license us to laugh at people who want to control our destinies and be treated like gods. Laughing at them simply degrades their potential for this, which is why in the unhealthiest polities satirists are murdered with such regularity by the henchmen of the high and mighty (this includes God, by the way). That they thus reveal themselves to be a hopeless bunch of whining snowflakes is entirely the point. Indeed, one of the most heartening things I've heard recently is how President Xi of China—who last year was elected by the National People's Congress the *de facto* leader of China in perpetuity and whose 'Thought', such as it is beyond worshipping Xi forever, has now been written into the Chinese Constitution. And yet recently Xi banned *Winnie the Pooh* from China because he'd been repeatedly drawn as the honey-loving bear of very little brain by the Melbourne-based dissident cartoonist Badiucao. When I interviewed him at Tate Modern last month, I asked Badiucao what it felt like knowing that the second most powerful man on Earth was frightened of him. He said it felt great, despite the dangers his drawings have brought down on him and his family.

But what happens when the lines of demarcation get seriously blurred? Last week, the Tories engaged in yet another so-fucking-ludicrous-you-couldn't-make-it-up exercise, when the *Daily Telegraph* ran an article by Boris Johnson asserting Jeremy Corbyn's attitude to billionaires was worse than Stalin's liquidation of the kulaks at the same time as some smirking goons in the Tory central office doctored TV footage of Keir Starmer to make him look gormless, *in precisely the same way as Stalin's own goons would doctor photographs to airbrush out his enemies*. So far, so standard. But it then became truly weird when Tory chairman James Cleverly claimed they were only being 'light-hearted and satirical'. Yeah, right.

The point here isn't that the usually satirized shouldn't invade our territory because they're rubbish at it (although they are: after a second's reflection, the reputedly hilarious Boris Johnson is revealed as truly, deeply unfunny except to sycophants and Tories and lands a punchline like the R101). During the European elections this May, you'll recall all those UKIP candidates laughing off their volleys of rape threats and racism as 'jokes'; Rod Liddle and his sniggering cadres on the *Spectator* peddle the same line on a weekly basis. The purpose, ultimately, is the opposite of satire. Instead of speaking truth to power by laughing at it, the intention is to just laugh things off to the point where nothing really matters because nothing is either serious or taken seriously. From there, it's a tiny step to printing your own licence to do absolutely anything at all, however serious—or even deadly—the consequences are for everyone else. And though no one tried out the 'it's only a joke' defence at the Nuremberg trials, I have the hideous feeling they'll sure as hell give it a go the next time round.

You really couldn't make it up. Just like Boris Johnson obviously isn't really a KGB sleeper agent. Obviously. Is he?

Foreword to Roland Elliott Brown's Godless Utopia

FUEL, 2019

In the summer of 1976, on the streets of Moscow in the depths of the Brezhnev Stagnation when the Soviet experiment was stumbling into its long, lingering death throes and where, by mid-morning, you were obliged to step over the drunks sleeping on the pavement, I was given a badge. More precisely, in exchange for a packet of Wrigley's Spearmint gum a small boy gave me a metal badge in the form of a red pentacle, at its heart a portrait, in silver relief, of the Infant Lenin.

I still have it, over forty years later, now pinned to the front of my Prince Henry cap (named after the Kaiser's brother and popularized by the afore-mentioned V. I. Lenin) as a satirical act of homage to Jeremy Corbyn, who I always draw wearing this particular item of millinery. Anyway, back in 1976 I was on a school trip to the Soviet Union, finally visiting a place that had beguiled and enchanted me for as long as I could remember.

This was partly because my father, a research virologist, had made several trips to the USSR and its satellite states in the late 1950s and 60s (including during that brief period when Stalin's mummified old corpse shared its mausoleum with Lenin, which my father saw shortly before the old monster was turfed out and dumped in a grave below the walls of the Kremlin). This meant I was aware from a very early age of the existence of a Somewhere Else, a fabulous, almost wholly unreachable Other, which wasn't only incomprehensibly exotic but also 'The Enemy', the appalling alternative it was worth blowing up the world to avoid according to the Manichean mindset of our masters.

Of course, that mindset in itself had been bequeathed to the men who own and rule England by nearly two millennia of Christianity, particularly in its corrupt form once it became the state religion of the Roman Empire and thereafter its successor entities, including both the British Empire and Tsarist Russia. At the same time as my dad was drinking Georgian champagne with commie virologists, I was getting my portion of that legacy in an extremely high-church Anglican prep school in the North London suburbs, endlessly colouring in maps of the Holy Land as creepy men in black dresses lied to us about the truth of the Gospels, one of them eventually, aged 80, being sentenced to ten years' imprisonment for half a century of molesting small boys.

Irrespective of the paedo priest, any inkling of faith they tried to browbeat into me failed to take hold, and as I grew into my teens, another attraction of the Soviet

416

Union, and another captivating aspect of its otherness, was its atheism. I considered this to be a comforting endorsement of my own fierce lack of faith even though, by then, I was far less starry-eyed about Soviet Russia: I'd read Orwell, genned up on the history of the October Revolution and the serial betrayals that came in its wake, working backwards from Trotsky's isolation and exile by Stalin to Trotsky's own suppression of the Kronstadt Rebellion, which was led by the same soldiers and sailors who'd been the vanguard of the Revolution and who now revolted against the Bolsheviks' instinctive authoritarianism.

Nonetheless, when I finally got to go there, aged 17, even though I now approached the place as a friendly sceptic rather than a pilgrim, I was still shocked by its shabby squalor, the ridiculous lies of the smooth young trusties we were permitted by the authorities to meet as they buttressed the crumbling ruins of the Revolution. Frankly, having come from London in the ferment of the first days of punk, I'd never been anywhere less rebellious, even though it was there that Soviet Russia's natural appeal lay for gobby teenagers like me, relishing the shock factor of talking about Karl Marx to maiden aunts and tight-arsed teachers: in short, all the things that guided me to be a satirical cartoonist, railing endlessly against the boring conformity of those in power who think they're somehow better and wiser than you and me. But even worse was the reality of Soviet atheism, which sank almost to Anglican depths of official, respectable dullness. Worse still, Soviet atheism—itself almost like a kind of reverse miracle—turned out to be no such thing.

Throughout history, atheism has been an insult hurled by those in power at any dissident who dares question their assertion that their power is bestowed by higher, non-human factors and is therefore unquestionable. Therein lies a great deal of its potency, although as often as not in the political sphere, atheism turns out to disguise differing degrees of anti-clericalism, that eternal struggle against the spiritual lackeys who prop up the power with their higher lies. In the English Peasants' Revolt of 1381, they beheaded the Archbishop of Canterbury, but that was because he'd introduced the poll tax which triggered the uprising. John Ball, one of the revolt's leaders, was himself a priest. Four hundred years later, Robespierre happily guillotined Catholic priests but also cultivated his weird cult of the Supreme Being. Indeed, his last speech to the Assembly before he was arrested and guillotined in his turn was a furious attack on the militant atheists who'd been daubing on the walls of Parisian cemeteries the fantastic slogan 'Death Is but an Eternal Sleep'. And the anarchists in the Spanish Civil War who put religious statues in front of firing squads were the same people who were tracked down for liquidation by Stalin's henchmen, more concerned with maintaining orthodoxy than with fighting fascists.

New Humanist, February 2008

In a way, Bolshevism had always owed more to Russian mysticism than to the Marxism it claimed to espouse. And that political philosophy itself, which presumed to apply to history the rigours of science, was also riddled with the attenuated Hegelian mysticism of German Romanticism. (You could argue that German Romanticism, in its various mutations, reached its apotheosis in May 1945 in the streets of Berlin, as its two dominant post-Hegelian strands, Stalinism and Nazism, dispatched yet more ghosts to evaporate in the roaring air above Hitler's bunkers as the sincerest homage to Goethe's *The Sorrows of Young Werther.*)

Claiming to be egalitarian, Bolshevism was rigidly hierarchical, being almost entirely a cult centred round Lenin; from the beginning it replaced the struggle for equality with the imposition of uniformity; its deeper mysteries, like those in the catechisms of dialectical materialism, were satisfyingly impenetrable. It was inevitable, therefore, that in practice Bolshevism turned into a new kind of Tsarism, propped up by state atheism as opposed to a state church. This time, personal rule was invested in Stalin, who encompassed infallibility, complete power and the kind of capricious murderous intensity normally reserved for gods. Even after Stalin's temple was desecrated by Khrushchev, the structures of the religion were too intertwined with the whole Bolshevik enterprise to dismantle as well, so—as is often the case with religion, where temples to the goddess Diana turned effortlessly into shrines to the Virgin Mary—the failed god was simply replaced with the old god of Lenin.

Hence my little badge. Hence, to a large extent, the ultimate failure of Bolshevism: the new religion laid over the old one turned out to be unsustainably ridiculous, unlike the Russian Orthodoxy it sought to replace. After nearly seventy years of deeply uncomfortable cohabitation and collaboration with the Bolsheviks, the Orthodox Church now thrives again under their successors, mostly former operatives of the Soviet security state who've effectively used a compliant church as a beard (deliberate pun) to distract the people from their wholesale plunder of the assets of the former Soviet state.

I visited Moscow again in 2016, forty years after my first trip. It had changed a lot, not least in the way the onion domes of Moscow's churches had all been freshly gilt with the money stolen by Putin's client oligarchs. Of Soviet atheism there was hardly a trace, but the continued presence of Lenin's relic, unrotting in its temple, sort of suggests it was hardly ever there in the first place. Beyond, that is, being a brutal tool of public control, which from my point of view is more or less the function of religion anyway.

As to the little badge, obviously you can now buy one anywhere. Just like pieces of the True Cross.

Covid Days: Plague Songs

Smokestack Books, 2021

On Friday, 3 January 2020, having filed my cartoon for the next day's *Guardian* early (it portrayed Donald Trump pissing fire onto Iran), I made the 20-minute train journey from Lewisham to Charing Cross and then walked through Central London to Soho to take some photos of Greek Street on my phone, as research for a commission.

On Thursday, 16 January 2020, I went to the launch of my friend Carol Isaacs' brilliant graphic memoir *The Wolf of Baghdad*, held at London's Cartoon Museum. I'd been feeling a bit odd—a tad fluey—for a couple of days, but didn't think much of it. To help me self-medicate, the Cartoon Museum's Alison Brown plied me with cocktails she'd devised specially to theme with Carol's book. I left early, feeling achier and achier, and when my wife Anna got home from her evening seminar she found me shivering and huddled in the kitchen with a temperature of over 100.

For the next two weeks I was incapable of anything, feeling more ill than I had for 50 years. Too enervated and exhausted even to draw, I slept most of the time, in between drenching night sweats, claustrophobic bouts of breathlessness and aching eyes and joints, my sense of taste not gone but twisted, so I felt enveloped in a headily sulphurous and slightly faecal miasma. I didn't imagine for a second I could possibly be suffering from the disease in China increasingly dominating the news.

But I was. An antibody test six months later proved the fact. I'd caught it almost before anyone else simply by catching a train and then walking through the streets of Central London in early January, a fact my late father, a virologist, would have relished. Almost exactly a year later, following unconnected surgery, wonderful, lovely, funny, brilliant Alison Brown died of it, like thousands and thousands of others before her.

On 23 March 2020, the British government belatedly announced a full national lockdown, although by then most people were stopping indoors of their own volition. On my last journey into Central London for months to come, on Thursday, 19 March, to stock up on arts supplies, I was reminded of the fragmentary Anglo-Saxon poem 'The Ruin', in which the narrator wanders through the abandoned ruins of a Roman city. Now, too, there was hardly anyone about. I gave a *Big Issue* seller a fiver but told him to keep the magazine and sell it to someone else. My mind was on infectivity rather than philanthropy.

A few days earlier, my friend the poet Luke Wright commenced on a programme of 100 nightly half-hour poetry readings on Twitter. I'd met Luke four years previously at the Laugharne Weekend in Wales, when he picked me up in a hotel bar. We rapidly established weird affinities, like being adopted, our adoptive fathers sharing an identical hobby, both of our little fingers being bent, having similar tastes and enthusiasms and much else besides. Indeed, I often suspect that we're both failed prototypes constructed by some shadowy and sinister intelligence, cack-handedly seeking to create the ultimate bumptious gobshite committed to strenuously avoiding ever getting a proper job. I'm not sure that Luke agrees with this analysis. Either way, we've done quite a few poetry gigs together and I've illustrated one of his books.

By early May his daily Twitter gigs were beginning to take their toll. I'd check in on them fairly regularly, and Luke was looking increasingly jaded and haggard. I proposed, therefore, a project to lift him from his languorous torpor, in which we would each write a daily poem just for shits and giggles. We should do it, moreover, on the Cartier-Bresson model, in honour of the great French photographer who only ever took one exposure of a subject: in other words, I wanted us to just knock the bastards out fast, forego agonizing revision in pursuit of elusive perfection and move on, thus keeping our minds fresh and nimble in those dark days of high spring in this foul and deadly year. Luke agreed, and naturally enough produced a couple of poems, moaned a lot and then scarpered (though, in fairness, it should be mentioned in mitigation he was also homeschooling his two young sons throughout).

I, however, persisted. From 11 May to 26 November more or less every day (saving most weekends and most of a snatched week in the Scottish Highlands in September), I sat down first thing after breakfast and wrote a poem, although later on five were written, as in the olden days, on trains. Whereas many found their lockdown solace in sourdough baking or growing beards, I was soon drawing mine from this regular matutinal mental throat clearing. Some the poems reacted directly to the cataclysm unfolding in the empty streets around me; others riffed on the latest political catastrophes of the day; some were old ideas I finally had time and discipline to beat into vague poetic shape; others yet were random thoughts or lines or sometimes just a word or two that flashed through my mind in the shower or while I was shaving or even in a dream, which I'd then lasso and let drag me across the scrub to see where the hell we were going to end up. Many are furious, some are meant to be funny; quite a lot, I hope, are both. And an awful lot, unavoidably, are about death—not least that of my beloved and very old friend Jon Medlam, who died of lung cancer in August.

After six and a half months, in the same way they'd started, the poems then stopped. If you want to read the unedited versions, you can find them on my website (martinrowson.com) published the day they were written, raw as a grazed shin.

And there you have it, and all that's left to me is to throw my darlings at your feet, and you'll either pick them up and cuddle them or stamp on the squirming sods. But whatever their fate now, this is a genuine daily response to a unique and terrible period in all our lives, in which thousands upon thousands of our fellow citizens died and a small number of our nation's governing party's chums made millions.

*

Pallbearers

Auntie Sarah's
Carer's
Pallbearers'
Nostrils flare as
They imperceptibly shift the weight on all four of them there.

And in a world that's been declared
As fit simply for billionaires
Don't fret you can't compare
Whether this or that is fair.
However clean the air is,
However loud the prayers
And however fixed the pallbearers'
Long, inscrutable stares,
It's invariably rare
That a shroud becomes its wearer.

21 May 2020

Look on the Bright Side

Then we chorused to the virus
    As it stepped towards the door
'But at least you've changed the World!'
    And someone cheered.
All the virus did was eye us
    And as it spat upon the floor

What it had instead of lips curled
    And it sneered.

'But everything is different now!
    Nothing can be the same!
It's the time to change our ways!'
    Everyone cried.
'The virus creased its many brows;
    Drawled: 'Didn't catch you names.
Though frankly I'm amazed
    You've not all died.'

We shuffled slightly nervously.
    With an embarrassed laugh
Someone said 'We baked some bread!'
    And then they coughed.
Hissed the virus: 'Heard of Malthus? He
    Could show you all a graph
To prove you're best off dead.
    Now just fuck off.'

'But virus!' we all cried at once,
    'At least you've made us pause
Our ecocide!' It roared loud
    'Christ! Stop whining!
You're just my scoff, you stupid cunts!'
    And left. Through our applause
Some of us thought, can shrouds
    Have silver linings?

10 June 2020

The Great Escape

What if their inner spies had tipped the wink?
Foretold the cruel incompetence of
    The callous cranks in charge
And whispered the full consequence
    Of the old's expendability?

What if, beneath the cover of Lock Down's deepest anxiety
They'd made a Great Escape, furtive through the hunkered towns
     Evading the gerontocide patrols
To secret airfields under clouded moons
     To be hissed aboard the waiting, looming airships?

And what if they'd then floated, silent as the streets,
Into the jet streams to be scattered through the safer world?
And what if it took months before their loved ones ventured round,
Knocking on unanswered doors before breaking locks and lockdowns,
     Simply to find a propped up, plugged in phone
Installed with apps to simulate an isolated chat with calls
Made automatically in rotation, a trillion algorithmic permutations
     Of familiar inanities, looptaping on Zoom?

What if that vast flotilla then had landfalled,
Tattered near volcanoes, smacked down beside a wadi in the desert,
     Silhouetted deflating languidly at the jungle's edge
While its passengers danced with gauchos on the pampas,
Lured lizards to the pot through termite mounds
Or crooned gently with macaques sat in the boughs
     Of monstrous trees?

What if What if? And what if some fifth columnists
Among the shackled vassals in Death's Realm
Had falsified the papers, sent their frailest charges
     Through the network of
The Secret Undertaking, trustworthy hearses,
Unapproachable morticians, unfilled pews,
Unwitnessed rites and unobservable cremations
     To safety and beyond? What if? What if?

And years to come, mysterious, coded postcards
All from the unlikeliest destinations, unsolicited
     And disturbing the still mourning
Are the only, vaguest hint of
     Something else.

22 June 2020

Plague Songs (Ripon: Smokestack, 2021)

Let's All Go Dunkirking

We beat the Hun, the Japanese
And now we've beaten a disease!
    VE – VJ – VV DAY! (V for Virus).
But before the second wave
Sweeps us all into the grave
    Don't forget a glorious moment to inspire us!

We didn't need the Yanks
Or brigades of Soviet tanks
    To define our mighty nation with their work.
The essence of True Brit
Is to roll ourselves in shit
    And pretend it's glory, just like at Dunkirk!

      So let's all go Dunkirking
      Because bugger all is working
        And the situation generally is dire
      And as everything gets murkier
      We chaps'll get Dunkirkier
        And victoriously sink into the mire!

It's because our Ruling Class
Can't tell its elbow from its arse,
    All these berks listed with peerages in Burke's,
Who drawl they've won because they've dared—
Ill-equipped and unprepared—
    To deny they've fucked things up, like at Dunkirk.

Posh, bland and mediocre,
Always in hock to their brokers,
    Complacent and inept, wrapped in their perks,
They'll still yowl of England's Glories
(Long since sold off by the Tories)
    With each fresh unfolding shitrain of Dunkirks!

      So let's all go Dunkirking
      Because the dying are just shirking

Whether cannon fodder or some wheezing codgers!
if our victory seems quirky
That's because we're so Dunkirky!
So let's drink all night to coast our ruling bodgers!

They'll claim the spitfire is their plane,
Churchill theirs, though Chamberlain
Is more their mark (or Churchill versus Turks)
And they then expect our thanks
When they dump the other ranks
At Gallipoli, and would have at Dunkirk

With their talent to appease
From dictators to disease
Winging the lot, pretending it's hard work,
Unprepared and ill-equipped!
Then little people's little ships
Save their bacon like they did once at Dunkirk.

So let's all go Dunkirking
As our wise rulers are jerking
Around the BEF or NHS
And if you think you're feeling perkier
You are just feeling Dunkirkier!
Dropped into one more god-almighty mess!

Because they'll lead you to your Death
With the lies upon their breath,
Each balls-up blanked with an infectious smirk,
And this is just the latest highlight
Of our never-ending twilight
That started falling on the beaches of Dunkirk!

So let's all go Dunkirking
Because bugger all is working
And everything they touch will turn to crap
So if you're feeling irky
Forget it all and get Dunkirky
And blow the whole damn bankroll on an app!

Let's all go Dunkirking
Although Nemesis is lurking!
    Sucking on a Duchy Original rusk
Hone your dirk until its dirkier
Slash your wrists to get Dunkirkier
    And dance across the beaches through the dusk

And we'll carry on Dunkirking
Until nothing more is working
    To be Dunkirky-wirky's such a lark
And then strap on that old merkin
And let's all go Dunkirking
    And reel all night Dunkirking! In the dark.

24 June 2020

Lines to My Dead Virologist Father

Now at last I feel that I can look your spirit in the eye
Now that at last the thing that poleaxed me back in January
Has been nailed down by a pin prick as the main event, the Plague,
That pig that left me sweating in freezing fits, embalmed in bed
In sulphurous miasmata, my joints like broken walnuts,
With hogtied eyeballs and less energy than dissipating smoke
Slowcooking me to Brexit Day, Pandemic's damp squib warm up act.

Now at last I know it's Covid, I can know that you'd be proud,
Proud in your quiet, unassailably determined way,
The way you were when I was eight and my endemic sore throat
Was, you proved, Coxsackievirus, by thrusting swabs between my tonsils
And drawing what seemed ponds of blood for growing cultures in your lab,
Also you'd be proud, I know, that I was in the avant garde,
Trend-setting and vanguarding the whole farce by getting iller
Than I had for fitly years or more, than when I'd had Coxsackie;
Fashionably early, struck down when our ministry of cranks was
Still too busy wanking about wrong types of isolation,
Back when the only vector was to be some foreign other
Back when they wouldn't test you till you're cradled in Death's radius.

Since when I've told the whole world how my virologist father
Would be laughing now sardonically at their hoarded folly.
So I know the pride you'd feel in your adopted boy's infection
Is bounced directly back, although you're now sixteen years dead.
And I repeat to all who'll listen how you told me in the 80s
When you'd overseen an autopsy on Britain's second AIDS death
That epidemiologically you thought AIDS was a dull disease
And that, getting down to basics, nothing that you couldn't catch
Standing fully clothed at a bus stap in broad daylight
Is all that much to worry you, if you take small precautions
But naturally, you added, the Establishment (the medical
As well as the political) assumed they'd smashed Infection
So the Isolation Hospitals sentinelling every town
Were closed, and as we spoke, now forty years ago, were bulldozed
To build neat estates of Barratt Homes, kindling Thatcherism,
Pump-priming the whole floating world of buy-to-let and outsourcing,
The neoliberal fantasy of privatizing track and trace,
The brittle hallow edifice that's left us 60,000 dead,
Tsunamied by a dream of greed, a fresh Somme for the veterans,
As if they'd built their New Jerusalem on a burial ground,
An uncleared Native Burial Ground, Yes, just exactly that,
And now at last that I can look your spirit in the eye
I see it twinkling because now we know we bloody told them so.

22 July 2000

The Guardian, February 2014

The Dolorous Countenance of Angela Merkel

The Guardian, September 2021

Among the repertory company of political actors cartoonists feature in their output, we can't help developing favourites, and often feel a sense of personal loss when they inevitably shuffle off the world stage. This is wholly divorced from either sympathizing with or viscerally loathing the politics—or even, quite often, the individual. It's just the buzz we get from drawing them.

When John Major resoundingly lost the 1997 election, Steve Bell told me he had lost his reason for living because of the Zen-like karmic thrill he got from doing the holes in Major's Airtex underpants. Likewise, George Osborne's departure from frontline politics still has me grieving: I loved drawing his head because it clearly has no bones in it. And I'm feeling a similar pang of regret at the imminent retirement of Angela Merkel, who I've been drawing regularly since 2008.

None of us, of course, can do much about the way we look, though public figures in positions of power often try—either through Botox or Photoshop. But while Silvio Berlusconi's eyebrows got pulled ever closer to his dyed hairline, it's significant that the woman he described as 'an unfuckable lard-arse' didn't appear to be that bothered about the face life had dealt her, clearly part of her political shtick as an ordinary and homely Ossi who, nonetheless, quietly succeeded in dominating Europe for over a decade.

Her face, in fact, is rather lovely, with more than a hint of the young Iris Murdoch about it. To a cartoonist's eye, however, she's obviously the MGM cartoon dog Droopy's long-lost twin sister. So her defining feature for me has always been the dolorous countenance of her face in repose. This, in turn, has informed the role she's played in the satirical narrative I found myself creating around her. Small, hunched and apparently unobtrusive; often passively observing some other idiocy nearby; when active, appearing to act more in sorrow than anger.

Even when she was helping immiserate the lives of millions of southern Europeans, particularly in Greece, in the Euro crises from 2011–15, I drew her as morose rather than gleefully malevolent. Whether that reveals the inner truth doesn't really matter: cartoons are journalism and therefore tend to be the first response to the immediate appearance of things.

But I reckon this portrayal does capture a hint of what, for want of a better term, we may call Merkel's soul. As she endured in office, I caught a definite whiff of long-suffering discomfort coming off her as she stood uneasily next to cavalcades of clowns and crooks at international summits, or in any meeting with any representative of the British government over the past 11 years. She tried her not-very-good best to disguise the general air of toe-curling embarrassment choking the atmosphere in the room, all of which was etched so eloquently on her expressionless face. Thus, albeit unconsciously, Angela Merkel smiled insincerely and squirmed inside for us all, and for that alone we should salute her.

Johnson on the Way Back?

The Guardian, October 2022

The Cartoon Museum's new show of Boris Johnson cartoons, *This Exhibition Is a Work Event*, chronicles Johnson's time as prime minister through the work of 50 different cartoonists (including a lot of regular *Guardian* contributors). But there is a question that, even now—as Liz Truss self-detonates and Tory members talk about the possibility of bringing him back—we must ask: were any of us actually delivering the coup de grace to Britain's worst-ever prime minister (up until then) by caricaturing his defining ridiculousness? Or did we merely frantically scramble to keep pace with the madness his premiership added in spades to the pre-existing madness of the past 6—or arguably 14, or even 5,000—years?

Many American cartoonists faced the same dilemma with Donald Trump. You couldn't, as many of them have told me, make this shit up. What are you meant to do when the targets of your satire are the masters of their own absurdity?

I once described Trump and Johnson to an American audience as two cheeks of the same arse (and then took another 10 minutes explaining what I meant), because both successfully controlled the laughter agenda, more or less from the beginning. And I mean from when they could first walk and fall over for comedic effect. Trump and Johnson are both sociopathic narcissists who feed, like vampires, on our horrified attention, using arsing about like any class clown. But herein also lies their Achilles heel. Almost their whole purpose in life is to get us to laugh with and not at them.

To give him his due, Trump can crack fairly effective, if brutal, jokes, whereas Johnson is merely a Tory's or newspaper editor's idea of funny and lands punchlines like the Hindenburg. Nonetheless, he has always understood the importance of the arsing about, hence the whole contrived 'Boris' act. Twenty years ago, commissioned to produce a *Spectator* cover when Johnson was editor, and increasingly enraged by his failure to confirm the precise specs I needed, I phoned him and got the usual Johnsonian harrumphing noises. I told him, maybe intemperately, for once in his life to drop the P. G. Wodehouse bollocks, to which he replied: 'What you call the "P. G. Wodehouse bollocks" has served me very well thus far.' And yet a couple of years later, when he was by then London mayor and was leaving a party at the Spectator's offices, I encountered him standing on the pavement. 'What's it like having responsibility finally thrust on your shoulders, eh, Boris?' I quipped, and his reply this time was abject. 'All these awful people like you keep doing these terrible drawings of me,' he whined, pouting.

Daily Mirror, May 2019

Part of the car crash of Johnson's personality is that he's a terrible liar. Not just like that, but because you can see in his face the precise truth as to his mood at any time. On this occasion he wasn't joking, he was whingeing, seemingly incapable of understanding why everyone everywhere wasn't laughing gratefully at his hilarious antics. Similarly, seven years later, he was due to open an exhibition of cartoons I'd drawn about London politics over a decade and a half. He pulled out of the event an hour before we opened, clearly unable to cope in real time, with TV cameras present, with the prospect of me pointing to a cartoon of him caricatured as a fatberg and be expected to take the joke in good part.

Ultimately, Johnson's fall was like Nicolae Ceaușescu's in reverse. The Romanian politburo knew the boss' days were numbered when the crowd at a rally started to laugh at him. We knew 'Boris' was stuffed when, at the final PMQs before his defenestration, the Tory benches stopped laughing. He'd finally completely lost control of the laughter agenda. Which, thank God, means it's back where it belongs, with the cartoonists.

I drew this when Johnson resigned to capture his defining entitled delusion. After his own side forced him out he carries on (as his Eton housemaster wrote of him) as if rules for everybody else don't apply to him. But behind the blustering bonhomie there remained a sullen, petulant, pouting manbaby, refusing to believe we'd all stopped applauding with joyous gratitude because he's so lovely. Various visions of 'Boris'—Trump the populist, Churchill the heroic war leader and Pericles the great orator—buoy up an unpopular coward barely able to string together a coherent sentence. Them's the breaks.

The Guardian, July 2022

The Love Songs of Late Capitalism (Ripon: Smokestack, 2022)

The Love Songs of Late Capitalism

An Excerpt

Smokestack Books, 2022

The minicab declutches at the lights,
Descants a Doppler shush and jolts to rest;
The heating in this car is turned too high;
The air-freshener cloys, chemically sweet,
Sways in gagging half-arcs from the mirror,
The oblong void against the windscreen's fringe
Where raindrops stream sideways in coral reefs,
Are pinpricked into gold refracted globes
Or speckle white to pixilate shut shops
Then smear off with a thud from wipers wired
With clenched intensity like mods on speed.
A thwack, a screech, some spray, a brutal sweep,
A Sisyphean mind-fuck written small,
Obliteration as eternal grind.
Then the lights, a greasy splodge, are changing
As music throbs out of the radio,
Music that is older than the driver,
Basses lisping, lung-hawkingly deep,
The trebles harmonizing with the ashtray,
A self-contained cacophony on wheels,
Capital Gold—Smooth, Magic—playing louder
The Easy Listening soundtracking our lives
That stays holding your hand long after midnight
And leaves my thoughts to segue in the dark.

The isle has always been too full of noises,
A sickle in an oak grove, rhythmic screams,
A lyre plucked, lies retold as plainsong,
Songs of murder yelled down drunken halls,
Chants in chantries, chancing deathly changes,
Full aisles muffling psalms of anxious pleas,
Feudal furrows shielding famished fieldsongs,

Coughs from dust blown in from stolen meadows,
The bawl of pistons orchestrating Hell.
The gold's percussion counterpoints the sighs,
Haphazard honks of brass grasp at salvation,
Young men in tweeds & cycle clips on raids
To hedgerowed hamlets sack old women's airs,
Anthems, chorales, arias, lovesick ballads;
Echoing dance bands swirl gauche pas de deux,
Songs round the piano in an air raid,
Concert party Pierrots down the pier,
Crooners crooning rationed maple syrup,
Songs of yearning grief & cheap pomade,
Genocidal oompah on the bandstand,
Rounds at rallies, rounding on the foe,
Sanitized to sing round guttering campfires,
Rousing roundelays to flay the flagging
Until the time the aisles grew wild with rockers,
Fairground flick knives flashing to the beat
That beats in time with klaxons on the dodgems,
Drowns out the silent screams of brylcremed kids
High on dads' dismay, young lust and danger
While being broken on the Ferris wheels;
The beat of forest drums, beats forgotten,
The beat of fear and night being repelled
Reawakened to reboot the Post War,
Equip the New Age with its potlatch props,
Grave goods for the pyramids of Boomers,
Its scooters, T-Birds, boys' haircuts, their shoes,
For culture wars waged by the rising side
With the heartbeat beat of being human
Expropriated from the mouths of slaves.

The Balls Pond Road's hedgehogging in the rain:
Once Twice Three Times A Lady. 4am
From Tower Hamlet's hissing thoroughfares
The City rises like a sneered affront,
Its hubristic fruit-machine high towers,
Their algorithmic auguries aglow,

Paying jackpot bonuses each second,
Chorused by designer bells and whistles.
The traders homeward long since roared their way,
Leaving the floors to cleaners and machines.
Buff humming tanks glide polishing between
The desks and termini, gilding the guilt,
Varnishing to sterilize the damage
Done the day before, resumed today,
The ceaseless round of pillage and returns,
Prophecy, propitiation, plunder,
Until time, in Swiss watches of the night
To pause, draw breath, get slaves to hose the decks,
The unperceived, the ancillary serfs
Now guiding all those laundering machines
Across the trading floors, like ploughmen trudged
Behind their straining teams, across unyielding
Rock-sewn land, all owned by someone else
Who always, always, always looked away.

Behind shutters hard due north of Shoreditch,
Too late even for inconvenience stores
(The rain's so hard the drunks have all gone home)
Hardened diasporas from everywhere
Beyond the Anglophonic Solipsism
Reach the time of night dreams dissipate,
Displaced by deep defragging sleep. Some scraps
Of previous dreams of former homes still jangle
Above rooms crammed with stock, the cheaper scree
And broken up moraine left by the glaciers
Of Global marketplaces grinding through
And bulldozing new landscapes while pursuing
The paths of least resistance into which
Fresh topographies of mass consumption
And glib geologies are to be crushed;
Dream places lives ago the Europeans
Claimed were undiscovered, Brigadoons
Which unperceived by white eyes stayed dark ghosts
Before we teased them out and made more ghosts,

Places where the trucks and kiosks rattle
With amplified tracks Westerners laid down
When small boys, as they watched the white men leave,
Felt the winds of change ruffle their blazers
And now, as old men, wear tops emblazoned
With Queen's tour dates in 1989
And children squat in shanty towns, in lycra,
Embossed with branded white boy bands' sour pouts,
Uncontacted tribes have traded sweatshirts
For arrow-heads or manioc or skins
And consequently end up advertising
Guns 'n' Roses or, maybe, The Fugees;
The bounty of the sweatshops, holey relics,
Indulgences both pirated and pure,
The ineffectual intellectual loot
Of corporations hawking bored elation,
Snapping on the wristband chains of freedom,
In new colonialisms of pure tat
As I board the midnight train to Georgia,
Born to Run to Galvaston or Nutbush,
Clarksville, LA, Memphis, Nashville, Tulsa,
Songlines mythologizing urban blight
And though from here it's five minutes to Dalston,
The radio plays on twenty-four seven,
Day after day, tied onto the tracks
Only interrupted by the ads,
The shilling, spiel, the barking for the heists,
Hard selling commodified rebellion,
Seeking selfish boy singer/songwriters,
New Dylans to revive the slumping shares
By bringing down Bastilles with t-shirt slogans:
8 billion individuals born to swarm.
Near the Tower, and indicating left,
Steady cicada throbs over the songs,
The car is still too hot, just like the World
And the music never ending, like the heist.

See! Quarries of light entertainers piled
In sacrifice appeasing Rock's cruel gods:
In plane or car crash, shot, inhaling vomit,
Or suicide; Nepenthe's pick 'n' mix,

Booze, fast living, bad behaviour, drowning
But always young enough, round 27,
To count as golden children come to dust,
Templating standard Romantic hard-ons,
Blue-jeaned Chattertons, slicked-back haired Keatses,
Shit-faced Shelleys or O'd-ing Christs,
Delicious easy deathfuls of dumb kids
Too high on fame, money and growing up,
Buddy, Ritchie, Jimi, Tupac, Amy,
Jim, Kurt, Sid, Nick, Tim, Janis, Gram, Brian,
Even Elvis dying on the toilet
Undergo tinselled apotheoses
To mount Olympus, squalor washed away,
And sacrament the lie: The Good Die Young.
No gods since the Aztecs' seem this hungry,
Frantically devouring young flesh,
Howling for a Paschendale of pop stars,
Doomed youth designed to go over the top.
Age shall not weary them, nor years contend
With celluloid or vinyl's ersatz aspic
That capture them in blobs now beyond Time:
The Beatles stay The Beatles as they ran
Through black and white industrial decline
That's now cemented in the past; they're present.
Like Ziggy Stardust, Bowie notwithstanding,
Should reek of power cuts and Three Day Weeks
And yet achieved escape velocity
From History's bonds, the Seventies' grey pall,
Transfigured into immortality
And Lenined like Snow White in glassed enchantment
Forever then and eternally now.
Transubstantiating thus, cheap music
Lignifies to tree rings, carbon dating

Exactly memories of time and place,
Evoking more than any hoarded totems –
Snaps and souvenirs, your dead mum's shit –
All those forgotten times we trail like skin scale,
In clouds that haunt like thickening ectoplasm,
Pinpointing memories like ethered moths,
Jerking your leash, a reflex that'll Proust you,
Getting Svengali'd by The Glitter Band,
Just jellyfish in Time's capricious currents.
The only option's worship or despair
Or queuing on your knees towards the tills
Of superstores, with racks of tabernacles
And sepulchres stuffed, stacked up to the skies
Filled with CDs, albums, LPs, downloads
Of packaged troubadours of caught, lean love,
Votive candles flickering rank on rank,
The tallow dripping meatily to sizzle
On cold mosaic floors of Halls of Fame,
Lit to the Trinity, the three-chord riff.

It's late. It's always late, and getting later,
40 years since Marvin Gaye was shot,
But still his voice, like Hamlet's father's, reaches
To me, like a seance in this fug.
The streets are empty as we cross the river,
London's Styx, reflecting Southwark's towers
Mirrored, pointing downwards into Hades,
Filled with the dead who sleep, bat-like, inverted.
The living boogie on. They keep on truckin'.
Stayin' Alive. Keith Richards' bingo wings
Flap at another gala for The Needy
Watched by Presidents and Queens and Kings
Who sway in time to much loved banging classics
About oppression, drugs, sex, blues and rape,
Pastiched by two Dartford boys who spotted
The Delta in the Thames for them to steal
Sixty years ago, though if you fold back
From then the way we turn to then from now,
Those boys would be obsessed with Marie Lloyd.

Mick yowls, his hair inhabiting continua
Divorced in time from what contains his face.
Paul McCartney's mouth, a feline anus,
Mewls words mewled a million times before,
A gerontology of rock and rollers,
Old boys on endless tours singing old songs
In forced communion with men they hate,
Bands of Brothers decayed to Cains and Abels
From decades knocking round and getting old,
Trapped and bored stiff in late adolescence,
Cursed, in shabby reworkings of Dante,
To tour forever Hell's provincial rings
To milk the last drying fungible drop
Of once being Rod Argent or in Mud
In atavistic senicults in Tring
Or Bailey's, Watford for the OAPS
Who hunch with spiders web tattoos across
Their mottled, wrinkled, lesioned once young faces,
Pates too bald or thinning for mohicans,
Anarchy in the UK droning limply
In another singsong in the care homes
While the fallen arches of their idols
Mark their mortality, deteriorating
Into cranks and codgers like their dads,
Mark E Smith recast with 20 woodbines,
Ian Brown van morrisoning crap,
Morrissey jekyll and hyding Farage,
Yet leavening the disappointment seeping
From daring to grow old before they die
Redeemed beyond the peonage of bores
Because their teenage avatars once channelled
The energy of not giving a shit,
Making their mates dance and then feel happy
Back in the time when they were first in love
While Brain Wilson glances at his watch
Halfway through *God Only Knows*, the closest
Any of them got to biting chunks of
Heaven directly from the foetid air.

The Christian skygod, since displaced, allotted
To man a span to live exceeded now
By the Hegemony of Teenage Kicks which
Globalized and monetized the yearning
Of nervous boys and girls who want to fuck.
Back catalogues in warehouses of memories,
Hawking nostalgia, evaporated youth,
Universalizing toddlers' dress codes
As Freedom's uniforms, infantilizing
Humanity to sell another song.
For merchants merchandise. It's what they do.
Ghettos of sub-cultures warp to brands;
Elitist and completist, young fans' need
For meaning through belonging twisted round
To opportunities to sell them back
Their dreams in furtive bags of their own shit
Spiked with lines of unquenchable sadness
At recollecting old scuffed leatherette,
Stacked speakers stickier with sweat than beer,
Slimier smoothnesses of mosh pit limbs,
Blissed rictuses and cleaned out fridgidaires,
Composty pagan prog rock comeback tours,
More detestable summer festivals,
Chemical toilets, Glastostomy bags,
Along with the spaced out, intense conviction
That any of this means a fucking thing.
Life's available through ticket agents:
Just psychotropic noises calculated
Like bland deceptive fascisms of sport,
To trigger massive endochrinal rushes
In every shop and restaurant and club,
Grand anthems that sell garbage no one needs,
Aspirational chord changes on games shows,
In madnesses of crowds in massive stadia
Attenuating into tyrants' fanfares,
To make you cheer or weep or shop or kill.
We're in Jamaica Road now, named by slavers
To honour wealth they stole from shackled toil,

Whose 'property', to break the chains within them,
Sang songs they'd smuggled on the ships from home,
Songs their captors eventually then captured
To steal the one last thing they hadn't grabbed,
Then, passed off and repackaged by hucksters,
Trickling down, enveloping the planet
In cauls of sentimental pomp, for sale,
Filling all the gaps between the atoms,
The Disco beats that broke the Berlin Wall
To bring an End to History, then Hope
To move beyond the Neverending Now,
Needily new, requiring fresh worlds
Each week for charts and markets to expand,
Like roaring air from bomb blasts, specks of dreams
Drowned in the flying debris of the cloud
Expanding and expanding beyond bounds
Of pointillistic possibilities,
To blast your ears and take your breath away,
Capitalism's love songs play forever,
Basically just there to fill dead air.
It's easy. Easy like Sunday morning.
I lean forward to the driver, and we speak.

The Prejudices That Haunt Us

The Guardian, July 2023

I've been a political cartoonist my whole adult life, and I believe what I do is important. Satirical cartoons weave together humour and weird forms of sympathetic magic to damage and thereby try to curb the excesses of powerful people through caricature and mockery, by means of metaphor and symbols; things signifying things other than themselves; allegories and allusions; tropes, if you like. They also require a lot of deniable ambiguity, because they undermine power by laughing at it, and power has a huge armoury of weapons with which to answer back.

Nonetheless, instead of the rather pompous definition of satire as 'puncturing pomposity', I've always preferred the punchline of the great Jewish joke where the kid comes home from work complaining to his mother about his new boss. She replies, with the wisdom of mothers, 'If he's so special how come he shits and he's going to die?'

In other words, it's my job to remind the powerful of their metabolizing mortality, which they share with the rest of us. But all those layers of ambiguity and diverse interpretation mean cartoons can be hazardous and potentially deadly, at both ends. So, because satire should only ever punch upwards and never kick downwards, years ago I drew up this simple set of rules for myself—

I should never attack anyone less powerful than me;

I should never attack people for what they are—their ethnicity, gender or sexuality—only for what they think and do;

And should I ever offend anyone I hadn't targeted, I would always apologize.

At the end of April, I drew a cartoon, part of which included a depiction of the former BBC chairman Richard Sharp as a typical employee after being sacked, carrying out their possessions in a cardboard box. After the cartoon was published on the *Guardian*'s website, another wholly plausible description was posted on Twitter by Dr Dave Rich of the Community Security Trust, describing it as brimming with vicious anti-Semitic tropes.

You can read my account of what I thought I'd drawn on my website (martinrowson.com), written within hours of Rich's initial tweet. In the same piece, I apologized unconditionally and took full responsibility for the enormous hurt and upset I'd unintentionally caused. But how could both things be true? I had drawn an anti-Semitic cartoon, yet I'd not been aware I was doing so.

Having unwittingly broken my first two rules, I'd quickly acted on my third. But soon this no longer mattered. Intentionality became irrelevant. I could now only see what Rich and thousands of others saw, and saw it for what it was. I was now consumed with deep, devouring shame. That coming Friday, I was due to draw a cartoon covering the coronation, but by this stage I'd long since lost all sense of moral authority or even agency to draw anything or judge anyone, and two days after the Sharp cartoon was published I asked for time off.

All of this matters so much because this mistake—though 'car crash' comes closest in my mind to describe the jagged intermeshing of accident, chaos, loss of control, damage and huge hurt to blameless bystanders—happened within a context I'm very conscious of.

Since that Saturday, I keep remembering my late colleague Simon Hoggart's story about travelling out of London with Alan Coren to record an episode of *The News Quiz*; how, when they boarded the train, Coren, who was Jewish, went into a kind of psychic shock. He'd been triggered, somewhere in his subconscious, by the role trains played in transporting millions of European Jews to their murder.

I also keep remembering one of the most chilling scenes in Claude Lanzmann's *Shoah*, where a historian displays the receipts for block-booking excursion tickets for the Nazis' victims' journeys to the death camps. I also keep thinking of the suitcase packed and ready by the front door in preparation for immediate flight.

This is the banality of evil continuing to terrorize: the everyday things where evil lurks in train timetables and tickets; disguised, who knows, in your neighbours; in a stupid drawing laden with otherwise unperceived meanings steeped in death in a cartoon in your morning newspaper, God forgive me.

It gets worse than that. Bite the air in Britain and you can taste the racism, the homophobia, the sexism and all the prejudices that constitute the real cancel culture that pervades our society. It's the thousand tiny cancellations people suffer daily not because of what they think or do, but because of what they are; cancelling their right to go where they choose and feel safe, do what they want and feel at ease, read what they like and not be triggered by a blunder blithely evoking genocide.

It's even worse than that. I'd like to think that I'm not even remotely anti-Semitic, but what do I know? As a visual artist operating in a genre dependent on exaggeration and mockery, I also swim in a swamp being constantly fed with poisonous slurry from two millennia of European Christian art portraying Jews as ugly, avaricious monsters.

Worse, 50 years ago, with the Holocaust rawly fresh in everyone's minds, at my Anglican school the chaplain dismissed the suffering of the Jews as punishment for

Christ's crucifixion. And 25 years ago, a senior figure at a major UK charity, thinking I was Jewish because he'd mistakenly assumed 'Rowson' is an anglicization of 'Rosen', instantly told me an anti-Semitic joke on discovering I wasn't. Far, far worse manifestations of anti-Semitism continue unabated. This is the air we breathe; the miasma many of us choke on.

These facts should not be ambiguous, though what I do as a cartoonist depends on ambiguity. But while all of it is about power and its control through mockery, within this context, individuals have multiple identities and multiple roles as these matrices constantly shift.

Take Sharp, a friend of Boris Johnson, whom I believed I had drawn in a particular, fairly unkind way, reflecting what he does and thinks. But at the very instant that depiction was seen—as it was, whatever my intention, by many deeply shocked and frightened people—as a cruel depiction of what he is, a Jewish man in his sixties, caricatured grotesquely (though in hideously familiar ways), the power dynamic completely collapsed. The public, satirizable appearance of Sharp dissolved to reveal the real, breathing, victimized human being beneath. Worst of all, victimized and bullied by me, in ways wholly anathema to me both personally and professionally. Carelessly and terrifyingly easily, I had utterly and comprehensively failed. It was and is inexcusable on every level.

What I do in my work is a twisted and dreadful magic, and it needs to be practised with extreme care. Over the past few weeks, clambering through the wreckage resulting from my last cartoon, I have been talking to lots of people, prominent and otherwise, from across the Jewish community both to atone and to help me understand how I could have done this terrible thing.

I thank all of them enormously for their generosity, their time and, let's be frank, their forgiveness. And they've helped me learn, bit by bit and ahead of my return to these pages in September, to remember what I already knew. The business of satire has never been to give indiscriminate offence, and nor is it my job. Its price therefore must always be eternal vigilance.

The Dance of Death: Vanitas (London: SelfMadeHero, 2019)

Communards

Left Cultures, June 2024

I knew I wanted to be a visual satirist more than anything else when, aged ten, I picked up my sister's school text book *An Illustrated History of Britain 1780–1950* and found it was full of cartoons, from Gillray and Cruikshank, via Tenniel, to David Low. It immediately infatuated me, and I was soon pillaging my father's old desk to find some ancient steel nibs to teach myself to draw the way Gillray etched.

About four years later, my art teacher Alan Whitney then entirely transformed the way I came to see the world. He must have given this talk scores of times during his career (he was a year away from retirement when I heard it) and probably knew it hardly ever made any impact, but his description of how to view everything in blocks of colour rather than in outline worked with me. The next day I was seeing things I'd never guessed were there—patches of sunlight or dampness, a shop front reflected in a gutter, dust sparkling on a moon beam. I'm pleased I was able to tell him this, decades later, shortly before he died.

Neither of these, though, contributed to my politics, the origins of which remain shadowy. Maybe they arise from the circumstances of my adoption, about which I've always known. Though having met several members of my birth family, my leftiness appears to be unique and clearly not congenital. Maybe I was aware, early on, of the capricious injustice in the way I'd been rocketed up the social classes. Perhaps that's the point from where I began thinking and raging about all the other injustices around me.

Who knows? Though in 1971, one thing made a real difference. It was two years after my adoptive mother had died and my adoptive father was still making a fist of being a single parent before remarrying two years later. Actually, he'd already laid a lot of the ground work of my politics—and certainly my satirical contempt for power—without me even noticing. He was a virologist and exemplified the scientific principles of healthy scepticism while also weaving in his own sense of anarchic mischief, mingled with the utter conviction that everyone in authority over him was, by definition, an idiot. When I was very small, he gave me the wisest advice of my life, even if it took me decades to work out what it meant: 'Never obey orders, including this one.'

As a struggling single father he worked out a wonderful way of dealing with me in the school holidays. His laboratory was in Gray's Inn Road, and each day we'd drive into King's Cross and he'd basically send me off on my own for the day with instructions to be back by 5. Thus, aged 11 and 12, I took personal possession of London.

Left Cultures, June 2024

I'd haunt bookshops, art galleries, cathedrals and museums for hours and hours, weaving between them to create my own songlines across the heart of the capital. And returning to Gray's Inn Road, my favourite rat run was always through the British Museum, through the main entrance then right and then left through book-lined corridors ringing the British Library off to Chinese porcelain, Dürer's great arch of paper, originally printed to brown nose the Holy Roman emperor (I've dreamed of producing a satirical update on the same scale for over fifty years) outside the Department of Prints and Drawings and then down to exit onto Montagu Place, thence to make off through the dimly lit streets to the east.

I think, though, I deliberately sought out the corridor exhibition marking the centenary of the Paris Commune, displaying pertinent documents in a handful of glass-topped tables. I particularly remember a cartoon of a Communard addressing a statue of Napoleon about to be pulled down (plus ça change, as they say in Paris) with the words 'We toppled your nephew so we can topple you!' And 53 years later, I can still feel with photographic clarity the comforting clonk of thoughts and factors finally coming together in my mind as I glimpsed what the Commune truly meant: that alternative, to capitalism and emperors and kings and priests and hierarchies a hundred years after Thiers' provisional government suppressed the Commune by killing 50 times the number of Parisians killed in Robespierre's Terror in two per cent of the time. Because I also saw and understood the desperate savagery the powerful will unleash to prevent the tiniest erosion of their power. My 12-year-old self was enraged. I still am.

Cartooning the Tory Years

The Guardian, June 2024

For the past five weeks people have repeatedly said to me, 'You must be really busy!' I've had to explain that elections aren't like that; in fact, from the point of view of cartoonists, they're boring. The only real fun comes when the wheels fall off the party machines and their careful choreography collapses into farce. But in this election even the Tories' serial weapons-grade balls-ups are becoming a bore, serving merely to remind me of the universal truth that reality will always, always be weirder than anything satire could think up in a million years.

That said, in the empty hours of this interminable death watch while we've waited for the Tory tumbril finally to trundle to the guillotine, I've been reflecting on the past 14 years, and how the worst government of my lifetime has been succeeded five times by one that was even worse.

Take David Cameron, Britain's very first gap-year prime minister, whose congenital complacency and effortless sense of entitlement had already equipped him with fathomless depths of risibility. Ever since he had been elected Tory leader, I'd drawn Cameron as Little Lord Fauntleroy, with an added dash of Basil Fotherington-Tomas. It's always best to go for the obvious joke. (For the past year I've been touring a show about the nine prime ministers I've been paid to draw over the past 42 years. When I reach Cameron I show a slide of a mortadella sausage. Some punters think this references his complexion, but actually it's about Luis Buñuel's assertion that Benjamin Péret's belief that mortadella was made by blind people was the ultimate Surrealist statement. Until, that is, Cameron attacked the kids looting TK Maxx during the 2011 riots for having 'too great a sense of entitlement'—or that may have been Boris Johnson, yet another Old Etonian using our country as his personal playpen. Either way, irony's corpse hit the pavement screaming.)

Then, because Cameron's charm (George Osborne described it as the Tories' secret weapon) signally failed to win a majority against Gordon Brown's crumbling Labour government, his comic potential was massively augmented by the forced coalition with the Liberal Democrats. I admit, halfway through the 2010 election campaign I still couldn't draw Nick Clegg, because hitherto there'd been no real occasion to.

However, when I watched the first leaders' debate (the one that spawned Cleggmania) I saw that he had a very noddy head, and physically was a weird amalgam of Private Pike from Dad's Army and Pinocchio. I opted for the second trope, the little wooden boy who wanted to be a real politician. The readers got it instantly, and

The Guardian, April 2010

The Guardian, November 2023

for five happy years Cleggnocchio was sawn into bits, dismantled, then reassembled as everything from deckchairs to gibbets.

That foul coalition government still makes me think of a spiteful 11-year-old boy smashing an Enigma machine with a mallet, just for fun. Though here I have to confess to the almost indecent degree of pleasure I got from drawing Osborne. This is a common occupational hazard among cartoonists, a weird variant on Stockholm syndrome whereby we fall in love with the public figures we satirize.

We may deplore everything about them, but just love drawing them. With Osborne, it's not just the weird nose, weak chin and cruel eyes, but the fact he clearly has no bones in his head, his skull replaced by lard and gristle. Then there's his mouth, ruby red and always in danger of smirking its way round to the back of his neck. And in 2014 he had a makeover and completely changed colour, from spectrum red heavily diluted with titanium white, to a rich, oligarchish raw sienna. Pure bliss.

Theresa May, though, was much more of a challenge. She had been part of the repertory company of characters who populated my cartoons for six years by the time she became prime minister after the Brexit vote. Shoulder pads were the signifier I chose for her, and she had chosen the leopard-print shoes herself (politicians often deliberately provide props for cartoonists; Harold Wilson smoked a pipe in public, but cigars indoors).

However, after she got the top job, I spent a truly dark weekend of the soul trying to capture her to my satisfaction and make her look, in the great cartoonist David Low's phrase, more like her than she does. But somehow I was never entirely confident I'd 'got' her, with my hand up her soul. Then, contemplating an undignified end to my career, I lowered her eye fractionally down her face and there she was. This is the weird, shape-shifting magic of caricature, and I've no idea how it works.

It was after her disastrous performance in the 2017 election, and after the Grenfell fire (the most significant political event of the past 40 years if we weren't too dumb to recognize why) I started drawing her as a ghost, until she finally faded away in 2019, the fourth Tory prime minister to be destroyed by her party's inability to reconcile its love of global capitalism with its hatred of foreigners.

Johnson I didn't want to draw at all, just to starve him of the oxygen of publicity. However, like all attention-seeking narcissists, although his skin appears inches thick, it's actually microns thin, and I know from several sources that he truly hates the way I portray him. Which is heartening, because he appears to pose a challenge to satirists, by doing the jokes himself. In fact, he lands punchlines like the Hindenburg, in his desperate need to be laughed with rather than at. It has been the defining aspect of the pathology he has had in the stead of a political career.

Ivory Towers

The Guardian, June 2017

The Guardian, December 2019

The Guardian, October 2022

This will sure as hell see off those AI monsters!!!

The Guardian, November 2023

By now farce was repeating itself as farce, on a rapid turnover. I had finally succeeded in truly capturing the essence of Liz Truss—nose like a little chisel, eyes as far apart as is physically possible on a still human skull, and gawky gawping mouth sinking into her clavicle—when she collapsed under the weight of her own contradictions. Then Rishi Sunak. When the Tories were governing exclusively in the interests of the Eurosceptic press, obviously they made a newspaper columnist prime minister; when that ended in tears, they got a sock puppet for the Tufton Street thinktanks, in whose interests they now ruled; after that disaster, as they now only represented the hedge funds that owned them, they gave a hedge fund manager the job. When I first noticed him, Sunak was so immeasurably pleased with himself, I gave him three rows of grinning teeth. I'm not sure yet if they'll feature much more after next Thursday, with or without him.

Either way, it's clearly high time that we re-established some proper demarcation here, that the jokers stick to politics and leave the jokes to us professionals. All in all, we need a bit of boring earnestness, that will eventually, like everything in politics, collapse into comedy gold.

Until then, maybe someone can make a stab at clearing up the mess left by all that Tory slapstick, while we, the cartoonists, sharpen pencils again to depict the fresh meat.

Past It Post

Afterword

Chris McLaughlin

Sometimes you don't know what you've got till you take another look in the store cupboard. That's how it was when Martin Rowson came up with this reassembled canon of work from the last two and a bit decades.

As his editor at *Tribune* for 14 of those years, I had the tremulous responsibility of discharging into the world Martin's regular excoriations against the 'craven, incompetent, cruel and callous clowns that lead us'. He pushed the boundaries—of style and offence. In a uniquely relentless, resolute endeavour to puncture a truth-suffocating miasma of political cant.

To say the arrival of his 'As I Please . . . ' column was a joy would be only half the truth. It was also an editorial headache, requiring a wary legal eye to be on the lookout for danger. Every piece was an exhilarating ride, you held your breath not knowing which way, or how far, it was going to go. But there never was any need to amend or pull the column for legal reasons. (Note to the aggrieved: it's too late now!) In fact, Martin was only once forced into silence, by a previous editor who thought a suggestion that Prime Minister Tony Blair should fake his own death was a step too far. I think I would have published.

Martin was a double jeopardy for *Tribune*. He was also our most prominent, leader-page cartoonist, a position carrying that special licence to break boundaries held by all cartoonists. He once described his cartoon work as 'visual journalism', as seen in the *Guardian*, *Daily Mirror* and many other outlets. This collection is conclusive evidence, in my opinion, that the national political discourse would be much improved by the more regular appearance of Martin's written journalism too.

Regrettably, all the columns and cartoons were removed from *Tribune* when it acquired new ownership in 2018. I am the current squatter, to borrow Martin's own term for himself, of the 'As I Please . . . ' column, most eminently launched and occupied by George Orwell, the paper's literary editor, under Aneurin Bevan's editorship. I'd like to think I'm just keeping it warm for Martin's return.

In one of these essays, from June 2003, Martin says: 'The enduring power of Orwell's satire demonstrates that nothing much changes, that human politics has always been debauched by power and that humankind has an infinite capacity for inhumanity.' It's one of many prophetic statements in what, read as a whole in a single retrospective collection, brings penetratingly truthful order to the kaleidoscope of history. Those who have read or dipped into the preceding pages will be familiar with the territory.

From international diplomatic upsets caused by Martin's eighteenth-century cartoon hero James Gillray through to the Iraq War, New Labour, 9/11, Northern Ireland, the power of Rupert Murdoch, Brexit, Jeremy Corbyn, Keir Starmer and a few diversions into Syd Barrett, David Bowie and the death of the Queen Mum, Martin takes a freewheeling, sometimes revelatory and irreverent tilt at events with the power to wrench us into uncomfortable realities. Or offers copious treasurable gems. Should I have known that Jim Morrison named The Doors after Aldous Huxley's iconic *The Doors of Perception*?

He retains a prominent place at the jagged cutting edge of what passes for political and social discourse, championing offence against those who would weaponize offence to shut down honest debate, such as the equating of criticism of the Israeli government with anti-Semitism.

It amounts, as Martin himself puts it, to '30 years of screaming my head off'. But nothing much changes.

Now—ever more an age he once dubbed the 'hegemony of the accountants', with its multiplying squillionaires, a growing, permanent underclass and shrinking democracy—it's time the screams were heard.

Chris McLaughlin was the editor of Tribune *from 2004 to 2018.*

Acknowledgements

Throughout the more than 40 years I've been a professional cartoonist, I've often told my text-journalism colleagues that the following truths are self-evident:

That drawing—like jumping, jokes and genocide—is one of the defining things we do as a species; and it is this, in fact, that makes us humans unique, as we recreate the perceived world about us by recreating what we see, hear or experience in what's now called 'safe mode' through art, music and narrative, acted, spoken or read. The earliest known drawing is about forty-five thousand years old and is of a pig on a cave wall in Indonesia.

That writing, on the contrary, is only five and a half thousand years old and is merely a by-product of accountancy. The original function of making marks on clay tablets was to record the size of the grain surplus in the hands of the emerging elite; thereafter, it recorded the tax paid to the elites, in grain; thereafter to list those who hadn't paid up and were due for execution. The purpose of writing, therefore, is as an occult code used by an elite of murderous thieves and tyrants the further to oppress the rest of us. Drawing, on the other hand, is about being truly human.

The point, obviously, is to annoy, like all jokes, while simultaneously evening up the score between all those newspaper columnists and editors, knocking back champagne flutes forever full of gravitas on the high table of the establishment, and us cartoonists down in the servants' kitchen drinking bathtub gin out of thimbles. And equally obviously, this volume gathers some of the thousands and thousands of words I've written over the past three decades in newspaper columns and articles. Most of these appeared monthly between 1997 and 2017 in the 'As I Please . . . ' column in *Tribune*, originally occupied by George Orwell in the 40s. I've also included things I've written for everywhere from the *Guardian* and BBC Radio 3 to underground comic magazines like *Black Eye* and *2000AD*, and the Russian/UK/US anti-art provocation *Artenol.*

My thanks are due to many people, starting off with Naveen Kishore and Diven Nagpal at Seagull for publishing and editing this collection. I must also thank my various other editors over the years, including my great friend, the old editor from *Sunday Today*, Bill Hagerty, who first introduced me to *Tribune*; thereafter, Mark Seddon, editor of *Tribune* from 1994 to 2004, for letting me add the 'As I Please . . . ' column to my other contributions to the paper, and to Chris McLaughlin, Mark's successor, for keeping me at it and providing the enormously kind and generous afterword to this book. Thanks, too, to my old friend Kevin Maguire, whose *Daily Mirror* column I illustrated for ten years until they sacked me in 2023, for his equally generous and touching foreword. All the other editors who commissioned me over the years deserve a nod too, even though it would be too long to list them all here. But particular thanks to Ryan Standfest of *Black Eye*, who was unstinting in pushing me to places no one should ever really go, and to my friend and regular correspondent Patricia Bargh, who was invaluable in providing a clearer eye in choosing what's included here from all the hundreds of thousands more bloody words I seem to have churned out over the years when I should have been drawing something instead.

Martin Rowson
London
June 2024